Philosophical Arabesques

Nikolai Bukharin, 1888–1938

PHILOSOPHICAL ARABESQUES

Nikolai Bukharin

translated by RENFREY CLARKE

with editorial assistance by GEORGE SHRIVER

MONTHLY REVIEW PRESS
New York

Translation copyright © 2005 MONTHLY REVIEW PRESS
All rights reserved

Library of Congress Cataloging-in-Publication Data

Bukharin, Nikolaæi Ivanovich, 1888–1938.
    [Filosofskiye Arabeski. English]
    Philosophical arabesques / by Nikolai Bukharin ; with an introduction by Helena Sheehan.
        p. cm.
    Includes bibliographical references and index.
    ISBN 1-58367-102-1 (cloth)
    1. Dialectical materialism. 2. Philosophy, Marxist. I. Title.
    B809.8.B75613 2005
    355.43'092—dc22
    ISBN 9781583679531   2005000249

MONTHLY REVIEW PRESS
122 West 27th Street
New York, NY 10001
www.monthlyreview.org

10 9 8 7 6 5 4 3 2 1

Contents

Introduction: A Voice from the Dead *by* HELENA SHEEHAN 7

Editorial Note *by* MONTHLY REVIEW PRESS 31

Author's Foreword 34

Author's Introduction 35

1 — The Reality of the World and the Intrigues of Solipsism 37
2 — Acceptance and Nonacceptance of the World 47
3 — Things in Themselves and Their Cognizability 67
4 — Space and Time 68
5 — Mediated Knowledge 81
6 — The Abstract and the Concrete 83
7 — Perception, Image, Concept 92
8 — Living Nature and the Artistic Attitude toward It 98
9 — Rational Thought, Dialectical Thought, ...
    and Direct Contemplation 104
10 — Practice in General and the Place of Practice ....
    in the Theory of Knowledge 113
11 — Practical, Theoretical and Aesthetic Attitudes ....
    toward the World, and Their Unity 124
12 — The Fundamental Positions of Materialism and Idealism 131
13 — Hylozoism and Panpsychism 139

14 — Hindu Mysticism and Western European Philosophy 146
15 — The So-called Philosophy of Identity 154
16 — The Sins of Mechanistic Materialism 163
17 — The General Laws and Relations of Being 170
18 — Teleology 177
19 — Freedom and Necessity 186
20 — The Organism 193
21 — Modern Science and Dialectical Materialism 200
22 — The Sociology of Thought: Labor and Thought ....
    as Social-Historical Categories 207
23 — The Sociology of Thought: Mode of Production ....
    and Mode of Representation 214
24 — On So-called Racial Thought 224
25 — Social Position, Thought, and "Experience" 232
26 — The Object of Philosophy 241
27 — The Subject of Philosophy 248
28 — The Interaction of Subject and Object 255
29 — Society as the Object and Subject of Mastering 262
30 — Truth: The Concept of Truth and the Criterion ....
    of the Truthful 269
31 — Truth: Absolute and Relative Truth 275
32 — The Good 282
33 — Hegel's Dialectical Idealism as a System 292
34 — The Dialectics of Hegel and the Dialectics of Marx 308
35 — Dialectics as Science and Dialectics as Art 331
36 — Science and Philosophy 339
37 — Evolution 345
38 — Theory and History 352
39 — The Social Ideal 359
40 — Lenin as a Philosopher 369

Notes 377
Index 395

A Voice from the Dead

HELENA SHEEHAN

This is a voice from the dead. It is a voice speaking to a time that never heard it, a time that never had a chance to hear it. It is only speaking now to a time not very well disposed to hearing it.

This text was written in 1937 in the dark of the night in the depths of the Lubyanka prison in Moscow. It was completed in November on the twentieth anniversary of the socialist revolution to which its author had given his life—the revolution that was in the process of devouring its own true believers, the revolution that was not only condemning him to death but demanding that he slander his whole life. This text lay buried in a Kremlin vault for more than half a century after its author had been executed and his name expunged from the pages of the books telling of the history he had participated in making. After decades, his name was restored and his memory honored in a brief interval where the story of the revolution was retold—retold in a society to which it crucially mattered, just before that society collapsed to be replaced by one in which the story was retold in another and hostile way, a society in which his legacy no longer mattered to many. Only then, due to the determination of his biographer and family, did the thousand-plus pages of his prison writings emerge from the vault to be published into a world he could never have imagined.

Perhaps the most remarkable thing about this text is that it was written at all. Condemned not by an enemy but by his own comrades, seeing what had been so magnificently created being so catastrophically destroyed, undergoing shattering interrogations, how was he not totally debilitated by despair? Where did this author get the strength, the composure, the faith in the future that was necessary to write this treatise of philosophy, this passionate defense of the intellectual tradition of Marxism and the political project of socialist construction?

Nikolai Ivanovich Bukharin was a tragic true believer. He was the youngest, most intellectual, most sensitive, most sparkling of the original Bolshevik leaders. He was extremely popular, both at home and abroad. Lenin held him in particular affection and esteem, despite polemicizing against him in key controversies along the way. Such was possible then. The early years of the revolution were full of problems and possibilities, of dreams and dilemmas and debates. The Bolsheviks were stunned to find that they had seized state power and they scurried about trying to figure out what to do with it. They were trying to do something that had never been done before. Everything was open to question. Everything needed to be rethought and re-created. They were in new territory with no maps to guide them. Bukharin was energetically engaged in exploring and mapping the new terrain. He was involved in virtually all of the important debates of the era: from agricultural and industrial policy to scientific and artistic questions. He was always on the move, striding around Moscow in his peaked cap, Russian blouse, leather jacket, and high boots, generating an atmosphere of intellectual excitement and fun, embodying "an aura of Bohemia come to power."[1]

Bukharin is the personification of a path not taken. His life and death will always be particularly poignant because of that. He was twenty-nine at the time of the revolution and forty-nine when he died. He was a member of the politbureau and central committee of the Communist Party of the Soviet Union, editor of *Pravda*, head of the Communist International. After the death of Lenin, he was at the pinnacle of power and was a possible successor. He advocated the continuation of the new economic policy, a conciliatory approach to the peasantry aimed at achieving agricultural productivity and steady industrialization. Stalin sided with Bukharin against the "left deviation" associated with Trotsky, Zinoviev, and Kamenev, which emphasized world revolution, rapid industrialization and collectivization. When this strategy was defeated in 1927 and its exponents expelled from the politbureau and even the party, Stalin reversed himself and turned on the "right deviation" associated with Bukharin, Rykov, and Tomsky, and in 1929 defeated them in turn. They were removed from the politbureau and higher echelons of power, but remained on the central committee and worked productively in industry, trade unions, and academic institutions. Bukharin was editor of *Izvestiya*, a member of the USSR Academy of Sciences (and head of its commission on the history of knowledge), and still active in many sectors of Soviet life, from the arts and sciences to economic planning.

Bukharin stood for what he called "socialist humanism"—socialism with a human face, socialism with an open mind, socialism with an honest voice, socialism with an outstretched hand. He advocated a more evolutionary path to socialism, an opening of a process where a society would grow into socialism, where those who questioned might be persuaded and not necessarily coerced or executed, where theoretical questions were settled by theoretical debates and not by accusations of treason, purges of editorial boards, and disappearances in the night. Bukharin was inclined to be bold and passionate in open polemics and to be somewhat guileless and sometimes even naïve in the face of covert political maneuvering. It has been the downfall of many a politician intellectual. It is a sad fact of life that unscrupulousness confers a decided advantage in struggles for power.

After this most consequential struggle for power came the frenzy of the first five-year plan, a titanic and turbulent struggle to collectivize agriculture, to build heavy industry, to achieve in ten years what took a hundred years in other countries. It was declared to be the time of "the new turn on all fronts of socialist construction"—the time of "shattering transformations," not only in politics, industry and agriculture, but in philosophy, art, education, science, in absolutely every aspect of the social order. There was intensified pressure to "bolshevize" every institution, every academic discipline, every artistic form. The intelligentsia was told that the time for ideological neutrality was over. They had to declare themselves for Marxism and for the dialectical materialist reconstruction of their disciplines or evacuate the territory. All the debates that had raged in the 1920s—whether between Marxism and other intellectual trends or between different trends within Marxism—were sharply closed down through the 1930s. There was to be one correct line on every question. Any deviation was considered to be not only mistaken but treacherous. There was resistance in many areas. Geneticists fought back against attempts by brash Bolshevizers to override the process of scientific discovery. Bukharin sided with those such as Vavilov who were standing up to Lysenko.

In philosophy there had been a debate throughout the 1920s between those who were grounded in the empirical sciences and emphasized the materialist aspect of dialectical materialism and those who were more grounded in the history of philosophy, particularly the Hegelian tradition, and emphasized the dialectical dimension of dialectical materialism. It has been an ongoing tension in the history of Marxism and it was healthy and natural for it to play itself out in the atmosphere of intellectual ferment and institutional transformation in the early days of Soviet power. Philosophy was considered integral to the social order. Political leaders, particularly Lenin and Bukharin, participated in philosophical debates as if these issues were matters of life and death, of light and darkness. Even while preoccupied with urgent affairs of state, they polemicized passionately on questions of epistemology, ontology, ethics, and aesthetics. [2]

Bukharin developed in and through these debates. At first he sided with the mechanists. At one point, he even confessed to "a certain heretical inclination to the empirio-critics."[3] He believed that Marxists should study the most advanced work in the natural and social sciences and cleanse themselves of the lingering idealism inherent in quasi-mystical Hegelian formulations. In *Historical Materialism,* published in 1921 and used as a basic text in higher party schools, he interpreted dialectics in terms of equilibrium: of conflict of forces, disturbance of equilibrium, new combination of forces, and restoration of equilibrium.[4] Although Bukharin was not uneducated in classical German philosophy, others who were more steeped in this tradition emphasized the origins of Marxism in this intellectual culture and criticized Bukharin accordingly. Lenin was one who did so and stated that Bukharin, although he was the party's outstanding theorist, had not quite understood dialectics.

Prominent Comintern intellectuals, such as Korsch and Lukacs, associated with a neo-Kantian, neo-Hegelian interpretation of Marxism, which went even further in this direction than the Soviet neo-Hegelian school of Deborin. Both criticized Bukharin. Korsch did so quite bitterly, even shouting during a speech of Bukharin at the fifth world congress of the Comintern. Lukacs accused Bukharin of bias toward the natural sciences, but saw this as being in conflict with his frequently acute dialectical instincts. At the fifth Comintern congress, Zinoviev railed against Korsch and Lukacs in a display of shameless anti-intellectual demagoguery. Bukharin made his criticisms of them in more intellectual terms as relapses into outmoded Hegelianism. He refused to go along with the bullying proletarian anti-intellectualism and saw fit to remark that a worker was not always right, no matter how black his hands. Interestingly, Deborin also criticized Korsch and Lukacs for going too far in the direction of Hegel and being hostile to the natural sciences.[5]

Although there was growing pressure to short-circuit such debates with demagogic rhetoric, Bukharin considered contending arguments seriously. In the midst of these debates, Engels's *Dialectics of Nature* and Lenin's *Philosophical Notebooks* were published and both sides were emphasizing different passages and claiming the texts as authority for their views. Bukharin seriously studied them and was particularly influenced by Lenin's *Philosophical Notebooks,* which dealt with problems in philosophy and the natural sciences, but paid great attention to the history of philosophy in general and Hegel in particular. He also reflected on Lenin's earlier criticism of him on the question of dialectics. In his writings in the 1930s, he came to a new understanding of dialectics and to the relationship of Marxism to its philosophical progenitors.

In 1931 Bukharin led the Soviet delegation to the international history of science congress in London. His paper, published in the ensuing book *Science at the Crossroads* and translated into many languages, indicated this philosophical transition. He set out to convey the intellectual vitality of Marxism to a skeptical audience, placing it within the context of all contemporary currents in philosophy and emphasized how dialectical materialism had overcome the narrowness of mechanistic materialism by superseding its ahistoricism, its quietism, its individualism.[6] Reading it in his prison cell in Italy, Gramsci still thought that this did not represent a significant change in Bukharin's tendency to emphasize materialism to the neglect of the dialectic and wrote an extended critique of Bukharin, whom he regarded as the embodiment of a positivistic tendency within Marxism.[7]

In 1933 Bukharin edited *Marxism and Modern Thought,* a collection of essays published by the academy of sciences to commemorate the fiftieth anniversary of Marx's death. Here he took greater note of the Hegelian roots of Marxism. He underlined Marx's excellent knowledge of the history of philosophy and argued that Marxism took up all that was rational and progressive in the thousands of years of philosophical development. He considered dialectics to be the "algebra of revolution," demonstrating the transitory character of every form, the interrelatedness of all things, the indivisibility of analysis and synthesis, the logic of contradictory processes and universal connections. Nevertheless, he still put a heavy emphasis on natural science and repudiated "Hegelian panology." His polemic contrasted Marxism with all other philosophical trends of the times, even while acknowledging the grains of truth in all of them: logical positivism, pragmatism, gestalt, neo-Kantianism, neo-Hegelianism.[8] These were the themes he took up again at much greater length in his prison cell in 1937 in this manuscript.

Bukharin was a cosmopolitan intellectual, exposed to an array of intellectual influences and accustomed to mixing with intellectuals of many points of view and arguing the case for Marxism in such milieux. So were others who found themselves between the covers of *Science at the Crossroads* and *Marxism and Modern Thought*: Hessen, Zavadovsky, Vavilov, Kolman, Uranovsky, Deborin. They were coming under increasing pressure from a younger generation who had come up under the revolution, never been abroad, knew no foreign languages, had no detailed knowledge of either the empirical sciences or the history of philosophy, had never read books enunciating other points of view. They were brash and often ruthless, more inclined to cite the authority of the classic Marxist texts and current party decrees than to engage in philosophical argument. They were taking over as professors, directors of institutes and members of editorial boards, increasingly occupying positions of authority over learned scholars of international reputation. Not that all of the younger generation were in this mould. There were others, many of them trained by and loyal to Bukharin, but they did not survive. They were arrested, interrogated, and executed.

These developments in Soviet intellectual life were inextricably tied to the rhythms of Soviet political and economic life. The way forward with the first five-year plan was far from smooth and uncomplicated. There was violent resistance to the collectivization of agriculture and peasants were burning crops and slaughtering livestock rather than surrender. There was one disaster after another in the push to industrialization. There was a fundamental contradiction between the advanced goals that were to be achieved and the level of expertise in science, engineering, agronomy, economics, indeed a general cultural level needed to achieve them. There was panic and confusion and desperation. There was reckless scapegoating. Breakdowns, fires, famine, and unfulfilled targets were put down to sabotage and espionage. There was a blurring of the lines between bungling and wrecking, between association with defeated positions and treason, between contact with foreign colleagues and conspiracy with foreign powers.

The country was pictured as full of spies and wreckers and agents of imperialist powers who wanted to disrupt every aspect of Soviet life in every possible way, from agriculture and industry to philosophy and physics. Fascism was on the rise in Europe, but there was little evidence of a Nazi fifth column within the Soviet Union. There was in fact little evidence of sabotage or espionage or even organized opposition on any significant scale by this time. Nevertheless the population was urged to revolutionary vigilance, to root out traitors in every form of Soviet activity in every corner of Soviet society.

The assassination of Kirov in 1934, of which Stalin was probably both prime mover and chief mourner, simultaneously eliminated a rival and provided the pretext for a new wave of repression. These purges swept through the entire population. There were no strata where the NKVD did not reach to uncover spies, wreckers, and traitors, but the accusations bore down most heavily on party members. Every day brought new reports of arrests of commissars, army officers, trade union officials, central committee members, Komsomol leaders, old Bolsheviks, foreign communists, writers, doctors, philosophers, scientists, economists, agronomists, engineers, construction workers, teachers and even children, and finally the agents of the purge themselves. Interrogators found themselves in prison and on trial with those they had only recently interrogated. The accusations and arrests brought a frenetic turmoil to the institutions from which the accused and arrested had come. Those remaining were called together to denounce the accused and to criticize themselves and/or others for not unmasking the traitor sooner. This often led to further accusations and a terrifying atmosphere of accuse or be accused. It escalated beyond all rationality and morality. Under threat and even torture, false confessions were extracted and esteemed colleagues and close comrades were implicated in the most fantastic conspiracies.

Through these years, Bukharin could feel the social order unraveling. His own room for maneuver was constantly shifting. He was often denounced, but occasionally honored, in the official discourse. In response to periodic demands that he not only accept defeat but renounce his views, he sometimes refused, sometimes capitulated, often compromised. He was always negotiating the terms in which he could speak or act. He continued to embody a critical alternative, although in increasingly Aesopian forms of expression. While he sincerely acknowledged the successes of the five-year plan, accepted the drive to intensified industrialization, and threw his energies into state planning, he continued to advocate freedom in intellectual and artistic life and agonized over the climate of fear overtaking every area of life. "Cats are clawing at my soul," he told the young Anna Larina.9

His relationship with Stalin was a merry-go-round of mixed signals. Stalin played with him, expressing admiration and affection, all the while scheming against him, jealous of his intellectual acuity and all-round popularity and vengeful against any alternative to his absolute authority, as his megalomania swept all into a hurricane of destruction. Bukharin had reason to know of Stalin's personality and plotting, and he did know, yet he was sometimes seduced into believing in a better side to him and hoping that appealing to it would bring results. They lived and worked in close proximity to each other, first in exile and later in the Metropol and Kremlin. After Stalin's wife Nadya committed suicide, Stalin asked Bukharin to change apartments with him, as the memory was too painful. In the same bedroom, where she was driven to her death, Bukharin went through his last agony before his arrest, feeling all the possibilities of life closing down on him. Nevertheless, all through the terror, right to the very end, he wrote letters to "Dear Koba," refuting the charges against him, protesting his innocence, believing, not believing that, if only Stalin could see what the NKVD was doing, where things were going wrong, he would put it right.

There were three spectacular show trials in which the whole original nucleus of the party, with the exception of Lenin and Stalin, were represented as involved in a fantastic conspiracy to assassinate party leaders, to sabotage industry, to foment peasant uprisings, to spy for foreign powers, to overthrow socialism and to restore capitalism. Zinoviev, Kamenev, and others were sentenced to death in August 1936. Radek, Pyatakov, Sokolnikov, and others were sentenced to death or long terms of imprisonment in January 1937. There was much testimony at these trials implicating Bukharin, Rykov, and Tomsky, preparing the scenario for the third trial.

To Anna Larina, who became Bukharin's wife, we owe an intimate account of his last months as he awaited arrest, humiliation, and death. For the most part he confined himself to the bedroom of his Kremlin apartment "like a caged beast." His mood changed constantly. He received mounting depositions of testimony against him, much of it from trusted comrades, describing a vast conspiracy to subvert Soviet power, to restore capitalism, to cede Soviet territory to foreign powers, to assassinate Lenin, Kirov, Stalin. At times he was totally mystified by what seemed to be "some inexplicable witchcraft." At times he became numbed to the horror of deceit and betrayal and wild irrationality, growing detached and listless. Then it would seem sharp and vivid again and he would flare suddenly into a fierce rage. He plunged into the depths of despair. He felt "banished from life like a leper." He heard of the suicide of Tomsky. He considered suicide himself, as did Rykov. At other times, he had surges of hope that the truth would triumph and he would be vindicated. He imagined scenarios in which he might live in the countryside with his young wife and see his new son grow and pursue his interests in art and science. There were times when he found the composure and commitment to write a book on the culture of fascism. He went on hunger strike to try to bring the central committee to its senses. He was immersed in an excruciating internal struggle:

"Nikolai Ivanovich both understood and refused to understand."[10] He attended the central committee and was confronted with monstrous allegations, face to face with his accusers impeaching themselves as well as him. He returned home to say, "I have returned from hell, a temporary hell, but there can be doubt that I will fall into it for good."[11]

He resigned himself to this hell, this disgrace, this death. He decided to reach across the hopelessness of his time to hope in posterity. On the eve of his arrest, he composed a letter to a future generation of party leaders and asked Anna to memorize and then destroy it.

> I am leaving life. . . . I am helpless before an infernal machine that seems to use medieval methods, yet possesses gigantic power, fabricates organized slander, acts boldly and confidently. . . . Storm clouds hang over the party. . . . I knew nothing about secret organizations. Together with Rykov and Tomsky, I expounded my views openly. Since the age of eighteen, I have been a member of the party, and always the goal of my life has been the struggle for the interests of the working class, for the victory of socialism. These days the newspaper with the hallowed name *Pravda* prints the most contemptible lie that I, Nikolai Bukharin, wanted to destroy the achievement of October, to restore capitalism. . . . If I was more than once mistaken regarding methods of building socialism, may my descendants judge me no more severely than did Vladimir Ilyich. We were the first to pursue the same goal by an as yet untrodden path. The times, the mores, were different. I turn to you, the future generation of party leaders, on whom will fall the historic mission of clearing the monstrous cloud of crimes that in these terrible days is growing more and more grandiose, spreading like wildfire and smothering the party. . . . In what may be the last days of my life, I am certain that sooner or later the filter of history will inevitably wash the filth from my head. I was never a

traitor. I would have unhesitatingly traded my own life for Lenin's. I loved Kirov and never undertook anything against Stalin.... Know, comrades, that the banner you bear in a triumphant march towards communism contains a drop of my blood too![12]

It was many years before that letter could be received by those to whom it was addressed.

On February 27, 1937, Bukharin said goodbye to his family. He assured Anna that truth would win out and he exhorted her to raise their son as a Bolshevik. He proceeded to the plenum of the central committee where he, along with Rykov, was expelled from the party and arrested for treason. Bukharin and Rykov had declared all accusations against them to be slanderous. Bukharin insisted, "I am not Zinoviev or Kamenev and I will not tell lies against myself."

For thirteen months he was imprisoned and interrogated in the Lubyanka. For three months, he resolutely refused to confess. Then came a period of extended negotiation, threats, and promises. It is likely that he made concessions to save the lives of his family and to have his prison writings published. He had little reason to believe that any promises made to him would be honored, but he held on to whatever thin thread of belief he could grasp.

During this period of thirteen months between his arrest and execution, he wrote four book-length manuscripts.[13] He also wrote letters to Stalin about his prison writings, begging him to let them be published:

I wrote [the prison manuscripts] mostly at night, literally wrenching them from my heart. I fervently beg you not to let this work disappear.... Don't let this work perish.... This is completely apart from my personal fate. [14]

The first was *Socialism and Its Culture,* a sequel to his book *The Degradation of Culture and Fascism* that he was writing before his arrest. Together these were to constitute a two-part work to be called *The Crisis of Capitalist Culture and Socialism.* Bukharin considered the quick publication of this work "at a crossroads of history" to be an urgent matter, devoted as it was to positioning the Soviet Union at the forefront of the anti-fascist struggle. He begged Stalin to have it published, even under a pseudonym if necessary, and to write a preface himself. There was no chance of this, as Stalin was already engaged in the secret diplomacy heading in the direction of the Nazi–Soviet pact of 1939 that had such tragic consequences for the anti-fascist movement.

The next was a collection of poems entitled *The Transformation of the World*. Most of them were poetic reflections on the same themes as preoccupied him in his prose writings. These were of epic scope, sweeping through the history of the world and positing socialism as the culmination of a centuries-old humanistic struggle. Some were also a chronicle of his emotional state, his love for Anna, his longing to be free.

The third was *Philosophical Arabesques*. This loomed large in his struggle to speak in a substantial voice to his own times as well as times to come. He desperately hoped that it could be preserved and somehow published. He must have had surges of expectation that this could be possible, in spite of so much evidence to the contrary, to invest such a massive effort in it and to address the world in it as he did. He wrote to Anna that she would be given the manuscripts in his cell at that time, putting particular emphasis on *Philosophical Arabesques:*

> The most important thing is that the philosophical work not be lost. I worked on it for a long time and put a great deal into it; it is a very mature work in comparison to my earlier writings, and, in contrast to them, dialectical from beginning to end. [15]

Philosophical Arabesques was an ambitious and systematic work of philosophy. The title might arouse an expectation of a collection of fragmentary or even whimsical epigrams, but it was not that. It marshaled the motif of Arabic art to refer to a series of discourses on various themes interwoven with each other to form an intricate pattern. This approach to philosophy set Marxism within the whole history of philosophy, within the whole battle of ideas of world culture of his times. It was a highly polemical text, engaging seriously with virtually every major intellectual trend of its times. It displayed an astute knowledge of the intellectual life of the epoch and the world-historical context from which it emerged. He saw the grain of truth in every previous philosophy and saw Marxism in continuity with the centuries-long struggle to conceptualize the universe. He acknowledged the partial perspectives in each of the contemporary trends contending with Marxism and argued that Marxism superseded every one-sided view of the world to bring philosophy to a higher synthesis than had ever been achieved. It was an integrative and grounded way of thinking that offered a fresh way into the complex new problems of the era.

This was in contrast to another approach to Marxism, which was prevailing in the Soviet Union at that time, isolating it from all outside forces, shutting down all internal debate. Marxism was reduced to a simplistic scheme where canonical formulations were recited repetitively, where all philosophical arguments were set in the past, where all philosophical questions were presented as basically settled. The philosophers busied themselves with writing textbooks, dictionaries, encyclopedias. In doing so, they stuck closely to the classics of Marxism and to current party decrees.

Bukharin began his treatise in a sweeping world-historical style, characterizing the epoch with exuberant energy as a time of titanic struggle between an old order dying and a new order being born, a time of revaluation of all values. As an integral part of this struggle, Marxism was proving to be the ultimate philosophy, holding its head high, winning the battle of ideas, interacting and arguing with all other philosophies, uniquely aware of the socio-historical context of all texts, supremely involved in shaping the world that other philosophies only conceptualized at a distance, indeed going onto the street as a fighting force. He portrayed opposing philosophies as turning away from an integration of reason and emotion and action into one cul-de-sac or another, each seeking one at the expense of the others, whether fixating on exact sciences or categorical imperatives or solemn hymns to blood and iron. From this launching pad, he addressed his readers (presumably the world audience there for his previous books):

> Here the author wishes to proceed along an avenue of thought, an avenue lined with enigmatic sphinxes that have torn many brains apart, but have also been able to play on the sublime harp of creativity. Let us go then to look once again at these old familiar figures and to gaze into their mysterious eyes.

There were shifts of style in the manuscript, some of them due to the circumstances in which it was written, which allowed for little proofreading or revision, but also because he was consciously making concessions to the style in which philosophical polemics of the day were written in order to convince adherents of alternative positions on their own terrain that their arguments were full of holes. Some of these passages, taking up battle on the "field of pure reason," on the terms of adversaries, might have been a bit tedious, but certainly no more so than the texts being addressed. He was at his best, however, when putting their arguments into wider and earthier context and highlighting the contrasts in the light of day.

In his polemic against solipsism, for example, he called attention to the irony of a world where people ate and drank, killed and died, made stone axes and electric generators and learned to determine the chemical composition of stars, while philosophers argued that it was all an illusion, that the whole symphony of the world played only in the solitary consciousness. Arguing constantly that ideas were social products and not immaculate conceptions in the minds of philosophers, he linked solipsism to the trajectory of class societies and how thinkers had become more and more remote from material practice. Going through a whole panoply of forms of subjective idealism, encompassing a cast of characters from Pyrrho to Kant to Eddington, he played out the polemic in several acts: from a purely logical exercise, where they at first seemed invincible, but could on closer inspection be reduced to a series of non sequiturs; to a demonstration of the contradiction of word and deed, where the world inevitably asserted its iron priority against the arrogance of spirit attempting to swallow all; to an argument based in sociology of knowledge, showing how class societies divided all of humanity's vital activities and fixed them in different sections of the population and could not achieve an integral overview.

So he argued on multiple levels, traversing the whole history of philosophy and taking on the whole array of modern currents, showing their roots in previous ideas as well as in contemporary experience. He engaged in polemics against positivism and mechanistic materialism, but the weight of his emphasis was on many forms of idealism, from Hegelian rationalism to primitivist mysticism. Always he stressed the resurgence of the world and the flesh against the arrogance of spirit and the tendency of the "I" to consume the world. He traced this through the evolution of the division of labor in which the theoretician became possible, but became one-sided, impoverished, atomized as mental and manual labor became increasingly disconnected. With the degeneration of capitalism, its radius of cognition tended to diminish.

There was a strong emphasis on the sociology of knowledge. Every concept was a condensation of collective labor, a product of centuries of social history. Every mode of production generated a characteristic mode of thought. He portrayed capitalist intellectual culture as flying off in all directions, chasing one myopic version of reality after another and argued that only socialism could generate a unified vision.

The picture of socialism articulated here was by this stage highly romanticized, but it was an attempt to reconnect with the vision of the society that his generation had sought to create and had believed was really coming into being. Indeed something had been created, however imperfectly, and he was clinging to it in a kind of desperate hope that it could reassert itself against the forces that were destroying it. His prison writing was a struggle to play a role in that still.

The gap between the picture of Soviet society in the text and the society imprisoning and defaming its true believers was a product of prison conditions and complex bargaining and compromising in order to achieve publication. Certainly the genuflections to Stalin as great thinker as well as great leader must be read primarily in this way. Nevertheless I believe that there was a more complicated, more conflicted psychology involved. There had to be some kind of complex dialectic of hope and despair, a striving that was surging and falling, powerful and powerless, not only in relation to his own fate, but to the whole world-historical experiment in socialism, playing itself out within him for him to persist in this work. He still believed, despite everything, that the foundations for true human liberation were being laid in a new mode of production and a new mode of representation.

There was much attention to classical German philosophy. He wanted to prove himself, even posthumously, to Lenin, on questions of philosophy and to vindicate himself against the charge that he had not adequately grasped the meaning of the dialectic and that he had not given due weight to the origins of Marxism in Hegelian philosophy. His knowledge of the history of philosophy was impressively erudite and his references were remarkably accurate, particularly considering the scant resources available to him in prison. He did have access to a number of philosophical texts from the prison library and through the indulgence of his somewhat intellectual interrogator, Kogan. He did become more consciously dialectical, but he did not go in the direction of a neo-Hegelian interpretation of Marxism. Quoting Lenin, he was wary of the "mysticism of the idea" and remained resolutely materialist in emphasis.

He stressed the study of the empirical sciences as well as the history of philosophy. He believed that theoretical tensions in various disciplines, including the natural sciences, were at root questions of philosophy, but that problems of philosophy could only be resolved by a transformation of the social order. Only Marxism provided the grounding for a unity of theory and practice, for a new form of theoretical practice (a term not invented by Althusser). A synthesis of knowledge was only possible in the movement toward socialism. There was formidable thinking being done along these lines, thinking at the foundations of science, but it was being done by those who were being purged, by those who were dying. N. I. Vavilov did not have long to live, nor had Hessen or Uranovky, but Lysenko and Prezent were thriving and denouncing Bukharin as representing the "powers of darkness" for Soviet science. Nevertheless Bukharin wrote in glowing terms of what was being accomplished by Soviet science, not only in compromised conformity to the stultifying official discourse, but in buoyant aspiration for it to be so.

There are other passages that might make a contemporary reader wince. His references to "old women of both sexes" as an image of cringing superstition make it hard for a twenty-first-century feminist, and a no longer young one at that, to come to his defense. He was a man of his times, an advanced thinker and an ardent revolutionary, but still a man of his times.

Perhaps the most jarring note to those of us who live today is the breathless talk of capitalism in its death throes. He exuded a strong sense of living at a time of an old order dying and a new one being born. Perhaps my generation had our own sense of a crisis of social order and radical new possibilities during the rise of a new left that an old Bolshevik would have found strange indeed. But we have lived on to see capitalism not only survive but thrive and to be succeeded by another generation, who might or might not be critical of it, but find it increasingly impossible to imagine an alternative to it.

And what a sad story to tell them is that of the attempted alternative that was the USSR. Some of us still struggle to do this, sometimes like Sisyphus rolling his rock up the hill, but it is vital to tell it in a way that defends its ideals and its accomplishments against slanders that are relentless even now. It must be done without in any dimension or detail failing to look fully into the face of the dark side of it. As I have been writing this, I have been playing a song called "I see a darkness" and imagining the terrifying darkness of the world Bukharin inhabited as he wrote this text. Yet the last words of this manuscript were astonishingly "full of the joy of life." The song playing too proclaims, "I have a drive to live I won't let go."[16] Anna Larina, writing of these horrors from her own experience, as she was transported deeper into a world where a child began each letter to his grandmother saying, "Once again I did not die," nevertheless proclaimed:

> Despite all the horrors prepared for us prisoners by fate, life went on. Life! It is all powerful! It cuts a path for itself, like the delicate fairy-ring mushrooms pushing up through hard thick asphalt.[17]

This, along with the particular determination of one who had at core a philosophical vision and a political cause, is all that could explain what Bukharin wrote next, the last thing he ever wrote. It pulsed with energy and zest for life. It was an autobiographical novel called *Vremena* (literally *The Times*), published in Russian in 1994 and in English in 1998 as *How It All Began*. The title reflected his desire to show the origins of the revolution in the higher impulses that gave birth to it. It represented a radical shift in style from his previous writings. It was more personal, more vivid, more earthy, less alienated. Communists of his generation were not much inclined to write in an experiential mode. It was virtually a memoir, even if names were changed. He must have believed, even if by a tattered thread, that this would give it a chance of publication, even if under a pseudonym. There was, however, no chance. As Stephen Cohen, who played such an important role in finally bringing it to publication, observed:

> Multicolored pictures of pre-1917 Russia, sympathetic portraits of doomed classes, and humanistic characterizations of future Leninists were already forbidden. And writers were being shot for less literary sedition than Bukharin's fleeting mirror images of Stalin's regime in its considerably paler Tsarist predecessor. [18]

The book was beautifully written. It was full of the color and detail of the natural world, of social classes, of religious traditions, of literary texts, of philosophical systems, of political debates. The portraits of personalities were psychologically astute. In contrast to his polemics on Kant in the philosophical manuscript he had just completed, he went back to his first encounter with Kant and conveyed how phenomena and noumena and antinomies and categories had all danced in his head like mysterious monsters, how transcendental idealism and categorical imperatives were like cold pieces of intestine that you could fill with whatever you wanted, but could give no living answers to living questions. He also recaptured his discovery of Marxism and how the world seemed in ferment and how arguments flared and passions blazed as Russia moved toward the revolution of 1905.

Knowing that he was about to die, he was reviewing his life and the very meaning of life. He did so in a way that was remarkably, even astoundingly, full of the joy of life, considering what tragedy was engulfing him and extinguishing the joy of life on such a grand scale. The book broke off in midsentence. Reading it, even knowing it to be an unfinished work ended by its author's death, there comes a jolt, bringing some kind of unexpected immediacy to the realization of what a living striving person had life seized from him, the sort of person who was taken to be shot dead just as he was writing this text so full of life. In his last letters, preparing to die, while still pleading to live, he had particularly asked not to be shot, but instead to be given poison "like Socrates." Nevertheless he was shot.

While writing the novel, he went on trial, one of the most famous trials in the history of the world. He confessed to the general charges, but he sparred with the prosecutor on specific charges, refuted testimony of others, denied even knowing some of his alleged co-conspirators. He formulated his very confession with subordinate clauses that virtually contradicted the main assertions:

> I plead guilty to ... the sum total of crimes committed by this counter-revolutionary organization, irrespective of whether or not I knew of, whether or not I took direct part in, any particular act. [19]

He was walking a tightrope, hoping that he was playing enough of the role written for him in this drama to save his family and his manuscripts, yet departing from the script enough to communicate as much of the truth as he could rescue within this act of the tragedy. He refuted charges of espionage. He denied any involvement in political assassinations, especially of Lenin:

> I refute the accusation of having plotted against the life of Vladimir Ilyich, but my counter-revolutionary confederates, and I at their head, endeavored to murder Lenin's cause, which is being carried on with such tremendous success by Stalin. [20]

The voice of the true believer constantly burst through, even in the guise of a tortuous twisted logic:

> The extreme gravity of the crime is obvious, the political responsibility immense, the legal responsibility such that it will justify the severest sentence. The severest sentence would be justified, because a man deserves to be shot ten times over for such crimes. This I admit quite categorically and without any hesitation at all. I want briefly to explain the facts regarding my criminal activities and my repentance of my misdeeds. I already said when giving my main testimony during the trial, that it was not the naked logic of the struggle that drove us, the counter-revolutionary conspirators, into this stinking underground life, which has been exposed at this trial in all its starkness.

> This naked logic of the struggle was accompanied by a degeneration of ideas, a degeneration of psychology, a degeneration of ourselves.... As this process advanced all the time very rapidly under the conditions of a developing class struggle, this struggle, its speed, its existence, acted as the accelerator, as the catalytic agent of the process which was expressed in the acceleration of the process of degeneration.... It took place amidst colossal socialist construction, with its immense scope, tasks, victories, difficulties, heroism. And on this basis, it seems to me probable that every one of us sitting here in the dock suffered from a peculiar duality of mind, an incomplete faith in his counter-revolutionary cause.... Hence a certain semi-paralysis of the will, a retardation of reflexes ... this was due not to the absence of consistent thought, but to the objective grandeur of socialist construction.... A dual psychology arose.... Even I was sometimes carried away by the eulogies I wrote of socialist construction, although on the morrow I repudiated this by practical actions of a criminal character.... We came out against the joy of the new life with the most criminal methods of struggle.... The logic of this struggle led us step by step into the blackest quagmire. And it has once more been proved that departure from the position of bolshevism means siding with political counter-revolutionary banditry. Counter-revolutionary banditry has now been smashed, we have been smashed, and we repent our frightful crimes. [21]

As other commentators have suggested, his trial testimony, as well as his prison manuscripts, must be read as a coded attempt to communicate covertly something sometimes utterly at odds with what he was asserting overtly. Certainly this final declaration in court was that. The dual psychology could better be read as an analysis of the prosecutors rather than the defendants.

Nevertheless, despite all the codifications and equivocations and refutations, he admitted to leading a counter-revolutionary bloc engaging in terrorist activities devoted to restoring capitalism. It was a bitter slander against himself and his comrades. It was acquiescing in deception and humiliation. His declarations of loyalty to his prosecutors, most particularly to Stalin, were insincere or conflicted, but his affirmation of the cause of socialism was utterly sincere. Looking back on his testimony and trial, Anna Larina asserted:

> But the most amazing thing is that, despite everything, the time of shining hopes had not passed for him. He would pay for these hopes with his head. Moreover, one reason for his preposterous confessions in the dock—incomplete, but sufficiently egregious confessions—was precisely this: he still hoped that the idea to which he had dedicated his life would triumph. [22]

The sentence of death was passed on Bukharin as well as on Rykov, Yagoda, and others, including Trotsky in absentia. The world looked on. A number of international observers were convinced, as were many Soviet citizens. Those who were not convinced were often fearful or confused. Communists abroad were disoriented, even traumatized, by the drama. They might have found the scenario of betrayal and espionage unbelievable, but the alternative interpretation was unthinkable.

The whole history of the revolution was rewritten. Books by Bukharin, indeed by all the purged, disappeared from libraries. Photographs were doctored to erase their presence from seminal events. Soon after the trial came the publication of *The History of the Communist Party of the Soviet Union (Bolshevik): Short Course*. It set the trials within the panorama of a brazenly falsified version of Soviet history. Millions of copies were printed and it became the basic text for the study of Marxism in the USSR. The section on dialectical and historical materialism was hailed as the preeminent work on philosophy, such that nothing else ever needed to be said. As philosophy for the masses, it was pedagogically astute, but it was highly derivative and had a stultifying effect on the further development of Marxist philosophy.

The interaction between philosophy and politics in these decades was quite complex. During the political debates and the purges and accompanying all the abrupt twists and turns of Comintern policy, the exhortation to "think dialectically, comrade" was used to justify the wildest irrationality and arbitrariness. When war came, Stalin worried about the suppression of habits of rationality and ordered that textbooks on formal logic be written and disseminated in the belief that rational thinking was necessary to the war effort. There was a corresponding de-emphasis on the dialectic and on Hegel. Stalin declared Hegel's philosophy to be an aristocratic reaction to the French Revolution, a position which had as much to do with whipping up anti-German feeling after the Nazi invasion of Soviet territory than with any considered judgment on the history of philosophy. There was an increasing emphasis on Russian patriotism, even in the approach to history and science and philosophy. Many theories and discoveries deriving from elsewhere were reattributed to Russians.[23]

After the war, life normalized in some respects, but the stultification of intellectual and political life continued. There was a new campaign against bourgeois cosmopolitanism that reinforced all of the worst tendencies to intellectual conformism and cowardice. After the death of Stalin in 1953 and a new struggle for power came the twentieth party congress in 1956 and

Khrushchev's devastating revelations and condemnations, full of vivid details of false accusations and mass repressions, even quotes from agonized letters of the accused and their last words before execution.

There was a time of thaw when truth was spoken in public, when victims were released from camps, when economic and political reforms were debated. Bukharin's wife and son were reunited. Many of those who had been purged were rehabilitated, including a number of defendants in the big show trials. Bukharin and the other high-profile defendants, Rykov, Zinoviev, Kamenev, were not rehabilitated, even though the quashing of the charges against their supposed co-conspirators made the charges against them even more incredible and incoherent. There was ongoing resistance, especially from those implicated. It applied particularly to Bukharin, because of his association with an attractive alternative. In 1961 Anna Larina finally delivered Bukharin's last testament to a party control commission investigating the case for his rehabilitation. In 1962 Pospelov, a central committee member close to Khrushchev, stated unequivocally to an all-union conference of historians that neither Bukharin nor Rykov was a spy or a traitor.[24] However by 1964 opponents of reform were again ascendant and Khrushchev was replaced by Brezhnev.

There was a revival of Bukharin's ideas, even though his name was still under official ban, from 1956 in the Soviet Union and also in the newer socialist states of Eastern Europe. The cause of reform communism, of socialism with a human face, flared up particularly powerfully in the Prague spring of 1968. It might have been put down in the east later in 1968, but communist parties in the west did not fall into line in giving their support to the "fraternal assistance" rendered by Soviet tanks. Substantial sections of most of these parties criticized or condemned the invasion of Czechoslovakia. Eurocommunism flourished for the next decades. It made Bukharin's name and ideas still dangerous to neo-Stalinist forces intent on holding on to power. For years, his widow and son had petitioned the party to clear him of criminal charges, to restore his name, to readmit him posthumously to the party. In 1978 there was an international campaign for the rehabilitation of Bukharin, which drew considerable support from Eurocommunist quarters, particularly from the PCI in Italy.

I lived in Moscow for five months of 1978. I resided at what was called, on official documents, the Institute of Social Sciences but was the semi-clandestine Lenin School where foreign communists were educated in Marxism. I did not attend classes, as I had during my first visit there in 1977, but pursued my own research program investigating Soviet philosophical debates for the chapter on Soviet Marxism in my book *Marxism and the Philosophy of Science: A Critical History*. At a meeting with Soviet philosophers at the Institute of Philosophy of the USSR Academy of Sciences, I asked why Bukharin's name did not appear in the *Great Soviet Encyclopedia*. They replied, "He has not been rehabilitated." They seemed not to grasp what a weird, crude, and alien concept *rehabilitation* was for a western academic, even if a communist. I had read the western Sovietological literature on these debates and had access to a number of primary sources in western libraries, but I wanted to penetrate further and to get Soviet perspectives on these debates. I rarely got direct answers to direct questions. I constantly had to guess what the rules of the game were, so as to calculate whether I was up against breachable barriers or insurmountable walls. I discovered that I had an interesting space in which to move, that I could do certain things that Soviet academics couldn't do because I was a foreigner, and certain things that other foreigners couldn't do because I was a communist.

On one occasion, when I was asked to give a lecture outlining my research at the Institute of Philosophy, I spoke of Bukharin as well as Trotsky, Sten, Hessen, Uranovsky. It almost didn't matter what I said, which was controversial, of course, but it was the fact that I had mentioned the unmentionable names at all. The atmosphere in the hall was amazing. It was the frisson of forbidden fruit. I can't remember what anyone actually said, but I got the clear impression that many were delighted that I had done it and got away with it, even if they couldn't or wouldn't do so. I became known to the precursors of glasnost and perestroika and was sought out to speak at various events, to broadcast on Moscow Radio, to write for various publications (not that the articles always appeared) by those who wanted to push out (or even test) the boundaries. I also encountered a bruising backlash, but that is another story. I fared better than foreign communists who had done lesser things in the days of the Comintern. I did not disappear. I did not die.

Despite fabricated charges, forced confessions, judicial execution, banned books and falsified histories, Bukharin did break through to posterity and did so with a frayed but unbroken thread of continuity. Wolfe asked in 1957:

> Why is it that [Bukharin's] heresy, so often condemned, so often refuted, so often punished, is so often resurrected? Why does this ghost not keep to his grave, though the stake is driven into his corpse again and again? [25]

He was known, not only to scholars who wanted to know history truthfully, but also to activists who wanted to shape history meaningfully and progressively. He had been a prominent political figure internationally in the 1920s. He was known throughout the world as a theoretician of the revolution. His books were published abroad in many languages and many editions, particularly *The ABC of Communism* and *Historical Materialism*. They were manuals in political schools. Even after he fell from power as a politician at the highest level, he continued to publish at home and abroad in the 1930s. He led the Soviet delegation to the international history of science congress in London in 1931, where he made a lasting impression on the British intelligentsia. The book *Science at the Crossroads,* hastily put together from the Soviet papers at that congress, was a milestone in the development of history, philosophy, and sociology of science. He addressed an audience of French intellectuals and workers at the Sorbonne in 1936. His international audiences were somewhat stunned and disoriented by his arrest, confession and execution, but his name could not be expunged from books in international libraries and continued to be known.

Bukharin was fortunate to have attracted a biographer of the stature and persistence of Stephen Cohen. His work *Bukharin and the Bolshevik Revolution,* published in 1973, brought Bukharin to life for me as for many others. It was an important source in writing about Bukharin in my own book, *Marxism and the Philosophy of Science,* that I was writing in the 1970s. It was influential in keeping the profile of Bukharin alive and clear of corrupting calumnies. Bukharin's son Yuri Larin discovered it and began a prolonged underground project of translating it into Russian. Among those who read it eventually was Mikhail Gorbachev. The other key figure in mediating between Bukharin and future generations was, of course, his young wife Anna Larina, although it was decades before she could break into the public arena to say what she had to say. She knew him from the time she was a child, as a daughter of a prominent Bolshevik and friend of Bukharin. She never saw him again after his arrest in 1937 and suffered prison, exile, separation from her baby son. When widow, son, and biographer teamed up in the 1970s and began to gather others, his path to posterity opened into the process that would eventually bring his prison manuscripts out of dark vaults into the light of day.

With the ascendancy of Gorbachev came glasnost and perestroika and recovery of history. These were ideas associated with the legacy of Bukharin as well as ideas creating an atmosphere favorable to his rehabilitation. This time it happened. Bukharin was judicially exonerated of all criminal charges and restored to party membership in 1988. What followed was a Bukharin boom. The memoirs of Anna Larina were a publishing sensation. After years of captivity, then obscurity, she became a celebrity. There were many books, articles, broadcasts, films, plays, and exhibitions featuring Bukharin. His last testament was finally given to the mass of party members. It was read at party meetings to tearful and powerful responses. For many Soviet citizens, it was "an emotional excursion into their long forbidden past." [26] It was highly charged and much of the charge from this spread to other socialist countries in Europe and also China. It was not only part of a revelation of the past but also a revaluation of paths into the future. There was a strong sense of hope, of renewal, of possibility of really building socialism with a human face, socialism with economic efficiency, socialism with political democracy, socialism with cultural creativity. Everything opened up just before it closed down again.

Then came the next act of the tragedy. The world turned upside down again. In 1992 Anna Larina finally received a letter written to her in 1938. Bukharin, on the eve of his fateful trial, exhorted her to "Remember that the great cause of the USSR lives on, and *this* is the most important thing. Personal fates are transitory and wretched by comparison." [27] She read it in a world in which the USSR had just fallen.

We read it now in a world in which the USSR has disappeared from the map. We encounter these manuscripts in a world that has moved on and considers socialism to have failed and to be forever off the agenda. A first-year student at Dublin City University, who heard a colleague of mine refer to the debate about whether socialism had failed, asked, "What is socialism?"

Nevertheless it persists in collective memory and higher human aspiration, even to the point where those who insist that it is dead believe that they must vanquish any vestige of mourning from those who keep coming to the grave and speak of what they have lost; that they must wipe the wistful smile from the face of anyone who takes pride in having ever called another "comrade" and remembers meaningful common effort; that they must not allow another generation to imagine a future in continuity with this past. [28]

Whatever may come in the future that may draw something deeper than dominant ideology cliché from this past, the USSR is gone. Nevertheless this past keeps pouring into our present. Neither those who honor it in whatever conflicting and complex ways nor those who revile it will let it go. Its story is one of the most momentous in the history of the world. Its story must be told fully and truthfully. Bukharin's life and work and death constitute a major stand in this story. So are the stories of all who built, as well as all who betrayed, the movement that sought to put the world into the hands of those who labor in it. Although the allegations against original Bolshevik leaders were finally and fully exposed as ludicrous and false, it seemed that their communist party did eventually give rise to leaders who would conspire to restore capitalism. There were enormous forces in play and a movement of history that was perhaps inexorable, but the role of communists turned anti-communists adds a note of bitter irony to the story of how it all began and how it all ended.

This manuscript is one document of that story. Its author had the astonishing composure and commitment to want to move the narrative onward, not only in his life but after his death. He believed that the brightness of the original vision was strong enough to overcome the darkness. It did break through somehow throughout all of those years even if the darkness prevailed. Those who accused those who dreamed of socialism of conspiring to restore capitalism, those who kept the truth of it in forbidden vaults, were the ones who sowed the seeds of reaction and restoration.

He could not have envisioned when laboring in his bleak cell to write the 310 tightly handwritten pages of this text that it would be buried in a vault for fifty-four years, that it would be published in a Russia that had renounced the legacy of the USSR, that it would come to me via forty-one email attachments from New York to Dublin in 2001 as I faced the task of bridging his world and ours. We all write into a vast unknown. We imagine an audience, but our published words move into the world along paths previously unimagined.

So how relevant is this text written so long ago and now published in our world of gloating, globalized capitalism? Is it only a record of doomed dreams or is it a voice from the dead saying something substantial to our postmodern post-philosophical times? I believe that it is a voice reminding us of the capacity of Marxism to take on the battle of ideas in our own times, to signpost the blind alleys of our own era, to rise up in the world again as an illuminating and transforming force. It is a voice inciting us to deal with the darkness of our own days and to reach for the future.

Editorial Note

Our aim in publishing this translation of Bukharin's *Philosophical Arabesques* is to make his text accessible in English to scholars and general readers.

With this purpose in mind, the text has been edited and annotated in such a way as to provide translations, references to sources, and background information that assist in making the text accessible, while at the same time avoiding a cumbersome apparatus. Bukharin was not able to edit his own text. Quite probably, he was not able to complete it. It is likely that he began Chapter 3, for example, then cut it short, and intended to continue with it, had death not intervened. We have not attempted to edit or complete it for him.

Any translation differs from the original in the myriad ways in which one language's tone, nuances, and emphases are not captured in another. Leaving these aside, the translation offered here differs from the original in the following, more systematic, respects:

1. We have broken up long paragraphs, in which one step of an argument leads into another without a paragraph break. We have done this when the insertion of a paragraph break made the argument or exposition clearer. Bukharin often used very short paragraphs for effect, sometimes just a few words. We have left these as they were.
2. We have kept phrases or sentences in languages other than Russian in their original languages only when they have a special sense in that language that will be lost in translation. Bukharin included, in almost every chapter, phrases and sentences in German and Latin, above all, but also in French, Italian, English, and ancient Greek. In some cases, but not all,

he followed the foreign phrase with a Russian translation. We have sometimes made use of this device—that is, including both the German or Latin word and the English in the text—when this does not result in an overly clumsy sentence. When the foreign phrase carried no special meaning that was lost in English translation, we have simply translated it into English. Nothing is gained, for example, by keeping the expression that "the wish is father to the thought" in the German in which Bukharin used it. For longer phrases or whole sentences that have been kept in the original language, English translations are provided in the notes.

3. In a small number of cases we have included brief editorial additions in the text, placing them in square brackets. We have limited such additions to the handful of passages that cannot be understood correctly without them. None of the material in square brackets is by Bukharin. However, Bukharin often interpolated his own comments in passages that he quotes. These comments are placed in parentheses, and followed by the word *author*, when that is necessary to indicate that the words are Bukharin's rather than those of the source quoted. Bukharin often included brief reference to the source of a quotation or citation in parentheses in the text, at the end of the quotation. We have kept them there, usually in the original language.

4. In a small number of cases, where it is overwhelmingly likely that the Russian edition of *Philosophical Arabesques* relies on a mistranscription of Bukharin's handwritten text, we have corrected such mistranscriptions. These corrections never involve more than a single word at a time, but sometimes alter the meaning of the sentence completely. In one case we have explained the change in a note.

We do not believe that these editorial interventions make the translation significantly less accurate, or change the meaning of the original text beyond the extent that is unavoidable in any translation. Taken together, they result in a text that is accurate in all essentials and considerably more readable.

In addition, we have provided references to the current English translations of sources quoted in the text and mainly biographical information relating to contemporary authors and works discussed by Bukharin that are now less well-known than when he wrote or less well-known outside Russia. Bukharin's translations into Russian of Hegel and other authors frequently carry a different emphasis from the current English translations. We have generally followed his translations rather than those of the current translations. We have not indicated differences in emphasis or terminology in the notes. On several occasions, Bukharin identifies the text from which he quotes in ways that are misleading or mistaken. Some of his apparent quotations are, in fact, paraphrases of the text. We have generally indicated these in the notes.

Biographical details are given in the notes only for the first references to a specific figure or text. These notes usually indicate dates, national origins, and significance very briefly and are not intended to be exhaustive.

The publishers gratefully acknowledge material for the annotations provided by George Shriver, who also checked and modified the translation of the text by Renfrey Clarke. He drew on the notes to the Russian edition of *Philosophical Arabesques*, but has also often improved on them, tracking down references that had eluded the Russian editors.

Author's Foreword

This book consists of a series of sketches bearing on important philosophical questions from the point of view of dialectical materialism. Especially in the opening sections, the argument at times has the character of journalistic commentary; nevertheless, the author has tried to follow a definite plan linking the "arabesques" together into a single whole. All the issues touched on are examined on their merits, but the stress is on the dialectical side of the questions. As his starting point, the author has taken a number of new points of view developed by Lenin in some remarkable drafts and fragments.[1]

Author's Introduction

Our age is characterized by a great crisis of world history. The struggle of social forces has reached an acute level. For old women of both sexes, these are apocalyptic times. We are witnessing the birth of a new world for humankind. For the revolutionary class it is a time of great heroic feats, and for the dying, departing order, it is a *Götterdämmerung*. All the old values are crumbling and collapsing. A general reevaluation of habits, norms, ideas, and world views is taking place, a demarcation and polarization of all material and spiritual potentials. Is there anything surprising in the fact that philosophy as well is being drawn into this whirlpool, into this titanic struggle? And is there anything surprising in the fact that the philosophy of Marxism, about which professional philosophers spoke with contemptuous smiles a few years back, has now risen to its feet and is thrusting its head high into the very heavens?

Marxism has not only come out into the street as a fighting force; it represents the supreme generalization of the theory and practice of socialism, of the new social system which now exists as the greatest world-historical factor of life. The enemies of Marxism try to attach compromising labels to it, describing it as a new religion, as eschatology and messianism. But a fine religion this is—one that is materialist! A fine eschatology (speculation on ultimate human goals), when socialism is already a fact! A wonderful messianism (understood as utopia), when it is seizing hold of hundreds of millions of people, and what is most important, is winning! And how it is winning! In direct class struggle, in production, in technology, in science, in scholarship, in travel, in heroic feats, in philosophy, in art—in short, in all spheres of the marvelous and tragic theater of life! Marxism covers the rubbish pits of history with sand and sprays them with disinfectant. To the horror of God-fearing women and cunning priests, livid with spite and rage, it abolishes even religion, this "spiritual perfume" of the old society—a society ruled by money, the "universal whore, universal procuress of people and nations"; a society ruled by capital, which came into the world "oozing blood and filth from every pore."[1]

Today's working-class hero is totally unlike the young ignoramus in Fonvizin, who asked, "Why do I need to know geography, when carriage drivers exist?"[2] It is the workers' enemies who are playing the role of ignoramus. It is they who are increasingly turning their backs on the intellect, which refuses to serve their ends. It is they who snatch up stone axes, the swastika, the horoscope. It is they who are starting to read haltingly from the book of history, sounding it out syllable by syllable. It is they who pray to stone goddesses and idols. It is they who have turned their backs on the future, and like Heine's dog, to which they have fitted a historical muzzle, they now bark with their backsides, while history in turn shows them only its a posteriori. Fine battles are now breaking out amid the grandiose festivities, and conflict envelops all areas.

Philosophy has often been Janus-faced; one of its faces has been turned to humanity, and the other to nature. The dictum of Socrates, "Know yourself!" corresponded to a crisis in Greek life, when the bewildered "subject" was seeking a place in society and opening his eyes wide, was asking what he was, what he had to live for, and what "good" itself was. Philosophy too unearthed multitudes of questions of a social and moral nature. But Bacon of Verulam thought this almost an idle pursuit.[3]

Bacon posed other questions, about the nature of things, about the physical world, about truth. The rational consciousness of new people, the people of bourgeois society, went forward and smashed the stocks in which feudalism had kept its prisoners immobilized.

Great crises blow apart all of the old systems of life, and pose anew the question of the human individual and the question of the world, since both the old social bonds and the old world view fall apart, just as they are doing now. What leaps, what pirouettes, the philosophical spirit of the present-day bourgeoisie is performing! They have gone from Christianity, with its rose-colored anointing oil, to the cult of Wotan.[4] From Kant's categorical imperative to solemn hymns to blood and iron. From the worship of reason to intuitive-mystical contemplation. From exact science to the barbaric worship of the most primitive superstitions. Indeed, the "drunken speculation" of idealist philosophy was a titan beside the wretched but insolent trolls of present-day mysticism, of whom even their spiritual ancestor Nietzsche might have said: "I sowed dragons, and reaped fleas."

But these are fleas only in the intellectual sense. In material terms they are still armed with first-class weapons, and they have to be resisted primarily with material force. As Marx wrote in *The Holy Family*, "Ideas can never lead beyond the bounds of the old order; they always lead merely beyond the bounds of the ideas of the old order. Ideas in general can never implement anything; the implementation of ideas requires people, who have to apply practical force."[5] But theory is also a force when it seizes hold of the masses. The people who apply practical force need to be people armed with ideas. This is why the battle of ideas is so important, especially in times of crisis. Socialism, the giant of the new material world, has become the giant of the new world view. The people of the new world have become new people, integrated individuals, people of will and thought, theory and practice, feeling and intellect, heart and mind, soul and spirit simultaneously. The profoundly tragic German writer Hölderlin lamented in his *Hyperion*: "I cannot imagine a people more torn asunder than the Germans. You see artisans but not people, thinkers but not people, clerics but not people, masters and servants . . . but still not people."

The unfortunate Hölderlin did not understand that class society dooms human beings to an inhuman existence. But it is precisely this inhuman existence that fascism elevates into an eternal law of hierarchy, in which "noble estates" are destined to rule forever over the "rabble" and in which people are bound forever to their trade and class. In our country all this has been overturned. As a result the corresponding categories of thought have been overturned as well, the kind of thought that characterized the *Domostroi*, which is still being preached and put into practice in the former land of philosophers and poets.[6]

In the *Domostroi* of the old "true Russia" it was said, even in regard to infants: "Do not hold back from beating a child, for if you beat him with a rod he will not die, but will be healthier for it; when you beat his body, you save his soul from death." This is becoming the height of wisdom in the fascists' paradise, and the same patriarchal lash rules in their world view. How much further can you go than to seriously proclaim as the epistemological criterion of truth the thinking of Herr Hitler? Even Papism could not dream up formulae of such genius! And now the fascists have managed it.

The way in which their thinking has fallen into this cesspit is symptomatic. But in the great struggle there are many paths, and even well-paved roads, that lead to this pit. In the demarcation of ideas, therefore, it is also necessary to confront with fixed bayonets the people who try to divert the course of development away from the broad highway of dialectical materialism. Unfortunately, there are a great many such people. Often, they do not understand what they are doing. But as was first said long ago, *ignorantia non est argumentum*—ignorance is neither an argument nor an excuse....

Kantians, positivists, agnostics, phenomenalists, and others—make your choice! Time is running out.

Here the author wishes to proceed with his readers along the avenue of thought, an avenue lined with enigmatic sphinxes that have torn many brains apart, but which have also been able to play on the sublime harp of creativity.

Let us go then, to look once again at these old, familiar figures, and to gaze into their mysterious eyes.

1

The Reality of the External World, and the Intrigues of Solipsism

Future generations will learn with surprise how the old world of class society—Hellenic antiquity, the Indian sages, and the refined philosophy of capitalism alike—left in its wrinkled, time-yellowed books, written in forgotten scripts, a monstrous theory concerning a human individual who had disclaimed everything else in the world and all other human beings. People ate and drank, killed and died, procreated, made equipment ranging from stone axes and arrowheads to diesel motors and electric generators, engaged in production, and learned to weigh stars and determine their chemical composition. Philosophers, meanwhile, argued that all this was a dream, an illusion, a *fata morgana*, a Chinese shadow play flickering in the consciousness of a solitary *solus ipse* of a madman who imagined that nothing existed apart from himself, and that everything was played out in his consciousness.[1] Our descendants will also recall that these philosophers died, and that in their place came new philosophers who read the works of their predecessors, were infected by them with solipsist stupidity, and—oh, the comedy of it!—denied even the poisoned sources from which they had imbibed their wretched wisdom. A world that could produce such people truly deserved to collapse!

But alas, these walking dead, these living corpses, remote from material practice, "pure thinkers," intellectual human dust, still exist, and most importantly, continue to infect the air with the excreta of their brains and to cast their nets, fine, sticky nets of arguments which to many people still seem convincing.

Well, then, let the game start, the fun begin! Let the swords flash, and the shields clash together!

The devil of solipsism is a cunning spirit. It drapes itself in an enchantingly patterned cloak of iron logic, and it laughs, poking out its tongue. How many people, after reading Bishop Berkeley, Hume, Mach, and the agnostics (the names of these philosophers are legion), have pressed their fevered brows to the cold wall or the window frame and asked themselves in bewilderment: "How can this be? After all, I can beat my head against this window frame. How can it not exist?"

But here Mephistopheles appears, and curling his lips ironically, says: "Oh, what a crude argument, my dear, naive child! How vulgar! You will go on to say that you eat bread and meat, digest them, and excrete the wastes. But is this kind of discourse worthy of a philosopher? This is an argument for the rabble out in the street, of whom the poet Horace wrote: *Odi profanum vulgus et cereco*—"Despise the profane multitude." This argument is for the vulgar, with their soiled hands, for the people who touch dirty things and engage in vile, filthy work. To people like this, such commonplace and, to tell the truth, gutter-level conclusions are convincing. But for you, my fine young man, for the heroes of pure thought, for the knights of the spirit, it is shameful to resort to such arguments. How do you know that the world exists? Is it not from your sensations that you know about everything? But these are *your* sensations, and yours alone! You will never be able to leap out of them. And whatever you create, whatever theories you might construct, you construct out of these blocks. From what else? Be consistent! Is this frightening to you? Are you afraid of solitude? Does the idea of the world becoming extinct scare you? Do you want the stars, love, and finally—the devil take it!—to perform deeds, great feats, perhaps? You have all this, the stars, love, and pursuits to occupy yourself with. You can enjoy yourself, love, read, and even work, if this interests you so much. But all this is within you, yours, for you. Within you is the whole symphony of the world. Isn't this enough?

"And anyway, my young friend, why do you need consoling? Isn't this an affront to your dignity? Whatever the truth is, you must look it in the face. Be consistent! Be fearless! Ha, ha, ha!"

And so, the wretched youth wipes his sweat-laden brow and squints at the window frame, where once again he fancies he sees the devil of logic poking its tongue out at him...

But let us leave this imaginary game of our imaginary young man and his tempter. Let us move on to the essence.

In reality, where is the seemingly convincing strength of the arguments of the solipsists, who appear so forthright and consistent (but in fact are so little so), and of the agnostics with their "obscurity of themes"? It lies in the impression they give of logical purity. Everything is strictly consistent. There is nothing superfluous. Everything is "from experience." Nothing is "thought up." "I am given my sensations." There is the whole stock of equipment. Everything else proceeds from this: all thinking, all opinions, all science, the entire "positive picture of the world." There is no escaping this situation. All that is possible is to reorganize these "data." No leap, no *transensus* or going beyond the senses to some other framework. Nothing else exists; the hypothesis of some alternative is groundless, since there is only this, "my sensations," and within their bounds the whole game is played out. Everything else is metaphysics, idle concoctions. True, it is possible to believe. But that is already a departure from empiricism, from experience, to believe that something exists beyond the bounds of "my sensations." *Sapienti sat.*[2]

These arguments seemed to many people to be so convincing, that even so powerful a critical mind as that of Georgy Plekhanov somehow let slip into print a sentence to the effect that philosophy had to perform a life-saving leap of faith, a *salto vitale* (as opposed to *salto mortale*, or death leap) in order to be able to continue its work. Here, indeed, we cannot fail to recall the Metropolitan Filaret of blessed memory and what he said in his *Catechesis*: "Faith is a notification of things for which we hope, a revelation of things that are unseen"!

How all the empiriocritics, empiriomonists, and empiriosymbolists have grasped at this "faith"! With what aplomb they have mocked the "holy matter," the *transensus*, and the "theology" of dialectical materialism, these people who have preached idealism, God-building, and God-seeking against a background of decadent social psychology during the times of reaction! That is what things were like! In the field of theory, meanwhile, Plekhanov for all his errors was a figure of the first rank, and Ilyich more than once described him as "an eagle." Krylov instructed us: "Eagles at times descend lower than chickens, but chickens never soar into the heavens."

Did the eagle, however, really have to descend lower than the chickens?

Indeed, he did not. No *salto vitale* is needed. Moreover, this *salto vitale* is indistinguishable in practice from a *salto mortale* with its lethal results, ending in death rather than in flight. The eagle should not have descended into a moldy, dung-strewn chicken pen!

Let us examine the question in still more depth. So much digging! We are also ready, temporarily, to make a major concession of principle. Because the "crude" refutation that comes from practice is a very powerful refutation. It is an enormously important idea. But we are also ready to take up the battle in the so-called "field of pure reason," that is, on the terms proposed by our adversaries. If you please, kind sirs!

Hence: "I am given only my sensations."

Who is this "I"?

It is obvious that the "I" is the solipsist philosopher, or the agnostic. An adult human being, cultured in his or her fashion, who has read books, written them, and so forth. To simplify the argument, we shall perform a certain hypocritical reincarnation, a temporary masquerade. This philosopher, this "I," writes the lines that follow.

So then, "I am given my sensations."

When?

Obviously, at each minute, each moment of my experience. At present I am writing. The paper is a complex of white, hard, smooth, cold. The pen is a complex of black, hard, and so forth. In short, according to all the rules of Berkeley and Hume, and all the norms of Ernst Mach's "analysis of sensations." This is given to me. From these sensations I piece together the paper, the pen, my own hand. *Mutatis mutandis*, I do the same with the remaining "sense elements." But allow me—are things really like this? Is such a "pure description," of which the philosophers of the schools listed above are so proud, really true? Do they describe things purely? Did I make up something? Indeed, I just created a pure invention that was, as it seemed, given to me.

This was something untrue and impure. The content of my "consciousness" was not at all like that. My "experiences" were described inaccurately. It is true that here there were black and white, smooth and cold. But this is now also linked indissolubly in me with the concept of the object. I do not have *pure* sensation. This virginal, innocent quality of sensation does not exist. I experience (to use the terminology of the adversary) black, white, and so on, and these elements are already entering into the concept of the things to which I, moreover, relate in an active, practical fashion. I see the paper; I know what it is and why I need it; I use it. I have to perform intellectual work; I have to make an effort in order to break open the shells of all these sensations, in order to isolate them from the bond of the concepts of the things, the objects, which in reality are not passively given to me, but which I use in one way or another. The sensations here are a product of analysis, a secondary, not a primary product, not raw material. They represent an end point, not a starting point. For me, now (the stress is on this context), these sensations have been obtained as a result of thought. I am not Eve, only just created by "the Lord" from Adam's rib, without a single idea in her head, knowing nothing and surrounded by a chaos of sounds, of colors and hues, with a head overflowing solely with sensations that have poured in for the first time. Though not a woman, I encountered the serpent of wisdom long ago, and have more than once tasted the fruits of the forbidden tree of the knowledge of good and evil. So why do they want to return me to an innocent-virginal-barbaric state of paradisiacally blissful, stupid, brainless, unthinking existence?

To make a long story short: It is not true that "I am given my sensations." I do not have pure, unadulterated sensations. That is an abstraction from what I have in reality, a distortion of my experience. Sensations sit within me in the pores of ideas. I do not begin the process *ab ovo* on behalf of all humanity. Nor do I repeat my own experience *ab ovo*, from the day I was born. I do not only sense; I also think and work. I sense and think at the same time. My sensations are not imparted to me in isolation, and are in no sense primary data. This, gentlemen, is where reality lies, not in your abstract fiction, not in a metaphysical illusion brought in under the guise of anti-metaphysical "positive science." A characteristic of vulgar empiricism (or creeping empiricism, as Friedrich Engels called it), and of people who treat dialectics with scorn, is that accompanied by the drums of anti-metaphysical battle, they fall into genuine metaphysics. Bang-bang! Bang-bang! Down with metaphysics, and long live pure description! But wait, gentlemen! It is you who have torn metaphysical sensations out of their real setting. It is you who have divorced sensation from understanding, feeling from thought. It is you who have set apart in time that which happens simultaneously. It is you who, in crudely anti-dialectical fashion, have destroyed the real bonds and the real processes!

Sensations are thus intermixed with understanding in a single stream of experiences; they interpenetrate one another at each given moment of experience. (We are conducting the debate here in our opponents' terms; let that be a consolation for them in "this vale of tears.")

Enormously important conclusions flow from this. Ideas are social products, and are inconceivable as purely individual products in just the same way as language, which can develop only in society among people living together, working together, communicating and interacting with one another. An individual as a biological unit, an individual in his or her essence, can and does experience sensations. But only a socialized human being thinks. An unsocialized human being is a crude abstraction. He or she is not a human being, much less a philosophizing human being, still less a philosophical "I." Every idea represents a departure from the individual, a departure from subjectivity. No color-blind person could discover that he or she was color-blind if he or she was *solus ipse* (the self alone). Consequently, any idea and any word adequate to describe it—that is, any act of thought and any act of speech—carries within itself the presumption "we." It is a negation of isolation and of the solitary "I." Moreover, it presumes thousands of years of human history, in the course of which ideas were shaped. Thus it is already presumed that "we" (and consequently, also he, she, and they) are inhabitants of the same social space, and are common participants in thought, since thought is a characteristic of the socialized human being.

Consequently, we have social human beings, or to use the language of Avenarius, *Mitmenschen* or "co-people." But because social human beings exist, there is absolutely no logical basis for objecting to the recognition of non-human beings, that is, to the recognition of natural things and processes, of the world of objects, of external reality in general. The breach has been made. Once I have recognized other human beings, in all their bodily reality, then by virtue of this I also recognize trees, grass, earth, and everything else. Through this breach a stream of reality has immediately poured, a stream of the real external world, objectively existing independent of its recognition by a subject. In our argumentation, therefore, social human beings are merely a bridge, a logical bridge. The entire real world breaks in, as data, defying the crazy narrow-mindedness of the solipsist.

The virginal purity and innocence of solipsist argumentation thus collapses. The immaculate conception of the world in the head of the philosopher, without the intervention of the external world, that is of the world outside the human brain, turns out to be just as much a myth as the immaculate conception of "the Lamb of God" who takes away the sins of the world.

But here our opponent comes running up, red-faced, gasping for breath, and in a strange state of indignation. Like a machine gun, he fires off his angry tirades:

"What? Do you deny that a child first has sensations, then forms ideas from them, and then...."

And so on, and so on.

Calm yourself! It's not good for you to get excited. And don't seize on an innocent child, because there is no way, absolutely no way, that it can help you. We agreed that we were talking about an adult, a philosopher. But if a grown philosopher needs the help of a tiny child, and for fear of drowning clutches at this straw, then we can talk about the little one as well. What, kind sir, are these directly perceived data of yours?

The child is not you, but someone else.

You cannot experience in the way a child does.

There is not even a trace of "my" sensations here. We are now talking about the child's sensations (that is, you have already jumped out of the category "my"). Moreover, you are not talking about a particular child, but about children in general. That is, you are making a summary and a generalization of your observations of a number of children.

In other words, you are assuming that a whole series of little subjects exist as well as yourself (and consequently, whether one wishes or not, that the world around them exists as well). In order to deny the world, you seize on an affirmation of the world. Perhaps this is also dialectics, but if so, let the immortal gods save us from it!

Here you are making a *salto vitale* which turns out to be a *salto mortale* for your entire rotten philosophy!

This confirms the total logical bankruptcy of the entire school of the solipsists, the agnostic-positivists, and *tutti quanti*. Their directly perceived data are not directly perceived; they are the product of what in logical terms is extremely bad analysis. In this way, we arrive at the conclusion that there are other people, and that there is an external world. We reach this point without any *salto*. It could not be otherwise. The proposition that logic and thought, which is the continuation of practice, could turn into absolutely distinct, totally counterposed, eternally estranged premises is quite monstrous. In practice, it would transform this world, which the theory denies exists. Real experience, which rests on the gigantic development of humanity and on the totality of human practice, in essence on all of life, speaks of something completely different. The solipsists have neither a grain of dialectics in them, nor a grain of the historical. They have only a kind of wooden lunacy, the rigidity of a hermit, the supreme poverty and spiritual destitution of an intellectual artisan, and a sterilized world crammed into their little skulls.

Hold your tongue, Mephistopheles!

Hold your dissolute tongue!

2

Acceptance and Nonacceptance of the World

As we have seen, the arguments of the solipsists are full of holes. But all philosophical currents that resemble solipsism, subjective idealism in general, agnosticism, and skepticism—which Hegel in his *History of Philosophy* spoke of as "invincible"—seem more or less imposing only when we are concerned with the so-called purely logical battle with them, though here as well they are doomed to defeat. In philosophy it is acceptable to pursue a discussion on the restricted plane of the most elevated abstractions, but it is not considered proper to undermine and destroy those abstractions from below, taking as one's starting point the most diverse types of human activity. Let us examine solipsism, with its "I," from this angle. What sort of "I" is this? "I" here is a known whole. But this whole is finite. No "I" can remember itself in the infinity of time, but only from a particular age. Even if we invoke a Platonic recollection, this is of little help, since it is evident that here there is no given, but a speculative explanation. And what was there before "I"? What will there be after "I"? Solipsism provides absolutely no clarification on these elementary points; it is not done to pose such questions. Why, exactly? Because this, you must understand, is the "vulgar" way of posing the question. But who said that a monstrous abstraction was superior to a diverse palette?

The subjective idealists are on the attack. It is necessary, however, to put them on the defensive.

The "I" eats, drinks, and engenders children. Is this merely prosaic? So be it. But all the same, does the "I" eat and drink? Or doesn't the "I" eat and drink? Does the "I" have a body or doesn't it?

Does the "I" have a brain or not? It is completely absurd to assume that a pure spiritual substance, "I," exists on its own without a material substrate. Otherwise, how would this pure "I-spirit," this "pure consciousness," become conscious of its own corporeal existence, of its organism with its sicknesses, bodily needs, and urges—that is, of the states of consciousness that in consciousness itself are linked with corporeal existence? And if this corporeal existence is in one way or another a fact, where does it come from? Implicit in this are such things as parents, as time, as the evolution of species, as nutrition and digestion, as the external world, and so on and so forth. Let the solipsists answer all these questions! Let the burden of proof lie on them for a while! But amidst these problems, the solipsists will immediately feel themselves like fish out of water. All questions of material life (such as food, drink, production, consumption, reproduction, and so on), of all culture, and of all mastering of the world (both theoretically and in practice) become impossible to explain, while wonderful mysteries issue from the very body of the notorious *solus ipse*.

Or else the above-mentioned "I" has to proclaim itself incorporeal, outside of time and space, an essence in whose eternity the difference between present, past, and future vanishes. No one, however, has yet been daring enough to perform such a *salto*. Perhaps a general "I" will save the day? Not the "I" of the solipsists, but an "I" in the Fichtean sense? Alas, if the question is posed in this way the attractiveness of the consistency (an almost-strictly-empirical consistency) which distinguishes the school of Berkeley and Hume and their recent satellites, along with the camp of positivist agnosticism and phenomenalism, is no more. This is because the "general I" is in no sense an original given, and its nature as a general abstraction of the intellect, as generic consciousness, is obvious at first glance. On the other hand, it is stronger for the fact that the other empirical "I's" come and go, while humankind remains. But here, too, the same questions are not to be escaped. What was there before humanity? What about the entire history of humanity—was this a myth? Do we have to send all of geology, paleontology, biology, and so on to the devil? All pile-dwellings, stone axes, bows and arrows, spears, catapults and ballistae, pyramids, canals, and steam engines? All human history in general?

Let us return to our *solus ipse*. Is this he or she, masculine or feminine? Or perhaps androgynous?

They will say to us: "What questions! What stupidity!" But why? If we are dealing with strict (ha, ha, ha!) empiricism, then consciousness along with everything else has to include attractions of a sexual variety (since emotions, fits of passion, and so on are not denied). Hence we will judge the issue not on the basis of external indications, but according to the facts of consciousness. If we are talking about a male principle (the "M" of Otto Weininger in *Sex and Character*), this means that there is also a woman, a real woman, outside of consciousness. If the principle is "F," that means there is also a man. And so on. Just try to evade these questions! It is, of course, possible to strike a pose for a while, arguing that such questions are "inappropriate," that they profane the snow-white mountain summits of thought. But this is a cheap indignation—if you please, the "nobility" of a card shark who has been caught in the act.

It is said of the Greek Skeptic Pyrrho that, taking his lead from the certainty of the untrustworthiness of the senses, he walked directly into the path of a chariot that was rushing toward him, and that his friends forcefully pulled him back and saved him from inevitable disaster. *Se non e vero, e ben trovato* ("If it isn't true, it's well thought up"). This is a unique case of consistency. In reality, there is not a single skeptic, agnostic, or solipsist who, if in imminent danger of being killed, would refrain from doing whatever was necessary to save his or her life. Why? If these people's beliefs are serious, how are we to explain this bifurcation, this polarity of theory and practice, of belief and behavior? Perhaps it is the behavior that is serious? In this case, is it not clear that the belief rests on sand? The accepted view is that arguments "with legs" are not arguments. So why the paradox? Because until now the people who have philosophized have been, so to speak, legless, defective people whose theory has been divorced from practice, and in whose consciousness the real world has been replaced by a world of mental abstractions and symbols.

Just look at the number of inconsistencies in the life of a solipsist or agnostic! If everything were acted out only in this person's pure consciousness, what would be the point in him or her even moving? A thousand times more consistent in this regard are the sages of Hindu spiritualism who spend years contemplating their own navels, considering the world of the senses to be the veil of illusion. Here the approach of not accepting the world is pursued much more consistently, though alas, even the frail body of the ascetic cannot distance itself entirely from its prosaic water and dish of rice, roots, and fruit. Of course, from the point of view of accepting the world or not accepting it, it makes no fundamental difference what your tastes are—whether they run to locusts and wild honey, or to roast beef, fruit, and champagne. In this case one might at least say: *Ut desint vires, tamen est laudanda voluntas* ("Even if the strength is lacking, the desire is praiseworthy"). To Western European philosophers who refuse to accept the world such a lack of discrimination seems scandalously hypocritical. But here, of course, what interests us is not the "moral" aspect of the matter—that side of things can go to the devil. What interests us is the fact that, here, behavior disproves a theory which flees into the bushes when confronted by the most ordinary facts of ordinary everyday life. Among Buddhists and pre-Buddhist Hindus, "brahma-nirvana," or "nibbanam," also meant rejecting the world of the senses in the name of an ideal supersensory world that for them possessed a reality outside of temporal being. Subjective idealists and solipsists, meanwhile, do not even have this. Their arrogance of spirit swallows everything, and at the same time is dialectically transformed into a miserable game which, in a multitude of conflicts with reality, beats a cowardly retreat literally at every step.

In nirvanic practice, the will is directed toward overcoming itself through rejecting the world of the senses and through self-absorption; this provides relief by reducing the sphere of action in general—that is, the sphere of active relationship to the outside world. But how are solipsists, who do not accept the existence of the world, to extricate themselves, when at the same time as rejecting this world, they act, that is, walk, eat, drink, work, love, make objects, engender children, and so on. It is one thing when people hold forth on the nonacceptance of the world from the point of view of passive contemplation. Here even their own corporeal being dissolves and evaporates, as it were, since the assumption is that it does not function, or at least, that reasoning proceeds from a fiction, from an "as if"—as though the corporeal being did not exist. This corporeal being does not weary anyone's spiritual eyeballs, since it does not crawl out onto the surface. Things are more difficult for the solipsists, in whose case we are talking not merely about passive "sensations" but also about acts of will (also, esteemed Sir and Madam, a fact of consciousness!), and of bodily movements corresponding to these acts of will and directed toward physical objects.

Here everything is interconnected, one thing with another. Nonacceptance of the world leads necessarily to the disclaiming of bodily movements directed toward this world; to disclaiming the corporeal being of the subject himself or herself; to transforming the subject into a purely spiritual substance, eternal and unchanging, in which time, space, the entire cosmos, history, life and death, all become extinct. It emerges that even the very body "I" is a creation of this "I" as "pure spirit." But alas, not even spirits are capable of catching Berkeley, Hume, or any of their followers. On the other hand, the actual multitude of claimants to the single, universal psychic monad destroys this oneness, and together with it, this uniquely mad philosophy.

In reality, every practical act leads the subject beyond the bounds of his or her "I," representing a breakthrough into the external world, which remains even when this subject itself ceases to exist and is transformed into nothingness. Here the subject, which in illusory fashion devours the world while creating it, is devoured by this world which he or she has supposedly created. The world asserts its iron priority over the transient solitary being of the individual, even if this individual is the most inveterate solipsist, refusing to accept the reality of the external world.

From the point of view of solipsism, the subject is a thing in himself and for himself, with no relationship to friends, with no ties, since he himself is everything. But try, for the sake of experiment, to approach this subject.

"Kind sir," you say to him, "since you are the sole monad, while I, poor sinner, exist only in your consciousness, and your body likewise, and this rapier as well, allow me to pierce with it your swinish (pardon me!) heart. Since all this is being played out in your consciousness, it stands to reason that my rapier will not harm a single drop of your essence."

"Help!" cries our solipsist.

Next, we can perform another experiment.

Suggest to the invulnerable philosopher that he should not partake of the fruits of the earth, and that proceeding from the independence of the spirit, that is, from pure consciousness, he should renounce anything as crudely prosaic as food and drink. He will look daggers at you.

Meanwhile, of course, it is clear that from the point of view of his supposedly invulnerable position all this is merely occurring in his consciousness, which cannot perish from such causes.

You will be told that all this is crude. But the argument is not about whether it is crude. The argument is in your experiments, and in the solipsist's reaction to them.

The same will apply if we call to account not a solipsist, but, let us say, a Hindu ascetic, who does not accept the world of the senses. Try taking his scanty food ration away from him. He will either die (if he agrees), or more likely, he will not give it up. Both answers will be arguments in favor of the external world. No cunning twist of thought, no scholastic contrivance, can refute these "crude" arguments.

The whole point is that in reality, the starting point is not the "datum" represented by "my sensations," but the active relationship between subject and object, with the latter having priority as a quantity independent of the consciousness of the subject. Here we see revealed the whole significance of Marx's argument (see his notes on the book by A. Wagner, his "Theses on Feuerbach," and *The German Ideology*) to the effect that in historical terms, the objects of the external world are not "given" to human beings as objects for contemplation, but that the historical starting point is the world as the object of practical action. It is the process of assimilation (through food, drink, and so on), mediated by one or another form of production, that is the historical (and hence also logical) *prius*, and by no means "my sensations" or a passively contemplative relationship between object and subject.

Therefore, as will later be shown in detail, it is only from the point of view of intellectual "purity," that is, of a monstrosity detached from the totality of vital functions, of an abstract and hypostatized intellect, that practice and arguments from practice are not a theoretical-cognitive criterion. The illusions of subjective and objective idealism, the denial of the world in general and the denial of the materially sensible world, represent an ideological distortion. They constitute a reflex that results from losing touch with the practice involved in the genuine mastering of the world, in its real transformation. It is not by chance that Oriental quietism (the Brahman and Buddhist "nirvana") and the *ataraxia* of the Greek skeptics coincide with the most extreme forms of denial of the sensible-material world, with the view that it is unknowable in principle, with all categories of being transformed into the single category of appearance.

In his *Phenomenology of Spirit*, Hegel discusses freedom of consciousness, and while analyzing and evaluating Stoicism and Skepticism, provides *en passant* a convincing critique of Skepticism from precisely this point of view.

Hegel here describes as servile consciousness a consciousness that is completely dependent on life and existence. Stoic consciousness, on the other hand, represents the indifference of self-consciousness; stoic consciousness is unfettered even when material fetters are placed on the human being involved. "This freedom of self-consciousness when it appeared as a conscious manifestation in the history of Spirit has, as we know, been called Stoicism. Its principle is that consciousness is a being that *thinks*, and that consciousness holds something to be essentially important, or true and good, only in so far as it *thinks* it to be such."[1]

The stoical imperturbability of the spirit, *ataraxia* (the virtue of the sage, a virtue known also to the main Oriental philosophical and religious currents), thus has as its basis a consciousness of the insignificance, to a greater or lesser degree, of the world of the senses. Skeptical philosophy, in which all objective knowledge is compromised, including certainty as to the existence of the world, is therefore (as Hegel put it) a slave to Stoicism. Stoicism is the master that frees Skeptical philosophy from any attachment to the perceptible, to the values of things and of the necessities of life. Stoicism destroys everything, including all contrary arguments, leaving intact only conscious indifference, *ataraxia*.

In his *History of Philosophy*, Hegel considers Skepticism irrefutable from the point of view of isolated consciousness. "We must," he says, "agree that Skepticism is invincible, but it is invincible only subjectively, in the view of the human individual who can stubbornly defend the view that philosophy is of no importance to him and who can recognize only negation ... it is impossible to change his mind or to force him to accept a positive philosophy, just as someone who is paralyzed from head to toe cannot be forced to stand up."[2]

In *Phenomenology of Spirit*, however, Hegel vigorously propounds not only the idea of the "solitary individual" but also the contradiction between theory and practice, word and deed, which is so characteristic of all skeptical philosophy. The skeptical consciousness...

> .... occupies itself with destroying the immaterial content in its thinking, but by virtue of the fact that it does this, it comes to represent consciousness of the immaterial. It pronounces a sentence of absolute disappearance, but this sentence exists, and this consciousness is a sentence about disappearance. It affirms the worthlessness of sight, hearing, and so forth, but at the same time it itself sees, hears, and so on. It affirms the worthlessness of moral decisions and at the same time makes them the masters of its conduct. Its words and actions contradict one another endlessly, and it thus represents a dual contradiction, the consciousness of immutability and of equality with itself in complete fortuitousness and variance with itself.[3]

When, however, this duality within itself becomes conscious of itself as duality, that is, becomes a duality for itself, that is, when self-consciousness recognizes its own duality, then a new form of consciousness, which Hegel terms unhappy consciousness, comes into being. This acknowledges a split between theory, on the one hand, and practice, on the other; that is, it intrudes here as a factor of primary importance, alongside the dualism of the world of "essences and appearances" (more on this later). Unhappy consciousness is "an unfortunate consciousness, bifurcated in itself."[4]

In his own fashion, where the point of view is that of objective idealism and of idealist universalism (in the pores of idealism there is a good deal of mysticism), Hegel seizes on two basic elements:

a) counterposing to a single skeptical consciousness the fact of general human experience, that is, of the experience of many people, of social experience;
b) counterposing to skeptical theory the principle of practice, including, and above all, the practice of the exponents of skeptical theory themselves.

Consequently, what in the mouths of apologists for skepticism (and also of supporters of consistent subjective idealism, or solipsism) appears to be a crude and unphilosophical argument is in reality a philosophical argument of huge importance, an argument that deals a crushing blow to "self-consciousness," which can stand on its feet only when it is blind in relation to its own content, and which becomes unhappy consciousness as soon as its blatant bifurcation in itself is transformed into bifurcation for itself, that is, when this bifurcation of consciousness becomes clear to the consciousness itself.

A revered aristocratic philosopher states:

> Imagine an underground dwelling, like a cave, with a long entrance open to the light. The inhabitants of this cave are chained to the wall, and cannot turn their heads, so that they can see only the rear end of the cave. In the distance far behind them, a torch casts its light from above. In this intermediate space there is a road up above, and also a low wall. Behind this wall, facing the light, are people carrying all sorts of statues of people and animals, like the dolls in a puppet theatre, raising them above the wall. These people sometimes talk to one another, and at other times are silent.... The people in the cave, since they are chained to the wall, would be able to see only the shadows falling on the wall opposite, and would take these shadows for real beings. What the people carrying the dolls said to one another would carry through to the

cave only as echoes, and the people in the cave would take these sounds for the speech of the shadows. If it so happened that one of these chained people was freed, so that he had the chance to turn round and see the objects themselves instead of their shadows, he would think that what he now saw was a dream, an illusion, and that the shadows were the true reality. And if someone managed even to release the people from the cave in which they had been confined, and took them out into the light, then they would be blinded by the light, would see nothing, and would hate the person who had brought them into the light, seeing in him someone who had robbed them of the truth and had given them in return only sorrow and misery. (Plato, *De Republica*)[5]

Here on the one hand we have people chained up like convicts and arriving in the vale of the non-authentic world of the senses. On the other, we have the world of ideas, of pure forms, of abstract essences, (*ton eidon*), that are inaccessible to human senses; of ideal prototypes of things which people can merely think of. Not far removed from this is the telephone handset of Karl Pearson (*The Grammar of Science*).[6]

Kant's world of noumena, of secluded "things-in-themselves," counterposed to the world of phenomena, of occurrences, also stands on the far side of the world of the senses, having a "transcendental" relationship to it. There is no way that a human being can make the leap into this frigid kingdom. Such is Kant's sad thesis. The real essence of this problem was already formulated brilliantly by the ancient Skeptics, especially Pyrrho, whose "tropes" were recounted by Sextus Empiricus.

Hegel, who especially in relation to Kant was not given to mincing words, stated in his *Philosophy of Nature* that with its doctrine of unknowable things-in-themselves Kant's metaphysic was like a contagion, and more stupid than animals, which throw themselves on perceptible objects in order to devour them. This is true, and represents a profound observation, since any practical step toward the real mastering of the world of concrete objects, that is, toward its alteration and transformation, goes beyond the bounds assigned to the "transcendental subject" in Kant's *Critique of Pure Reason*. However "crude" this proof and this summons to practice, they are also totally convincing from the point of view of the theory of cognition, though Hegel refers with irony to the way in which Diogenes proved to Zeno that movement is possible. He did it by walking—that is, with his legs. Through acts of will, people in fact change the world of objects as they wish, at the very same time that the idea is being hammered into them that they cannot, as a matter of principle, be cognizant of this material world. This is a special topic, an exceedingly important one, and we are still trying to raise lumps on the thick skulls of the agnostics over this question. Nevertheless, we are prepared here to make a temporary concession of principle to our adversary. We shall reason in "purely logical" fashion, even though this understanding of logic is false, excessively restricted, and even trivial. We shall do this for the reason that to the extent that we introduce considerations of practice as proofs, this practice crosses into the realm of theory, itself becoming a theoretical argument.

What is the essence of all the constructs arguing in favor of the unknowability of the external world? (We are not talking here of denial of the world, something about which we have already had a jocular conversation.) This essence consists in the subjective nature of perceptions, ideas, occurrences, and phenomena, in contrast to the objective, to the thing-in-itself, to the "noumenon." Color, sound, sweetness, bitterness, hardness, and so forth—these are all subjective influences, signals issuing from the noumenal world "in itself." But what is the world "in itself" like? What does a rose smell like, when there is no one smelling it? How can we mentally remove (*abdenken*, to use the term preferred by Avenarius) the subject? And if we mentally remove the subject (which according to Avenarius is impossible), what then remains? How can the world be presented to a human being in non-sensible form? And if this is impossible, that means it is impossible to know the world "in itself"; it remains an eternal riddle that is insoluble in principle. Perhaps the world is matter, or perhaps it is spirit. Perhaps it is a totality of monads. Perhaps it is a kingdom of Platonic ideas. Or perhaps it is something utterly unfathomable? Here we have the realm of faith, of fanaticism, of pure contemplation, of mysticism, of irrationalist "cognition." Work it out by reading your coffee grounds! Everything here is a "case apart"!

The way that Pyrrho sets out this question is striking for its clarity. Sextus Empiricus records the following "trope" of Pyrrho: "The first point is the difference between animals, thanks to which various creatures have different conceptions of one and the same object, and one and the same object arouses different sensations."[7]

The same applies to people. Someone suffering from jaundice sees white as yellow. This is just like Mach, with his example of the drug santonin (*The Analysis of Sensations*). It follows directly that subjectivism has a dual character. In the first place, it is individual (jaundice, color blindness, and so forth). Secondly, subjectivism also has an overall human, generic character.

So what about things-in-themselves? What existence do they have, outside of these two subjective colorings? What are they objectively?

The chorus replies: we do not know. The skeptics maintain: we do not know. The agnostics and Kantians say the same. Nor, all of them insist, will we ever know. *Ignoramus, ignorabimus*.[8] Ah, what fat-headed cretins!

A wise response to Pyrrho's trope is provided by Hegel. Though an idealist, Hegel due to the extreme objectivism of his idealism stands on the boundary of idealism's opposite, materialism, and hence often turns his heavy artillery on the agnostics and Kantians. "If they (the skeptics and Pyrrho) also deny the identity of sensations," Hegel observes, "and consequently deny this universality, then another universality takes its place, since universality or being consists precisely in that we know. In the overused example of the man suffering from jaundice, things seem to him to be of a particular color. That is, we know an ineluctable law, in accordance with which he experiences changes in his perception of color."[9]

This is a superb key to the problem, a genuinely dialectical approach to it. The "thing-in-itself" and the human being, the object and subject (supposing a subject exists), are bound together, are in a certain relationship. If the object remains the same, while the subject changes, and we know the specific character of the subject and the law of the relationship between the object and the subject, then we already know something. We know that the "thing-in-itself," that is, external reality, has the objective characteristic of arousing quite specific sensations in some subjects and quite specific sensations in others. As is well known, Kant in his *Critique of Pure Reason* gnawed his way through every connection between subject and object. For him, even the category of causality was a priori a category of pure reason. It is only the blatant inconsistency that tears his whole system apart that can explain the fact that for the same Kant, things-in-themselves "affict" our feelings—that is, that in this case a causal relationship is present.[10]

This is an incontestable failure, an undoubted fiasco, the collapse of an elegant structure.

We thus already know: (1) that things-in-themselves are the causes of our sensations; and (2) we know the law of relationship, that is, that it is an objective property of things that they produce particular sensations.

This is from the side of the object. On the side of the subject, one of whose objective characteristics is the property of having sensations, we see that thought removes subjectivity by understanding it as such.

Here, however, we need to stress something that Hegel missed, and that had to be emphasized by Marxist dialectics. That is the following:

First, the fact that the (relative!) subjectivism of the color-blind man or the jaundice sufferer is understood and defined by thought could arise only out of comparing the experiences of numerous individuals. That is, it could be "given" only in the process of human communication, of which ideas, systems of ideas, and science as an increasingly correct reflection of the objective world are all products. Second, the fact that we understand subjectivism (also relative) of a generic, all-human variety (a subjectivism, as it were, of a second category) is also the result of cooperation between people and of a rich experience of comparing different organisms, an experience that already extends beyond the bounds of human beings (ants, for example, see rays that are invisible to people).

Nevertheless, it does not follow from this that sensations are purely subjective. That is a one-sided, metaphysical view. The same applies to phenomena, that is, to the phenomenalist "map of the world." What is manifested in phenomena is the world. Phenomena are not arbitrary, one-sided figments of human consciousness (neither individual nor social phenomena, nor sensations, nor ideas, nor concepts of the first category, the phenomenalist map of the world). A phenomenon is always a relationship, a connection. There would be no color if there were no objectively existing light rays. There would be no phenomenalist map of the world if there were no world. Here objective reality is transformed into its own opposite. Or, as Hegel says in *The Science of Logic*, "A phenomenon is not simply immaterial; it is the manifestation of an essence." If we translate that into our language, a phenomenon is a manifestation of the objective world in the categories of human sensations.[11]

To regard sensations as purely subjective, with no connection to objective reality, is absurd. This point was already well formulated by that "Hercules of the ancient Greek world," Aristotle, who in *De Anima* wrote that for sensations to be felt, it was essential that "something which is sensed" be present. That is, sensation presupposes something outside, some external reality which is independent of the subject and connected to the subject, and which the subject senses. He or she senses it; it is sensed by him or her. Lenin in *Materialism and Empiriocriticism* provides an even sharper formula concerning light: the energy of external irritation, he observes, is transformed into the sensation of color.

Ergo: material rays of a certain wavelength and velocity act on the tissues of the retina, nerve impulses are transmitted, the brain functions, and the other-being of this is sensation. For this very reason, Ilyich in his *Philosophical Notebooks* puts forward the thesis that sensations do not separate human beings from the world, but link them to it, bringing them and the world closer together. Here we find the mutual interpenetration of opposites, the existence of dialectical links between them, and not one-sided subjectivity, not an absolute rift between object and subject, not the denial (as in the *Principled Empiriocritical Coordination* of Avenarius) of the reality of the external world, as if the world were not mighty enough to exist without the subject. This opposition to *realité* arose historically when nature created and singled out from itself a new quality, the human being, the subject, the historico-social subject.

Pyrrho's eighth trope is also extremely interesting. It states: "In this trope we conclude that since everything exists in relationship to something or other, we shall refrain from saying what it is in itself and in its nature. It is necessary, however, to note that we are using the word 'exists' here only in the sense of 'it seems'."[12]

Pyrrho, consequently, speaks here of relationships in a dual sense: first, in relation to the subject who is doing the interpreting, and second, with regard to the relations between objects, that is, the relation of one object to another, to other objects or processes. We have already discussed the first of these; now for the second. Here it should be noted that a thing-in-itself is Kantian, that is, a "thing" taken in isolation from any relationship to another thing. As such it is an empty abstraction, stripped of any concrete attributes, "that is, nothing, a *caput mortuum* of abstraction," as Hegel put it.[13] What, for example, is water if we do not define the temperature, the pressure, and other conditions? What is water "in itself"? The question is absurd, since "in itself," that is, outside of any defined relations, it is nothing, an "empty abstraction devoid of truth," as Hegel aptly observed. In *The Philosophy of Nature*, Hegel formulates the question as follows: "It is impossible, on the basis of the fact that air, fire, and so forth behave in particular ways in one sphere, to draw any conclusions concerning their behavior in another sphere."[14]

Essentially, then, there are no facts in isolation from laws, and no laws without relation to facts; the two make up a single whole, since a law is an essential relationship, the link between one thing and another, the transformation of one thing into another, becoming, metamorphosis, and so on. It is not therefore the physical, chemical, organic, or other properties of bodies that express relationship. Electrical conductivity, volatility, thermal conductivity, elasticity, weight, fusibility, ductility, time, motion, and finally, even the properties of feeling and thinking are all objective properties of bodies in particular relations to one another, laws as relationships. It *is* possible to "mentally remove" the subject. Cognition, proceeding from the senses, strips away subjective factors of the first, second, and other orders, arriving at the objective properties of things and processes, at the relationships between them, independent of the relationship to the subject. Contrary to the doctrine of the empiriocritics, the being of nature in the absence of a thinking subject was the historical being of the earth before the appearance of humankind. But it does not follow from the fundamental possibility and necessity of "mentally removing" the "fundamental empiriocritical coordination" that it is possible to mentally remove all natural relationships. Here the so-called bald syllogism, over which the sages of antiquity wearied their brains, comes into play; here quantity is transformed into quality.

It follows that the skeptics are correct only when they argue against purely mental, metaphysical, anti-dialectical definitions, operating as things-in-themselves, in isolation from all outside relationships. One cannot have knowledge of such a thing-in-itself, for the simple reason that it does not exist. It is a nothingness, an empty abstraction, a metaphysical illusion. We take so-called distinct entities (electrons, atoms, chemical elements, individual beings of the organic world, and so on) in their relative independence, but always in particular, artificially chosen, stable relationships, which precisely because of their relatively settled nature are left out of account and are not noticed. A human being, for example, would be a sight to behold in a perfect vacuum, and at a temperature of absolute zero! What would the person's "nature" be like then? Or else, let us recall what Engels in *The Dialectics of Nature* has to say about "the eternal character of the laws of nature." These laws exist if certain natural-historical conditions are present. In their essence, these laws are just as historical as any law of society, only the time scale is quite different. The recent researches of Eddington, for example, have proven that in astrophysics, at colossal temperatures and pressures, bodies do not expand when heated, but shrink, in total contrast to the usual earthly relationships—that is, as a result of different relationships between objects and processes.

Such are the changes that occur in nature. Here too we find revealed the whole absurdity of treating light, sound, and so on as merely subjective, since:

1) experiencing sensations is an objective property of the subject, whom we also, perhaps, regard as an object;
2) this sensation appears as a result of the influence of an object.

After all, we might consider the relationship between object and subject itself to be an objective relationship, and the property of giving rise to sensations will then be an objective property of the object, while the property of experiencing sensations will be an objective property of the subject. If we know that in the subjects a, b and c the object x produces the sensations a, b, and \, then by virtue of this we know certain objective properties of the object. Let us take an example, paradoxical at first glance, which we mentioned earlier: that of a poisonous spider. If the spider bites someone, that person gets sick. What exactly is the poisonous nature of the spider? It is an objective quality, of which the person has cognition. Outside of the relationship of this property with a human being, it no longer exists. A tarantula might bite a tree, and no poisonous qualities will be evident, but these qualities will be apparent if the spider bites a person. Consequently, this quality of being poisonous is something related to the subject, and outside of this relationship, the quality does not exist. All that exists is the quality of emitting a particular fluid of a certain chemical composition.

True, it is possible to object here that we are talking about the subject as a physiological entity, while the question of sensations involves a specific difficulty. There, what is new is the psychological aspect. There, moreover, the question is not merely of sensation as a process, but also of sensation as a reflection of the external, and of the relationship between the content of this reflection and that which is being reflected. This is true, but it is not what we are arguing about; it is not an objection.

What, in reality, is the question about? It is about whether Kant was right to transform the relative subjectivity of phenomena into absolute subjectivity, and to conclude from this that things were unknowable in themselves. To this, we raise objections, and the analogy with the spider is again apposite. The essence of the matter is that we, to use the words of Hegel, know the law of relationships. The poisonous nature of the spider is an absurdity, an *Unding,* to use the German expression, outside of the relationship to the subject. From this point of view the poisonous character is itself something subjective. But it also reflects an objective property, and knowing this objective property (that is, the objective relationship between the spider and human beings), we cognize the spider from a certain angle. This signifies: every time the spider bites someone, such-and-such will happen to the person. The spider, we conclude, is poisonous. Not "in itself," but relative to something. When we say that a rose is red, this means that every time a person looks at the rose, the sensation "red" arises in that person. To produce the sensation "red" is an objective property of the rose. The rose is red. Not "in itself," but relatively. We repeat, however, that producing the sensation "red" is an objective property of the rose. Being cognizant of this property, we are also, by virtue of this, cognizant of the rose. But just as the poisonous nature of the spider is underlain (outside of its relationship to human beings) by the spider's property of emitting a fluid of a particular composition, light of a specific wavelength underlies the redness of the rose.

We thus see here a whole dialectical relativity of concepts. The sharpness of the thorns of a rose is an objective property of the thorns, but in relation to the body of a human being or other animal; outside of this relationship the concept of sharpness is meaningless. However, this does not prevent the concept from expressing a certain objective relationship between the object and subject.

Knowing the law of relationships, we are also aware of the relative character of this property. But this is something totally different from non-cognition, which would be our conclusion if we were to follow the "spurious idealism" of Kant.

We are also concerned, however, with connections and relationships that do not depend on the subject. If an electric current is passed through water, the water breaks down into oxygen and hydrogen. We see the whole process, broadly speaking, through the spectacles of our subjectivity. (Moreover, we know the "law" of these "spectacles.") But the relationship between the current and the electrolysis of water does not depend in any way on the spectacles; it is objective. Here there are two relationships: 1) the relationship between the current and the water; and 2) the relationship between the whole process being observed and the subject who is observing it. But the relationship between the current and the water, in its specific nature, is independent of the second relationship, the law of which, in any case, we know. Are we cognizant of this first relationship? Of course we are. But this also means that we are cognizant of the objective properties of things and processes. Every time we pass a current through water, the water is going to break down into oxygen and hydrogen. This process is applied both in the laboratory and in industrial production. What is there that we do not know about the objective property of an electric current to electrolyze water, or of the objective property of water to be broken down under the action of electricity? Who can say that these are not objective properties? What is subjective here? The color of water? Its smell, and so forth? But we are not even talking about this. We are casting aside this "subjectivity." We are talking about the fact that water is electrolyzed, something that is an objective property of electricity in relation to water, and an objective property of water in relation to electricity. And we know this. The situation is exactly the same with an enormous and ever-growing quantity of things and processes in their relationships and interrelationships. These, to be sure, are not Kantian "things-in-themselves"; they are real things and processes in their real associations, transitions, and movements.

In his *Phenomenology of Spirit*, Hegel provides a detailed analysis of all the forms and gradations through which the "spirit" proceeds (objective consciousness, self-consciousness, absolute consciousness). Examining objective consciousness, Hegel describes a transition from sensible apprehension to perception, and from perception to understanding, providing a wonderful picture of the contradictions and difficulties involved in the main question of the relationship between thought and being, and of the cognizability of things and processes. He gives a remarkable depiction of how contradictions impel consciousness toward thoughts of the universal bonds linking everything that exists, and states in conclusion:

> The link with another is the end of being for itself. Thanks to its absolute character and to its counterposed position, it exists in relation to other (things), and only this relationship has essential meaning; the relationship, however, is the negation of independence, and hence the thing perishes, precisely because of this essential property.[15]

Here, according to Hegel, the object is no longer a "sensuous being," but "*absolute universality*, and consciousness here for the first time truly enters the realm of the Understanding."[16]

This ought not to cause us any disquiet, since what is involved is only rational categories. The above conclusions, however, cannot be let pass without certain objections. For Hegel, the relationship between things, as particular objective entities, has a tendency to turn into a pure relationship with nothing relative about it, just as in his *Philosophy of Nature*, for example, matter is defined through the unity of time and space and their interrelationships, and not the other way round—that is, not so that time and space are defined as forms of the existence of matter. If things do not exist outside of relationships to other things, this by no means signifies that they perish, that is, cease to exist; the negation of the isolated thing is not the negation of the thing. If a relationship exists as an essential property of something, then when this something perishes, the relationship must perish as well. To separate the one from the other is impossible; this is an anti-dialectical, purely intellectual operation. A thing presupposes relationships, and negates the concept of the thing-in-itself as something abstract and empty of content. A thing is always and everywhere both for itself and for others. It is itself a dialectical contradiction, and it is as a dialectical contradiction that philosophy must deal with it.

Discussions of the question of cognition often arouse a certain dissatisfaction due to the fact that people do not think of the cognition of the objective world, but of something else; that is, they do not think of receiving a reflection (an accurate reflection) of an object, but of receiving the object itself. In other words, they think of transforming themselves into objects.

This desire arises in relation to an analogy with other people. If subject X observes another living person, Y, he judges Y by analogy with himself. He considers that he knows Y when he reproduces experiences of Y in his own consciousness, on the basis of Y's facial appearance and expression, bodily movements, and so on. In other words, he knows Y when to a certain degree he himself is transformed into Y, re-creates that object within himself, although at the same time he distinguishes himself from this other object. But presumed here is a generic uniformity of the structure of specific living matter, and a generic uniformity of consciousness, as a property and other-being of this consciousness. The consciousness of each is at the same time (at a particular stage of historical development) also the object of itself. This is self-consciousness. The stage of self-consciousness, as Hegel defines it in *The Phenomenology of Spirit*, represents "the authenticity and truth of the self," and is thus different from objective consciousness. However, this difference also consists in the fact that while cooperation or struggle between people in their bodily form is also cooperation or struggle of their consciousness, the relationship between a human being and unbounded nature is quite different. Here it is quite impossible for a log, as a log in its bodily sense, to be situated in human consciousness. The log can be reproduced only "spiritually" (*geistige Reproduktion*, as Marx puts it). The log is without consciousness, just as the entire inorganic world is without consciousness (we will discuss this later in more detail). If the subject were to be transformed into a "log," that is, into a part of inorganic nature, the subject's consciousness would disappear as well, and for this subject all the problems of the world, including the problem of the log, would disappear as well. Such is death. In death, following decay, that which was a thinking subject becomes as one with inorganic nature, and expires in its nonchalant indifference and indifferent nonchalance. Failure to understand this fact is linked with various deceptions and illusions, when diverse types of consciousness intrude into nature, attribute spiritual qualities to it, transform it into a god, and then wish to commune with this divine paradise, in their naivety imagining that this represents a higher type of cognition.

The "nature of things" and their laws are the expressions of eternal movement, of fluidity, or flux, of incessantly changing relationships and bonds, of the world-dialectic of becoming. The process of cognition, which has its origins in indications from the senses, thus becomes rooted in history. It sheds its covering of subjectivity, understanding this subjectivity and its relative nature, knowing its "law," and providing itself with a map of the world that corresponds more and more closely to reality.

Roughly speaking, we can list the properties here of three categories:

1. the most general properties, expressing universal relationships: time, space, motion, form, mass, and so forth.
2. qualitatively specific properties that express relationships independent of the subject: physical, chemical, and biological properties, hardness, liquidity, gaseousness, electrical conductivity, crystalline character, thermoconductivity, volatility, and so forth; the capacity for assimilation, movement, and multiplication; the capacity for feeling; social and historical properties; the capacity for thought, for speech, for active adaptation to nature, and so forth.
3. the property of producing sensations in particular types of specially organized matter (sensations of color, sound, and so forth), and properties in interrelationship with the subject in general (for example, the poisonous nature of the tarantula spider).

The first two series of properties express the variable, mobile, unstable, dialectical relationships between things and processes independent of a conscious subject. The last series expresses the relationship between external reality and its direct manifestation in the sensations of the subject, historically, in the process of thought, growing into a more and more adequate picture of the world, the reflection of the world, its copy (though by no means a duplicate of reality!), and also the objective relations between the object and subject in general. A rose "in itself," that is, solely in relation to nature, reflects light waves of a particular length. In relation to the eye of a normal person, it is red; in relation to the eye of a color-blind person, it is green. We know the rose, or more precisely, we are cognizant of it, both through the objective relationship and the relationship with the subject, and we come to understand the laws of relationships, that is, the properties of things and processes in their dialectical interrelatedness and instability.

In the historical process of cognition, therefore, we follow the historical changes of the objective world, the rise of new qualities, for example, the origins of organic bodies out of inorganic nature, the evolution of organisms, the evolution of human societies, and so forth. It is not the slogan of Du Bois-Raymond, *ignorabimus,* that is correct. The truth lies in the countervailing slogan of Ernst Haeckel: *Impavide progrediamur!* "Fearlessly we shall go forward!"

3

Things-in-Themselves and Their Cognizability

Hence, the external world, the abstraction from which (independent of "my" consciousness, and even of "our" consciousness) is the "I" of idealist philosophy, actually exists. Conditionally, it can be designated as things "in themselves," that is, "things" independent of the subject.

However, this cannot be done in the Kantian sense. Hegel in his *History of Philosophy* notes very wittily that Kantian criticism is the worst form of dogmatism, since it posits both "I-in-myself" and things-in-themselves in such a manner that the two elements of this opposition absolutely cannot meet up. Kant's great unknowable X, the eternal mystery, the Isis behind the impenetrable veil, the bugaboo of all modern philosophy, in essence has a history dating back thousands of years. A widely familiar example from more than two thousand years ago is Plato's myth of the cave, in which he expounded in graphic form this same doctrine of the world of ideas as opposed to the world of appearances. [The text of this chapter breaks off here.]

4

Space and Time

One of Plekhanov's most serious philosophical errors, associated with his theory of "hieroglyphs," was his essentially Kantian interpretation of space and time. "That time and space are subjective forms dependent on our viewpoint was known already to Thomas Hobbes, and no materialist will deny this," wrote Plekhanov in his well-known polemic with Bogdanov (*Materialismus Militans*).[1]

This was Plekhanov's most vulnerable point, and it is no wonder that whole battalions of his theoretical opponents immediately rushed into this breach. Thus, for example, Vladimir Bazarov very wittily objected: if time and space are subjective forms, to which something merely corresponds in the objective, noumenal world, that is, in the world of things-in-themselves, then it is obvious that motion is also a subjective category, since it presupposes time and space.[2] Consequently, all that objectively exists is something corresponding to motion, as its subjective hieroglyph. From this stems the conclusion that matter lacks even the attribute of motion.

It is possible to develop this argumentation still further, turning it loose, for example, on the concept of causality. Plekhanov quite rightly exposed the flagrant contradiction of Kant, according to which the category of causality is subjective—a priori—while, on the other hand, "things-in-themselves" are the cause of the world of phenomena. But if time is subjective, then the relationship of causality cannot be objective either, since a consequence follows a cause in time. This leads ineluctably to the conclusion that the world of things-in-themselves cannot be the cause of our sensations, and that causality itself is not an objective category; it merely ought to "correspond" to something. In other words, causality too is a hieroglyph, which cannot as a matter of principle be deciphered in its objective meaning.

Such are the elements of Kantianism that have crept into Plekhanov's materialist philosophy.

The question of space and time is one of the most difficult in philosophy. To resolve it correctly, it is essential to reject a particular predisposition, namely, the inclination to suppress or disregard the qualitative diversity in the forms and associations of being. This prejudicial inclination makes it extremely difficult to understand real associations and relationships. We had cause to be convinced of this when we analyzed the question of the cognizability of "things-in-themselves." In reality a "thing-in-itself" does not exist; a thing exists solely in its relationships. Yet there are people who want to have it "in itself." In reality, any object gives rise to sensations only in connection with a subject, but these people want to imagine properties apart from the subject, in isolation from this connection, in the categories of "pure" sensation. In reality, the relation between the brain and the mind, or psyche, is a unique case of a relationship of "other-being." But people want to imagine this unique relationship as a sensuously perceptible model for other relationships, and so forth.

Here we see a total obliviousness to dialectics, which encompasses contradictions, transitions from one thing to another, and all the multifarious associations and relationships in existence in all their specificity and qualitative uniqueness. Thus, when these people set out to solve the problem of space and time, using other forms and properties of being as a model, they most often end up wide of the mark.

After these preliminary remarks, we shall move on to the essence of the question. As our starting point, we shall take a definition that appears in a work by N. Morozov: "The Function (A Graphic Presentation of Differential and Integral Calculus)."[3] Here we read:

> ...the full algebraic expression for any object, U, that exists in nature, is:
>
> $U = x, y, z, t$,
>
> where x = length, y = breadth, z = height, t = time. U (signifying "any object that exists in nature") is a function of four variables, four dimensions, three of space, plus time. That is,
>
> $U = f(x, y, z, t)$.

Even from a cursory glance at this formula it is obvious that, despite what its author says, it cannot be considered complete, since nothing is present except the four dimensions. No other physical, chemical, organic (biological), or other qualities or properties are contained in this "complete" formula, nor can they be. The formula speaks only of space and time; it is abstracted from everything else. It deals only with quantitative relationships of space and time, and with nothing else; it does not, so to speak, contain a grain of substance in general, nor of substance in its determinate qualitative being. In reality, endless properties, associations, and mediations are present, and U is f times all of them; it is the point of intersection of countless influences, and exists in their mobile and multifarious network. In Morozov's formula, the predicate thus acts as the substance, the form as the essence, one aspect of being as being itself, a property as the whole, *pars pro toto*.[4]

In Hegel's *Philosophy of Nature*, we find the following definition of nature: "The primary or immediate determination of nature is the abstract *universality of its self-externality*, its unmediated indifference, i.e., *space*. It is on account of its being self-externality that space constitutes collaterality of a completely ideal nature; as this extrinsicality is still completely *abstract*, space is simply *continuous* and is devoid of any determinate difference."[5]

Here nature is defined through pure space, and not space through nature. Space is torn apart from natural being; space, in its isolation, universality, and indifference to everything else, is transformed into a thing-in-itself; that is, "a being already essentially mediated within itself, an external other-being," so that this "other-being" of nature turns into a natural "being in itself." But on what basis, essentially, does Hegel assert this? He makes two other assertions:

1. "The content of space has nothing to do with space itself."[6]
2. "One cannot point to a part of space which is space *for itself*; for space is always filled, and no part of it is separated from that which fills it. It is therefore a non-sensuous sensuality and sensuous insensibility."[7]

If the second statement is correct, however, what are we to say about the first? Here there is a contradiction, but the contradiction is by no means dialectical. If space is always full of space, then it is obvious that space is a form of the existence of nature, of the universe, of matter, an expression of extent, a universal property of everything material. Hence "pure quantitativeness," universality, undifferentiatedness. Aristotle put forward complex arguments against the notion of a vacuum, of "empty space," as an independent quantity in which bodies were situated. But the question of space, like any other question, cannot be resolved a priori, "out of one's head," in purely speculative fashion. Modern science speaks of various kinds of waves and "corpuscles" filling space in endless quantities. But even if pores of absolute emptiness were discovered, spatial relationships would still exist as relationships between bodies, according to the law of relationships between material things.

On the other hand, if there were no bodies at all, space would be transformed into total nothingness, an abstract expression of pure negation. Hence it is not space that is the starting point, but the material world, whose form of being is space as a universal norm.

Space in physics is different from space in everyday consciousness, but it is more capable of explaining objective reality. The infinity of space is not an infinity of a particular substance, but the spatial infinity of the endless universe. Any finite quantity, however, is in turn infinite by virtue of its endless divisibility. Hence space is contradictory in itself, and the contradictory natures of the finite and infinite interpenetrate one another. Space is a particular universal norm of the existence of matter, and must be understood precisely as a particular norm. Therefore, it cannot be considered along with, say, the combustibility or transparency of bodies. Aristotle, we find, understood this point.

First, for Aristotle space is not itself a body: "Is place a body? It cannot be a body, since otherwise there would be two bodies in one and the same place."

Second, "Place is not the material of things, since there is nothing that consists of it. Nor is it form (here we are concerned with form in Aristotle's sense of entelechy, the soul, the active principle, not in our sense—author), or concept, or purpose, or a motivating principle, and yet it is something."[8]

Here we find expressed quite well (though only in negative fashion) the specific character of space, as distinct from other properties of matter and of being in general.

Time is a similarly all-encompassing form of the existence of the universe. Here it should be said that time:

a) is in no sense an independent quantity, a particular substance;
b) is not something within which processes of change take place, but merely an expression of those processes, as also proceeds from the first proposition.

Hegel puts this particularly well: "It is not, however, in time that everything appears and passes away; time itself is this process of *becoming*, arising and passing away; it is the *abstraction* that has being, the Chronos which engenders all and destroys that to which it gives birth." Time is not some kind of container, says Hegel, in which everything is borne away and swallowed up, as in the flow of a stream. Time is merely the abstraction of this destruction. And in that which does not exist in time, processes do not take place.9

In other words, it should not be imagined that on the one hand there are processes, and that these real processes are situated in time as if in a box. On the contrary, a process is a process to the extent that it is already occurring within time. Consequently, when we say that things do not arise and are not destroyed within time, but that time itself expresses the process of becoming, we mean that a process occurs within time, but in a stricter sense of the word, since time is already implicit in the very concept of a process. It is not implied that there first of all existed a sort of extratemporal process, which was then located within time, taking on temporal characteristics. But in Hegel, as in his doctrine of space, there is also a hint of a rupture between time and matter, and a clear tendency to define matter itself through the unity of time and space, and not the reverse. In reality, the unity of time and space is the unity of the basic general forms of the real world.

Time, like space, is both discrete and continuous, and of course, infinite as well. The present exists because there is no longer a past; it is the negation of the past. The non-being of the being of the present, that is, its negation, is the future. Only the present exists, but it is the result of the past, and it is pregnant with the future.

> The flight of gray time is threefold:
> The future moves
> With sluggish step,
> The silent past
> Stands still forever,
> And the present flies
> Like a winged arrow....

Objective time, reflected in the scientific concept of time, is uniform. Subjective time may flow more quickly or more slowly (the "boredom" and slowness of time, the rhythms of life of particular organisms, the speed of biological processes, the perception of time, and so forth).

The question of the relationship of time and space and of their unity is a special case. "Here" is also "now." "The truth of space is time," is the way Hegel phrases it. This unity is expressed directly in the motion of matter, since a shift in spatial coordinates is also a shift in time, and the quantity of movement is the product of velocity and time. This unity of space and time is the basis of a theory (that of Hermann Minkowski), which regards time as a fourth dimension of space. There can be no doubt that time represents a general dimension, that is, a universal form of the existence of matter. In the same way, there can be no doubt concerning the unity of time and space. This, however, is a dialectical unity, and not identity. The specific character of time must not be merged with the three-dimensional space of being. "Space and time," Hegel writes, "are generally taken to be poles apart: space is there, and then we *also* have time. Philosophy calls this 'also' into question."[10]

This is both correct and incorrect—correct, since space and time are mutually conditioned forms of being, and incorrect, since they are not identical forms. They constitute unity, but not identity. In precisely the same way, they are bound up with matter as attributes of material substance, as its objective properties.

The objective character of time and space is confirmed by experience through countless indices and through all the senses, which yield one and the same result. The formulae for velocity, for the quantity of work, for the transformation of energy, along with the formulae of geometry, physics, mechanics and so on, all corroborate from various angles this functional dependence on space and time as objective forms of matter in motion. All the preliminary calculations of the processes of productive technology, of scientific experiments, and so on, employ the quantities of space and time. Practice, experiment, and prediction confirm the objective nature of time and space. But time and space are not independent quantities. Hegel, who had a tendency to define matter in terms of the unity of space and time, was not correct, and neither are a series of outstanding present-day physicists who are inclined to consider time and space "the true substance" of the universe. This is for the reason that defining the world through the equation $U = f(x,y,z,t)$ means taking only one side of things and approaching the question in an abstract, formal manner, substantializing its attributes in anti-dialectical fashion, isolating the question from real substance, and "mathematizing" being.

The fact is that when time and space are divorced from reality they themselves perish as time and space. Instead, they are transformed into dead abstractions, into dry mummies of abstract, rational, purely quantitative thinking, which considers phenomena to be subjective expressions of the objective world. In the first case, colors, odors, and sounds; in the second, atoms, waves, rays, and so forth. It is worth comparing, for example, the well-known passage about light in the first volume of *Capital* with a number of passages from *Anti-Dühring*; the *Philosophical Notebooks* of Ilyich (in particular, the summaries of *The Science of Logic*) with *Materialism and Empirio-criticism*; and the commentaries [by Lenin] on Feuerbach with those on Hegel. To the superficial mind, the mind of the non-dialectician, this will seem like contradictory vacillation. But what is present here is a dialectical contradiction, with its basis in the fact that "essence" is implicit in "appearance" and that the subjective cannot be treated as merely subjective.

Here, however, we want to examine this question from the point of view of the process of cognition, of the historical process of cognition.

What, for example, about modern empiricism (the whole school of Mach and Avenarius, the immanentists, the philosophizing mathematicians and physicists grouped around the journal *Erkenntnis*, the fictionalists, positivists, and others)?

For them, the process of cognition is merely the conversion or rearrangement [*Umformung*] of perceptions, of the "direct data of the senses." This is how they interpret the dictum *Nihil est in intellectu, quod non fuerit in sensu*.[11]

There is nothing new here. The process of cognition is presented as though a bear were shifting a "given" heap of boulders, and setting them up in such and such a fashion. It is all just *Umformung*, undertaken in order to make thought more simple, convenient, and economical. Here, in truth, "simplicity is worse than theft"!

Hegel in *The Philosophy of Nature* mocks these primitives. "We start from our sense-knowledge of nature," he writes. "If physics were based only on perceptions, however, and perceptions were nothing but the evidence of the senses, the activity of a natural scientist would consist only of seeing, smelling, hearing, etc., so that animals would also be physicists. It is, however, a spirit, a thinking entity, which sees and hears, etc."[12]

There can be no doubt that in the process of history, cognition has proceeded from "sense-knowledge of nature." The same, in abbreviated fashion, is also true for the human individual—a situation that recalls Haeckel's phylogenetic law, according to which the human embryo reproduces the evolution of the species. Such an evolution from feelings to thought has occurred over thousands of years in language: *videre* (Lat.), *videt'*, *videnie* (Rus.), *wissen* (Ger.), *vedenie, vedovstvo* (Rus.), *eidos* (Gk), *idea* (Lat.), *schauen*, *Anschauung* (Ger.), *zret'*, *mirovozzrenie* (Rus.); *concipere, conceptio* (Lat.); *greifen, begreifen, Begriff* (Ger.); *yati, poyati* (Old Rus.), *ponyatie* (Rus.), and so forth. The eye and hand have played an especially important role.

However, the fact that the evidence of the senses is the starting point for the historical process does not by any means signify, as crude empiricism maintains, that thought adds nothing new. It is only necessary to ask oneself: how can this be so? If thought adds nothing new, how does the miracle occur through which theory brings practice to fruition? Through what miracle is science becoming a gigantic lever changing the world? How is it fulfilling this vital function if it is merely a convenient summary, the simplest possible, a simple *Umformung* of sensory data? After all, it is impossible to claim that "complexes of sensations," these beloved categories of "warm," "cold," "red," "green," and so on, can serve as instruments for changing the world, for its authentic transformation. This means that the result of thought is something different in qualitative terms from the cognitive raw material represented by sensations. A new alloy has been fused together *in intellectu*, a product distinct from the original material and from intermediate products.

Here we are not concerned with "innate ideas," or with the a priori categories of Kant; nor with pure Platonic ideas (accessible only to the mind), nor with a logical *prius* of the extra-experiential, implanted miraculously in a "transcendental subject"; but with the fact that as people worked together over hundreds of millennia their experience devised objective forms of thought, and gradually altering these forms, came to assimilate ever-new portions of the sensorily-defined world. The transition from sensation to understanding, from feelings to abstract thought, from the subjective to the objective (here, not in the sense of something material, but in that of a copy adequately reflecting the objective world); from the individual to the social, existing in the heads of socialized and collaborating individuals (collaborating in one way or another, which does not exclude struggle but presumes it); the new quality of the products of thought; all this, so far as the empiricists are concerned, is a book sealed with seven seals. Engels was justified in calling such people creeping empiricists and "intuitive asses." (This barb is less than polite when applied to Isaac Newton, but it is meant as a statement "for itself"; many people fail to understand this, and are very offended on behalf of the great scientist.)

The reworking—*Umarbeitung* and *Übersetzung*—provided by Marx (see the foreword to the first volume of *Capital*) transforms cognitive raw material in the same way as practice transforms the world of concrete objects. From a certain point of view, the output of production contains nothing new, and at the same time everything is new—its use value, for example. There is no miracle of transubstantiation in abstract thought, but there is the fact of new qualities which arise through the active process of thought, and which are in no way divorced from practice even though in various socio-historical formations they are linked to it in different ways (for example, natural science as defined by Marx is the theoretical side of the productive process). People do not only taste and sniff; they also think, and work, and act jointly. The great Goethe remarked aptly that nature plays hide and seek with individuals, and that it can only be comprehended and mastered by society.

In the historical process of cognition, people have broadened the sphere of their perceptions by gigantic amounts, extending their organs (despite the Bible) and increasing the number of their senses (contrary to Feuerbach) through creating powerful, complex, and extremely sensitive scientific equipment, apparatus for perceiving reality on the macro and micro levels. At the same time, people are deepening their cognition, stripping off the covers of subjectivity—of individual subjectivity (color blindness); of generic subjectivity (the subjective coefficient of perception); of terrestrial subjectivity (overcoming the geocentric point of view—compare this with the trope of Pyrrho on position); and so forth. From the primitive idea of the sun as a round, shining disc hanging from the firmament, people have advanced to a highly sophisticated understanding which reflects a huge and very diverse complex of the objective properties of the objective body and of its relationships and mediations: volume, mass, chemical composition, qualitative forms of matter, temperature, types of motion, position in the solar system and in still more gigantic systems emitting radiation of various kinds; its relationship to the earth, and to the transformation of light and heat energy on the earth in innumerable varieties and qualities, and so on to infinity. (Here we are not even analyzing the "reflections" of the sun in consciousness, from the simple "disc" to sun worship...) Physics, chemistry, astrophysics, geology, zoology, botany, history—all the sciences contribute their material! And instead of the primitive "complex of sensations," we have a concept of the sun, a concept that includes a vast range of qualities and which is adequate (in terms of cognition) to the objectively existing heavenly body.

If we seek out the rational kernel in Hegel's idealist dialectics, in its interpenetrating concepts of being (that is, being, immediate being, and being for itself), of essence, of appearance, of reality, and so on, then we find here a mighty attempt to embrace levels of cognition corresponding to those of objective being itself. In a good many of the polemical passages in Hegel, therefore, the philosopher is dragging his adversary by a lasso out of the subjective bog into the objective world, even though—with his collar turned inside out—he understands this in idealistic terms. Following on from Marx and Engels, Lenin understood things in the same way. When Lenin spoke of a reflection, what he had in mind was not the dead, and to a substantial degree, passive "mirror image" of the world registered by the senses. He was referring to the *Umgearbeitete* and the *Übergesetzte*, that is, to a reflection as reworked by abstract thought (see the foreword to *Capital*).

In his *Philosophical Notebooks*, Lenin wrote the following:

> Cognition is the reflection of nature by a human being. This is not a simple, direct, or integral reflection, but a process involving a range of abstractions, a process of formulation, of the formation of concepts, laws, and so on; these concepts, laws, and so on (abstract thought, science = "the logical idea") also encompass conditionally, approximately, the universal principle of eternally moving and developing nature. [13]

Actually, objectively, there are three elements involved here: 1) nature; 2) the cognition of humanity = the human brain as the highest product of nature; and 3) *the form in which nature is reflected in human cognition—this form also includes concepts, laws, categories, and so forth*. A person cannot embrace = reflect = represent nature in its entirety, fully, in its "direct wholeness." All a person can do is to eternally approach this, creating abstractions, concepts, laws, a scientific picture of the world, and so on and so forth.

Meanwhile, the above-mentioned abstractions and laws are not formal-logical abstractions, that is, abstractions with a unified content. On the contrary, they "reflect nature more profoundly, truthfully, fully." Although abstracted from reality, the concept of the sun of which we spoke earlier is at the same time invariably richer than the brilliant fifteen-kopeck coin of sensory perceptions, and far richer than a coin of much greater denomination.

Consequently, we repeat, these are not empty abstractions but concrete abstractions. From this point of view it can be seen that if one of the sides of cognition is exaggerated, cognition is led onto false paths. If, for example, we take the path of abstraction from all mediations and qualitative definitions, we finish up eventually with a *caput mortuum* of abstraction, a truthless and empty abstraction, a Kantian thing-in-itself.

If we constantly link the object with the subject, that is, if we consider abstraction from a thinking subject to be impossible, we finish up with "principled empiriocritical coordination," idiosyncratic idealism of the type of Mach and Avenarius.

If the generic features existing in the concrete (the so-called "universal," standing out among the "individual" and "particular") are inflated and hypostatized, that is, if they are endowed with an independent being, becoming transformed into substance, this leads by a direct road to objective idealism. If sensations are considered in isolation from their links to objective reality, if they are examined outside their links to that which is sensed, that is, not as manifestations of external "data," but in themselves, this leads to subjective idealism.

If practice is examined in isolation from the object of practice, this leads to voluntarism, pragmatism, and so forth.

If the formation (that is, social formation) of concepts is considered not as a process of cognition on the basis of reflection of the objective world, existing independently of the subject, then we have the rise of a social-myth-creating idealism of the type of Bogdanov's empirio-monism.

And so on, and so forth.

In other words, the process of mediated knowledge is fraught with many dangers. It has many facets, and the exaggeration or inflation of one of these out of proportion with reality creates a distorted, one-sided picture of the world. It need hardly be said that the corresponding distortions, along with their direction, the vectors of thought, are determined to a significant degree by the socio-historical environment, giving rise to what Marx called the means of representation, a correlate of the means of production. This, however, relates to the question of the sociology of forms of thought, which deserves separate consideration.[14]

Empirio-positivists and phenomenalists of all stripes set out to frighten people by arguing that recognition of external reality involves a duplication of the world, the same sort of metaphysics as, for example, in Plato's objective idealism. Hence their jibes about the "essence" of objective matter, and so on. Here we find a real bacchanalia of play-acting, of bad manners, of speculation on fear of metaphysics and fear of the obscurantist "nature philosophy" of the

Romantics, and so forth. Therefore, and logically enough, this type of philosophy has been especially widespread among philosophizing physicists. Nevertheless, these expressions of alarm and anguish have precisely no basis.

What is really at issue is not the multiplying of objective reality, which is always one and unique, though viewed as a diverse totality. The real question, to resort to a metaphor, concerns the various types of copies of reality, the various pictures of the world, which are more or less accurate, adequate, faithful, profound, and so on. However many copies there might be, how is this a multiplication of the world? Why is there some kind of duplication? According to Plato, there were two realities, one "real" and the other "not real." Such was Plato's view. Such duplication can very often occur where there is a belief in the dualism of soul and matter—for example, in various religious doctrines where the real world is sensual, material, carnal, and sinful, while above it there exists a world that is spiritual, paradisiacal, free, and divine. But what is the point of all this when we are examining the question of various forms of reflection of the world? What duplication or multiplication of reality can there be in this case? It is clear that the whole question is posed quite wrongly. To a certain degree, meanwhile, an objection to "duplication" was raised by Avenarius (and later by Petzoldt) with the so-called doctrine of introjection. This objection, to a certain degree, provided the inner polemical fire for the whole school in its struggle against metaphysics, which was considered to include materialism. It is true that at that time almost none of these philosophers were familiar with dialectical materialism, but it is typical that they were concerned not with overcoming the one-sidedness of a mechanistic and vulgar materialism, but with combating materialism as such.

Just as in the question of sensations and of the reality of the external world the philosophers concerned were suborned by "pure experience," here they were won over by the struggle against the duplication of the world and against metaphysical essences. None of this, however, has any relation to the question we are discussing, of the process of cognition as posed by dialectical materialism, and of the various degrees of adequacy of "reflections." The process of cognition also consists in changes to these reflections, which have advanced from the crudely primitive drawings of a savage on the walls of a cave, to highly complex photographs and X-ray images, from the chaos of confused sensations to the sublime scientific picture of the world.

The constant rejection of particular "copies," and the shift to more advanced, comprehensive, profound ones, increasingly adequate to objective reality, is this very process of unending cognition of the world. Dialectical materialism does not consider copies of the objective world to be the objective world. The objective character of a copy is not the objective character of the external world; it lies in the correspondence between this copy and the objective world. This is the only way the question can be posed.

5

Mediated Knowledge

The thesis of the sensationalists—*Nihil est in intellectu, quod non fuerit in sensu*—is extremely radical.[1] Ludwig Feuerbach, in his (furious, holy, and just) war against the "drunken speculation" of Hegel, against the replacing of the world of reality, the material world, by a game of self-motivated ideas, and against the panlogistic gibberish of objective idealism elevated to the status of a grandiose universal system, raised the banner of feeling. In the broad cultural sense and in the historico-cultural context, this was at the same time the philosophical expression of a whole movement for the rehabilitation of the flesh, for defending it against encroachments by the disembodied spirit, the process described so wittily by Heinrich Heine in his brilliant and celebrated essays on the history of religion and philosophy in Germany.

"How stupid it is," Feuerbach wrote, "to want to make metaphysical existence into a physical one, subjective existence into an objective one, and logical or abstract existence into an illogical, real existence!"[2]

A savage war was fought, and Feuerbach did a great deal to expedite the disintegration of the Hegelian school and the formation of the "Hegelian left," within which the genius of revolutionary Marxism was born. Feuerbach took the sensationalist principle to such lengths as, for example, to write in his *Lectures on the Essence of Religion*: "Nor have we any grounds for imagining that if man had more senses or organs, he would also cognize more properties or objects of nature.... Man has just as many senses as are necessary ... to perceive the world in its totality...."[3]

Feuerbach's enthusiasm here is clearly excessive. Where is the reason for this predetermined harmony? A limited number of senses, in the face of the infinite qualitative diversity of nature? These "anthropological" enthusiasms, however, do not detract from the great services rendered by a fine philosopher.

To a reader who follows Marxist literature attentively, it might seem that the classics of Marxist thought themselves are marked by uncertainties in their interpretation of sense and thought, or (something that is an expression of this dilemma) by vacillation between "naive realism," which considers the world of phenomena to be the direct "essence" of the world, and materialism of such a persuasion.

6

The Abstract and the Concrete

Is it impossible to stir up a revolt against what has been described above? Seriously! We live in the world of the senses, we feel it, we batter our heads against its solidity, we meet its resistance. And despite all this you wander off into some abstractions and laws or other! Yes, this materialized Hegelianism with its "universals," its idols which have swallowed the concrete and living! Did not Marx write that, in Bacon, matter with its poetically sensual gleam smiled on humankind? Did not Marx write that materialism, with its grayness, its geometric forms, its abstractness, subsequently became "hateful to humanity"? Do you not head off into this cold realm of the transformed Hegel instead of living, working, and thinking in the sphere that smiles with its sensuality? We do not want these abstractions, these dead, plucked peacocks, out of which you have pulled all the luxuriant plumage! Apart from Marx, here are two more quotations for you:

1. A quotation from Goethe (Goethe on Holbach's *Système de la Nature*):

> To judge from the title, which loudly proclaims that the book presents a system of the universe, we naturally hoped that the author would hold forth on nature, on the goddess whom we have served.... But how great was our disappointment when we began to read his empty atheistic verbiage, in which the earth with all its beauties and the heavens with all their constellations sank without trace! Here we heard tell of eternal matter, which was in endless motion, and that this motion alone... was supposed to have created the endless phenomena of being. Even this would have satisfied us, if

out of his moving matter the author had really succeeded in unfolding the entire universe before our gaze. However, he knew no more of nature than we did, since after establishing a few general concepts, he immediately discarded them in order also to transform that which is highest in nature into the same material, weighty (though also mobile), but formless nature. (*Dichtung und Wahrheit*)[1]

Goethe, as is well known, was a pantheist, a hylozoist, and so forth. And here too is none other than your Hegel himself, in his academic cap!

2. A quotation from Hegel:

The more thought predominates in ordinary perceptiveness, so much the more does the naturalness, individuality, and immediacy of things vanish away. As thoughts invade the limitless multiformity of nature, its richness is impoverished, its springtimes die, and there is a fading in the play of its colors. That which was noisy with life, falls silent in the quietude of thought; its warm abundance, which shaped itself into a thousand intriguing wonders, withers into arid forms and shapeless generalities, which resemble a dull northern fog.[2]

We are posing these questions in a spirit of Socratic irony, spurring doubts, creating ferment, forcing thought to really work, prising it apart from its habitual laziness and inertia. But how can we come to grips with the real essence of these questions? What is involved here?

First, it should be noted that humanity in the social-historical sense has a multitude of different relationships with nature, not only intellectual but also theoretical. Humanity relates to nature both in practical ways (including biologically) and in artistic-aesthetic fashion. In reality, these diverse relationships are usually neither distinct nor consistent. They are merged in one proportion or another, interpenetrate one another, and are inseparable, though also dependent in various ways on the dominant historical ideas and the social-cultural climate, which is determined in turn by the material conditions of social development. Consequently, we shall not examine questions of emotional attitudes here at all. We bring them up only "to prime the material" and will return to them later.

Second, since we are dealing with an intellectual, cognitive relationship to nature, and since it is in this connection that the question of wealth and diversity (or, on the other hand, of poverty and sparseness) is posed, we have already answered this question in a previous exposition. But here, in order to satisfy the rebellious demon of irony, we shall examine it from the point of view of the complex relationships between the abstract and the concrete, that is, from the point of view of the transition from the particular to the general and from the general to the particular.

In this connection Hegel's doctrine of the dialectic, interpreted in the materialist sense, represents a huge acquisition, whatever the primitive worshippers of pure sensationalism might say and however indignant they might become.

And so, let us get down to work.

What is repellent, useless, harmful, and dead? Formal-logical abstraction when it is taken to the point of frivolousness. It is indeed a plucked, gutted, soaked peacock. Here the logical volume is inversely proportional to the content, the usual law of common scholarly logic. Abstraction is a bare, stripped, featureless pole, even the shadow of a pole. The universal here is universal in the poverty and sparseness of its emaciated definitions. It is the negation of a multitude of qualities; it represents a restriction to one or two characteristics, transformed into dry, wrinkled mummies.

Dialectical abstraction is concrete abstraction, which includes the whole wealth of concrete definitions. But surely this is rubbish, or some bizarre eccentricity! A classic case of a flat contradiction, or perhaps some kind of mocking conceptual game, the sort of logical mysticism and gibberish one finds so often in Hegel? No, the structure of dialectical concepts is precisely as indicated above. In them, the universal is singled out, while the whole diversity of concrete properties, qualities, relationships and mediations is retained and subordinated to the universal. This is not the primal chaos of concrete uncertainties, nor the chaos of the "first concrete," but the cosmos, the genuine richness of the world, subject to order, containing law and essence, understood in a way adequate to reality and its corresponding parts and aspects.

First the various "parts" of the object, its aspects and functions, are established analytically. They are isolated and examined in their isolation. Then the transitions from one to another of them are considered. Next, the thought process returns to its starting point, that is, to the concrete. But this concrete (the "second concrete") differs from the starting point (the "first concrete") in that now we understand its essence, its law, its universal nature as revealed in the particular and individual. Here, therefore, the object is understood in its conformity to natural laws. We understand the relationship between its components; we understand the relationship between this basic character and its mediations. There is nothing scanty here; on the contrary, compared with the first concrete we see a massive enrichment, since instead of indeterminate and arbitrarily selected aspects, the living dialectic of the real process is represented here. Marx in all his works made brilliant use of this dialectical method, which is simultaneously both analysis and synthesis. Let us take, for example, his concept of the circulation of capital (set out in the second volume of *Capital*).

First concrete: the circulation of capital, not yet understood, in its unity and indeterminateness; this is the starting point.

Then, analysis: distinguishing between the forms of money capital, productive capital, and commodity capital and their circulations; analysis of particular circulations in their abstract isolation; they are counterposed to one another; they exclude one another; they negate one another.

The relationship between them: the transition from one phase to another, from one opposition to another.

Next, synthesis: the process as a whole, the unity of opposites, the return to the concrete (the "second concrete"). Here, however, the circulation of capital is understood; its law-governed character is clear. All the concrete aspects of the circulation of capital are retained, but at the same time its essence is also distinguished, and is taken in all its mediations. The abstraction "the circulation of capital" is now concrete.

Or else, let us take such a highly abstract concept of the social sciences as that of society. For Marx, it includes the concept of historically changing social-historical formations, with all the interactions of base and superstructure, and with the basic laws distinguished. Here all the opposition between "generalizing" and "individualizing" methods, between the "logical" and "historical," which the school of Rickert worked up such a sweat in elaborating, is dialectically removed.[3] At the same time, we find here that Marx long ago scornfully refuted the antihistorical "wholeness" of modern-day fascist theoreticians, who in their fetish for a universal, hierarchical community, melt down everything in history that is concrete and specific. Marx's concept of society thus contains, in a nutshell, potentially all the possible definitions, in all their richness. Here the dialectical formula, like a gigantic capacitor, holds within itself the entire wealth and diversity of social life. Nor is it in any way wanting compared with other formulas or "reflections." Of course, real life is richer than any intellectual theory. From this point of view, Goethe was correct when he said, "All theory is gray, but green, forever green, is the tree of life"—an aphorism that Lenin was particularly fond of.

Cognition is a process, and encompasses reality only in its unending motion; it apprehends things only in the asymptotic sense (the notion of infinite approximation) and ultimately never fully grasps everything. But that is a separate question, quite apart from the one we are analyzing here.

Let us take the concept of matter, the most abstract concept in physics (in the broad sense of the word). The definition of matter in formal logic is exceedingly empty and impoverished, but the dialectical concept includes qualitative diversity, historical transformations of one type of matter into another, and concrete properties in their relationships and transitions. This is not the gray, mechanical, formless principle whose dullness so frightened and dismayed the young Goethe when he read Holbach's *System of Nature*.[4] This is a unity divided in a diverse multitude of ways.

Idealism of every stripe has always tried in some fashion to impart to the concept of the general an independent existence, a "true being," in contradistinction to the individual as an "inauthentic" being. The Platonic "idea" is nothing other than a hypostatized concept, a deified abstraction. The medieval debate between the nominalists and the realists finished up with the nominalists advancing the thesis *"Universalia sunt nomina,"*[5] while the realists asserted the opposite, *"Universalia sunt realia."*[6] In precisely the same way, concepts in Hegel's objective idealism are transformed into essences, and objective reality is measured against these concepts to see whether it corresponds to this true reality (taking this approach, Hegel really only accepts what corresponds to his own ideas!), instead of the other way round, with the concepts measured against real things and processes in order to test whether they correspond to the objective world. Hence Marx also considered that the first form of materialism was nominalism. How furiously Marx attacked the Hegelian replacement of pears, apples, and so forth with "fruit in general," of real objects with their logical shadows and reflections!

It is in this respect also that Feuerbach is particularly noteworthy. With what noble passion Feuerbach protested against the transforming of logical being into real being, and of real being into logical being! With this aspect of his system, Hegel turns the whole world upside down and forces it to walk on its head. Precisely for this reason, Lenin wrote in his commentaries on Hegel's *Science of Logic* ("On the Question of Dialectics"):

> Primitive idealism: the universal (concept, idea) is a *particular being*.... But is not modern-day idealism, Kant, Hegel, the idea of God, of the same nature (*absolutely* of

the same nature)? Tables, chairs, and the *ideas* of tables and chairs; the world and the idea of the world (God), thing and "noumenon," the unknowable "Thing-in-itself"; the relationship between the earth and the sun, between nature in general and law, *logos*, God. The dichotomy of human cognition and the *possibility* of idealism (= religion) are already *given* in the *first, elementary* abstraction ("house" in general and particular houses).[7]

Here, however, we want to stop in passing to clarify a point on which a great deal of confusion has frequently reigned. The individual too has its name, its "nomen." Corresponding to this nomen is a concrete, individual reality, a thing, a being, a process. The nomen itself is merely a reflection, a logical correlate of this reality of the external world (or of the so-called inner world, for example, the nomen "sensation"; this, however, is again a special question). Here, therefore, we cannot substitute one for the other. Now it might be asked: what is there in reality that corresponds to the general, as a logical category? Is there nothing? Or does something correspond to it after all? It is clear from what has been said above that an individual being does not correspond to it. But what corresponds to it, or at any rate can correspond to it, in reality? (We say "can" because an answer from the realm of fantasy, as Lenin remarked in expanding on some aspect of the question, leads to pure illusion, to which nothing corresponds.) What can correspond to it, and usually does, is one or another feature, property, or aspect, that exists in concrete things themselves, and that is repeated in a multitude of such things. This feature, property, or aspect does not exist apart from the specific individuals. Such characteristics are not the essence of the thing, its particular individuality. But they exist as properties of individual, concrete processes, of things, of beings. Such is the dialectic of the general and the particular, captured superbly by Lenin in the fragment quoted above.

> [The] individual exists only in the connection that leads to the universal. The universal exists only in the individual and through the individual. Every individual is (in one way or another) a universal. Every universal is a fragment (or an aspect, or the essence) of an individual. Every universal only approximately encompasses all the individual objects. Every individual enters incompletely into the universal, and so on and so forth. Every individual is connected by thousands of transitions with other *kinds* of individuals (things, phenomena, and processes), etc.[8]

Here, however, we might be teased a little by Socratic irony. How can this be? You have just sworn to the richness of dialectical abstractions, and here you are, talking about their incompleteness! And not in the sense that cognition at any given moment is finite, and that it is infinite and complete only at eternity, but in another, more prosaic sense: your "universal" is now also incomplete in relation to what you know, that is, to what is really accessible to you in one way or another, and which you can talk about!

Here it really is necessary to provide a substantial explanation. A dialectical concept represents a certain abridgement, condensation, abbreviation. The richness of concrete attributes is, so to speak, asleep in it; it is present in it potentially, and has to be developed. To put it crudely, the dialectical concept of capital cannot replace all three volumes of *Capital*, and it is simply comical to demand that it do so. Science, philosophy, and thought in general would be easy if this were otherwise! In this connection, there is yet another curious question that deserves close scrutiny.

In Hegel's *Philosophy of Nature* we encounter the following passage:

> If empirical natural science, like the philosophy of nature, also employs the category of universality, it is often in some doubt as to whether it should ascribe to this category an objective or subjective significance. We often hear that classes and orders are established merely for the purposes of cognition. This uncertainty is further manifested in the fact that we seek out the characteristics of objects not in the conviction that they represent substantial objective attributes of the things involved, but merely for the sake of our convenience (sic!), since we are easily able to recognize things by these attributes. If meaningful attributes were only marks (sic!) for the purposes of recognition and nothing more, we could for example say that an attribute of humankind is an earlobe which no other animal possesses. But here we immediately sense that such a definition is inadequate for the cognition of what is important in a human being.... There is agreement that types do not only represent general characteristics, but are the authentic inner essence of the objects themselves, just as orders serve not only to make our surveys of animal life easier, but represent ladders of nature itself.[9]

In [Hegel's] *Encyclopedia* there are also places where law, or the universal, is equivalent to the species (hence his concept of the species). This tradition goes back to Plato (see Hegel's *History of Philosophy*, vol. II). Here, however, we also find included a particular problem that does not coincide with the one of which we spoke earlier. In reality, can we speak for example of the concept of the human species, *Homo sapiens*, simply as the abstraction "humanity in general," like a "table in general" or a "chair in general"? Or is there something special here? And if so, what? There is indeed something special here, and something extremely important: the concept of the human species (a rung on the ladder of nature itself) is a collective concept. Corresponding to it in objective reality is a real totality of mutually interacting individuals, closely linked with one another, comprising a living unity, not a "body" analogous to an individual animal, but a specific unity, a unity *sui generis,* of which particular parts die while others arise, while in sum a biological species, changing in time, is present. Here there is a definite reality corresponding to the concept of a species.

Things are exactly the same with other collective concepts, if corresponding to them there is not just an intellectual totality (statistical or mathematical, for example), but a real one. By the concept of matter, for example, we can understand the totality of all matters in their mutual associations, transitions, and transformations. This collective concept of matter, which includes all its qualitative peculiarities, all its particular types, all its relationships and processes, corresponds to objective reality. Here, thought has also proceeded from the particular to the general, from the concrete to the abstract. But the general here is itself a particular, a particular of the second order, singular and plural, new, individual, a real unity, a real totality. Hence the debate concerning the objective reality of a species is by no means a simple repetition of the debate surrounding "nominalism" and "realism." A species exists not as particular traits of individual animals, but as their current totality. The synthetic function of cognition (a particular feature or facet of the dialectical method, which is both synthesis and analysis simultaneously) here consists not only in the unification of particular features and properties, subjected to analysis, but also in the (intellectual) unification of individuals, actually linked in real life, and by virtue of this relationship counterposed to the "other" (that is, to other species, to the external environment, and so forth).

The most supremely abstract of all concepts, the most concrete, the most general, the totality of all totalities, the relationship of all relationships, the process of all processes is the concept of the all, the universe, the cosmos. This most abstract of concepts is at the same time the totality of everything concrete. Opposition itself dies out in it, since it encompasses everything, and nothing stands in counterposition to it. All the storms of becoming are played out in it, and it itself "flows" in infinite time and space, which exist merely as forms of its being. This is the great substance of Spinoza's *causa sui;* it is *natura naturans* and *natura naturata* simultaneously, stripped of their theological baggage. Objectively, this is the richness of everything. In thought, in reflection, in conception, this is the sum of all human knowledge, worked out historically in the course of many millennia, combined and elaborated into a system, into the vast and grand scientific picture of the world, with its endless quantity of coordinated concepts, laws, and so forth. Anything that is merely "immediately perceived" (which in fact is not possible!) is truly *pitiable* compared to this immensity!

7

Perception, Image, Concept

In his *Philosophical Notebooks*, Lenin posed the question: "Is sensuous representation closer to reality than thought is?"

He answered: "Both yes and no. Sensuous representation cannot apprehend motion *of every kind;* it cannot directly perceive motion at a velocity of 300,000 kilometers per second. But thought can and must apprehend it."[1]

This question, as is readily seen, is the same one we were already working on, the question of the relationship between the perceptibly concrete and intellectually abstract, the question of mediated knowledge, but addressed from a particular angle. We shall pose this question again in this new context. When perception is being considered, the perceptible has to be present, that is, the object, matter, or process itself. Perception occurs only when there is direct contact between the subject and object. *Material* contact is needed between the subject and object as material bodies. There has to be some material action by the object on the material-physiological organs of the subject, so that the latter receives the material "irritants" whose psychological other-form is sense perception. In this sense, direct sensory perceptions are closest of all to the real world. "Closest" here signifies the immediacy of the process itself. This is the principle of sensation (sense perception) about which sensationalists of all shades and persuasions have carried on their discourse. Here we find the material action of the object on the subject. In this action, the object, according to Kant, "afficts" the feelings of the subject. The object, so to speak, materially penetrates the subject, bombarding it with light waves, sound waves, heat waves, and so forth. Since the external world here represents a diverse source of "irritants," and the energy of this external irritation is transformed into the "motion" of the subject's nervous-physiological apparatus, a "motion" whose other-being is sense perception (sensation), it is evident that such direct perceptions (or sensations) are closest of all to reality.

The image (or representation) is already a distancing from reality, and *at the same time* it is a step closer to reality. Why is this so?

Aristotle writes in *De Anima*: "... no one can learn or understand anything in the absence of the senses, and when the mind is actively aware of anything it is necessarily aware of it along with an image; for images are like sensuous contents except that they contain no matter."[2]

This means—Aristotle here is basically right—that an object can also be imagined if it is not directly present, but only on the basis of former sensations. Here, however, the element of *connection* among multiple sensations is overlooked, that is, an aspect of the whole is left out. An image reproduces in a merged or blended form various sensations as they relate to an object, and it is precisely the presence in the image of this connection among multiple perceptions that makes the image closer to the object, to reality. It is closer, however, not in the sense of directness (in this respect it is more remote), but in the sense of its being more complete.

The subsequent process of cognition (in essence, it is the historical process of cognition that is being depicted here in the abstract) leads to the formation of concepts; here, as we know, is the transition to the general. We have analyzed this process in detail, and for the purposes of the present question, we can sum it up as follows: in the respect of directness, for example, the "scientific picture of the world" is immeasurably further from reality than sensations and images. But it is the complex product of complex thought, and in the sense of the adequateness of the reflection it provides, it is immeasurably closer to this reality, fuller, closer, more variegated.

Here we are approaching the question from the same direction as Lenin, when he grasped it with such brilliant simplicity.

In fact, we shall use his example. The eye sees light. Light has a velocity of 300,000 kilometers per second. This velocity conditions the fact that the eye sees light in general. But the eye cannot observe the speed of light in the same way that it observes (sees) the speed of a moving automobile or train, where changes in the spatial relationship between the train and the surrounding objects are fixed visually. The subject cannot therefore imagine a speed of 300,000 kilometers per second in visual terms. The imagination is powerless here. But it is possible to think about such a velocity as much as one likes, and every physicist constantly works with this concept. All "astronomical magnitudes" exceed the bounds of the imagination, but all astronomers use them constantly. A light-year is unimaginable as a unit of distance, but in astronomy it is a standard measurement. Infinitely small and infinitely large magnitudes can neither be sensed in their infinite extent, nor are they imaginable. Nevertheless, we think about them, they are objects of scientific study, and in a whole number of instances in mathematics and technology they have great practical significance.

The relationship between the physical (more precisely, physiological) and the psychological as its other-being is not imaginable visually, but we nevertheless think about it. Let us turn once again, however, to the experimental sciences as usually understood. We do not have a sense organ that can directly perceive electricity, but by observing electricity with sensing instruments, we have developed an electromagnetic theory of matter. Detecting electrons individually and collectively in experiments, we create an electromagnetic picture of the universe. We cannot see ultraviolet rays, but we think about them in profound terms. We cannot directly sense or imagine the infinite number of alpha, beta, gamma, and other rays, with their enormous velocities and so forth, but we think about them and their velocities. We cannot see X rays; we cannot directly perceive or have a sense-based representation of the splitting of an atom of radium; we cannot directly perceive or have images of the temperatures and pressures inside the sun or some other star; but we think about all this in sophisticated fashion. And so forth.

What is the point here? The point is that our senses are limited, but that our cognition as a process is boundless. Beyond a certain threshold of stimulation our senses refuse to serve us. The limited nature of sensory images is connected with this. The actual number of senses we possess is trifling, something we can only regret, whatever Feuerbach might have said. Our senses are also very imperfect. As observed by Standfuss, the male of the Saturn fruit butterfly can detect the scent of the female at a distance of fifteen kilometers.[3] The visual acuity of eagles is well known; so too is the ability of dogs to orient themselves using their sense of smell, and so forth. If it were not for people's ability to think, they would not have made much progress in cognizing and mastering the world! In terms of their senses, dogs rate highly; they smell and hear better than we do. Other creatures can see incomparably better. How is it that human beings are "superior"? Without an understanding of the process of formation of the human brain and of the capacity for thought, a process that has developed historically among socialized human beings, making sense of this situation is impossible.

Let us go still further. A sensation furnishes the particular; it cannot embrace everything at once. You cannot perceive the endless diversity of nature (in this case, that is, see it, hear it, smell it, and so on). But we can think about it, and we must do so. In aphoristic terms, we might say that sensation is anti-philosophical, while thought on the other hand is philosophical. But where is this leading us? Are we not performing a somersault and finishing up showing an idealistic disdain for the empirical, for experience as derived from sensory data? Are we not turning into supporters of breaking off contacts with the sensory world, into supporters of mental as opposed to sensory perception? Are we not about to seek a Platonic "mental space," which we can only approach through the mind, spitting on the lowly senses? Are we not preaching extra-sensory knowledge? Are we not crossing over to a sort of universal apriorism? We might after all be asked: "How do you know about all this, about all your radiation, X rays, velocities, and everything else that you, in your own words, do not sense, that you cannot form a mental image of, but that you think about? What sort of mystification is this? Answer, if you please!"

The answer is simple: we know about all this from experience and through our senses. But the real question is: how? When I stand next to an electric furnace and look at the temperature gauge, I see various arrows and so forth, and on their basis I judge the temperature. I do not stick my finger into the furnace; I would not be able to sense the degree of heat, but would simply get burned, just as I would not be able to sense the cold of liquid oxygen if I put my hand into it, but would immediately lose my hand. I do not sense X rays directly, but sense the evidence of them provided by instruments. I do not see, do not hear, do not smell, and so on, the chemical elements of stars, but perceive the signals of instruments that perform the process of spectral analysis (that is, I mainly see the corresponding readings on the instruments), and I draw various conclusions from this. I see high or low temperatures indirectly; I see huge pressures as they register on a manometer; I see huge degrees of electrical potential by the arrows of measuring instruments. Here there are relationships in which one sense acts in place of another. Both experience and perception come into play here, but perception of another order. Here the object is not sensed directly, but it is nevertheless sensed indirectly.

In order for intellectual conclusions to be drawn, an enormous sum of previously accumulated experience has to be present; otherwise, it would be impossible to decipher these perceptions coming from the instruments. On the basis of the gauge, I determine the temperature in the electric furnace. I cannot sense such a temperature. Nor can I imagine it, that is, form a sensory image of it as warm or hot. But I can think about it. Why? Because thought is capable of comparing, of forming intellectual conclusions, of generalizing. I think of gigantic temperatures, of their influence on various bodies, of the velocity of molecules, and so forth, a whole list of relationships and mediations. I can think of a temperature of 1,000 degrees as being n times greater than any temperature that I have felt or can imagine in sensory terms, just as, to use Lenin's example, I can think of the speed of light as being a velocity known to me, multiplied by n times. I can think of this as an integral quantity, but I cannot imagine it in sensory terms, and still less can I perceive it. In all these examples, however, everything has its source in feeling and experience; without sight (the visual sensing of movement on the dials of instruments), without previous experience, without experience in general, no knowledge would be imparted. I identify the chemical elements in a star on the basis of experience and of perceptions, but not on the basis of the direct effect of this star on my sensory organs. I also identify them through intellectual work; I am not merely sensing and perceiving. Here we find a dialectical progression from sensation to thought, and their dialectical unity. It is significant that Hegel's idealism obliges him to show a disdainful attitude toward the data of empirical science, toward the sensory in general, despite dialectics. On the other hand, it is often possible, especially among scientific experts, to find that abstract thought is clearly underrated. Feuerbach's formula is inadequate, the one that states: "The senses tell us everything, but in order to understand their discourse, we need to link them together. To read the gospel of the senses in a coherent way means to think."[4]

Great intellectual labor is needed in order to establish this link—that is, the process of developing concepts, laws, interconnections, and ever more profound generalizations. It is in this process that we find "where the dog is buried."

Here, though, we return to the question we touched on right at the beginning of this work, when we were polemicizing against the solipsists. In examining the process of cognition, present-day bourgeois philosophy operates constantly with an imaginary Eve before her fall. This philosophy regards the subject as having a sort of idiotic holiness: when this subject encounters an object, he or she sees and hears for the very first time. The subject merely senses. But as we explained in some detail, there are no such subjects. All new perceptions are experienced simultaneously with images and concepts. In essence, for every subject the "sensations" remaining from direct perception ("warm," "cold," "red," and so on) are the product of analysis. In reality, people see, hear, and feel other people, trees, tables, bells, cannon, and so forth, having historically formed concepts of all this; they by no means start the entire historical process from the beginning, *ab ovo*. If it were otherwise, humanity would be running eternally in one and the same spot—that is, acting out some fantastic fairy-tale about a white bull-calf. Fortunately, things are not really like this; the tale of the white bull-calf is only played out on the pages of works of bourgeois philosophy.

Therefore, to speak crudely and metaphorically, when a person perceives he or she carries within himself or herself a developed system of concepts, more or less adequate to reality. Hence, the closeness to reality of which Lenin spoke actually consists also of the fact that direct contact with reality via the senses (something expressed in sensations) is accompanied by a fusion of these sensations with a whole, closely related (closely in the sense of reflection, that is, more and more truthful) system of concepts. Hence any socialized human being, that is, thinking human being, does not wander in the world like a sleepwalker, as a subject filled with a "chaos of sensations," but orients himself or herself more or less adequately in the external world. This is because the person in one way or another knows the world; he or she does not merely sense, but already knows. This knowledge is not a priori, but it is "given" at every moment before each new sensation, and sensation, which in the final analysis (in the final analysis historically!) is the source of thought, the fount of concepts, falls in any subject into a whole sea of already formed concepts.

But since these latter already to a considerable degree correspond in one way or another to objective reality, any further orientation in the world is nothing other than a further synthesis of sensation and thought, that is, transformations of sensation into thought, the sucking in by thought of new aspects of sensation. While becoming more remote from direct sensation, thought therefore draws closer to reality, testing itself directly through objective practice, in which the subject, actively mastering an object theoretically, actively, and in directly material fashion masters it practically, transforming its very substance and establishing the closest possible relationship with it.

8

Living Nature and the Artistic Attitude toward It

A commonplace objection to materialism has focused on poetry and feeling. Developed, for example, from the point of view of hylozoism and hylozoist pantheism (this theme was presented with particular force by Goethe, including in his critique of Holbach quoted above), this objection protests at the fading away of the directly emotional and poetical significance (according to Avenarius, "affectional," and positive) of colors, sounds, and so forth. In relation to this, we may note in lapidary fashion:

1. Holbach is not a "model." Dialectical materialism, as opposed to the mechanistic variety, affirms the qualitative diversity of the world, and the endlessly varied forms of its associations.
2. It is by no means true that dialectical materialism considers colors and so on to be merely subjective. A rose is red in relation to the eye.
3. A human being, while experiencing influences from the direction of nature, also feels (sees, hears, smells, and so on) an infinitely small part of the world.
4. When a human being has a "scientific picture of the world," he or she possesses an immeasurably richer whole (with an infinite number of properties, associations, laws, aspects, types, and so on). This aesthetic (if we are to look at the situation from this angle) is far richer than the aesthetic of primitive savages in their supposed (to a significant degree, illusory) capacity of "naive realists."

5. Into this picture, there also enters a sentient human being with all sorts of "copies of reflections" and so on—reflections of varying degrees, of varying depth and breadth.
6. This picture of the world is therefore adequate, to the extent that cognition allows, to actual reality, to the real universe, and is an infinite number of times richer than the picture with which the hylozoists and pantheists, when they contemplate it in direct artistic fashion, are so enraptured.
7. In particular, it should be noted that into our developing understanding of the infinite universe (infinite in time, in extent, and in respect of quantity and quality) there enters also an understanding of the possibility of the infinite change and development of nature and humanity, and also of cognition of the universe, since here, so to speak, we find an infinitely vast fund of hidden riches, revealed in diverse ways through the infinite cognitive process.

There is also, however, another side to the process: this is the theme of living nature, of the life of the cosmos.

Hegel in his *Philosophy of Nature* directly celebrates Goethe for his pantheistic-hylozoist attitude toward the life of the cosmos, for his vital understanding of nature. It is curious, however, that in the same work he observes that nature and the cosmos should not be confused, since nature is the cosmos, or the world, minus the "spiritual essences." Here Hegel betrays dialectics in two ways. First, "spiritual essences" are divorced from corporeality; thus, one aspect of a unitary being is hypostatized—that is, a metaphysical freezing of its spiritual nature takes place. The second betrayal, still more important, lies in the fact that thinking and perceiving beings are torn away from nature; that is, in place of a relative, dialectical juxtaposition, a bifurcation of something which is unitary in character, we find an absolute juxtaposition. In particular, human beings are regarded only as "anti-members" of nature, and not as part of nature. Humanity is regarded as a supernatural principle. If animals are excluded from the category of "spiritual beings," then human beings are also excluded from the organically evolved category.

However, let us return to our topic.

In what sense can we speak of the cosmos as a living entity? Not in the sense of Schelling's world spirit; nor in the sense of the monadology of Leibniz; nor in the sense of mystics such as Jakob Boehme, nor in the sense of *logos*, of religious cosmogonies, and so forth. So in what sense? In the sense that living matter is a fact. There exists a huge, complex organic world; there exists what Academician Vladimir Vernadsky termed the earth's biosphere, full of infinitely varied life, from the smallest microorganisms in water, on land, and in the air, to human beings.[1] Many people do not imagine the vast richness of these forms, or their direct participation in the physical and chemical processes of nature. Meanwhile, this wealth is so great that it once moved Lamarck to consider that all complex compounds present on the earth had been formed through the agency of polyphased living organisms. Hegel, for example, described the organic life of the sea in almost poetic terms, abandoning the mystifying gibberish which Engels termed "abstruse" and which Hegel's Pindar, Michelet, called "the mighty speech of Olympus."[2]

Further, it is unlikely that life exists only on earth. In the infinity of the cosmos, the opposite is millions of times more likely, and Kant in his early, "pre-critical" (and remarkable!) works on natural science spoke directly of living beings on other planets. And since the cosmos is also infinite in time, life in it is eternal. Somewhere, life is being born out of the inorganic. It appeared at a certain point on earth, arising historically out of nonliving matter. But when it did not exist on earth, it existed at other points in the cosmos, and so forth. In a word, life is immanent to the cosmos.

This life is linked inseparably to the "whole," and is part of the whole, one of its aspects, phenomena, facets, properties. It does not exist by chance, but is essential; it is inherent in the whole, as a stage in the historical development of its parts. On the earth, humanity is the most complex product of nature, its flower, so to speak.

In essence, Hegel is not far from this when he writes, using his own language:

> If the geological organism of the earth was initially a product in the process of constructing its form, now, as the individuality lying creatively at the basis, it takes off its deathly rigidity and opens itself up for subjective life, which, however, it denies to itself and gives to other individuals. Since a geological organism is vitality only in itself, then the authentically living is alien in relation to it.... That is, the earth is fruitful precisely as the basis, the soil, for the individual life found upon it. (*The Philosophy of Nature.*)[3]

It is true that Hegel later speaks of the life of elements and so forth and that, for him, this is not only metaphor but also mysticism. But in the passage cited above, a completely rationalist view of things is developed.

If human beings are both products of nature and part of it; if they have a biological basis when their social existence is excluded from account (it cannot be abolished!); if they are themselves natural magnitudes and products of nature, and if they live within nature (however much they might be divided off from it by particular social and historical conditions of life and by the so-called "artistic environment"), then what is surprising in the fact that human beings share in the rhythm of nature and in its cycles? Here we are not concerned with intellectual cognition, but with the practical or cognitive mastering of nature, when social and historical human beings are counterposed to it as subjects, as relatively antagonistic principles, as conquerors and tamers, as an actively creative force counterposed to the elements of nature and to the organically nonhuman world.

We are concerned here with human beings in their fusion with nature, with a bond expressed in anthropomorphic fashion, in the solidarity of human beings with nature, in their intimately sympathetic relations with it. Does not every human being experience a cycle of his or her own development, organic, natural, and biological (childhood, youth, maturity, old age)? Do human beings not experience the cycle represented by the rotation of the earth on its axis, with the alternation of day and night, wakefulness and sleep? Do not human beings, as natural magnitudes, also experience the orbiting of the earth about the sun, with the changing of the seasons? In spring, does not their blood circulate in more lively fashion? Are these great cycles, rhythms, pulsations of the earth and the cosmos not felt in common by nature and human beings, organically, in the blood, so to speak? There is absolutely no mysticism here, just as there is no mysticism in the springtime pairing of animals, or in the amazing migrations of birds, or in the migration of mice before an earthquake. The closer human beings are to having direct contact with nature, the more directly and naturally they experience its course. Hegel remarks on this point: "Primitive tribes sense the course of nature, but the spirit transforms night into day." Social laws of development transform these natural relationships, modifying them and giving them new forms, but do not do away with them.

Urbanized human beings are divorced from nature, but not entirely, and they sublimate springtime and youth in the form of lyric poetry. The eroticism of historical humanity takes on socially conditioned forms; the love lives of a medieval knight, a modern-day bourgeois, and a socialist tractor driver are quite different, but their biological basis remains, and the spring is the spring. The feeling of a bond with nature is present in human beings in the most diverse forms, and there is nothing accidental about the longing of townsfolk for sunshine, green fields, flowers, and stars. Biologically, a human being "takes delight" in nature just as he or she eats plants and animals and takes pleasure in food, drink, and satisfying the instinct to multiply. The wind, sun, forest, water, mountain air, the sea—to a certain degree these too are preconditions for maintaining a *corpus sanum* in which the *mens* is *sana*.[4] This is also a sort of requirement of nature, if we may use such a term.

In all such processes there is also the basis for an emotional bond between people and nature. But a human being is not "a person in general"; he or she is a social, social-historical person. Hence this original basis is complicated to a high degree and in various ways dependent on the individual's social psychology and type of thinking (which is concretely historical, involving particular ideologies). The factors at work here may include, for example, religious beliefs, a complex of poetical and metaphorical attitudes, or an expansion of knowledge of the universe and a realization of its eternal and infinite nature, of its motion, and of its great dialectics. Nature can therefore be experienced in emotional and mystical fashion, as a god; as a great all; as "primal mother earth"; in a relatively narrow, geomorphic sense; in a broader, heliocentric manner; or in the broadest possible fashion, as the universe, and so on. Artistic perception and contemplation passes over into thought, and back again, since emotional life is not isolated, and is not a distinct spiritual substance. One might also make an analysis and commentary from this point of view in regard to the ancient Greek concept of eros.

The process of biological adaptation, with all its enormously varied interactions, is a truly immense subject. It should not be forgotten that in this (in the broad sense) historical process all the so-called basic instincts became established, including the instinct for self-preservation and the instinct for the perpetuation of the species—mighty forces. It is therefore no accident that, for example, love and death, in sublimated and socio-historically conditioned forms, play such an exceptionally prominent role.

Biological adaptation, unlike the social variety, is passive. Hence the corresponding emotional basis of the relationship to nature, that is, the basis of the artistic-aesthetic attitude toward nature, of contemplation of it, delight in it, immersion, dissolution in it, and so forth, differs quite sharply from the basis of the actively practical and actively cognitive-intellectual attitude. Do we not have here the roots of the fact that aesthetics (the aesthetics of Kant in particular!) take the "disinterestedness" of artistic emotion as a constructive characteristic? We shall give warning in advance: this point of view is one-sided, and is far from exhausting the whole topic. Nevertheless, it encompasses that side of the topic that is most closely related to the aesthetics of nature. (It is far, far from embracing aesthetics as a whole! But for now, we are not concerned with the other aspects!)

Let us return to our starting point of living nature. The demand for a "living" study, seeing an object as a "living" process, and so on, is a terminology often encountered in the works of Lenin. When used in relation to objects that *stricto sensu* are not alive, it is of course a metaphorical reference to dialectical cognition as cognition of a fluid, mobile state of being, a reference to the flexibility of intellectual forms, and only this. But here, we are already passing on to another question, which will be taken up in the next chapter.

9

Rational Thought, Dialectical Thought, and Direct Contemplation

In the sea of philosophical and quasi-philosophical ideas, several currents are now in contention: rational thought, as put forward by the majority of natural scientists; dialectical thought, as represented by dialectical materialism and idealist neo-Hegelianism (which in essence is a surrogate for dialectics, a rancid margarine on the capitalist market of ideas); and intuitive contemplation, from its purest forms to the hysterical-hallucinatory mysticism represented primarily by the philosophizing sycophants of fascism, but also including other charlatans of suspicious type. They have now multiplied under the protection of the swastika, like mushrooms following a warm rain. The picture recalls the ideology of the period of the decline and fall of the Roman Empire, with mystical cults, horoscopes, miracle plays, processions, orgies, sorcerers, and hysterics. But enough of this.

Rational thought, resting directly on so-called common sense, is highly respected, and within certain bounds is completely legitimate. This is the realm of formal logic, with all its apparently absolute and unshakable laws: of identity, of contradiction, and of the excluded middle. Rational thought forms concepts, unearths facts, and makes analyses. Its favorite method is induction. It is empirical, solid, and apparently durable. It professes to be alien to everything metaphysical, to which it cries out: "Keep away, don't touch me!" It dissects the substance of nature and of the organic world. Measurement and weight, quantity, number—these are its element. For a long time it was the sole embodiment of rational cognition in general, and to many people it still seems to be so. Its services have been immense. To a large degree it was rational thought that assembled vast quantities of facts; distinguished between classes, genera, species, and families; established an infinite variety of classifications; isolated from the general relationships of the world an endless multitude of things, taking them as being identical to themselves and fixing them in science. Facts, things, the processes of isolation and dissection, analysis, induction, measurement, weight, number, experiment, instruments—these are such characteristic features of rational cognition that for the person who understands them, simple enumeration is enough.

But is this enough for the process of cognition? And to take the opposite tack: is everything above and beyond this the work of the devil? Is not talk of dialectics malicious trickery, logical double-dealing of the sort so beloved of the ancient Greeks who went about the public squares proving to everybody what agile mental acrobats they were, what daring gymnasts of thought? Other such people, like the Futurists in their yellow shirts thousands of years later, shocked their stunned contemporaries with unexpected paradoxes and improbable conclusions, and to this day we laugh at them along with that malicious scoffer, Aristophanes. Hegel too probably felt a certain resistance from the public when he wrote, switching suddenly from his extremely abstract language (to which you need to become accustomed in order to understand it at all), from his ponderous thoughts marching in their leaden boots, to a light-minded, casual style:

"The philosophical mode of exposition is not something arbitrary, a capricious wish to take a stroll on your head for a change after walking on your feet for so long, or just once, to see your familiar face painted" (*The Philosophy of Nature*).[1]

Nevertheless, this is incorrect. Rational consciousness does not grasp either motion, the transformation of one thing into something else, the contradictory nature of things, or the identity of opposites, their unity and integrity. Moreover, it transforms the law of identity into an incontestable dogma, considering the criterion of any "system" to be the exclusion of contradictions. It tries to see isolated parts of a whole as arithmetical parts; it is mechanistic "in itself," and consequently there is something numbing in its analysis. It is a great vivisector, armed with a powerful measuring apparatus, with delicate instruments, and the wonders of modern experimental techniques. Many thinkers have revolted against such limited cognition, among them Goethe, cited *con amore* by Hegel:

> *Encheiresis naturae* chemistry calls it,
> Mocks itself, knows not what befalls it,
> Holds the parts within its hand,
> But lacks, alas, the spiritual band.[2]

Goethe, indeed, saw perfectly well the limited nature of rational cognition. But in his criticism, he was often wide of the mark. He protested against experimental techniques. He rose in revolt against the diffraction of light, considering it an encroachment on the province of the Almighty. While equipped with an excellent understanding of the restricted nature of the quantitative, he tore quantity and quality apart. Observing the rationalism of the vivisectors, he tore off a part from the whole. Protesting against mechanistic materialism, he crossed frequently into the province of pantheistic contemplation, with a tendency to replace intellectual cognition with artistic emotion. Overall, no doubt, he already possessed significant portions of materialist dialectics, but these sprouted as suckers that led off in directions remote from rational cognition. Let this spoonful of tar not spoil the barrel of beautiful fragrant honey left to us by the great poet and thinker!

Our old Russian poet Yevgeny Baratynsky, in his artistically remarkable verses written on the death of Goethe ("and the wave on the sea spoke with him!"), rose in direct revolt against measurement, weight, analysis, and number; time and again he used symbolic examples, animals, birds, grass, fortune-telling, sacraments, and the voices of nature-sorceresses![3] Belinsky in his time remarked on the reactionary nature of such a world view, from which Goethe was thoroughly remote.[4]

Now we have to say directly: yes, rational cognition, formal logic, its laws and analysis are indispensable, but insufficient. Criticisms of rational definitions, criticisms of the one-sidedness of the quantitative, and criticisms of the analytic-vivisectionist method are encountered in the works of such philosophers as Henri Bergson, and these are often correct and very apt. To defend the one-sidedness and restricted nature of rational cognition in general, and of mechanistic materialism in particular, is not our goal. But this was all revealed brilliantly by Marx and Engels, without appeals to entelechy, intuition, or any other super-rational claptrap. And so, we repeat: rationalistic cognition is inadequate. It is highly useful, but it is not enough. It has not exhausted all the possibilities for a process of cognition that would be more complete in its methodology. So there is a need to go beyond its bounds. But in what direction?

In an intelligent direction, embracing the logic of contradictions, motion, becoming, wholeness, the universal connections among all elements of the universe, qualitative change, leaps, the interpenetration of opposites, the transformation of opposites one into another, the diremption, or differentiation, of the one into many and the resolution of many into one, and so forth. The use of formal logic, breaking things down and analyzing them, establishing fixed and unchangeable identities and opposites—this is merely the first stage of cognition, which can extend historically over a very prolonged period (all of rationalism is the embodiment of this kind of cognition). But the next stage involves motion, the shift to the opposite of what came earlier, to its negation. Later still comes the onset of a third stage, when the opposites are unified and we see the emergence of an integrated whole that includes everything that has been obtained through analysis, the dismembered whole, diverse and concrete, with its laws and with the totality of its associations. Here is the unity of opposites. Here is the ascent to the concrete. Here is the growth of content. Here is synthesis. Here is the resolving of contradictions, both their overcoming and their retention. Here is the negation of the negation. Here is true reason. Here is a higher stage of cognition.

If dialectics is taken in its rational form, that is, materialistically, then it contains neither mysticism, nor miracles, nor tricks, nor eccentricities. This is a more profound and all-encompassing method of cognition, which to narrow-minded "common sense" sometimes seems like a conjuring trick. In the same way, propositions concerning infinity, the formulae of differential and integral calculus, non-Euclidian geometry, the theory of relativity, and a great deal else all seem to "common sense" to be absolute rubbish. However, Zeno in his aphorisms on motion showed in essence the limited and inadequate character of rational thought. From his point of view, an arrow could not fly, and Achilles could not catch up with a tortoise. And what about the Skeptics? And Kant's "antinomies"? And the present-day problems of physics, with the contradiction between particles and waves, between the continuous and the discontinuous? If we reject contradictions from the outset or if we fail to see them at all, we cannot have a thorough understanding of anything modern, of anything qualitatively new. Antinomies will seem like an eternal mystery, an impassable barrier, and we shall never reach an understanding of the whole in its "living" mobility and in the diversity of its interrelated parts when those parts are considered separately.

The one-sidedness of the rational cognition of the part has as its total opposite the "direct contemplation of the whole," which leads beyond rational cognition altogether. On this, Hegel wrote in *The Philosophy of Nature*: "Even less acceptable are references to what has been given the name of contemplation, and which to previous philosophers has in fact been nothing other than a means through which ideas and fantasies (and also wild extravagances) act by analogy."[5] And elsewhere: "In children and animals we find a natural unity of thought and contemplation, a unity which at best can be called feeling, but not spirituality.... We should not head off into empty abstraction, should not seek salvation in the absence of knowledge...."[6]

This is polite, but very biting. Concealed here is a jibe at Schelling, who considered cognition to be the highest form of intuition, all things to be sensations, and all of nature "frozen" or "petrified" thought. To be fair, it should be added that, on the one hand, Schelling's works contain many elements that passed into Hegel's system and, on the other, Hegel himself, the historical Hegel, was not characterized exclusively by objective idealism. He was not a "dry" panlogician, but also a mystic in the most real sense of the word, and for him, nature without ideas was merely a gigantic corpse. But this is *en passant*, a digression.

The old "philosophy of nature" had a good many contemplative-mystical-intuitive features. In our own time, philosophizing sorcerers and soothsayers have erected a whole Tower of Babel of "theoretical" rubbish, truly worthy of animals. The term "direct contemplation" is self-explanatory. It is either artistic-aesthetic "immersion in nature," bound up with the sensing of a bond with nature and the experiencing of this sensation (as such, "direct contemplation" is both natural and legitimate, so long as it does not express a claim to replace thought, intellectual cognition, reason); or else, it is a religious-mystical attitude; that is, one formed under conditions of dominance-subordination, with recognition of the intuitive as the highest principle of cognition. In the latter case, it makes a blatantly importunate claim to substitute itself for everything rational and reasonable. Here the central idea is that of a hierarchical integer, a whole, a totality. But this "whole" is counterposed not only to the rational, dead whole assembled in one-sided, mechanical fashion out of its component parts, but also to the dialectical whole, existing in the realm of thought as a "second concrete," and reflecting a reality which is unified and at the same time diverse, the unity of which Hegel wrote, precisely in relation to nature:

> [A] theoretical and thinking consideration of nature...[aims] at comprehending that which is universal in nature as it presents itself in a determinate form, i.e., forces, laws, genera. Here the content is not a simple aggregate, but is distributed through orders and classes, and must be regarded as an organic whole.[7]

This means that reasoning thought, in contrast to the rationalist variety, is far from imagining a whole as a collection of parts; it thinks of it as a real, indivisible unity with internal relations between opposites, a whole of which any part, once separated, immediately destroys the whole, and ceases to be that which it was in the relationship of this whole. Rationalist cognition exists "in sublated form" within reasoning cognition, in the way that formal logic exists within dialectical logic. Reasoning cognition does not for a moment rule the quantitative out of account, but it perceives the transformation of the quantitative into the qualitative. It does not strike out the particular, but sees it in relation to the whole. It does not kill off oppositions, but embraces them both in their mutual interpenetrations and singly. The sorcerers and soothsayers of modern mysticism totally deny rational cognition, measures, weights, figures, analysis, synthesis, dialectics, rationality, and reason. They even counterpose the soul (*Seele*) to the so-called spirit, or mind (*Geist*). Tearing thought apart from feeling, they seek in intuition, in the unconscious, and in insensible immersion in the object, with mystical revelations, to find ideological assistance for themselves in their struggle both with the heritage of the Enlightenment era and, above all, in their struggle against Marxism, which throughout the world has raised the most prominent banner of the intellect and of rational cognition in general.

Whom Zeus wishes to destroy, he first deprives of reason. Reason is replaced here partly by mysticism, and partly by a foxlike cunning. The mystical "whole" turns out to be a cosmic hierarchy of fascist social values, the universalization of the caste ladder of fascism. The pronouncements of Hitler, seen as embodiments of suprarational grace, are taken to be the epistemological criteria for truth. Here all grounds for dispute disappear, since one cannot function from a reasonable point of view while using the categories of mysticism. This is the realm of faith and of charlatan quackery, of the cult of cruelty of German militarism, of the big bourgeois, of alcoholic and cocaine-addicted military officers, and of crudely bestial *Landsknechte*.[8]

Even the skepticism of Oswald Spengler was a thousand times cleverer than the belches of mysticism whose odor permeates all of fascist Germany. This is not the overcoming of the rational one-sidedness of so-called positive science, of solid British empiricism, of the ideology of the counting, measuring, inquisitive, inventive weigher of nature who from the times of Francis Bacon has understood perfectly that *scientia* and *potentia humana* coincide, but who has not yet had the wings to fly any higher, to make the transition from rational to consciously dialectical thought. On the contrary, the "theory" of the fascist hysterics is equivalent to advocacy of the pick and spade, of the power of the earth and the voice of blood, of narrow medieval corporatism, of rigid class-estates, of ossified hierarchy and the idols of the absolute.

This is not the petty-bourgeois sentimentality of the notorious philosophy of belief and feeling, the creation of Hamann, Jacobi, and Lavater, with their *schöne Seele* or beautiful soul. Their romantically mystical ideology of "stormy geniuses" was an expression of protest against Germany's feudal narrowness. Present in it were the concepts both of the strongman and of the weakling. Also present in it were protests against reason, in the name of "heart," "soul," intuition, and open-hearted faith. But what does the ironclad "contemplation" of the hierarchy of sorcerers, as bloodthirsty as the Carthaginians' Moloch, have in common with this? In what way does the *schöne Seele*, sensitive beauty of spirit, remind us of the cold "blond beast," whose blood sings over charred ruins? At the bottom of the vessel into which Heinrich Heine once looked as a guest of the goddess Harmonia, the haughty gaze of the beast sees an Assyrian hierarchy, crowned with a swastika, a cold monster whose talons rip the flesh of everything living. This is not a warm pantheism, not the naive immersion in nature of the Hindus with their preaching of love for animals, birds, the sun, and flowers. It is not artistic delight or aesthetic admiration. This is contemplation of the world with a religious tint (and with calculation!) along the lines of the table of ranks established by Herr Adolf Hitler in his Caesarian empire. We would like to see the cosmos "in its entirety," but alas, we see only uniforms, ranks, insignia, epaulettes, cannon, fangs, and estates.

The illusory empire of the fascistized *Universum* is the ocean in whose waves the modern mystics of blood and poison gases immerse themselves.

They take pleasure in themselves, so to speak, seeing in the mirror the mystical world they have created, a world in which everything is allotted according to the same estate-class-whiphandle order of precedence, just as in the constitution of a fascist state. This dark ossification and ossified darkness express the drawn-out, ignominious decomposition of modern capitalism, when its restless, incessant progressive labor, its motion and flights of thought, have come to an end; when the twilight of its gods has begun, and the owl of Minerva from the new world makes its mysterious flight into the future...

The Faust of the bourgeoisie has died. The former vitality of the capitalist world, its enormous dynamism, which in the realm of thought bore such fruit as the differential and integral calculus, Darwin's theory of evolution, Hegel's logic of contradictions, has been replaced by the rotten "associated capitalism" of Schmalenbach, interlinked by rotten "thought," by the search for a static, elemental absolute, by a return to an age-old hierarchy of forms like that of the holy father St. Thomas Aquinas.[9]

In Spinoza's *Treatise on Religious and Political Philosophy* there is a remarkable passage that describes how human beings in critical times vacillate between fear and hope, and how they then fall into mysticism and superstition, into a slough of tokens and divinations. Such is now the position of the bourgeois who senses that the real direction of movement of capitalism is toward extinction. Hence the new theodicy.

But in its "tones," this theodicy is the complete opposite of that of Leibniz! Its mysteries are enacted, not in bright Greek churches or even in Gothic cathedrals, but on the back lots of the fascist barracks, in the stables of Augeus, which await their proletarian Hercules. This time, however, Hercules must not only clean out the stables, but also cleanse the world of the infection from their stench. Then these insolent phantasms of the new "contemplation," drunken and barely able to stand on their feet, will disappear forever, yielding their place to a victory parade of human reason...

"There is nothing easier than inventing mystical causes, that is, phrases devoid of common sense," wrote Karl Marx in his well-known letter to Pavel Annenkov criticizing Proudhon.[10]

But Marxism and Marx's materialist dialectics, fighting for reasoned, rational cognition, are not at all rationalistic. Here, reason is not divorced either from the intellect, or from the feelings, or from the will. The conscious is not torn apart from the unconscious, and logical thought does not exclude either fantasy or intuition. Intuition itself, however, is understood not as a mystical process, but rather—since we are speaking of science and philosophy—as the scientific instinct, separated off and developed by the culture of thought. In no way does it negate either the intellect or rational cognition. Hence Marx, for example, wrote of Ricardo: "Ricardo possesses ... a strong logical instinct" (*Capital*). [11]

Lenin expounded superbly both on "dreams" and on "fantasies" (in science and philosophy). As is well known, he gave them their due. But he found truly great words in which to sing a celebratory ode to human reason and reasoning cognition. We are no longer speaking here of the immense, paramount significance of practice in the theory of cognition, something quite unattainable to dry, one-sided rationalism. This is why dialectical cognition is a far higher form than rational cognition, and simply cannot be compared with animal-like mystical contemplation. In Shakespeare's *Henry V* the archbishop says:

> The age of miracles is past,
> and we must seek causes
> for all that happens upon the earth....[12]

Cataleptic states, hallucinatory raving, lethargy, suggestion and other phenomena of hypnosis, elements in the actions of shamans and quacks, fakirs and Hindu sorcerers—all these have become objects of real cognition. This cognition drives out, as old, barbaric forms of consciousness, mysticism of any and all types and hues that has been elevated into an ontological principle, a principle of being.

Dialectics does away with the analytical disconnectedness both of nature and of humanity, with the rigid isolation and absolutization of various aspects of matter and spirit, with the metaphysical seclusion of isolated "things."

Dialectics bears on its shield integrity and unity, but not a solid and undifferentiated unity, and not elementary integrity, but integrity of an open, mobile, contradictory, diverse variety, with an endless range of characteristics, aspects, interlinkages, shifts, and interdependencies, and with the identity of its opposite.

Hoc signo vincis! [13]

10

Practice in General and Practice in the Theory of Cognition

Earlier, we dealt with the naive claim of the agnostics to be reasoning on the basis of their sense perceptions alone, and thus to be able to demonstrate the unreality or incognizability of the external world.

This claim proved to be baseless and comic. From this we may conclude that any philosophical reasoning, since it operates with concepts, which are a social product, the product of thousands of years of mental work, must because of this very fact operate on the broad basis of all the achievements of science, leaving behind all the fuss and bother of foolish subjectivists.

Science, however, tells us that in historical terms, the starting point was the active, practical relationship between humanity and nature. Not contemplation, and not theory, but practice; not passive perception, but action. In this sense Goethe's dictum "In the beginning was the deed," when counterposed to the evangelical-Platonic-Gnostic dictum "In the beginning was the word"—that is, logos, or reason—furnishes us with a precise expression of historical reality. Marx noted this repeatedly: in his notes on the book by Adolf Wagner, in which he heaps scorn on the closeted professorial view according to which objects are passively "given" to humanity; in his *Holy Family*; in his *Theses on Feuerbach*; throughout the whole text of *Capital*; and together with Engels, in the brilliant pages of *The German Ideology*.

Contrary to the ravings of idealist philosophy to the effect that thought makes worlds, and that even matter is the creation of spirit (for example, the creating "I" of Fichte), it is human practice that creates a new world, actually transforming the "substance of nature" in line with human wishes. Historically, it was social humanity, the social-historical human being, and not an abstraction of the intellectual side of humanity, personified by philosophers as the subject, that above all produced, ate, and drank. It was only later, through the division of labor, that theoretical activity became separated off and isolated as an independent (or relatively independent) function, becoming restricted to particular categories of people, "mental workers," with the various social and class modifications of this category. Theoretical cognition arose out of practice as well. The active, practical relationship to the external world, the process of material production, which, as Marx put it, conditions the "exchange of substances" between humanity and nature, is the basis for the reproduction of the entire life of social humanity. The chattering of the high priests of the so-called philosophy of life (*Lebensphilosophie*), including Nietzsche and a series of present-day biological-mystical hysterics, bypasses this fundamental fact, just as numerous representatives of classical idealist philosophy also bypassed it. Of course! After all, from the point of view of Kant the simple acts of sawing wood, smelting iron, or making liquid oxygen constitute a breakthrough into the "transcendental," that fearful transgression which is "impossible"! What a mess the "practical" bull creates in this china shop full of unknowably subtle statuettes!

In fairness to Hegel, that "colossal old fellow," as Engels affectionately called him, it should be acknowledged that although Marx and Engels had to wage a desperate, impassioned, and ultimately victorious struggle against the "drunken speculation" of Hegelian idealism, Hegel did have an understanding of practice, of labor and its tools. Moreover, the embryo of historical materialism, in the form of brilliant conceptions, was present in his works. We shall have cause to be convinced of this subsequently...

The field of practice, or of the practical attitude toward the world, can be understood in a broad sense that includes such processes as, for example, respiration—that is, the extensive material interaction of society and nature. In a more narrow sense, the word *practice* relates to production and consumption. Finally, it relates to the reproduction of humanity (see Engels, *The Origin of the Family*, etc.), the field of sexual relations, and intra-societal practice, that is, the practice involved in changes to social relations, to real, material social relations. Here, in this discussion, we shall touch above all on practice as the relations between humanity and nature, practice as it appears in the actual transformation of the material world, that is, of the very "things-in-themselves" on which so many philosophers have broken their teeth and before which they have beaten a retreat.

To know an object, Hegel observes somewhere, means to take control of it as such. This point of view is quite productive, and deserves to be developed. In particular, it should be developed in relation to the question of practice. Here it is particularly clear that for human beings, the matter of the external world is transformed into raw material, into objects of deliberate action, objects to be processed in line with a preconceived goal. Here, as Hegel defines it, the "feeling of singularity" stands counterposed "to inorganic nature, as its own external condition and material" (*The Philosophy of Nature*). Manifesting itself as raw material, that is, as the object of action, the substance of nature is transformed "artificially" into something else, into a different quality, into the object of direct assimilation. The real power of humanity over nature is revealed in this process:

> Whatever forces nature has developed and set in motion against humanity ... humanity always finds a way of counteracting them, deriving these means from nature, using nature against itself. Human guile is able to direct one natural force against another, forcing them to annihilate one another. Standing behind these forces, humanity is able to maintain itself intact. (*The Philosophy of Nature*)[1]

It should be said: not just to "protect and preserve himself," but "to develop himself." In the present case, however, this is of secondary significance. Hegel also saw the role of tools, in the case of animal-instrumental organs (see the morphological theory of Academician Severtsov), for human beings, above all the tools of labor. Hegel wrote directly of the latter in *The Science of Logic*:

> ...the plough is more honorable than are immediately the enjoyments [which are] procured by it and which are ends. The tool lasts, while the immediate enjoyments pass away and are forgotten. In his tools man possesses power over external nature, even though in respect of his ends he is, on the contrary, subject to it.[2]

Power, possession, force, and hegemony over nature for the purposes of life and the "direct expansion" of life are everyday categories for Hegel. Here, and in all his analogous constructs, the great idealist indeed stands on the verge of historical materialism. He is the living embodiment of "measure" and transition (in the person of Marx) into his own dialectical opposite.

The process of production is thus a process of taking control of the external world and of remaking it in line with definite ends, or goals, which in their turn are determined by a whole series of circumstances. But what does this process signify? It signifies a change in the qualities and characteristics of the objective world, and the creation of new qualities and characteristics, which were needed, which before the productive process occurred stood out as goals, and which, therefore, were posited in advance. This goal-setting activity is consummated, or achieves its realization, when the productive process reaches completion.

What is the outcome here from the point of view of agnosticism in general, and of Kantian agnosticism in particular? The same outcome encountered by Zeno, with his assertion that motion was impossible, when Diogenes demonstrated by walking that indeed motion exists. How can one assert that the external world is unknowable (both as a whole and in its parts), that the object of labor is incognizable, when this object is turned into another in line with the wishes of a subject who supposedly knows nothing about it? From coal, or with its help, we make cast iron, liquid fuel, benzene, lubricants, volatile liquids, paints, perfumes, a great multitude of items, but supposedly we have no idea, God help us, what this coal is in itself! Meanwhile, the question is resolved quite simply: we know the qualities and characteristics of the "thing-in-itself," depending on and in relation to other factors, to temperature, to pressure, to its relationships with various substances, and by altering these relationships, through our knowledge of the laws that govern them, we obtain "another" coal. All this expresses itself in Hegelian fashion; that is, in altered forms, new qualities, new "things-in-themselves" as parts of the objective world. Hence, we do know the qualities of coal!

Practice is "living," active proof of this knowledge, a proof arising through the objective process itself, in action, manifested in the process of material transformation, which goes ahead according to the "reasoned will" of the subject. Practice tells us convincingly that we know the qualities of things and their laws. The fact that the subject of this practice is himself or herself subject to these laws (both when positing goals and when using the laws of nature to realize these goals) does not disprove this knowledge, but on the contrary, confirms it. Freedom is cognized necessity. The fact that a technological process conforms to the laws of nature allows us to conquer nature while ourselves being subject to it. This point was understood perfectly by Francis Bacon, who provided a popular exposition of it in his work *Novum Organum* in 1620. Because the subject is "bound" by the laws of nature, and knows what these laws are, he or she is free. The fact that the subject creates "freely" proves that he or she knows. The real subject of history, that is, the social-historical person, in the process of reproducing his or her life (that is, social-historical life) is countless times convinced in practice of the reality of his or her knowledge and of the "this-sided" nature of his or her thinking.

Here it is appropriate to recall a semi-anecdotal incident involving Georgy Plekhanov, who in translating one of Marx's *Theses on Feuerbach* imparted to a particular passage a meaning precisely the opposite of the original. Marx wrote that through practice, a human being needed to demonstrate the "this-sidedness" (*Diesseitigkeit*) of his or her thinking; Plekhanov transformed this into "that-sidedness," evidently deciding that there was a misprint, and that Marx had meant to say that practice involves accomplishing a leap into the "transcendental." It is possible to express oneself metaphorically in this fashion, and there would not be any great error except for the fact that Marx's idea was different. He meant to say that no leap was required, that no process of transcendence was necessary, since there was nothing transcendental; there was no second, extra-rational, noumenal world, but only one, objective world, a single nature, in which human beings are also active, thus showing that so-called "this-sidedness" is also real, and has no need of any extra-rational duality.

It is typical that in most cases agnostics of the positivist stripe have skirted around the question of practice. The pure-blooded subjective idealists simply "created" the world out of themselves. Objective idealism presupposed an "authentic world" in the form of an idea; in its most aristocratic form, represented by Plato, it viewed ordinary mortals as prisoners for whom contemplation of the idea was unattainable, since they were fettered eternally in a cave. According to agnostics such as Pearson, human beings have only signs, symbols, and "empiriosymbols." These categories are all purely passive; we are not dealing here with Fichtean "creation out of oneself" (Hegel jokes that when Fichte puts on a coat, he thinks he is creating it), in which the world is like a spider web emitted bubble-fashion by the spider. This is not voluntarist and actualist pragmatism. No. Here we have signs, signals, conventional designations, "hieroglyphs." Practice, however, destroys all such concepts, since it alters the very starting point, presenting the subject in his or her active-creative instead of passive-contemplative functions. Least of all is the subject in the midst of external nature a prisoner in chains, confined to a cave by a "noble" slave-owning philosopher. Such a subject is not a slave, but to an increasing degree controls the surrounding natural world, despite also being completely dependent on it (another dialectical contradiction!).

Scientific categories are in no sense conventional signs, labels selected arbitrarily for the purpose of distinguishing between things, like Hegel's already mentioned human earlobe. Scientific categories are representations of objective characteristics, qualities, relationships, and laws of things and of real processes, objective processes, material processes. Practice, too, demonstrates this in thoroughly convincing fashion. As [Vladimir] Ilyich [Lenin] puts it succinctly: "The result of activity is the test of subjective cognition and the criterion of *objectivity which truly is.*"3

From a certain point of view it might be said that practice is superior to theory (conditionally, relatively!), since it is through practice that thought (theory) manifests itself in the objective, takes material shape, and is objectified in the real world. Simple syllogisms are syllogisms, the gyration and inversion of ideas, that is, movement in the sphere of thought. Metaphorically speaking, they are understood laws, reflections of laws, coordinated with subjective aims. Through practice, they become steeped in the objective; they take material form in the technological process and its satisfactory result, that is, they manifest their truthfulness, their correspondence with reality. The correctness of thought is embodied in the "correct" flow of the material process and in the "correct" material result—that is, a result corresponding to the goal. The process "flows" in line with the concept of a material law, on the basis of which this process was coordinated earlier with a certain goal to which it has also led. Its progress and its end result have already been presupposed, consciously anticipated. Figuratively speaking, thought has been projected into matter, and has been tested by way of the material, proving its own power through the power of practice. It is in this that the supreme theoretical-cognitive, epistemological significance of practice consists.

In this connection, let us recall the a priori categories of Kant. These are not treated by Kantians as "innate ideas," nor as a historical prius. For Kantians, they are a logical prius, indispensable forms of sensory experience which serve to impose order, mechanisms through which the chaos of phenomena is transformed into an ordered cosmos. As Kant himself states in his *Prolegomena*, they serve "as it were, for the storage of phenomena, so that these can be read as experience." Outside these categories, experience is impossible; it is something formless. Within them, experience takes on form, while they in turn acquire content. These categories, according to Kant, are extra-experiential; they themselves are conditions, indispensable, a priori conditions for any and all experience. Such are the categories of quantity, quality, relation (together with the categories of substance, causality, and interaction), and modality. Also, the forms of perception: time and space. What place can mere practice have amid such company?

All these categories and forms of perception, however, are considered to be a priori because they were formed on the basis of experience and have been confirmed by practice, billions upon billions of times over many tens of thousands of years. They represent the most persistent, general, constantly encountered patterns, perennially tested by practice, by all that endlessly diverse, immensely prolonged labor practice of humanity. On this basis, they have been retained as universal axioms of experience. We shall not enter now into a discussion of the four sets of three categories, or make examining them a particular topic. Here we are interested in other things. Let us take, for example, time. Is it really not clear that any act of labor presupposes an "orientation in time"? In hunting, agriculture, irrigation, seafaring, journeys through deserts—in each case, in the molecules of labor experience, and in the larger aggregations of such experience, the anticipation (or expectation) of certain temporal relationships has been tested and verified through practice. The measurement of time, and time as an objective form of the existence of the material world, have had a corresponding reflection in the human brain, a reflection obtained through experience and tested endlessly in practice.

Kant set out to subjectivize the objective, but in apriorism itself, the shadow of objectivity is already present. It is no accident that in the case of another "a priori" concept, the category of causality, the great Königsberg ascetic finished up in such confusion that he was again forced *volens-nolens* to objectify this subjective, which according to his doctrine was a category. This occurred when he constructed a bridge of causality between "things-in-themselves" and the subject, whose senses they "affict." When the priests of Egypt foretold the floods of the Nile and in this way oriented works of agriculture; when the Babylonians dug canals and built temples and palaces according to calendars; when irrigation works in China, and the building of the Great Wall, were conducted according to chronological indications; when Taylor introduced time and motion study; when gigantic five-year plans in the Soviet Union were implemented according to calendar schedules—what do you think? Was the notorious "a priori form of perception" not verified in practice in every wave of the flood of time? Of course it was. Not, however, as the a priori form of perception of Kant's transcendental subject, but as the objective shape of the world, reflected in the concept of time. The same applies to space, causality, and so forth. In short, here as well practice has played, is playing, and will play an exceptionally important role. How can we fail to understand the epistemological, theoretical-cognitive significance of practice?

But this category too, like everything on earth, is capable of being misinterpreted.

Will there be troubled times, or not?

Will only weeds grow in the garden?

Unfortunately, there have been weeds growing in the philosophical garden too. They have been sown by so-called pragmatism, and today's fascist "actualists" have turned them into a real narcotic, blooming in the garbage dumps of fascist ideology. William James expanded the concept of experience, including in it everything that is possible and impossible ("what you want, you ask for"), right up to the point of mystical religious experience (see his *Varieties of Religious Experience*). In his works, "practice" took on its own similarly universal character, encompassing any volitional situation, any activity no matter how manifested. The "practice" of religious feeling and of mystical raving was also "practice." The businessman, exploiting, trading, carousing, praying for forgiveness from his sins, a man making money, for whom time is money and not an "a priori form of perception"—this ultimate American philistine has found a fitting ideology in pragmatism. The practical criterion of truth has accordingly degenerated as well. The starting point here has ceased to be objective change in the objective world (which, from the point of view of theory, includes the verification of cognition through practice), but is now "usefulness," understood in an exceedingly broad and subjective sense. If a lie is useful to a swindler, then that lie is the truth. If religion comforts an old woman, then it is the truth. Here, in the "instrumentalist," "pragmatist" point of view, in "usefulness," everything has become degenerate. In social terms, this is the ideology of the bourgeois trader; logically, it is worthless, the prostitution of the concepts of experience, practice, activity, and truth.

Nevertheless, "practice in general" and "practice in the theory of cognition" have reached their extreme levels of degeneracy in the modern-day fascist "philosophers" (*sit venia verbo*—i.e., if I may be excused for using the word "philosopher" in this context). On the basis of their bloody belligerency and social demagogy, that is, of their whole system of deceptions, masks, and myths (the making of imaginary worlds elevated into a method with a principled foundation), a philosophy of extreme voluntarism arises. The subject is declared to be a "political being" (not merely a "social being"). Everything which is of use to the politics of fascism is true; truth, therefore, is an emanation of fascist "practice" (about which no more need be said). But since the degree of usefulness is defined by Herr Hitler, the criterion of truth, the epistemological criterion, lies in the hands of this gentleman, like Aaron's rod in the Bible. There is no "philosophy of revelation" to compare with this! Here things are much simpler: "revelation" flows directly from the eloquent tongue of the head bandit! Whatever would Schelling make of this? The old but eternally new principle of correspondence to reality (this absolute principle, which manifests itself in relative fashion on the scale of all cognition) here falls away completely. The fact that the thesis "the Communists set fire to the Reichstag" is advantageous to the fascist brigands means that it is true. Myth is raised here to the status of principle. As can readily be seen, this represents the extreme degree of degeneration of philosophical thought. To the extent that one can talk about cognition at all in this case, cognition negates itself. The object of cognition disappears, and in its place an illusion is installed; the ideology is that of deception.

Only this kind of social setting, which in its essence (that is, in the fundamental tendencies of its development) is aimed against these particular "philosophers" (as fabricators of ideology for and representatives of a decadent, rotten bourgeoisie), could engender its own negation in their heads. Hence also the pure voluntarism, combined with profound inner despair and pessimism, the latter drowned out by all sorts of bloodthirsty Horst Wessel songs and other products of fascist creativity. In this way capitalism, which as it progresses, is rushing toward non-being, from being to nothingness and otherness, also reduces to nothingness the process of cognition. For capitalism, dialectics is indeed tragic!

Practice, material practice, gives birth to theory. It has always lain at the basis of theory, since mental labor arose out of material labor, separating itself off and becoming autonomous. Practice engenders theory, since it continually places new tasks before cognition. Theory, which is an extension of practice and at the same time its opposite, enriches practice and broadens it. We thus see here a truly dialectical movement. Practice is something counterposed to theory; theory negates practice, and vice versa. But theory passes over into practice. The unity of theory and practice is the reproduction of life in its fundamental definitions. This was also expressed in idealist terms by Hegel, who spoke of "the unity of the theoretical and practical idea" (in his *Science of Logic, Encyclopedia, Philosophy of Nature*, and elsewhere). Hence, if we understand P as being practice, T as theory, and P' as enriched practice, the process as a whole is represented by the formula:

P-T-P'; P'-T'-P"; P"T"-P"' and so forth.

Out of the relationships between theory and practice there flows also the relationship between the criteria of truth. The practical, "instrumental" criterion coincides with the criterion of "correspondence to reality"; practical success is achieved because reason really was reason, because ideas corresponded to reality, and were a correct representation of it. In essence, the principle of economy also coincides with this, so long as it is understood in its rational form, and not in a form that justifies the saying "simple-mindedness is worse than thievery." Thought is "economical" precisely when it corresponds to reality, when there is nothing in it that is superfluous, that is, incorrect, not corresponding to reality. When thinking is economical, the whole process of thought, taken as a whole, is at its most productive, since it is not led off onto crooked paths.

The various mediating mechanisms that provide a link between theory and practice include scientific experiment. Here there is practical change, material change in the substance of nature (for example, in laboratories, under artificial conditions of a second order, so to speak), accompanied by a corresponding reworking of thought. Here we find the material tools for the process, highly complex apparatus, measuring instruments, marvelous technical devices which broaden our experience to an extraordinary degree (devices such as the microscope, X-ray equipment, microscales, and so on). The factory laboratory is an objectified complex in which knowledge and practice, industry and theoretical science make direct contact, and pass over into one another.

So far, we have touched on the variety of practice involved in changes to the substance of nature. But one can also speak of the practice involved in changes in social relations and in the theoretical side of this process (the social sciences). It is not hard to see that among the representatives of a mode of production that is doomed to perish, the radius of cognition inevitably diminishes, and science rapidly becomes transformed into apologetics; conservative, reactionary, counterrevolutionary practice has a corresponding ideological reflection. "Science" in this case becomes subjective, and its class subjectivism acts as a fetter on development, not as a form of it. Moreover, this "science" takes on forms that are actively hostile to the main tendencies of development, to a much greater degree than is the case with the theoretical areas of the natural sciences.

Marxism, by contrast, achieves the unity of great theory with great revolutionary practice; the practice of Lenin and Stalin brilliantly confirms their theory. Also stemming from this quality of Marxism are the brilliant predictions made by Marx and Engels, who foresaw historical events a century ahead. The French have a saying: *Savoir c'est prévoir*, "to know is to foresee." Not only to foresee, however, but also to act successfully. Knowledge, foresight, and brilliant practical successes are the characteristic traits of Marxism, as social theory and as practice. The course of the whole world-historical process, including the development of science, confirms the correctness of the mighty generalizations of Marxist materialist dialectics.

11

Practical, Theoretical, and Aesthetic Attitudes toward the World, and Their Unity

The starting point is a historical examination of the topic (an examination of that which is historical, dialectical, in the process of becoming). Marx and Engels, in *The German Ideology*, were justified in regarding history as an integral science that could be broken down, in line with a process of objective division of the whole, into the history of nature and the history of society. (Here, we are inevitably geocentric for the present, since we know nothing about the "people" of other planets; they exist for us merely as *dynamei* and not *energeia*, as Marx loved to say—that is, as potentialities, not realized potential.)

If we take the question of mutual interaction between humanity and nature, then historically (in the broad sense of the word) we have:

1. The process of biological adaptation. Human beings are not yet human in the proper sense of the word. They are merely becoming animals of the species *Homo sapiens* in their natural form.

This is not the "natural state" posited by Rousseau and the philosophers of the eighteenth-century Enlightenment. Such a state has never existed; it is a fantastic illusion in the minds of ideologues. The "human being" in this case is a gregarious semi-ape, beginning to walk on its hind legs, with a differentiating hand as a natural instrument of labor. The following points are of importance: the reproduction of the species; collaboration and the struggle for survival; instincts (the instinct for self-preservation, the instinct of perpetuating the species, that is, the sexual instinct); the formation of races; the influence of nature, climate, and of all the so-called "geographical factors." The process of adaptation is mostly passive and unconscious. Nature shapes humanity, while humanity does not as yet shape nature (if we employ a certain simplification, that is, if we speak relatively).

2. The process of active social adaptation. In line with the objective situation, human beings are regarded here as social animals that make tools (*Homo faber*!). This is why the qualities of subjectivity and activity come into play. The old materialism viewed human beings solely as products. Meanwhile, historical human beings had already transformed themselves into subjects. For this reason, Marx in his famous theses on Feuerbach insisted on viewing the relationship between humanity and nature in subjective, practical, and active terms. The word "subjective" implies a rejection of objective cognition; the idea is that the objectivity of cognition requires the taking into account of a new, higher, nonbiological objectivity once a subject has stepped onto the scene, when humanity with its tools is actively affecting nature and transforming nature in line with human goals, the basis for which is the process of labor as the process of "the direct production and reproduction of life." In this process of labor, human nature itself undergoes a transformation. Biologically, this occurs "in sublated form." It is therefore necessary to have done with the game developed by the "organic school" in sociology, political economy, and so forth.

Here we find a new quality, which has taken shape in a historical manner. The modern rebirth of "organology," of a bastardized "social Darwinism," together with the entire school of Othmar Spann and of rabid racism, is all repellent from the scientific point of view.[1] They have missed the mark!

Society itself divides up into classes, and a specific movement begins, the dialectics of social development, with all its contradictions and transitions from one socio-economic formation to another.

The subject here is the social-historical individual, a representative of a particular "mode of production," of a specific class and of a particular "mode of thinking." The "biological" is not done away with; it is *aufgehoben*, or elevated to a higher plane.

At their basic level, the relations between humanity and nature are of a triple character; they are practical, theoretical, and artistic-aesthetic. We have examined these three types of relationships separately and in their interactions. Now we are faced with the task of understanding them in their unity, as functions of a single process of the production and reproduction of life.

Practice in this case is the material, technical mastering of the substance of nature, and labor is the transforming of this substance, the material exchange of substances between society and nature. Theory is the intellectual mastering of nature, cognition of its qualities, peculiarities, and laws, of its "whole." The aesthetics of nature is a sympathetic shared experience of the rhythms of nature, an experience which has its ultimate roots in humanity's animal-biological origins. Corresponding to practice is the will, corresponding to theory is the intellect, and corresponding to aesthetics is feeling. Practice is the realm of material things and processes. Theory is the realm of concepts and ideas. Aesthetics is the realm of the emotions and of emotional forms and images. If we recast this in terms of processes, we come up with the following: the process of labor, the process of thought, and the process of artistic-aesthetic contemplation.

Theory and practice, as we saw earlier, are opposites that interpenetrate one another, and at the same time constitute a unity. This unity signifies an active relationship to nature, a relationship that is active in two ways at once, the process of mastering and subjugating nature. Here the subject stands opposed to nature, as an active principle. The subject does not "apprehend" nature, but regards it (and acts upon it) as material. The subject transforms nature materially in the process of labor, and thought mediates this process. Nature is passive, while humanity is active. Nature is transformed, while humanity does the transforming.

The situation with the artistic-aesthetic contemplation of nature is quite different. Here the subject becomes immersed in the object, dissolves itself in the object. The individual "disappears," becomes lost as such, is absorbed and sinks in the "all." In other words, nature here is active, while humanity is passive. The subjective retreats into the background. Sublime and grandiose, the rhythms of the cosmos make themselves felt, while rhythm is itself only an infinitesimally small part of the gigantic, unbounded fabric of the universe. The immensity of the universe is reflected in the emotions it arouses. Artistic-aesthetic contemplation is therefore the polar opposite of both practice and theory, as principles underlying the vital activity of humanity. This, among other things, serves to explain the fact that artistic contemplation, unlike theory and practice, cannot provide us with the criteria of truth. At the same time, artistic contemplation is contradictory in itself. While dissolving the subjective in the objective, it is extremely subjective. The emotions associated with the sympathetic experiencing of nature do not have the universal significance of, for example, concepts; this sphere is an ocean of sensations and of extremely volatile emotions, with a far greater coefficient of the subjective.

Nevertheless, just as the division by old-style psychology of all the so-called "spiritual attributes" into independent "essences" (mind, will, and feelings) had to be surmounted because of its one-sidedness, the three types of relations between humanity and nature that we are concerned with here are in no sense disconnected, but flow across, one into the other, and in sum, make up a stream of vital activity.

Let us take the field of sensual contemplation, of sensual-aesthetic pleasure in nature. It is quite obvious that the experiences which correspond to this are by no means pure emotion. Present here as well are concepts in the most diverse forms. When, for example, a modern-day person "admires" the starry heavens, his or her experience may also include, and does include, elements of a scientific picture of the universe (thoughts about stars, planets, the galaxy, of an infinity of worlds, of electrons, scientific hypotheses, and so forth). Moreover, depending on the social character, on the "mode of thought" of the epoch, determined by the "mode of production," the forming of emotions and thoughts is subject to certain dominant ideas, which fit within the general framework of the "mode of thought." For example, over the course of centuries artistic-aesthetic experiences have mingled with religious forms, with consideration of the world along the lines of dominance-subjection (as Marx puts it, relations of dominance and subjugation). This sociomorphism of thought has also been a sociomorphic principle in the sphere of aesthetics, not only among savages, primitive animists, "average people," the philistines of their epoch, so to speak, but also among the most refined thinkers. Hence, for example, to Pythagoras the "music of the spheres," the rhythm of nature, expressed in figures and embellished artistically, was a divine principle *stricto sensu*.

On the other hand, the aesthetic-artistic also penetrates its opposite, that is, thought. For example, it is worth reading how Hegel describes the life of the land, and especially, the life of the sea! Or take the scientific works of Goethe, not to speak of the German philosophers of nature, concluding with Schelling. As was noted earlier, Heine recommended that Schelling be a poet, not a philosopher.[2]

Here, therefore, we see an interpenetration of opposites, the passing over of one into another, and their unity. But the sphere of artistic-aesthetic contemplation itself, as it strives to reproduce itself, gives birth to *active* effort, producing art, music, poetry, painting, and so forth. This is now an extremely complex formation, extending far wider, encompassing all areas of life and with a diverse significance, including a cognitive significance. Basically, however, it operates through images, and it is no accident that poetic language is the language of metaphor and of personification. Its most profound origins lie in the sympathetic shared experience of the rhythms of nature and in bonds with it. In art, as creative activity, the passive principle becomes highly active; aesthetic emotion itself grows more complex and is enriched through acquiring an actively creative side (through experiencing the value of craftsmanship). The sphere of sympathetic shared experience is the authentic sphere of art and aesthetics; it is precisely for this reason that love and eroticism play such a prominent role; the principle of shared feeling is expressed with particular clarity here, and it has exceedingly profound roots in the hidden depths of humanity's biological nature.

Corresponding to the practical, theoretical, and aesthetic principles is the old trinity of goodness, truth, and beauty, fetishized abstractions drawn from the three main spheres of human activity.

By "good" ("happiness," "welfare," "the ideal") all systems understand a complex of vital goals which is presented as a single entity, a center of gravity, the "truth of virtue." Since practice itself is divided into the practice of transforming the natural world and the practice of human relationships, the practice of social changes, the corresponding concept of "happiness," "welfare," "the ideal" has in various proportions included an orientation toward useful things and virtues. It should not, however, be thought that these are isolated elements. In the final accounting, the production of material objects is also the production of use values, that is, of values for humanity. The value placed on "the good things of life" therefore enters into the general ideology of "values," and is included in various systems of moral-philosophical ideology (with hedonism and asceticism as the two poles). To the ancient Greeks, the concept of "the good" had a more or less clearly expressed intellectual character; this is the case with Plato, Aristotle, the Stoics, and Epicurus. "The good," therefore, is an abstraction of the vital purpose and of the norms of behavior associated with it, their abstractly expressed dominant idea. It has always been defined historically, that is, in terms of epoch, formation, and class.

By "truth" has usually been understood one or another correspondence (right up to the point of coincidence, that is, identity) with one or another "given" (whether consciousness, matter or spirit, a god, etc.).

By "beauty" has been understood the ideal of the external, sensible form; in a number of philosophical systems, it has been the sensible expression of truth. In reality, truth, as is clear from everything that has been said earlier, is that which is correct; that is, it corresponds to the object, reflecting it in the realm of ideas. The social significance of "searches for the truth" amounts to a mediating of the material process of production, a broadening of the sphere of cognition and a deepening of it, and a growth of human consciousness. The real meaning of beauty consists in a raising of the emotional tone of life. This is an abstract notion which manifests itself concretely in the most varied forms. The ideals of manly and womanly beauty are the supreme expression of external features (of the features of a sensible form), embodying ideal qualities and characteristics (mind, courage, nobility, tenderness, positive sexual traits, and so forth), conditioned to some degree biologically, and in part created and modified (and sometimes done away with entirely, for example, in decadent epochs and among decadent classes) by the social and historical environment. Nature makes its impact felt through its pulsation, which as we have seen, humanity experiences too, once again in a definite, socially conditioned manner. Social life evokes artistic images, which also raise the tone of life, disseminating the developing emotions through the externally sensible (as with music and poetry). And so forth. Plato was already well aware that it was this sensual side that was characteristic of aesthetics and of the aesthetic attitude toward the world; he spoke of the definiteness of the beautiful, which, unlike an idea, acts as a thing or as a sensual concept, that is, concretely.

Class societies are characterized by a rupture between groups of people. Different aspects of humanity's vital activity become fixed in different categories of the population. This has happened, for example, with the most profound division of labor, into mental and physical work; mental labor has become one of the functions of the commanding exploiter classes. In decadent class societies, the functions of vital activity may be transformed not only into antisocial functions but also into functions of the self-destruction of this class. Such, for example, is the case with the "aesthetic" of death and decay, and with the dregs of modern-day mysticism in "philosophy."

Here socialism achieves a radical turn-around, of truly world-historic importance. We can therefore speak of a new epoch, in which the real history of humanity has begun, after its agonizing prehistory.

Here classes are abolished. Here, integrated human beings grow and flourish. Here, consequently, the relations between theory, practice, and aesthetics become unified, and people have a multifaceted existence. Here, fetishistic straitjackets are cast off: religious forms, the forms of the "categorical imperatives" of external character, understood as divine command; the forms of absolutely "pure" art, "pure" science, and so forth, expressing their estrangement and isolation from the whole context of life; and so on. Separate aspects of life become elements in the lives of ever greater numbers of many-sided living people.

It is here, therefore, that the unity of theory, practice, and aesthetics finds its clearest expression. In (progressive) class societies this unity with all its aspects expressed the ascent of life (the might of the productive forces, the power of cognition, an increase in vigor) in struggle with numerous obstacles and under conditions in which human beings were disintegrated into one-sided subjects. But in real history, all the barriers fall, the entire process accelerates to an unprecedented degree, the disintegrated nature both of society and of the individual is done away with, and the unity of vital functions celebrates its historic triumph.

It is not difficult to see that an exaggerated understanding of one of the sides of vital activity gives rise to an ideological fantasy:

— the setting apart and isolation of thought, its estrangement from practice, and the autonomization and separatism of "the realm of thought" has a tendency to transform this thought ("concept," "abstraction," "idea," "the general") into the independent essence and substance of the world;
— the setting apart of practice from thought leads to crude empiricism, and with the divorce of practice from material objects (commercial practice, social practice, and so on), to voluntarism, pragmatism, and so forth;
— the setting apart of aesthetics results in a tendency to reject rational cognition and to transform artistic-aesthetic experience into mystical experience, leading to the adoption of a mystical-intuitive world view.

It would not be hard to demonstrate this using the actual historical development of philosophical thought. We are not, however, writing a history of philosophy, and the reader will forgive us if we call a halt at this point and pass on to another topic.

12

The Fundamental Positions of Materialism and Idealism

After a long interval, the demon of irony again makes his appearance.

"Have you had enough of 'my sensations'? Well and good. But is this really an affirmation of materialism? Or are you so naively interpreting the position of Lenin (that the philosophical concept of matter is a concept lying outside of 'me,' and nothing more)? As though Lenin denied there was such a thing as the consciousness of another. Or have you failed to understand that in objective idealism God does not by any means coincide with 'my' consciousness? Are you unaware (if we are to indulge your love for the authority of your holy fathers) that in the *Philosophical Notebooks* of the same Lenin it is stated plainly that from 'general' idealism a special 'essence' is formed, that is, something situated outside of 'me'?

"Well, and if you are not too stubborn (to be stubborn would not be very clever), why not take a 'spiritual' principle as the fundamental basis for the world? In fact, why not speak openly and without prejudices, and be so good as to allow a small digression. Look how your spiritual predecessors hunted down quacks and sorcerers, crying out 'It's all charlatanism!' and denying cases of successful cures. And now you yourselves admit there was something to it; only you talk about 'hypnosis.' Just like that. Well, there's more to be said along the same lines. Will you allow me?

"Consciousness is a fact. Are you going to deny that? Are you going to argue that the only things that exist are those you can beat your head against?

Are you going to maintain that the only thinking being is you? This would be contradictory from the point of view of your collectivism, socialism, and so on.

"This means that consciousness is a fact. Just to set your mind at rest, there is nothing miraculous, mystical, or supernatural in that. Consciousness exists—that's all there is to it. Consciousness, moreover, is an unmediated fact. From this, we have the maxim of Descartes, *Cogito, ergo sum*.[1] The fact of thinking beings, and of thinking in general, is fundamental.

"But if in my own being the fact of consciousness is fundamental, is not external 'matter' (or 'extension,' beginning from my body), an other-being, a manifestation, a passive form ('form' not in the actively creative Aristotelian sense) of my consciousness? For example, your spiritual essence is reflected in my consciousness as something corporeal, in just the same way as I am reflected in your consciousness as an external body. But 'in ourselves,' we are 'spiritual essences.' The same with everything else. With a rock, with a star, with the sun, and with the universe.

"Why do you dislike this 'picture of the world'? Great minds have approved it. Isn't that so?"

And the tempter fixes his mocking eyes on you. It is clear that he has his own logic. From this, we might say, Leibniz derived his monadology. In this construct, a different consciousness is reflected, and is reflected as something material. In essence, Bogdanov's empiriomonism was extremely close to precisely this type of idealism, if we consider his conception as a whole. According to Bogdanov, the world "in itself" is a "chaos of elements." In individual consciousness, these elements are linked by bonds of a sort of associative type; in "specially organized experience," they are reflected in a higher type of bond, becoming the "physical world." Hence the "physical world" is a reflection of a chaos of elements, like dissipated technical monads, although they do not possess a discrete integrity and individuality, as in Leibniz, and are only "elements." Proceeding along the pathways of this idealism, it is easy to reach God as well. He too, it could be said, turns out to be something almost extra-miraculous. To be specific: there are various monads of different degrees, a hierarchy of monads with corresponding degrees of material other-being. The monad of stone is reflected as material stone, and the monad of humanity as a human organism. But there is also a star "in itself," that is, the "soul" of the star; there is also a universal, all-encompassing monad, the general "soul" of the cosmos, God, whose materiality is the world in its material translation and interpretation.

Enough! This is already too conscientious, giving so detailed an account of the adversary!

We should note that all the boundary markers between objective idealism, Spinozism, and materialism are in evidence here. Yawning open before us are all the abysses of the "final depths" of thought about the world, and from a certain point of view, the transition from one world view to another is unusually easy; a slight turning of the wheel, and—there we are! In this instance, thought dances on the "nodal points" of the Hegelian "measure," where leaps are performed into new qualities: God as substance; the Hegelian world spirit; Leibniz's monad of the universe; the "world spirit" of Schelling (and earlier, of Plato, and in the Middle Ages, of Thomas Aquinas); the godless "god," *natura naturans*, of Spinoza; the denial of God by materialism; all these positions are crowded into the one philosophical space!

Let us begin with the "primary nature" of the fact of consciousness. Here the position of Cartesianism is weaker than that of Berkeley and Hume, since instead of "pure sensations," we are now given concepts as well, and as a result, we are given other people and the external world. But if all this already exists, and moreover, in all its corporeality, then why is consciousness "primary"?

There is not the slightest basis for such a conclusion.

In sum, if we no longer proceed from the "I" (and here the isolated "I" immediately disappears, along with the recognition of concepts), we enter the field of scientific examination of the genesis of consciousness, of historical examination. By virtue of this, we depart entirely from the sphere of primitive speculations about the primary, virginal data of consciousness, about the "given" which in essence is also the result of extremely complex analysis, the result of (fallacious) mediated knowledge. In this, there is an immense difference; here the virginal purity of the argument dies out altogether.

What do we in fact see?

1. The "self-consciousness" of a human individual comes over time. Only a cultured adult, a philosopher, could say *Cogito ergo sum*. It was no accident that it required Descartes to do this.
2. Consciousness is "given" together with its content; there is no consciousness from which content is absent.
3. Of the content of consciousness, 999 parts per thousand are "given" by the external world.

4. This world acts on human beings, "afflicting" their sensory organs. That is, the world is both a historical and logical *prius*, a primary cause.
5. Human beings actively influence the world in their corporeality, in their thinking corporeality. But in conquering the world, they are also subject to its laws.
6. A human being is the product of development 1) in society, 2) in the form of *Homo sapiens*, as part of the human herd; and 3) potentially, in the form of a humanoid ape and so forth, back in the evolutionary chain.
7. The organic world arises out of the inorganic world, and so forth.

Here, therefore, we make the transition to the province of the various sciences that are concerned with the evolution of matter and with the qualitative stages of this evolution. All the data tell us of the growth of new qualities, and impel us to treat consciousness as a property only of a particular type of matter. The only "evidence" in favor of a panpsychic conception is provided by anthropomorphic analogy, but is this really proof? This is a return to animism, in all its primitiveness. Also resting on this animist metaphor is the entire philosophy of Schelling, which Heine in his wisdom understood so well. (In this connection, it is interesting to recall Feuerbach's remark that poetry does not claim that its metaphors are real!) Science thus speaks of the historical origin of the organic in the inorganic, of living matter in nonliving, of thinking matter in unthinking. Here lies the truth of the remark (only superficially trivial) which Engels makes in *Anti-Dühring*, when he notes that the real unity of the world consists in its material nature, and that this is proved by the complex work of science, not by a couple of empty a priori theses which someone has sucked out of their thumb.

For precisely this reason Hegel with his idealist instincts sensed, as it were, that the idea of development in nature would refute idealism. His system therefore includes the following monstrous (and in no way dialectical!) contradiction. According to Hegel, nature does not experience development, and the forms of the organic are unchanging. This represents a gigantic step backward compared to Kant, whose views on natural science were extremely progressive for his time. Here the great dialectician, who raised the principle of movement and development to such heights, surrendered his main conquest as it applied to all of nature! Hegel was sickened by the atomic hypothesis, so brilliantly confirmed by modern physics, by the theory of the changeability of species, and by the very notion of evolution in nature! It should be noted that Hegel's artful thought is able to squirm out of this dilemma... Here dialectics perishes in the name of idealism. Literally for the greater glory of God, dialectics is slaughtered on the altar of idealist philosophy. Precisely for this reason, the development of dialectical thought raised the imperious demand for unification with materialism. This was achieved in Marxism—not, of course, on the basis of a separate "self-movement of ideas," but against the broad background of real life.

In Hegel, therefore, there are whole tangles made up of knots of mysticism. The spirit is outside time, but it develops (since it "develops" logically, as a concept). Nature is within time, but does not develop. The earth is the fruitful basis of life, the source of spontaneous generation, but species do not evolve; and so on. The problem here is the internal sickness stemming from the fact that the spirit is itself the outcome, the historical outcome, of matter, since living matter, that is, feeling matter, arises out of inorganic matter, that is, nonliving matter (not dead, not having died, but not having begun to live), while thinking matter in its turn arises only out of feeling matter. Hegel's wonderful doctrine of "measure," of "the nodal line of measure," of the interruptibility of the continuous, of leaps, of the transition from quantity into quality, of new qualities, and so forth, enters into conflict with his idealism, and unlike his idealism, is brilliantly confirmed by the data of science, although this science for the most part has not involved any notion of dialectics.

In order to have any arguments for the priority of consciousness, one would need to take a cinema film of the history of the world, and to run it backwards. Since this cannot be done, the conclusion is irresistible. We know for certain that until a particular period in the development of the earth, there was no life on it. We know for certain that life arose. We also know for certain that the presence of life became a fact before human beings appeared. We know for certain that human beings arose out of other types of animals. Initially, life was little pieces of living protein with rudimentary forms of the so-called "psychic" among its properties. Are we being ordered to consider this the great "World Reason," "God," and so on? What rubbish! The same rubbish as the teleology that Goethe mocked wittily in his *Xenia*, with the ironic assertion that cork oaks were created so that corks could be made for bottles. It is obvious that such primitive views of the universe are crudely anthropomorphic. Ascribing a "soul" to the stars, "reason" to the world, and so on is to judge things by analogy with human beings, while investing humanity with characteristics such as omniscience, all-beneficence, omnipresence, and so forth. It is true that analogies often contain something rational, and the history of science has repeatedly witnessed extremely fruitful analogies. But there are facts and facts. Nothing whatever can be said in favor of analogies such as those described above, which all science, all real science, serves to refute. So where is the basis for idealist arguments? Or for a reversion to the animism of savages?

Marx in his *Holy Family* wrote: "Hegel makes men and women people of self-consciousness, instead of making self-consciousness the self-consciousness of men and women, of real people, that is, people living in the real, objective world and conditioned by it."[2] An abstraction of human consciousness, torn apart from human corporeality, turned into "being" and transferred to the entire world—this is the stuff of idealism.

Here, however, it has to be said once again that this very abstraction contains a huge betrayal of dialectics. Once thought is abstracted from thinking, we also see the destruction of that integrity about which the same idealists sing like nightingales when they turn to discussing life. And here (that is, in the thesis on integrity) they are completely correct. So what is the end result? Is it really hard to see that when you tear the spirit apart from the body, you turn the spirit into nothingness, and the body into a corpse? It is simply comic to see how respectable people, after making fiery protests against crude empiricism, rationalism, vivisection, and the destruction of life, after triumphant odes in praise of integrity, unity, the individual whole, and so on, suddenly seize on a man or woman, tear them in two, sever the thought from the body, and imagine that in the process the body has become the body and thought has become thought! No, dear philosophers! No "self-development of ideas," no "procession of the spirit," and no other metaphysical devilry can really exist, precisely because you, despite the doctrine of dialectical wholeness, have destroyed this wholeness, slain the "body" and done away with the "spirit." Hegel, when it came to the fundamental question, sacrificed his brilliant dialectics to the idealist God. Molière in his *L'Ecole des Femmes* observed venomously:

> Unfortunately, madam, I note
> That I am made up of body and soul,
> And that my body and soul are very much connected.
> Perhaps, with the help of great wisdom, they could be separated,
> But heaven has not made me a philosopher,
> And in me, body and soul live together.[3]

It is true that an adherent of the "philosophy of identity" might object to this, citing the words of Schelling in the *General Deduction of the Dynamic Process*, which seek to demonstrate that there is no rupture here, since "all qualities are sensations, and all bodies are views of nature, while nature itself, together with its sensations and views, is congealed thought."[4]

But how, if you please, did you arrive at such a conclusion? The truth is that you have never observed thought without a human being. And before making your deduction, you carried out a simple operation: you tore thought out of the human being and projected it onto nature! A picturesque "deduction" indeed! Such consistency, of course, is a good thing. Your argument contains only a few small shortcomings. First, in extracting the thought, you killed the thinker; second, like a savage, you were satisfied with an empty analogy. "Only" everything.

Dialectically speaking, we see here the transformation of relative opposition into absolute, the destruction of a bond, and the metaphysical isolation of the spirit, that is, its transformation into a thing-in-itself, an empty nothingness, since it can only be taken in terms of its interrelationships, outside of which it does not exist.

Here, therefore, we see that dialectics, that is, objective dialectics, insistently demands a materialist point of view. Otherwise, it consumes itself.

In logical terms, every ideological distortion rests on some facet of reality, while inflating it in one-sided fashion, exaggerating it, and elevating it into some kind of essence. This is why Lenin wrote in his *Notebooks*:

> Philosophical idealism is nonsense *only* from the standpoint of crude, simple, metaphysical materialism. From the standpoint of dialectical materialism, on the other hand, philosophical idealism is *one-sided*, exaggerated, *überschwengliches* (Dietzgen's term) development (an inflation, distension) of one of the features, aspects, facets of knowledge to the point where it becomes an absolute, *divorced* from matter and nature, apotheosized.[5]

This is confirmed in striking fashion by the whole history of idealism, which has torn the characteristics of living matter out of matter, divorcing humanity from nature and the "spirit" from humanity, elevating thought into an absolute, and inflating this absolute to the point where it becomes a universal-cosmic ideal category.

But every ideological distortion, while resting on a preceding store of ideas, at the same time also expresses a particular "mode of presentation," which rests on a definite mode of production, if we are to speak of great ideas and of the dominant intellectual concepts of specific epochs. Idealism, as a world view, is undoubtedly such an ideological formation. What does it rest on in this particular sense? Where are its unconscious social roots? Marx and Engels answer this question in *The Holy Family* and *The German Ideology*. When they deliver a furious dressing-down to "critical criticism," they reveal the polarity of spirit and matter as a reflection of the polarity between "critical criticism" and "the inert masses" (the common people, the multitude, physical workers—it is, by the way, extremely interesting to trace the historical formation of the concept of physical mass and that of "the masses" as a broad sector of society). Social dualism is reflected in the dualism of spirit and body; the spirit directs the body and is superior to it in the same way as spiritual leaders direct the masses and stand on a higher level compared to them. In *The German Ideology*, Marx posits a direct link between all idealism and the movement of hypostatized ideas with the setting apart (class particularization) of mental labor as a function of the ruling classes. Of course, these observations provide only the most general framework; they are necessary, but not sufficient. But they do serve as signposts on the road to further research—research in the realm of *the sociology of thought*.

Is it not clear from this that the convulsions now being suffered by idealism constitute its death throes? Is it not clear that idealism cannot and will not have a future?

13

Hylozoism and Panpsychism

In the present connection, it is necessary to dwell in more detail on hylozoism and panpsychism.[1] Both systems of ideas take as their starting point the presence of the psychic in all matter. The usual substantiation advanced by the hylozoists is that matter in various of its forms has the property of being able to feel. Panpsychism, meanwhile, is idealist. Here the substance is provided by the ideal, revealing itself in material form; that is, the ideal has the property of acting as the material. Finally, there is also a third point of view, to which Spinoza was attracted, and which holds that the material and the psychical, or ideal, are two aspects of one and the same substance. Here we again see how readily opposites pass over into one another—how easy, for example, it has been to turn the Ionian hylozoists of ancient Greece, who saw all matter as animate, into modern panpsychists, and vice versa.[2] To gain a correct understanding of these questions, we have to approach them from the historical-dialectical angle.

Moving backward in historical time, we shall examine various forms and types of nature, beginning with humanity and passing on to less and less complex animals, in something akin to a Lamarckian "degradation." First we have human beings, with their developed brains, spinal cords, and nervous systems, with thought and "reason." Next we pass through a whole series of stages, with particular sensory organs (eyes, ears, and so on) disappearing. Then the brain disappears, followed by the entire nervous system. Maggots have neither a head nor eyes. Polyps have neither a brain nor nerves, and are without organs of respiration, a circulatory system, or organs of reproduction. Infusoria do not have any specialized organs.

Hence even Lamarck (on whom the "psycho-Lamarckians," with their unconcealed vitalism, place their hopes) wrote with regard to polyps and so forth (see his *Philosophy of Zoology*):

> There is no basis for saying that in the animals examined ... all these organs nevertheless exist (even in infinitely reduced form), that they are dispersed ... in the general body mass ..., and that consequently, all parts of the body can experience every sort of sensation, enact movements, demonstrate will, have ideas and thoughts.... It stands to reason that the study of nature does not lead us to such a hypothesis. On the contrary, it shows us that wherever any organ ceases to exist, the capabilities associated with it disappear as well. In no case can an animal without eyes see..., no animal without nerves, that is, specialized organs of feeling, can experience sensation.... In polyps, the parts of the body are capable of no more than being irritated ... these animals ... are not capable of feeling.[3]

By "the capability of being irritated," Lamarck, following on Haller, understood the property of the bodies of animals of recoiling from the action of external irritants.

It is quite possible that there is some sort of psychic quality that corresponds to this property as its "other-being." But despite, for example, Franse, it is clear that what cannot exist here is thoughts and "syllogisms."[4]

At one time it was fashionable to deride the notion that thought occurred in the brain. Avenarius in his *Critique of Pure Experience* advances various considerations on the theme that the brain is not the "seat" of thought. There is a rational kernel here in the fact that the brain does not exist "in itself," that is, as something isolated; it can function only in concert with the whole organism, and in this sense it is not the brain that thinks, but the whole person. However, a dialectical understanding of the part and the whole, and of their unity, does not in any way exclude the possibility of an organ having a specialized character and function. A person thinks, not the brain in itself. But the person thinks with his or her brain, not lungs, although the functioning of the lungs is indispensable for that of the brain.

As Lenin noted in his *Philosophical Notebooks*: "Hegel, though a supporter of dialectics, failed to grasp the *dialectical* transition *from* matter *to* motion, *from* matter *to* consciousness—especially the second. Marx corrected the error (or weakness?) of this mystic." Lenin also noted: "It is not only the transition from matter to consciousness that is dialectical, but also the transition from sensation to thought, and so forth."[5]

This signifies that the issue cannot be posed in the following way: a human being has a lot of consciousness, a dog has less, a polyp less still, a plant even less, and a basalt cliff still less again. This would be to take a purely quantitative, mechanical, anti-dialectical view of things. Real development is both continuous and interrupted, gradual and proceeding by fits and starts, quantitative and qualitative. Hence there are qualitative degrees of the "psychic," representing specific forms of a qualitatively diverse structure within the bounds of the organic world itself. To have an instinctive inclination is not to pose a reasoned goal; to formulate a reasoned goal is a qualitatively specific ability. To take another angle, a plant is not an animal, though both are alive; a human being is not a polyp, though both are animals. The transition from sensation to thought is dialectical; that is, thought is a new quality of consciousness. It is impossible to cook everything all up together without any discrimination. To consider historical evolution to be purely quantitative change, the continuous increase of one and the same, means not only to betray dialectics, but in betraying dialectics, to turn one's back on reality. For materialists, the point is not that something should correspond to a "concept," but that concepts should correspond to reality.

From experience, we know that thought is a faculty of an organism of a particular type, with a brain, with the hemispheres of the brain, and with a nervous system. It is absurd to impute dialectical thought to a tapeworm or a polyp. In the process of our scientific investigations we see the historical phases of development of a living creature; we see the various historically composed structures of this creature, and their qualitative peculiarities. In nature, however, we also see the leap from the inorganic world to the organic one. The fact that such a leap exists is obvious simply from the fact that until now we have not managed to create living matter artificially.

Life represents a whole series of qualitative peculiarities, and among these peculiarities, as a specific form of a particular (organic, material-animate) property, is the property of the "psychological." There is not a single hint in the natural world to provide us with grounds for imputing psychological life to stones, oxygen, the incandescent solar mass, the frozen moon, a log, or a steel ingot. The path from inorganic to organic nature leads by way of a dialectical leap.

This does not mean, as the vitalists maintain (we shall have more to say about the vitalists later—they will be dealt with too!), that by virtue of this, living organisms are not subject to the basic laws of nature. It does mean, however, that new properties take their beginnings from this point, and that the general laws of nature manifest themselves here in specific form.

Some wiseacres among the ultra-positivists conclude that we cannot talk even of the consciousness of other people, and that what is present here is judgment by analogy, the transference of one's own consciousness onto another person, whose consciousness we cannot sense in any way. But as we noted not long ago, there are analogies and analogies. Every hour, in every act of collaboration and struggle, in theoretical or practical work, the correctness of this "analogy" is confirmed. We foresee someone's actions; we understand his or her verbal reactions; we act in accordance with this, and witness the corresponding result. The fact that the consciousness of "another" is not directly "our" consciousness worries us exceedingly little; we are cognizant of this consciousness through objective factors such as motor reactions, mimicry, so-called facial expressions, and so on. This testifies once again to the indivisibility of spirit and body; it is not an argument for cheap agnosticism, but for dialectical materialism.

Let us take another historical process, that of the domestication or taming of animals—horses, cows, sheep, dogs, and so forth. Is it really the case that all the practice (over thousands of years!) of this process and of the process of making use of these animals has not taught us anything about their psychological existence? Materialism does not, as some people claim, deny the existence of psychological life, but regards it as a particular form of objective-physiological process. (Despite this, many people who imagine themselves to be materialists say things like, "That's just nerves!" Meanwhile, this "purely psychological" might be psychological at the same time, and on the same level, as it is physiological and nervous! Or else, such people counterpose the more purely physiological, or "physical," to the "nervous"!)

But to return to our mutton, in this case literally. Any hunter knows which of his dogs is smartest, and appreciates that the dog understands him, the hunter. Here, it will be said, there is also an analogy. Quite so. Not the sort of (stupid!) analogy that in totally anthropomorphic fashion would attribute to the dog the full power of human reason, but nevertheless, an analogy. This analogy, however, is confirmed by gigantic, infinitely prolonged, and endlessly diverse practice.

The entire historical experience of humanity confirms that the phenomena of consciousness (in the broad, psychological sense of the word) are connected with organic life. As for plants, we are simply constructing a hypothesis that here there might be something resembling instinct; something of the sort, for example, can be observed objectively in the case of heliotropism and geotropism. When we speak of the entire animal world, we have a basis for extrapolating from the things we have observed and of which we are firmly convinced, while qualitatively lowering the level of the psychological. But when we make the leap to inorganic nature and fail to make a corresponding leap where its properties are concerned, this contradicts all our experience. Meanwhile, there is absolutely no evidence to confirm the existence of consciousness in the inorganic world. Consequently, there is no basis even for hylozoism, not to speak of the panpsychic concepts which seduce people with their "elegant simplicity." Here stupidity is indeed "worse than theft." Logically, we would expect to find here a clear simplification of reality, not an expression of real simplicity.

Here we find one of the properties of reality inflated in one-sided fashion, exaggerated and unjustly generalized in an unhistorical and anti-dialectical manner. Something that actually exists only under particular conditions is universalized. Instead of the diversity of nature, which is revealed in its unity, we are urged to accept its nonexistent uniformity. Instead of development by leaps and bounds and the appearance of the new, we are offered continuity, with rejection both of the new and of a leap in the most decisive area. Instead of the historical emergence of consciousness, we find the argument that it has been constant in all ways and all places. In fact, the most important feature of the dialectics of nature is precisely the "splitting into two" between organic nature, possessing a psyche, and inorganic nature. Here we also find a real, historical, objective process of diremption, of a splitting into opposites. But these opposites pass over into one another; the inorganic passes over into its opposite, the organic; the organic, when it dies and decays, passes over into its opposite, the inorganic. The unity of both aspects is nature as a whole, which thinks and reflects exclusively through humanity as a constituent part of nature. No one has as yet discovered the miracle of thought without a brain.

Meanwhile, the most enthusiastic supporters of hylozoism are characterized among other things by their search, so to speak, for the supreme forms of mental life; they seek these forms in "sublime individualities" such as the sun, stars, the universe, and so on. Here, hylozoism crosses the boundary into hylozoist pantheism. When we analyzed the question of the artistic-aesthetic relationship to nature, we saw that human beings shared in experiencing the rhythms of nature, "living nature." But at the same time we also explained that nature "lives" only in a relative sense, and that it is impermissible to identify this feeling of oneness with nature with assertions about the presence of spirit in all things, impermissible to allow the one to grow over into the other.

Meanwhile, it is quite legitimate to confront the hylozoist sun-worshippers with the question, monstrous at first glance: Do you maintain that in this gigantic ocean of incandescent gases there is something that functions as a brain, as a nervous system, or as higher forms of such organs? It is an absurd question. But it is absurd because the entire hylozoist position is absurd, even though this position has many enticing features: the substantiality of matter, an understanding of the universality of interrelationships, a grasp of the integrity of all things, and so forth. This also imparts to the hylozoist position a sort of exalted intellectual tone. However, rigorous thought cannot survive without strict self-criticism, and the point of view of the hylozoists, and still more, that of the panpsychists, has to be rejected. It is not worth elaborating particular arguments against the panpsychists, since it is clear to everyone that if hylozoism collapses, panpsychism collapses along with it.

We thus arrive at a historical series:

1. inorganic nature;
2. the leap to the organic via *generatio aequivoca*;[6]
3. very simple forms of the organic, with embryonic forms of the psychical;
4. the leap to more complex forms possessing sensations;
5. the leap to still more complex forms, with images, concepts, and so forth;
6. the leap to social humanity, with human thought.

Naturally, all these leaps do not occur at a historical gallop. Here we are merely anxious to stress once again the dialectical nature of the historical process. It would be naive to throw into one pot, as the Germans say, stones, mountains, planets, electrons, dogs, infusoria, and people.

In the novel *Nikolai Negorev, or the Fortunate Russian*, by the largely forgotten novelist Ivan Kushchevsky, there is a character who speaks very amusingly on this topic:

> I think that the earth is also a person. We, perhaps, live on his finger, and our millennia seem like an instant to him. If he bends his finger, it will be the end of the world for us, and everything will be destroyed. He—this giant, the earth—doesn't even

imagine that we live on his finger and build cities there; he can't see such tiny animals as us through his magnifying glasses. This giant, for whom our millennium is only a moment, also lives among other people—other giants like him—and perhaps he is also studying at the moment in a gymnasium. Perhaps he is now reading Margot,[7] a single comma which covers a space a thousand times greater than all Europe; otherwise, he would not be able to see the comma. He put his finger on a page in order to turn it, and that is when our world began!![8]

And so on.

This school-pupil fantasy, depicted rather vividly over several pages of the novel, is very reminiscent of hylozoist theories. To tell the truth, many of us in our youth gave ourselves over to similar thoughts, since we all think of an infinity of worlds and about the infinite nature of the world as a whole. There is a question here, the question of "the universe," and with the discovery of the structure of the atom it has become a question of extraordinarily compelling interest! But why do we have to resolve this question in school-pupil fashion? Is it not time to understand that with socialism, humanity has now entered university, and that in this *universitas rerum et artium*[9] it is now time for people to abandon old dogmas? In humanity's school days these ideas would still have passed muster, but they have now clearly grown old and decrepit, having outlived their epoch. Is it not time to understand that it is simply comic to return to the era of Assyrian-Babylonian astrology, to amulets, to Chaldean magic, to the divine astral beings of Plato, Aristotle, the Stoics, and so forth? Is it not time to replace illusory relations with those of reality?

14

Hindu Mysticism and Western European Philosophy

Among a number of bourgeois philosophers and the philosophical "caste" in general, the flight from the clamor of collapsing capitalist civilization arouses a craving for mystical primitivism, although in these circles this primitivism is distinguished by a particular refinement. The influence of Chinese and Indian philosophies, in their spiritual and mystical variants, is especially evident. Hegel encouraged the prejudice that the East has not contributed anything positive either to science or to philosophy. In this case Hegel manifests the same white nationalist line which induced him to see in Prussia and the Prussian state the seat of the world spirit; in Alexander the Great, a demigod taking vengeance on the Greeks; in Asia, a drunken sensual bacchanalia; and so forth. This quite preposterous thinking, which simply justifies the German saying that the wish is father to the thought, and which directly contradicts objective reality, later acted as one of the components of fascist "Aryan race" ideology. Along with it, one usually finds an artificial selecting out of the spiritualist and mystical currents in Eastern philosophy, an omission of everything that even smells of materialism, and a distortion of the whole picture of the philosophical development of the East. Here, therefore, we have the use of a method of falsification common in the history of philosophy, a method mocked in Russian literature by the prematurely deceased Dmitry Pisarev. In his article "The Idealism of Plato," Pisarev observed bitingly:

In accounts of the history of Greek philosophy, it is usual to refer condescendingly to the Eleatic school, to Heraclitus and Democritus, to Pythagoras and Anaxagoras; then, with indignation, to recall the Sophists; then to be moved by the personality and fate of Socrates; to perform a deep bow before Plato, his Demiurge and Ideas; to describe Aristotle as his great pupil, who was often unjust to his great teacher; then to scold Epicurus, laugh at the Skeptics, and express benevolent sympathy for the exalted valor of the Stoics.

This is accepted; this is demanded by the interests of morality, which is guarded so jealously by so many pseudo-artists and by many real toilers in the broad ... field of scholarship.[1]

So it is that materialism is made subject to a code of silence, and is cast into the depths. So it is that all available energies are put into blowing up the bubbles of idealism. It is no wonder that in circumstances marked by extreme intellectual turmoil and by the reevaluation of all values, when the bourgeois individual often stands in confusion "beyond good and evil," the longing for spiritual peace, for consolation, for refuge from a stormy reality should be expressed through immersion in a Buddhist nirvana, which unlike the *dolce far niente* of devil-may-care *lazzarone*, has its complex philosophical correlative, a whole mountain of thoroughly sublimated intellectual categories, combined into peculiar mystical-philosophical systems.[2]

For the official philosophers of fascism, mysticism has the character of the voice of the blood and of the actualism of imperialist janissaries. But for philosophers who are fleeing from the field of battle, or who have got lost and are seeking rescue wherever it might be had, mysticism has the character of an Eastern Rousseauism. Such philosophers seek spiritual solace in the great ages of Indian mysticism, in the holy Ganges of mystical contemplation. The stream of Indian mysticism (which in Western European philosophy rests to a well-known degree on Arthur Schopenhauer) is very strong, mainly among German philosophers; Paul Ernst, Count Keyserling, and Theodor Lessing (killed by the fascists) reflect with considerable clarity this admiration for the spiritualism of the East.[3]

In connection with this, it is interesting to pose once again a number of basic philosophical questions that we have discussed earlier, and for purposes of illustration, to take the works of Lessing both in their critical and in their positive aspects.

In his work *Europa und Asien*, Lessing provides a scathing critique of rational cognition in general. It is curious, above all, to dwell on his detailed criticism of "the scientific picture of the world." In making this criticism, he uses the example of light. His thesis can be summed up as follows:

1. The first stage is cognition of seven colors and of the transitions between them. This is science on the first plane.
2. Then follows science on the second plane, the "second reality"—waves of various lengths. Here we find the process of *desqualificatio*: the phenomena of the first plane grow pale, and in place of colors, the movements of the mental substrate come to the forefront.
3. Next follows a "still stricter science"; a further process occurs in which the surface phenomena of life fall away and a "third reality" appears. Maxwell and Faraday teach us that behind light waves there are electrical forces.
4. Does the matter reach its conclusion with this? No. Beyond these stages are energy processes with purely quantitative attributes.
5. Does the process of *desqualificatio*, and of shedding surface phenomena, end with this? No!

    The world, bereft of light and luster, a purely numerical world of mathematical physics, is transformed into a world of atoms, of space, time, movement, of "process above all."

    The atom is regarded only as a planetary system susceptible to calculation and regulated by quanta, that is, by pure relationships.
6. "Light" has been "explained." But what has remained of it? A useful, serviceable formula. This "Western European" calculating science kills life. Counterposed to it is the symbolic knowledge of the East. So argues Professor Lessing.

Let us dwell on this for a little. As we can see, there is nothing here that is fundamentally new to us, with the exception perhaps of the clear and systematic way in which everything is set forward. In essence, however, we have already answered the author's objections. The reality is:

First, this criticism only has meaning as a criticism of "physical idealism," in which the substance of the world is represented by a mathematical formula, that is, a symbol. But the author takes quite a liberty in interpreting the "scientific picture of the world" this way! In fact, the "formula" does reflect objective reality.

The formula is not the substance; it is the formula of the substance, its reflection, a picture of it. That is by no means the same thing.

Second, despite what Lessing says, what exists here is not various "realities," a first, second, third ... up to a sixth (along with, we might add, an unspecified number of "planes"). What exists is one and the same reality. The first "plane" is reality taken in its relationship to the subject. The second and all subsequent planes are the same reality in relation to its various aspects, more general and less general. In principle electrons can also be broken down into smaller components. But these still undiscovered components of electrons do not destroy electrons, just as electrons do not destroy atoms, atoms do not destroy molecules, molecules do not destroy the earth, the planets and the sun do not destroy the solar system, the latter does not destroy larger astral systems, and so forth. The one exists within the other, and passes over into the other. Here we have a diversity of associations within one reality, not a diversity of realities.

Third, contrary to Lessing there is no question here, for anyone with a dialectical understanding of the process of cognition, of annulling qualitative aspects, since we also find present qualitative peculiarities of the elements and qualitative characteristics of their diverse connections and relationships. This is all the more obvious since if we move upward from electrons, atoms, and so on, we also have living matter, the organic world, passing beyond the bounds of physics and chemistry. In relation to the subject, the object does have luster, color, and so on; this enters into the general picture of the universe, which also includes the subject, as we explained in detail in the chapter on the cognizability of "things-in-themselves," where we criticized the Kantian conception of these "things-in-themselves." Lessing's idealist criticism is therefore correct only when it is directed against idealism in general, and specifically, against "physical idealism" of all hues. His criticism does not in any way affect the positions of dialectical materialism, of which this venerable philosopher does not in any case have the slightest notion.

Collapsing along with this are all of Lessing's subsequent arguments, which are concentrated in the following two main positions:

1. We experience only the image (the *brahma-vidya* of India).... We become bereft of life at that moment when, growing estranged and making our departure, we "objectively gain cognition"....
2. Becoming familiar (directly familiar) with the growing, producing, dreaming image is something that must be sharply distinguished from the judgments and evaluations of consciousness. With the latter we pass beyond nature, and in this sense physics and

psychology represent a passage beyond nature. "In relation to the directly perceptible world, physics is therefore metaphysics."

Lessing also bravely formulates the following paradox:

> It sounds preposterous, but it is absolutely correct that the only person who penetrates into the depths of nature is the one who remains on the surface of its phenomena. Not an experimenter in the natural sciences! Not a psychologist! Not a physicist! Not a mathematician! And so forth. On the contrary, the person who experiences this profundity is the one who believes the sun to be a shining disc the size of a fifteen-kopeck coin, suspended from the firmament.

That is putting it plainly! (Keyserling says much the same in his *Reisetagebuch eines Philosophen*.) Unmusical, uncreative natures, with their arithmetization, their quest to understand the world, their "logification" of the world, do away with life. Direct experience is placed in doubt. The focusing of microscopes, telescopes, and *camerae obscurae* comes to intervene between humanity and nature; people become prosthetic beings. And so on and so forth.

Though sometimes witty, these arguments are in essence bankrupt. If human beings through the use of scientific apparatus are able to extend and broaden their sensory perceptions, then according to Lessing, they take their leave of nature; a process of denaturing occurs. But from this point of view a dog or an infusorium has a better knowledge of nature than a man or woman.

So what is all this about? How are we supposed to put up with such rubbish? What grain of rationality might there be in it (since one never encounters absolute rubbish)?

Let us analyze it.

Lessing advances the following thesis: "The human sense of power is growing. But the human sense of being is disappearing." The sense of power, however, rests on genuinely growing power. How can this power be possible in the absence of real cognition, that is, penetration into the depths of nature? One can laugh as much as one likes at Bacon's proposition that power is linked to cognition, but this link is a real one. Here the mystics display a clear ambiguity. On the one hand, they seem to acknowledge that a human being in his or her own fashion actually does have some kind of reality, though this reality is not the one they are really looking for. On the other hand, they assert that the scientific picture of the world is merely a bare formula, which leads beyond nature. But if it led beyond nature, that is, if it announced itself to be the substance of the world, then where would this power and the corresponding "sense of power" have appeared from? The entire concept is clearly splitting at its seams.

What lies concealed behind all this? To answer this question, we have to turn our attention to the following argument of our philosopher. "The sun is indeed what it is. Experience this, and you know it. Nature does not lie. But what is going on here, if the reality of knowledge gives me a sun quite different from the one that the eye can see, that the senses can perceive? This scientific sun, of course, is real. But it can be perceived only as a concept.... I, however, confine myself to that which is experienced." Clearly opening up here is a dual "reality"... "reality never exists without some form of behavior on my part. It is one thing when I am active, and another when I am passive. For me, a logical-ethical and a religious-aesthetic orientation mediate different realities."

> Europe takes a wilful attitude (to the object), and Asia, a contemplative one. Europe resists nature in an active manner; Asia stands passively within it. The European individual actively transforms nature, overcoming its resistance; the Asian breathes rhythmically and contemplates passively, like a plant, an animal, or a child.

So argues Lessing. We shall leave his absolutization of the differences between Europe and Asia without detailed refutation; it is enough to point out that no anchorites, mystics, or philosophers, of the Brahman, Buddhist, or any other persuasion, could exist even in India if it were not for the fact that in the same India there are people who work to support them, that is, relate actively to nature and, in one way or another, rationally cognize it. It is true that Lessing was enraptured with the arguments of the Chinese sage Confucius, according to whom you will not be burnt by a fire if you love fire; you will not be drowned by water if you love water; you will not be torn to bits by a lion if you love the lion; and according to whom it is better, if you want to prevent or extinguish a fire, to obey your parents than to construct a pump. However sublime this love for all nature, the real links and relationships bypass these illusions, and in Asia people have worked, and at times shed their blood as well; they have never had time to fall into nirvana or into pure contemplation.

Among mystical philosophers (if not among Asian people "in general"), contemplation has been a fact. But what follows from this? Has there, as Lessing argues, been a different reality? Of course not. There has been a different perception, a different reflection of reality, and insofar as passive mystical contemplation is concerned, this "reflection" is not of an intellectual type. Here, consequently, we are not talking about cognition, but about a different type of relationship—that is, not about a cognitive reflection, although cognitive aspects are not excluded entirely, since vital activity is an integral whole, and even mysticism in practice has rational features, located perhaps in its pores, especially when this mystical "experience" (forgive the expression) is subject to logical reworking (which no "system" can do without).

It should be noted in particular that in Hindu spiritual systems the subjects adopt an active attitude toward themselves. This involves an enormous training of the will, including exercises with breathing and the pulse, directing the activity of one's organs, and so forth. This has a number of positive results in the areas of physiology, psychology, and hypnosis. But this is a special question; in essence, there is nothing mystical here.

As for attitudes toward nature, and the mystical contemplation of nature, passive contemplation of course yields a different "picture of the world," or more accurately, a different sensation of the world. This proceeds along lines which we have termed the sphere of shared experience of nature. This shared experience confers no advantage in cognitive terms. Its mystical-religious form yields no cognitive results, and neither, therefore, is there any increase in human knowledge or in the power of humanity over nature. Lessing is in raptures over animism, natural gods, demonology, and so forth, but these are sociomorphic forms of primitive cognition, the roots of which are as clear as noonday. What is there to be envious of here?

The rational kernel of all this mysticism, however, consists in the yearning of despiritualized capitalist humanity for nature. Shut up in a stone coffin, the urban neurasthenic, deprived of sun, forests, waters, and air, overwhelmed by the din of machines, transformed into a screw in a gigantic mechanism, yearns for a ray of sun, for light, for greenery, for the purling of a brook. Such a person is damaged, deformed. His or her biological nature protests at being torn asunder from the natural world. This is the problem, and its solution lies in socialism. The problem is not, however, one of cognition, but of people's way of life. It does not have to do with a higher type of penetration into the secrets of nature; it is a problem of achieving a greater fullness of life. The need for the shared experience of nature, that is, for the enjoyment of nature, for closeness to it, for links with it, for aesthetic love of it, is a legitimate need and a rightful protest against the abnormality of the crippled, one-sided urban human being of capitalist culture. But in exactly the same way as this does not justify rejecting machines and theoretical science, it does not justify rejecting rational cognition either.

Under socialism, people will enjoy nature and feel its warm breath. But they will not turn into primitive animists. Nor, for people under socialism, will poetic metaphors take the place of the rational cognition that develops along with the practical power of humanity's technical equipment. This rational cognition does not by any means lead beyond nature; on the contrary, it makes possible a deeper and deeper penetration into nature's secrets. But of course, no microscope can substitute for the biological enjoyment of mountain air, or for the glow of the dawn sky. Science also has its aesthetic. But neither science nor the scientific aesthetic can take the place of the biological need for direct communion with nature, since cognition cannot take the place of food, drink, and erotic life. To deprive someone of sexual pleasures is to cripple that person. But it does not flow from this that sexual delight can substitute for intellectual cognition, or that erotic oblivion and ecstasy are the highest form of cognition, more profound than rational cognition in general.

Meanwhile, the arguments of Lessing and others are very much along these lines. Self-emasculation is the killing of life, and in just the same way, becoming divorced from nature is the killing of the fullness of life, that is, the partial killing of life. This, however, has no relation to the question of the type of cognition. It could even be said that drawing close to nature, improving the general tone of life, bringing about the healing of humanity, will lead to an even greater flourishing of rational cognition, to the dying-out of mysticism, and furthermore, to the defeat and destruction of any and all idealism, which will disappear together with the disappearance of its social base, will disappear along with the division of labor into mental and physical, urban and rural, supervisory and nonsupervisory. Vanishing along with them will be the dichotomy of "Europe" and "Asia."

15

The So-Called Philosophy of Identity

Fichte, Schelling, and Hegel, who stand side by side in the history of Western European philosophy, sought to resolve the basic philosophical question of the relationship between thought and being from the point of view of identity. However, both Schelling and Hegel, not to speak of Fichte with his distinctive subjective idealism, are justly included in the category of idealists. The result is that for these philosophers, identity is not identity at all, since in the formula A = A, the second A can be shifted to the place of the first, and vice versa; the two elements will coincide just as before, since they really are identical. The concept of other-being is not a formula of identity, since it is not at all the same thing to say that spirit is an other-being of matter, or that matter is an other-being of spirit. The property of being an other-being is a special one that denotes a particular type of real link, in which identity is not simply identity, but where primacy is retained by a particular side in the identity equation. Properly speaking, what is involved here is not even A = A, but the formula A = other-being B, which is far from the same thing.

To Fichte, the "I" represents the underlying principle in the whole system. This is not an empirical, individual, concrete "I," qualitatively defined in its individuality, peculiarity, and separateness, but an "I" in large letters, that is, general or so-called pure consciousness, or to put it differently, the transcendental unity of self-consciousness with its indispensable forms or acts. Its primary act is the will.

This abstract "I" presumes its own existence, distinguishes opposites and unifies them. In other words, the basic philosophical question is hidden in the "I" as if in a sack. "Everything that is occurs in the 'I' and through it," is how the active, energetic side of the process receives emphasis. From this, however, the following would seem to flow: if "I" = everything, then everything = "I." Inverting the formula, we immediately come up against the difficulty that was noted by Hegel when he spoke out in concert with Schelling. Hegel observes (*Hegels Werke*, v. 1. *The Difference Between the Philosophical Systems of Fichte and Schelling*) that Fichtean identity is an identity of a special type; to Fichte, the "I" is simultaneously both subject and object, that is, a "subject-object"; this "subject-object," however, is a subjective "subject-object." This also means that here, in essence, there is merely the appearance of identity; the problem has not been solved, but is reproduced in a new form.

Hegel provides an astute description of this Fichtean "I":

> This monstrous arrogance, this mad self-conceit 'I,' which at the thought that it constitutes a single whole with the universe, that eternal nature acts within it, takes fright, experiences revulsion, and falls into depression; this tendency to be horrified, to grieve, and to be repelled at the thought of the eternal laws of nature and their subordination to stern, sacred necessity; this despair at the thought that there is no freedom, freedom from the eternal laws of nature and their strict necessity; these inclinations to consider itself indescribably unfortunate because of the necessity of this obedience; all these feelings presuppose the most commonplace point of view, devoid for the most part of all reason.[1]

The Fichtean "I," according to Hegel, has the same relation to things as an empty purse has to money.

To Fichte, therefore, the "subject-object" is subjective.

How, then, does Schelling cope with this task?

For Schelling, the starting point is the absolute (undifferentiated identity, absolute identity), cognizable only through intuition. This is a primary essence, "complete indifference to the subjective and objective." Various degrees of development proceed further. The real world, as an endless world of isolated things, falls into two parts: the real (nature), and the ideal (spirit). Nature can be reduced to reason, and reason to nature, while the universe is the identity of both: "There are not two different worlds; there is only one and the same world, in which everything is contained, including that which in ordinary consciousness is counterposed, such as nature and spirit" ("On the True Concept of Nature Philosophy").[2]

In the first place, however, there arises here a dualism of the Absolute and of the world, of an undifferentiated identity and of the identity of the differentiated. Secondly, the subject-object is presented in such a way that the subject itself is objectified, while its relationship with the object, and consequently its disintegration, remains. On the other hand, the verbally proclaimed identity is not in fact identity, since nature is merely an other-being of the spirit. As we saw earlier, Schelling in his *General Deduction of the Dynamic Process* wrote: "All qualities are sensations, all bodies are ideas about nature, and nature itself, together with its sensations and ideas, is, so to speak, congealed thought."

The constant, unchanging spirit has given rise to nature, and the development of nature is the arousing of this spirit from sleep. Nature is thus an other-being of the world spirit.

In Hegel, Schelling's opposition between the undifferentiated Absolute and the world is done away with, since according to Hegel, the history of the absolute spirit is the history of the world. However, for him, the spirit is not an other-being of the world at a particular stage of development, but on the contrary, the world is an other-being of the spirit, a particular, distinct stage of it.

Consequently, the "philosophy of identity" is not in fact a philosophy of identity.

Fichte transfers everything into the "I," and in this abstract "I," which is also an idealist starting point, a comedy which is both divine and human is played out.

In Schelling there is absolute motion, but it is the spirit that gives birth to nature.

In Hegel, the action of the world spirit has nature merely as its other-being. In *The Phenomenology of Spirit*, Hegel writes: "Reason is the conviction of consciousness that it constitutes all of reality; this is how idealism expresses its idea."[3]

According to Hegel, the absolute spirit passes through three stages. The first is that of the logical idea; the second is that of nature; and the third is that of the absolute spirit. In logic, the idea moves in the abstract sphere of thought; in nature the same idea appears in another, counterposed form, not in the form of pure logical concepts, but in that of perceptible objects. The development of nature is not development in the normally understood sense, but merely a distinct reflection of the logical development of ideas, of a development which in its dialectical movement reveals the potentialities inherent in the idea.

On closer examination, therefore, the identity here proves to be merely verbal, a purely linguistic identity.

No one has ever disputed, and no one now disputes, that the philosophy of Schelling is mystical through and through. But the so-called panlogism of Hegel is not, in essence, a "dry" panlogism either, since as we earlier noted in passing, it has a great many purely mystical features. In general, it should be noted that Hegel inherited far more from Schelling than is usually thought. There can be no doubt that Hegel's philosophy contains a huge quantity of "alien" elements (from Plato, Aristotle, Spinoza, Schelling, and so on) in borrowed form; this is clear to anyone who has studied the great idealist. It is widely known that in the early phases of Hegel's development, when he was collaborating with Schelling, he found a Schelling-style mysticism perfectly acceptable. Also widely familiar is his philosophical *profession de foi*, set out in the poem *Eleusis*:

> The mind loses itself in contemplation,
> That which I called mine disappears;
> I surrender myself to the infinite.
> In it, I am everything, and only it.
>
> ....
>
> Fantasy brings the eternal close to the mind,
> Uniting it with form....4

An entire program is contained here. Contemplation stands on a higher level than rational cognition; in the very highest forms of relationship with the world, reason dies out and is dissolved, along with the "I." The "eternal" is brought close to the mind through intuition and fantasy, or imagination...

Rosenkranz cites an interesting passage from the early Hegel:

> Mental life selects from among particular forms—the mortal, the transient, the eternally contrary, the contending—that relationship which is free from disappearance, which does not contain in itself anything of the dead (here, therefore, the dead = the vital and active!), of elements of complexity that annihilate one another (sic!—author); that which is not a unity, not a conceivable relationship, but an all-vital, all-powerful, eternal life, and calls this God.

> If human beings envisage eternal life as the spirit of the integral, also existing outside of itself since it is itself a limited essence; and if they envisage themselves as also outside of themselves, as limited beings; if they elevate themselves to the living, and unite themselves with it in the closest possible fashion, then they worship God.5

Subsequently there appears to Hegel what might be called a "logicized" God, stripped of many alluring baubles. It seems to us, however, that mysticism is not dispensed with here, but becomes a special kind of mysticism—one mediated by logic and thought. Hegel was a great hater of all naivety, and had an uncommon regard for the culture of thought. However, his whole giant philosophical machine was constructed, ultimately, to allow him to shelter in the quiet harbor of the absolute spirit. To this end, he also forces the "idea" to cast off various costumes in order, *post factum*, to confirm the mystical kingdom. He sets out to prove and justify mysticism, doing away with its animal-savage-childish form, and to elevate it into a higher class. In all his works, therefore, in the very style and exposition, we find numerous devices which at first sight seem to be only artistic-poetic metaphors, but which in fact have not only this but also another, more "profound" meaning. When we speak of mysticism, we are not, of course, speaking only about God. It is well known that the World Spirit, God, Reason, and so on, play an enormous role in Hegel's grandiose system, so that to demonstrate this would be to break down an open door. The same applies to the relationship with this God, and to the character of this relationship. Discussing religion in his *Phenomenology*, Hegel himself defines mysticism in this fashion:

> The mystical element consists not in the hidden nature of some secret, or in the lack of knowledge, but in the fact that the self knows its unity with the essence, and that this latter manifests itself in this way. Only the self reveals itself to itself; or, that which reveals itself to itself achieves this only in the direct truth of itself.6

Religion and philosophy have one and the same content, but in religion this content is expressed in the form of revelation, and in philosophy, in the form of an idea; here, it constitutes the highest form of consciousness of which the *Phenomenology* speaks.

Unity with the "essence" is unity with God. This mysticism in ideas is formulated by Hegelian philosophy, in which mysticism in the narrow sense is supposed to be present "in sublated form." However, since a depiction is provided of motion in its entirety, mysticism enters into the discourse uncommonly often and openly.

In *The Philosophy of Nature*, for example, Hegel in relation to inorganic nature, its elements, planets, and so forth uses the categories of tension, torment, revulsion, striving, and so on in the spirit of Jakob Boehme (*The Torment of Matter*) of whom, in the relevant volume of his *History of Philosophy*, Hegel speaks for the most part very positively.[7]

Or else, Hegel speaks in the spirit of Paracelsus, for whom nature has as many elements as there are major virtues. We see that "the preserving of a grain in the earth ... is a mystical, magical action." In the same *Philosophy of Nature*, however, the sun is a variant form of eyesight, water of taste, and air of the sense of smell. Here the idea, the sensory principle, and nature are combined in completely monstrous fashion. The objectivism of Hegel's idealist philosophical system passes over into flagrant subjectivism.

The counterposed variants (the Fichtean on the one hand, and the Hegelian on the other) of the "philosophy of identity" (which in reality, as we have seen, is not a philosophy of identity at all, and which bears this label quite falsely) are therefore not so different. Solipsists such as Berkeley and Hume stripped consciousness from the living integrity of the empirical personality. This stripped-off consciousness was summarized by Fichte, who transformed it into a universal "I." Hegel objectified it, turning it into "spirit." Hegel quite justly and in delightful artistic fashion mocks Fichte's "I" as a manifestation of "monstrous arrogance" and "mad self-conceit," but this reproach can in essence be made against Hegel's entire system. Here, ultimately, the same thing is at issue. The endless diversity of the infinite universe—in which inorganic nature "gives birth" to organic nature, which comprises a minor part of it, while organic nature gives rise to thinking humanity, which is part of this organic nature—is replaced by the cosmic spirit, to the rank of which human consciousness is elevated under various pseudonyms.

Hegel directs very well-aimed shafts against naive mysticism. Discussing, for example, the question of the divided "unhappy consciousness," which rushes back and forth between the world of the other side and the world of this, while seeking unity with the world of the other side, he notes that this striving is "pure consciousness," but not "pure thinking"; since, so to speak, it merely *tries* to think, but ends up instead in [nothing more than] a reverential mood. Its thinking, such as it is, remains a cacophony of bells or a warm, misty phenomenon, "musical thinking (quite so!—author) that does not produce an idea, which would be an immanent objective image." It is "pure emotion." And so forth.[8]

So what is the result? The outcome is to be found in a "reason" in which everything is immersed, and this universal flood is, as it were, the vanquishing of dualism on the basis of identity. In practice this means that human reason has as various of its forms the sun, the moon, the stars, the Milky Way, and the entire universe. In some respects this lightens the task; if, for example, things are the same as ideas, the question of cognition becomes especially simple, and the difficulties practically disappear. This disappearance of the problems is achieved, however, at the price of a gigantic distortion of the actual relationships. At its core, Hegel's philosophical system is closer to religion than to science. Despite this, Hegel's dialectics is a great treasure trove of thought. All that has to be remembered is that dialectics is acceptable to us only in its materialist form. This means, however, that one cannot limit oneself simply to placing a different mathematical sign in front of dialectics. Form depends on content; this Hegelian proposition is absolutely correct. From this flows an especially critical attitude toward the greatest philosopher of the bourgeoisie. To read Hegel "materialistically," as Lenin recommended, means to alter him, systematically correcting him on the basis of the knowledge provided to us by the gigantic growth of modern science.

Hegel himself in many places formulated with uncommon clarity the link between his own objective idealism and religion. For example, in *The Science of Logic* (*Die Wissenschaft der Logik*, vol. V of his *Werke*) he writes:

> It is wrong to think that we are first of all given objects that make up the content of our ideas, and that we join to them our subjective activity, drawing off and seizing their general features, and that in this way we form concepts. Ideas exist prior to objects, and objects owe all their qualities to that idea that lives and is manifested in them. Religion recognizes this when it teaches that God created the earth from nothing, or in other words, that the world and everything in it came from one common source, from the fullness of divine thoughts and designs. This means that thought, or more precisely, the Idea, is an infinite form, a free creative activity, which translates its content into reality without any need for outside material.[9]

This passage from the "Great Logic" clarifies in marvelous fashion the thesis of *The Phenomenology of Spirit*, where Hegel states that religion and philosophy have the same content, but that philosophy captures in an idea what religion captures in an image. Both express the same thing: these are phases in the motion of the same ideal principle that is the idea, the spirit, God. Revealed here in all its fullness is first of all the fact that the philosophy of identity is not a philosophy of identity, and secondly, the fact that the development of idealism inevitably leads it to religion. In this sense, the movement of idealism from the subjective to the objective is internally contradictory; the more objective idealism becomes, the closer it approaches—somersaulting, as Lenin put it—to materialism, and at the same time, the further it distances itself from materialism, joining directly with religion.

Especially interesting is the starting point of Hegel's *Logic*. It is well known that for Hegel, logic is at the same time ontology. Here Hegel poses the question: where to begin? He answers it as follows:

> We find here ... a solution which can also be considered arbitrary, a decision that we want to examine thought as such. The principle must therefore be absolute or ... abstract; it must presuppose nothing, must not be mediated by anything, and must not have a basis. Rather, it must itself be the basis of all science. Therefore, it must be absolutely unmediated, or rather, must in general be unmediatedness itself. It cannot have any definition in relation to anything else, and to the same degree it cannot include in itself relations of determination; it cannot have any content, since this content would involve a distinction and a relationship of this distinction to another, that is, a mediation. The principle is thus "pure being."[10]

From this tirade it follows 1) that a "decision," and moreover, an arbitrary decision, is present here; 2) that the content of science is thought; 3) that the examination of this thought begins with pure being; 4) that between thought as such and being, there is an "equals" sign (or more precisely, a sign of identity); and 5) that it is thought that has priority.

All this is intimately connected with the "system." But where is there even a hint of substantiation of the initial position, that is, the idealist position? There is not even a trace of it. On the contrary, Hegel insists that the beginning has to be immediate and spontaneous. One can, of course, follow Kuno Fischer in his *History of Modern Philosophy* (v. VIII; *Hegel: His Life, Works, and Doctrine*) and consider that this immediacy arose on its own, and that it is mediated by the entire "phenomenology of spirit."[11]

But to this one can justly object: why is it necessary to begin with the phenomenology of spirit? It is clear that philosophy could not arise prior to any thought whatever. Consequently, philosophy is doomed to rest on "positive science." But where in this science is there a basis for rejecting the materialist point of view *a limine*?

This is why Marx, taking over the revolutionary side of Hegel's method while rejecting and demolishing Hegel's idealist system, was compelled to create his own materialist dialectics, in which Hegelian dialectics is present only in "sublated form." Marx's dialectics reaps the harvest of the dialectics of Hegel; it is its preservation, negation, and elevation to a higher level, its *Aufhebung*. This German word combines the senses of *conservare*, *negare*, and *elevare*.[12] Marx's philosophy is dialectical *materialism*, and materialism is opposed to idealism of all varieties; it is *dialectical* materialism as opposed to "stupid" (Lenin), "vulgar" mechanistic materialism, which has to be overcome just like the "intelligent" idealism of Hegel.

16

The Sins of Mechanistic Materialism

The history of materialism has still to be written. The great service rendered by Plekhanov consists, among other things, in the fact that he overturned many of the distortions to which materialism had been subjected as a result of the arguments of its idealist opponents (for example, the Kantian Friedrich Lange). One of Plekhanov's most important works here is his *Beiträge zur Geschichte des Materialismus*.[1]

How spiteful idealism can become, even when its greatest, most talented and authoritative exponents are concerned, is clear from the example of Hegel. He rejects Leucippus and Democritus, and does his best to purge all the materialist elements from that giant of ancient Greek thought, Aristotle. Hegel violently abuses Epicurus, a thinker who two thousand-odd years ago defended atomic theory, foretold the movement of atoms along curved paths, formulated a hypothesis on radiation that involved minuscule particles, and centuries before the so-called modern era paved the way for the Lockean doctrine of primary and secondary qualities, driving all teleology out of philosophy and, in the words of Hegel himself, "initiating empirical natural science and empirical psychology." The same Hegel scornfully pats on the shoulder all the eighteenth-century materialists, praising them mostly for their Gallic wit and defending their revolutionary enlightenment against excessively vulgar attacks (as if to say, the customs that prevailed in France were intolerable—simply swinish!). It is typical that in all these attacks

Hegel directs his fire not so much against the antidialectical nature of the old materialism, as against the fact that it was materialism. "Flat," "banal," "trivial," "empty," "meager," "non-thought," "absence of thought," "dullness" and so forth—these are Hegel's characteristic comments on the materialists; none of these philosophers, he maintains, have matured enough for "speculative" thought, "higher" thought, and so on. Meanwhile, how much respect and how many pages are allotted to Jakob Boehme, a thoroughly cretinous mystic and "holy fool"!

It goes without saying that for their time, Democritus, Epicurus, and Lucretius were mighty philosophers; that the real Aristotle, not the one scholasticized in the Middle Ages, often came to the very threshold of materialism; that in England, Hobbes and Bacon were great thinkers; and that the pleiade of the *encyclopédistes* will remain forever as a shining constellation in the history of thought. The "vulgar materialism" of Büchner and Moleschott is on a much lower level; it is no accident that Engels called them "blockheads" compared to the idealist Hegel, while even Lenin (quite logically) preferred intelligent idealists to stupid materialists (see his *Philosophical Notebooks*).[2] For the sake of historical justice, however, we shall recall the role which even this vulgar materialism played in Germany, and among us in Russia. It is no accident that *Kraft und Stoff* figures in Turgenev's *Fathers and Sons*.[3]

Nor is it any accident that such people as Dmitry Pisarev were enthusiastic admirers and propagandists of Büchner's materialism, or that the people influenced by Büchner included such great minds as Sechenov, the author of *Reflexes of the Brain*.[4] Sechenov blazed the trail for one of the leading figures of Russian science, Ivan Pavlov, and laid the basis for the so-called "Russian physiological school." Lenin himself affirms that the Marxists criticized Mach and Avenarius "in the manner of Büchner...."[5]

It would, of course, be stupid narrow-mindedness not to see the hidebound nature of all the old materialism, which on the whole (despite the great differences between its various currents) was a mechanistic materialism. Its restrictiveness and other shortcomings were revealed with exhaustive thoroughness by Marx and Engels precisely because the latter thinkers combined materialism firmly with dialectics, creating dialectical materialism.

It is extremely useful to dwell once again on this question, even if only in brief, summary fashion. This is because the most difficult problems of modern science and philosophy cannot be solved using the methods of mechanistic materialism, while this materialism simply nourishes idealist currents, such as the so-called idealist physics, and in biology, "vitalism," not to speak of the philosophical trends that provide cover for them.

The old materialism was antidialectical, which in essence says everything. But it was capable of being developed.

The outstanding question here is that of quantity versus quality. Mechanical materialism had a clearly expressed quantitative character. It proposed an atom without qualities, an identity of atoms. Their quantity and quantitative determinants (number, velocity, and so on) lie at the basis of everything. The laws of their movement are the laws of mechanical motion, that is, of simple displacement in space. They themselves are the indivisible, unchanging building blocks of the universe. The various quantities of them provide the subject with sensory diversity. Quality, therefore, is on the whole rather a subjective category. The task of cognition is to bring qualitative diversity to the genuine relationships, that is, the quantitative ones. The sole type of link is mechanical causality; everything else has to be discarded. Qualitative integrity is the sum of its parts (or something of the kind); it is subject to decay, and has to be expressed in a quantitative formula. And so forth.

There was clearly a real enthusiasm here for mechanics and mathematics. In the noble quest to banish theology and teleology from the realm of science and philosophy, this materialism grossly oversimplified reality, forcing it into servile conformity with bare mechanics. In a particular historical period, this effort was profoundly progressive, but it quickly became transformed into its dialectical opposite, creating insurmountable difficulties for moving the boundaries of knowledge forward.

Even in the most "extreme" concepts of mechanistic materialism, its restricted nature is still evident. Its atom, without qualities, unchanging and indivisible, has turned out in fact to have qualities, and to be divisible and mutable. Atoms differ according to their qualitative properties. An atom of hydrogen is not the same as an atom of oxygen; it possesses a whole range of specific, individual properties, and behaves in relation to others quite differently from an atom of oxygen. The incorrectness of the notion that atoms lack qualities can be seen even at this initial level.

Hegel revealed his own negative "quality" when, as an idealist, he protested in several passages in his works—protested stubbornly, persistently, and abusively—against the very concept of atoms, considering them a worthless illusion. Modern-day idealists and agnostics, who until quite recently denied the existence of the atom or considered it merely a symbol, a model, and so forth, have been shamed on this point along with Hegel. As a dialectician, however, Hegel turned out to be completely correct when he asserted the impossibility of the atom being indivisible, unchanging, and without qualities. Mechanistic materialism sought to consign everything qualitative to the area of the subjective (though inconsistently!), and in each case to dissolve the qualitative in the quantitative. Meanwhile, qualitative diversity is an objective category. Quality is quality of being; it is immanent in being in just the same way as quantity, with each interpenetrating the other. From the limited character of the mechanistic materialist outlook flowed the interpretation of all organic, animate, and thinking life according to the model of the mechanical, to which it was "reduced" (the problem of so-called "reductionism"); *l'homme machine* is the symbolic designation of the above-mentioned tendency. The transition from physics to chemistry, from chemistry to biology, from biology to sociology, and so on through the use of the category of measure; that is, the leap to a new quality, a new integrity or integrated whole, a new type of motion, a new regularity, was beyond the reach of mechanistic materialism.

Mechanistic materialism tended to view any whole, any totality, as a mechanical aggregate, differing from other aggregates in the number and position of the atoms making it up. Meanwhile, the fact that the whole was not an aggregate, and was not equal to a heap of its constituent parts, its sum, was lost from view. Even the solar system is not the sum of various bodies, but with a particular bond present, is a specific entity. Separating a live, organic body into its parts turns this whole into a corpse; Aristotle explained this point brilliantly, although he also brought it beneath the roof of idealist "entelechy" (there will be more about this later). In the organic world, consequently, a new quality and a new integrity are present. In just the same way, society is something distinct from the human species; it differs from the latter in its specific properties, qualities, and laws. These are all completely objective properties and qualitatively different "integrities," existing independently of the subject.

If matter varies qualitatively, its motion and "laws of motion" are also varied, and cannot be reduced simply to aspects of mechanical movement. It is necessary to dwell on this point a little. Usually, when the question of "reduction" is being discussed, the following controversies arise. One side argues that the other, when it protests against reduction, retains a mystical sediment, an undissolved residue which in biology is "entelechy," a mystical *vis vitalis*, or "vital force," and so on. The other side rebukes its opponents for rejecting qualitative specificity, that is, for committing the fundamental sin of mechanistic materialism. In reality, the question can be resolved quite simply. A new quality is by no means an addition to the properties of the earlier elements, entering into a new relationship. It is not lined up in a row with them; it cannot be placed in a single rank. It is a function of aspects related in a special way. If this relation is destroyed, the function is destroyed as well; there is no place here for any "residuum." The constituent aspects exist in a new "integrity," but they exist in "sublated" fashion—to use the language of Hegel. They have become transmuted aspects of a new whole, and have not simply been crammed into it like potatoes into a sack.

Even in a field so beloved of mechanistic materialism as mathematics, quality plays a huge role, including in the highest areas. An example is the transition from finite magnitudes to infinite ones; in the case of the latter a whole series of concepts, perfectly apposite where finite magnitudes are concerned, no longer apply.

Associated with this is another blatant inadequacy of mechanistic materialism. It is oblivious to development; it is antihistorical. In fact, if any entity is mechanically flat and not dialectical, not contradictory, if it is not making the transition to a new quality (ontologically, in its real being), then a true understanding of development, which consists in the appearance of the "new" and the disappearance of the "old," becomes impossible. Hence, for example, in the notorious "theory of equilibrium," a refined variant or manifestation of mechanistic materialism, a crudely mechanistic interpretation is given of productive relations (the coordination of material "living machines" in the field of labor is "social matter," and this is the same thing as matter in physics!); on the other hand, equilibrium (even though mobile!) is taken as the starting point, despite the fact that equilibrium in general can be seen only as a particular instance of movement.

The French materialism of the eighteenth century was rationalist, connected with the idea of the "natural state" and the "social contract"; it failed completely to comprehend the real motive forces of history, and interpreted the sins of the present as the result of violations or "misunderstandings" of eternal natural laws. According to this materialism, the laws of nature and society were not historical, changing, transient, the expressions (on various scales of time and space) of transient processes, but eternal and unchanging relationships, like geometric theorems as usually understood. The naturalistic interpretation of social law, inevitably bound up with a rationalist-static, that is, metaphysical, that is, antidialectical, understanding of it, flowed, as is obvious from the above, out of the whole conception of mechanistic materialism.

In its discussion of the contentious question of soul and body, the "vulgar materialism" of the nineteenth century was on an even lower level than the materialism of the eighteenth century. A number of French materialists advanced the correct position that thought was a property of matter organized in a specific way, while the vulgar mechanistic materialism of Büchner and Moleschott inclined to the thesis that the brain emits thought in the way the liver emits bile, that is, oversimplifying the whole question to an extreme degree, crudely reducing it to processes that have other specific features.

It was thus as though mechanistic materialism plotted the whole diversity of the mobile, three-dimensional world on the flat surface of the single dimension of mechanics. This simplified world was rendered gray and trivial, something which horrified the rich, full-blooded sensible-artistic nature of Goethe.

Marx, however, noted another trait, another shortcoming of the old materialism, which afflicted all materialist philosophers up to and including Feuerbach. In theoretical terms, the old materialism was passive; it viewed human beings almost exclusively as products, in a purely objective manner. Meanwhile, as Marx noted in his *Theses on Feuerbach*, idealism succeeded better in developing the active side of humanity. We have already touched on this in passing, and will not repeat ourselves here. In this connection as well, Marx had the honor of making an abrupt turn of the wheel, that is, of viewing the object as the object of practice, and the subject as the subject of practice, rather than simply of mental theorizing; of introducing the category of practice to the theory of cognition as its very center, and finally, of treating the subject of cognition not as "I," "I in general," "humanity in general," but as social-historical humanity, a category unknown either to the old materialism, or to Feuerbach, or to philosophy in general. The old materialism here shared in a general failing, and its "subject" was the same one-sided, extra-historical, and extra-social intellectual abstraction as it had been for philosophers of other persuasions, and with a lower coefficient of activity.

All these inadequacies, the one-sidedness and the antidialectical character of the old materialism, were overcome by dialectical materialism, the brilliant creation of those geniuses Marx and Engels. In the development of philosophical thought in general, a new epoch, in the literal sense of the word, begins from this point.

Mechanical materialism was materialism, but it was passive in its theoretical view of the subject. Idealism, the negation of materialism, was active. Dialectical materialism is materialism, but active materialism.

Mechanistic materialism was antihistorical, but revolutionary. The evolutionary theory that followed it (in history, the historicist school; in geology and biology, the doctrine of gradual evolution, and so on) was historical, but antirevolutionary. Dialectical materialism is both historical and revolutionary at the same time.

Mechanistic materialism is materialism, but antidialectical. Hegel's dialectic is idealist. Dialectical materialism combines these opposites in a brilliant unity.

A great deal of rubbish has been written about the relations between Marx and Hegel. In the same rank with Plenge in this field is the gray-haired maestro, Herr Werner Sombart, who from a position of sympathy with Marxism crossed over to a profitable sympathy (as the Germans would say) for the gangsters and janissaries of fascism.[6] Out of the whole crowd of the highly-trained German scholarly fraternity only Troeltsch recognizes that Marx preserved and developed the valuable dialectical heritage of Hegel. Nevertheless, the same Troeltsch maintains in his *Historismus* that nothing of materialism remained in Marx![7]

Troeltsch writes:

> It (that is, Marxism) is an extreme realism and empiricism on a dialectical basis, that is, on the basis of logic, which by Marx's own admission explains the reality of experience not in the same way as the unmediated and abstract materialism of the French rationalist tradition, not as comprised of material elements and complexes of them, but as a concrete, mediating dialectical philosophy, flowing out of a law that constantly splits up and reconciles everything, that dissolves every distinct entity in universal motion.

This is from the writings of one of the most intelligent, knowledgeable, and conscientious of these people. What are we to say about the others?

17

The General Laws and Relations of Being

In Lenin's *Philosophical Notebooks* there is a remarkable passage, which will be cited here in its entirety:

> When one reads Hegel on causality," writes Vladimir Ilyich [Lenin], "it appears strange at first glance that he dwells so relatively lightly on this theme, beloved of the Kantians. Why? Because, indeed, for him causality is only *one* of the determinations of universal connection, which he had already covered earlier, in his entire exposition, much more deeply and all-sidedly; always and from the very outset emphasizing this connection, the reciprocal transitions [or interpenetration], etc., etc.[1]

To Kant, in his *Critique of Pure Reason*, the category of relation has within it three concepts: substance, cause, and interaction. Hegel's thinking, of course, was incomparably richer; his dialectics is more developed than that of Kant. But how can we understand Lenin from the point of view of the whole state of modern science? Does the totality of scientific knowledge confer on us the right to draw Leninist conclusions? Does it confirm these conclusions?

It confirms them brilliantly. The above-cited proposition of Lenin also in fact opens up a new stage, turning a quite new page in the history of philosophy as a whole and in the history of dialectical materialism in particular. It is not only Kantians who have put forward causality as virtually the sole type of relation. This point of view has also exercised unconditional dominance throughout Marxist literature. This is a fact that can be confirmed using countless examples. And what is surprising about this? Lenin himself writes (as we have seen) that in the twentieth century, Marxists criticized the Machists more in the manner of Büchner than in that of Marx in the strict sense of the word. This is true, and Lenin is not ashamed to admit it.

But what does this proposition of Vladimir Ilyich mean from the point of view of the gigantic sea of orderly empirical data that makes up the "economy" of modern science? We isolate a cause from the whole complex of relations and mediations as something that in acting on something else, passes over into it. A cause is an active principle; the "other" is passive. The chain of causes is infinite; it is always possible to ask "why?" It is in this sense that Hegel says:

> A cause is itself something for which it is necessary to seek a cause, passing in this way from one to another in an evil infinity which signifies an inability to conceive of and present the general, the fundamental, the simple, consisting of the unity of opposites and hence immobile, though leading to motion." (*The Philosophy of Nature*)[2]

The critical part of Hegel's view is dictated by searches for the Absolute, for repose. However, the *type* of connection is nevertheless presented here: interaction or reciprocity is another type of relation which consists in the fact that both the active and passive roles are present here on both sides of the relation. In *The Science of Logic*, Hegel defines interaction as the causation of substances that are conditioned one by another. This type of relation is not different in principle from causation. It presupposes, however, that behind the backs of the interacting factors there stands a third quantity, of which they are a feature. Is the sum of the real bonds and relations exhausted by these concepts? Not in the slightest. When, for example, I pull a trigger and a gunshot resounds, its cause is the pressure on the trigger. However, if there were neither powder, nor shot, nor cartridge, not to speak of more general conditions, the gunshot would not have occurred either. The relation here is diverse, and a whole series of conditions have to be met for the gun to fire. It was on the basis of this, among other things, that so-called "conventionalism" was formulated in its time (see for example the works of Max Verworn); this proposed replacing the concept of causation altogether with that of conditions, or conventional factors. However, it can readily be seen that, to use the earlier example, the fact of pressure on the trigger has a specific sense and meaning; here work was performed (in the physical sense), and this work directly conditioned the transformation of energy, having been modified itself.

Certain conditions are therefore necessary for a cause to bring about a particular result. If these conditions are lacking, the consequence will also turn out to be different. We have already cited the example of the seemingly "eternal" law according to which heating a body causes it to expand (the cause is heating, and the consequence is expansion). In astrophysics, however, heating serves to compress a body through the operation of quite different "ambient conditions," that is, other relations and mediations. These cannot simply be thrown overboard, and here, consequently, we see a type of conventional relation, which in no way excludes or replaces either causation or interaction. Next, we can for example recall mathematical relationships, which express typical real relations. If, for example, we formulate the so-called theorem of Pythagoras, which was already known to the ancient Egyptians and which states that the square of the hypotenuse is equal to the sum of the squares of the other two sides, this is again a special type of relation. Here one thing does not flow from another, as in the relationship between cause and effect, but the one is given simultaneously with the other. If we take the theory of functions, we have something that is similar, but dynamic. This means that we still have two types of bonds and relations that do not fit within the frameworks of the above categories.

Let us, further, take the relationship between "thinking" and "being," between the "mental" and "physical," between thought (or sensation) and the brain (or the bodily organism). The designation "physical" here is not precise, since the subject is exclusively living matter, and not simply the physical body, which as we have seen, is not the same thing. Can it be said here that the brain is the cause of thought, that the relationship is of the causal type? We think that strictly speaking, it cannot. Two completely different issues are intermingled here: the question of the genesis of spirit, and that of a specific relationship. Thinking matter arose out of inorganic matter. In this sense matter is primary, and spirit secondary. In this sense, matter is the cause of spirit. We cannot, however, tear spirit away from matter, since matter did not simply give birth to spirit in isolation, in an impossible isolation; matter gave rise to thinking matter through a chain of sensing matter. The relation between the body and spirit of a subject is not a causal relation for the simple reason that these are not two different objects, one extensive and the other nonextensive, but are one and the same. The thinking body has the property of being conscious of itself and others; consciousness is not an object, but an other-being of a thinking body. The function of consciousness is a particular form of the nervous and physiological functions of the hemispheres of the brain, as part of a whole outside of which the brain is not a brain. If it were ever proven that the brain "radiated" some specific energy, this would not in essence change the question at all, since the energy concerned would then have its own, sufficient, distinct form.

The theory of "psycho-physical parallelism" is unacceptable because it establishes a relationship between two "substances" when these do not exist. In its descriptive part it is correct: in the language of psychology, this and that "corresponds" to the nervous-physiological process. However, there are not two processes here, but one and the same. The specific nature of the bond and relationship is that the dialectical opposites coincide in their direct identity as one, equal to itself.

The usual breaking of heads on this point occurs because people search either for a visual representation (almost since the time of Spinoza, for example, they have been searching for two sides of the arc), while a visual representation, a sensible image, is excluded here *a limine*; or, people want to set forth this peculiar and specific type of bond, this special category of relations, the category of other-being, in concepts that correspond to other specific categories, which is also impossible. Meanwhile, the problem here is a false one; this relation exists as a special, unique association, a special type of real bond, and it is necessary to formulate it mentally, that is, "in conception," as a special type, in all its originality, specificity, and relative opposition to other forms and types of relation. None of this excludes the existence of relations of a special type on the plane of other-beings themselves; such relations include, for example, laws of association.

Let us now take the type of relations expressed by the so-called mathematical-statistical law. The usual example employed here is that of the law of large numbers, illustrated by the act of flipping a coin. The greater the number of throws, the more nearly the number of heads (or tails) approaches half the total (an elementary illustration for people beginning to study the theory of probability). To treat a mathematical-statistical law as something outside of experience, with no relation to reality; to consider "pure mathematics" as something having no contact with earthly life, is "pure" rubbish. We are no longer talking of the concept of number, and so on. Here, it is obvious that behind the back of the mathematical law stands the correct minting of a coin, giving it a symmetrical form. If the center of gravity of the coin were shifted, the results would be different as well. Here, too, we therefore find a definite type of real relation, a special type. The debates conducted in the field of modern theoretical physics around questions of statistical laws, concerning the "nature" of laws in the macro-cosmos, are founded in real problems. At any rate, we have the question here of a new type of relation. This is yet another example confirming Lenin's thinking.

Further, let us take the laws of dialectics. In *Anti-Dühring*, Engels described these laws as general and all-encompassing principles embracing nature, society, and thought. In *The Dialectics of Nature*, he provided brilliant examples of dialectical materialism as a method of research in the highest reaches of theoretical science. Marx in both his historical and philosophical works proved himself an unsurpassed master of this method. All of *Capital*, from start to finish, is also permeated with the spirit of dialectics. It was not by chance that Ilyich in one of his aphorisms noted that many Marxists did not know Hegel, and therefore did not have a thorough grasp of *Capital*.[3]

But just what are dialectical laws? For example, the law of diremption [the splitting or sundering of the single whole], the interpenetration of opposites, the negation of the negation, the transition from quantity to quality, and so forth. Are these laws of causation? No. Are they "conventional"? Again, no. Statistical? Still less so. What, then, are they? They are laws of dialectics, yes, laws of dialectics, particular, specific laws, laws that are *sui generis*, and moreover, of the most general type.

This is only one question as regards the general types of laws. But in this connection, we must also recall what was said earlier about particular and specific laws relating to each type of motion of qualitatively different types of matter, in the first instance physical, chemical, and biological, then social, and so on. As we have seen, the woodenness, narrowness, and relative stupidity of mechanistic materialism was founded on incomprehension of the category of measure, of leaps, and of specific qualities. Consequently, the difference between the above types is further multiplied by the specific nature of the laws that flow out of the nature of the object itself, and by the specific, immanent character of the subject.

Here, however, indignant voices interrupt us: "This is too much! The devil only knows what the author has agreed to here! Don't you know that this is pluralism of the first order! Nothing remains here of the monism on which Marxists have always prided themselves since the time of N. Beltov's book that caused such an uproar (the work by Plekhanov, *Development of the Monist View of History*).4 All the laws are split up and on different shelves—each has its special shelf, everything is partitioned off. Outside of the "specific," everything is smashed and destroyed—and here we are before the old trough of pluralism! This is truly shameful dialectics, and for us, a shameful transformation into our opposites!

"How terrible, comrades! More terrible than we can even express!"

What is the problem? The problem is:

First, that qualitatively different objects are related among themselves. They are both individual and specific, and at the same time linked with "others," interpenetrating one another. Here are to be found diversity and unity, and unity in diversity. In line with this, the laws as well are united here (just like real objects) by the laws of dialectics. Finally, all the laws of dialectics are tied in a single knot of necessity, the opposite of which, chance, is itself a form of necessity. Necessity is the "supreme" category, which expresses unity, monism.

Monism does not reflect a flat, trivial, calm, comfortable unity, akin to inadvertence. It represents a diverse, disintegrated, contradictory unity, with various opposing parts and aspects that interpenetrate one another. Here there is not even a scent of pluralism. And neither is there an aroma of vulgarism.

Our opponents, however, dream of revenge. They are rising in revolt, and already we hear voices:

"Well then! You have surrendered the materialist position! Contrary to Marx, Engels, and Lenin, you consider that spirit is an other-being of matter! Be so kind as to tell us, is this not in reality the position of the philosophy of identity, that is, of idealist philosophy? That's fine materialism!"

To which we reply:

In the first place, our worthy opponents are no doubt aware that Plekhanov defined Marxism (of course, with a grain of salt) as a type of Spinozism. And we all know what Spinozism is.

Secondly, it is by no means a matter of indifference whether we say that spirit is an other-being of matter or that matter is an other-being of spirit. If it were all the same, then Hegel, for example, would not be an objective idealist, but a materialist; Schelling would not be a mystic, but a materialist, and so on. The argument turns into its own opposite.

Thirdly, dialectical materialism is characterized by a historical view of the subject. After giving paramount importance to the origin of thinking matter in organic matter, by this very fact we have assigned paramount importance to this inorganic matter as a historical and logical *prius* (an absolute opposition between the historical and logical here does not exist, and cannot!). A stone does not think; the earth as a whole does not think, and there is no "spirit" of the earth, no "soul of the earth," no world spirit, and so on, of which an other-being might be the material universe, nature, or the earth as a planet. On the earth, it is people who philosophize, and there is no other "spirit" weaving spider webs of philosophical ideas. Idealism therefore rests on the ultimate concept of teleology and of a freedom that posits goals, while materialism rests on the idea of strict necessity. This does not mean that materialism fails to see, anywhere, purposefulness or regularity of purpose. However, materialism subordinates this regularity to the strict concept of necessity, so that it occupies a special place and is at the same time an expression of necessity. In idealist systems, meanwhile, this regularity of purpose is the demiurge of the world. However, we have deliberately kept this question separate, so as to analyze it in a special chapter [on teleology], especially since this idea has now become very fashionable both in philosophy and in science, particularly in "vitalist" biology.

18

Teleology

In Aristotle's *Metaphysics*, we read about the organization of the universe:

> We have to investigate in what way the nature of the whole contains within itself the good and the best; whether it contains them within itself as something separate and existing on its own, or as an order, or whether they are present within it in a dual fashion, as we see, for example, in the case of an army. In an army, the good consists both in the order that prevails within it, and in the commander. The latter represents the good of the army to an even greater degree than the former, since the commander does not exist thanks to the order, but the order exists thanks to him. Everything is coordinated in a certain manner, but not everything is coordinated identically. Let us take, for example, live swimming creatures, live flying creatures, and plants. These are not ordered in such a way that none of them has any relation to another; they exist in mutual relationships. Everything is coordinated in a single system, just as in a house people are not by any means permitted to do just as they like, but on the contrary, everything or most of what they do is regulated. Slaves and animals (sic!), on the other hand, do little that is aimed at the general good.... The principle of every creature is its nature....

To back up his idea about the "commander" of the universe, that is, God, the great philosopher and sage, the tutor of Alexander the Great, cites Homer: "To have more than one leader is always harmful; let one person be the ruler."[1]

This "position" of Aristotle immediately reveals the social-class underpinnings of his theoretical constructs: the "mode of production" is reflected in this "mode of presentation" in a truly inimitable, truly "classical" form.

What is at issue here is not the rich content of Aristotle's philosophical work; it would be an appalling vulgarization and oversimplification to see some social-economical or political category behind almost every philosophical idea. Aristotle observed the object of science while resting on an intellectual heritage. He gathered a gigantic volume of empirical material, and was himself scientifically and philosophically creative. But the overall stylistic forms of his thought reflected the general style of the epoch, of its military-slaveowning "spirit," which was conditioned by the "mode of production." What is involved is precisely the "mode of presentation," to use Marx's expression.

Why have we picked on Aristotle? For the reason that, right up until the present, all teleological philosophers and scientists have in essence chewed over what Aristotle provided in his initial concept, of which more below. And why did we begin with the above-cited passage? Because it is also the key to a logical and social-historical understanding of the teleological concept. This will be confirmed in full measure by the account that follows.

According to Aristotle's doctrine, the activity of a "form" is required if matter is to exist. "Form" here does not imply one or another external appearance or real structure of matter, but something quite different: an active principle. Matter in itself merely represents a possibility (*dynamis*) ; it is transformed into reality, acquiring the form of reality (*energeia*) only in the presence of an active principle. This active principle is *entelechy*, free activity, containing within itself a purpose and representing the realization of this purpose. Entelechy is pure activity, activity from within itself. Absolute substance is the unity of "form" (in the specific sense indicated here) and matter, containing, that is, good, the universal purpose, God. The purpose is, therefore, the good in each thing, and in general, the very best or the "highest good" in nature. The soul is entelechy. "It is not matter that moves itself, but the master." Entelechy moves that which constitutes the object of desire and of the thinker, but is itself immobile. This is the purpose, the beautiful, the good. In order to understand nature, it follows from this point of view that it is necessary to distinguish two main categories: 1) the purpose (*causa finalis*); and 2) necessity (*causa efficiens*). By the purpose is understood not an external aim, but an immanent one, present internally in the object as an internal striving which may also reveal itself as the mind in the absence of thought. Necessity is merely the external, materialized, objective manifestation of the purpose.

This, in sum, is the doctrine of Aristotle, which has been elaborated in all its details, especially in relation to the living, that is, to the organic. (Here, as we have already observed, it has become the basis of vitalism.) It should be noted, however, that in this sense Aristotle understands all nature as being organic, that is, as life.

Consequently, the order of the universe is a copy of the slaveowning order, a microcosm projected onto the macrocosm, the "all." At the head of the universe is a master who determines the goals, and whose goals are objectified in "order," in each thing in which the "good" (or the "beautiful") constitutes a purpose. At the same time, this purpose is a molecule, so to speak, of entelechy, both of the general entelechy, the active "form" of the world, and of its motive principle; matter and the object are merely an embryo that develops according to a norm established in it and to a purpose immanent in it. This latter is also the force of development whose external manifestation is necessity. Paramount importance is thus assigned to the *causa finalis*, to which the *causa efficiens* is completely subject.

Intellectual reworking may have made this system elaborate and refined, but its anthropomorphism, or more correctly, its sociomorphism, with a thoroughly animist core, is as plain as the palm of one's hand.

Hegel, in his *Lectures on the History of Philosophy*, cannot find words sufficient to express his delight at this aspect of Aristotle's teaching. (This aspect, by the way, lay at the basis of the positive reception given to Aristotle by the medieval Catholic church. It was precisely because of this that Aristotle was proposed for canonization as a Christian saint, while St. Thomas Aquinas many times drank the waters from the teleological-theological spring of the illustrious Greek.)

In *The Philosophy of Nature*, Hegel wrestles with the concept of an external goal, but stands like a mountain for immanent teleology, in which the "wisdom of God" is expressed:

> The concept of a purpose as immanent to the objects of nature embodies their simple determinateness, in the same way as, for example, the germ of a plant already contains, in real potential, everything which is later found on the tree, and consequently this germ, representing purposeful activity, strives purely for self-preservation. This concept of a purpose in nature was already familiar to Aristotle, and he termed this purposeful activity the nature of the thing. True teleological understanding—such understanding is the highest (sic!) form—therefore consists in nature being regarded as free in its distinctive living activity.[2]

External teleology is considered here to be unauthentic. Through its crudity, it clearly has discredited itself and the notorious "workings of the Lord," that is, all of teleology. Hegel ridiculed the idea that "sheep were created in order to be shorn"; just as Goethe did the idea that the cork oak exists in order to provide corks; and Heine, the idea that lambs and other animals exist in order to provide soup. These and other absurdities clearly show the impossibility of "external teleology." True, immanent teleology is on the other hand recognized by Hegel as the supreme form of cognition of nature.

The social genesis of the idea of immanent teleology is perfectly obvious, and we shall not waste words on it. But what does the conception propounded by the teleologists rest on in logical terms? What trait, facet, or quality of real relations was "inflated" or exaggerated here, transformed into an essence, perceived in an illusory relationship instead of a real one?

Serving as the "material" for this conception were the general order and regularity of the world; objective regularity in general; the evident purposefulness in organic nature, which expresses the relatively well-adapted nature of biological species (morphological regularity, as the most striking instance; the purposeful character of coloring, and so forth); the instincts of animals, which are sometimes striking for their purposeful character; and the goal-positing activity of human beings, their reasoned activity, in which the aim precedes the action and is realized in purposeful activity.

Let us dwell first on biological fitness.

Aristotle's *Physics* contains a remarkable discourse in which the author takes issue with the brilliant insight of Empedocles, who foretold Darwin's theory of evolution. This is astonishing but true.

Aristotle argues that when drought damages a grain crop, this is a natural phenomenon that is quite accidental in relation to the grain. Here the relationship is external, and it is in this that the accidental nature of the cause consists. There is, however, a necessary relationship of things involved, an external necessity.

"But if this is so," Aristotle continues:

> what is there to prevent us from accepting that something which appears to us as a part, for example, a part of an animal, might of its nature behave in the same arbitrary fashion? For example, the fact that front teeth are sharp, and well suited to biting through food, while back teeth are broad and are suited to grinding food, may be the result of pure chance; this may not have occurred from necessity, with the teeth being fitted for a

> given purpose. In exactly the same way, this reasoning can be applied to other parts of the body which, as it seems to us, have a particular purpose, so that in this case the living being in which by chance everything turned out in such a way that it served a particular purpose, survived precisely because everything turned out as it did, although initially this expedient arrangement arose by chance, on the basis of outside necessity.3

Aristotle goes on to say that this objection pertains to Empedocles, who argued that the world was originally inhabited by monsters, and that these monsters perished because they were ill-adapted.

What objections does Aristotle raise against Empedocles? And how does the Aristotle of the bourgeoisie, Hegel, come to the aid of the slave-owning Aristotle?

The arguments directed against Empedocles by both philosophers are pompous, unspecific, and at the same time worthless. Nothing is directed against empirical science apart from the arrogance and superciliousness of the "pure idea"!

Hegel mocks the term "emergence," describing this as senseless development; meanwhile, the word "senseless" is used with a dual meaning, so as in this way to glorify the "sense" of the "purpose"! Hegel's vituperation is obviously naive, because the claim of "senselessness" has a compromising function when there ought to be thought but is not, and does nothing to compromise that which lies outside the very category of thought. The abuse is founded on *petitio principii*.4

Meanwhile, what are Aristotle's objections?

> Nature signifies precisely that whatever something becomes, that is how it has existed since the very beginning; it means internal universality and self-realizing expediency, so that the cause and the action are one and the same, since all the separate elements are correlated with this single goal.

> On the other hand, the person who accepts the arbitrary formation described earlier destroys nature and that which arises out of nature, since (sic!) that which arises out of nature is that which has in itself some fundamental principle through which, in incessant motion, it achieves its purpose.5

Hegel is in raptures. Here is "the whole of the true profound Notion of life"! Beautiful, exalted, and so forth. But where is there even the shadow of proof? One decree, one logical manifesto addressed to an "army," and one complete repetition, in the guise of a proof, of something that ought to figure only as a conclusion.

In his commentaries on Aristotle, Hegel himself advances the following considerations:

> Aristotle's concept of immanent purpose has been lost beneath the influence of two factors: mechanistic philosophy and theological physics. Theological physics has put forward the idea of an extraterrestrial intellect as a universal cause; that is, it has also appealed in its own fashion to the external. Mechanistic philosophy has placed at the basis pressures, stimulus, chemical relationships, and as a rule, always external relationships, which, it is true, are immanent to nature, but which (listen to this!) do not flow out of the nature of the body, but represent an alien appendage supplied from outside, like a color in a fluid.[6]

Hegel then goes on to praise Kant for his concept of life as an end in itself.

Here an otherworldly God is placed on the same level with otherworldly matter (the "holy matter" of our empiriocritics, who mock materialism and external reality, showing that there is something in history that repeats itself after all!). Once again, Hegel in essence does not argue, but simply lays down the law, rendering his concept of nature so profound that he proclaims natural relationships to be something alien to nature, like tiny particles of coloring pigment suspended in water! But if these relationships are alien, whose are they? What world were they borrowed from? If they are alien both to the spirit and to nature, then what are they even from the point of view of Hegel's philosophy? To this, there is no answer.

In this way, the urge to throw off real nature whatever might happen leads (true, without the "purpose" posited by Hegel) to manifestly "senseless development."

But let us move on to the essence of the matter. In the sense of the relative adaptation of species to the external environment, conformity to purpose is a fact. The aim of the exercise is not to deny this fact, but to reveal its real content, and to locate it within the general dialectical relations of nature.

Empedocles addressed this question in thoroughly correct fashion. A mutation—accidental, as was noted earlier—is caught up in the process of selection; those individuals of the species who possess a useful mutation have greater chances of surviving, while those that are less fitted for survival perish. The process of selection sifts out the best-adapted, which remain alive; when arranged in a single line, they provide a picture of conformity to a purpose.

But what is this process really about? However we might interpret the mutation (in Lamarckian fashion or in some other way, for example, as the product of the crossing of various individuals with different "genes"), there is no predetermined goal here; the fitness of a number of individuals, as a result of selection, is a necessary consequence, the reverse side of which is a savage million-fold "nonconformity," that is, the death of a vast, infinitely great quantity of the ill-adapted. The conformity to a purpose appears here *post factum*, and not as a motivating aim. It is, so to speak, a by-product of necessity; only in this sense and with this meaning can it find a place for itself. In other words, the conformity to a purpose is an aspect of necessity.

This was not understood by Aristotle. Nor by Hegel, nor by our half-baked Russian anti-Darwinists, such as Danilevsky, nor by the modern-day vitalists headed by Hans Driesch.[7]

Thus, the whole teleological conception collapses. It can also, however, be destroyed from the other end. The expedient tooth of the tiger, outwardly representing a "boon" for the tiger and an example of entelechy, represents a negative for another creature, let us say, a fallow deer. For a deer, "herbivorous" teeth represent a boon in relation to grass. Meanwhile, they are negative from the point of view of the grass, negative from the point of view of the deer in relation to the tiger, and positive from the point of view of the tiger in relation to the deer. So where is the "boon" of universal entelechy? In the fact that human beings in one way or another make use of the grass, the deer, and the tiger? Where is the "higher goal" in this? There is no alternative, no other solution! If this is so, however, we return happily to the "theory," ridiculed by all, according to which a cork oak exists in order to stop up bottles, a lamb for meat and soup, a sheep in order to be shorn, and lettuce to be eaten with a roast.

After taking our leave of this naive, philistine, stupid conception, we cheerfully return to it from the other end, in circular fashion. "Immanent" teleology reveals its immanent nature and manifests its essence, namely, the fact that it is merely a refined variant of vulgar teleology and that it is vulgarly teleological, with the "master," that is, God, arranging everything for humanity, although he often acts quite incomprehensibly. But on this point, we already have Tertullian's *credo quia absurdum*.[8] We see the same "transmission belt" to vulgar teleology in Hegel, who, forgetting how he has mocked this vice, defines a plant, for example, as follows: "A plant is a subordinate organism whose purpose is to serve a higher organism and to be an object of its use" (*The Philosophy of Nature*).[9]

The situation is more difficult with instincts, that is, with the capacities of animals to perform actions that correspond to particular goals, ensuring the survival of the species and of the individual (the instinct for self-preservation, the sexual instinct, the instinct of love for offspring, and so forth). These are inborn and unaccountable factors, uniform and powerful, which objectively and physiologically appear as unconditioned reflexes, while psychologically, most likely, they appear as a dim inclination, an unconscious or obscurely conscious urge. Here, to please Aristotle, there is already a transition to a purpose, the purpose of *dynamei* or potentialities. But this purpose is precisely an aspect of necessity, and here as well, all our previous arguments remain completely valid.

Instinctive inclination is transformed into purposes in thinking human beings, passing through a series of intermediate stages on which we need not dwell here. In human beings a new quality comes into being, that of purpose in the real sense of something posited in advance and brought to fruition. We now have the emergence of a subject, a reasoning subject, a subject that formulates goals. This is something fundamentally new. Here we have a leap, though generally speaking, it is prepared by the preceding development, and what we have here is unity of the interrupted and uninterrupted. This, however, is a special, side issue, though it is important in another respect. Here there really are goals, goals *stricto sensu*, and purposeful activity. Marx in the first volume of *Capital* cites a well-known example when he compares an architect to a bee. The architect has an image, a plan of the structure as the purpose determining his or her activity. The bee does not have this, and builds unconsciously.

In humanity, nature undergoes a bifurcation; the subject, which has arisen historically, stands counterposed to the object. The object is transformed into matter, into the object of knowledge and of practical mastering. A human being, however, represents a contradiction, a dialectical contradiction; he or she is at one and the same time both an "anti-member" (to use the term of Avenarius), that is, a subject counterposed to nature, and a part of this nature, incapable of being torn out of this universal, all-natural, dialectical relationship. When Hegel introduced his trinomial division into mechanism, "chemism," and teleology, he in essence used idealist language to formulate (that is, if we read him materialistically, as Lenin advised) the historical stages of development, of real development.

Idealist philosophy, however, performs the following operation here: it transforms a category that has appeared as a result of historical development, as an aspect of natural necessity, into an initial given quantity, universalizing this category. Then this given quantity, supposedly primary and universalized, describes a gigantic circle and returns to itself. In essence, this trick is not at all difficult, but it has to be understood in its development and according to its nature, as we do here. From this, however, it flows in completely obvious fashion that only the rupture with dialectics, the antidialectical tearing out of teleology (or, in other works of Hegel, "the organic") from the context of natural histocial necessity can lead to purpose being elevated into a primary form, that is, the active-reasonable basis of all principles. In reality, however, a human being as a biological and social-historical individual is at the same time a goal-positing subject, and a link in the chain of natural necessity. The purpose here is an aspect of this necessity, although it is no longer a metaphor, is not the embryo of a purpose, is not *dynamis*, but an actualized purpose, *energeia*. An understanding of this makes itself felt in Hegel as well, for example, when he says that a human being, in pursuing his or her aims, depends on nature and is subordinate to it.

Consequently, we find here, among human beings, a thoroughly real purpose, the posing of objectives, teleology. This is something that actually exists. Teleology itself, however, is an aspect of necessity, an aspect which has arisen in historical fashion. A purpose, at least on earth, is a human purpose. It is quite impossible to project a purpose onto the earth and onto the universe as general entelechy. If in relation to everything earthly we can say that the earth has purposes, then these are human purposes, the purposes of humankind as a product of the earth and of nature, and not superhuman planetary purposes, an emanated particle of which abides, as it were, in humanity. Dialectical materialism does not treat human beings as machines; it does not deny special qualities, does not deny goals, just as it does not deny reason. But dialectical materialism views these special qualities as a link in the chain of natural necessity; it views human beings in their contradictory duality as antagonists of nature and as part of nature, as both subject and object, while viewing the specific teleological principle as an aspect of the principle of necessity. This corresponds to the real relation of things and processes, while the illusory relation has to be destroyed completely and without mercy. This is how the question of teleology is posed in its general formulation.

19

Freedom and Necessity

The above also in essence provides an answer to the notorious question of "free will" and necessity.

At the outset, it should be noted: freedom in the sense of an absence of cause, of indeterminism, "pure freedom," is nothing other than the will taken in isolation, without relation to anything outside itself, that is, the same absurd, empty abstraction as the Kantian "thing in itself." In *The Critique of Pure Reason*, therefore, it goes in harness with God and the immortality of the soul as one of the postulates of practical reason. In this hypostasis and isolation of pure "free will" is the essence of all the moralizing ethical and "cultural-ethical" chatter of the epigones of Kantianism.

Another preliminary note must also be made, this time about necessity. Aristotle distinguished between several concepts of necessity, pointing to a triple significance of the word "necessary"; it referred 1) to constraint, "that which is counter to inclination"; 2) to "that without which good does not exist"; and 3) to "that which cannot exist otherwise than absolutely."

This differentiation is extremely important. The revolt which is raised by idealist philosophers in the name of "free will" (overwhelmingly, these philosophers are ideologues of earthly goals!) usually appeals to the feeling of freedom, to the perception of the act of free will; precisely this perception is testimony to the feeling's lack of cause and definition, to its purity in itself and self-sufficiency! Lenin therefore wrote, in his commentaries on Hegel's "Great Logic" (*The Science of Logic,* Part II), analyzing the question of practice: "Mechanical and chemical technology serves the aims of humanity because its character (essence) consists in its definition by external conditions (laws of nature)." And subsequently: "In fact, human goals arose out of the objective world and presuppose the existence of this world, as given and immediately present. But it seems to human beings that their goals are taken from outside the world, and are independent of the world ('freedom')."[1]

This is precisely the same view that Spinoza presented in his renowned *Ethics*, a view he "demonstrated" *more geometrico*, or in an exact "geometric manner."

Spinoza protested in every possible way against the widespread view that "human beings have unlimited strength and depend on nothing apart from themselves." Spinoza seized brilliantly on this fundamental, this abstract vacuity of "pure will" taken "in itself," that is, outside of all relationships. Pure will is in fact a myth, although the sensation associated with an act of will may be one of complete freedom: "A child thus imagines that it freely wants the milk that feeds it; if it gets angry, it thinks that it freely seeks revenge; if it gets scared, that it freely wants to run away."[2] But here, as we see, what is always involved is necessity in Aristotle's third sense, and it is only about this necessity that we are talking in the present instance. This necessity is the main object, the center of the whole problem; in no way is it the "constraint" mentioned by Aristotle.

Therefore, the negation of "free will" and the recognition of necessity is not at all equivalent to the notion of a human being bound hand and foot. This is a quite different question, which does not coincide with ours and does not encompass it. The essence of the philosophical question does not consist in the contradiction between will and the world, when the latter dumps mountains of volcanic ash on you, as at Herculaneum, or when it makes your wishes unattainable, or when it restricts them. The core of the philosophical problem lies in whether a free act is free in the sense that it is independent and not determined by others, or whether it is a link in a chain of natural necessity that manifests itself as subjective freedom. This is an extremely difficult question.

The answer to it is that present within this freedom is necessity. In the free desire of a child for milk, in the child's inclination, a natural law manifests itself. In the powerful sexual instinct, a natural law manifests itself. In the free urge to satisfy hunger and thirst, a natural law manifests itself. And so forth. Here the natural law is the nature of the subject itself, revealed by the subject in acts of will. The will here is really that of the subject; it is a manifestation of the subject's nature. Since, however, the subject outside of nature is nothing, an abstraction, an illusion; and because the subject himself or herself is the product of nature and part of it; the law-governed character of the subject's nature is a natural phenomenon. The "free will" of idealists is freedom not only from the external world, but also from the nature, the real nature, of the subject himself or herself. In other words, here there is not only the abstraction of an isolated subject, and not only the abstraction of his or her consciousness, but the abstraction of part of that consciousness elevated to an absolute and revolving about itself. In exactly the same way, in the analysis of the process of cognition, idealist philosophy operates with a universalized abstraction of the cognitive aspect of consciousness. Having taken the cognitive aspect "in itself," it performs exactly the same crudely antidialectical operation with the will, that is, with another aspect of consciousness. In light of this, Schopenhauer was ill-advised to interpret the world as "will and representation"!

Oh, let fools forgive us (the clever will understand!). The dogs of the late Academician Pavlov, however, provide a marvelous scientific key to the problem. The experiments conducted with unusual rigor over long decades in the laboratories of Ivan Pavlov revealed and explained the processes involved in the formation of reflexes, which from the objective-physiological angle characterize behavioral acts, acts of will, in their relationship to external stimuli. In his last works Pavlov, with all the stringency and methodological caution characteristic of him, turned to human beings, and from these concisely written works, in which huge layers of factual material lie concealed beneath every word, objective laws of human behavior, both "normal" and "pathological," gaze out at us with extraordinary clarity. Just as Darwin revealed the conformity to scientific principles, that is, necessity, underlying the conformity to goals of the lives of species, so Pavlov revealed the conformity to scientific principles, that is, necessity, at work in the lives of individuals; here, biology received a worthy addition in the field of physiology. The nervous-physiological substrate of an act of will is understood here in its relations and mediations with the environment, and its dialectical motion is revealed. In the process, the nature of its other-being is also revealed as an aspect of the general conformity of nature to scientific laws.

Supercilious fools can giggle as much as they like at the shift from dogs to the "realm of nature," in just the same way as philistines and God-fearing old women of both sexes giggled in their time over "monkeys" when confronted with Darwinism. This is the way of the philistine rabble, to mock the brilliant discoveries of human reason. Meanwhile, reason is something of which this philistine rabble is quite bereft, even though its members imagine they are standing up for the honor and dignity of the intellect. Such are the ironies of history!

In this way the teleology of individual behavior, that is, of reasoned, purposeful behavior, of acts of will, is included in the chain of necessity; that is to say, it is understood and interpreted scientifically.

The question of the social behavior of social humanity also has its own particular, specific, and, moreover, historically determined aspect from the point of view of the problems of "free will" which we are examining.

In his essay on Feuerbach, Engels observes that in history nothing happens...

> without a conscious intention, without a desired goal. It is only very rarely, however, that what has been willed comes to pass; in most cases numerous desired goals cross over and collide in the struggle. In the historical arena, the collisions of numerous wills and individual actions thus bring about a state that is fully analogous to the phenomena that hold sway in unconscious nature. The goals of actions figure as wishes, but the results that in practice follow from these actions are not the object of the wishes, or else, to the degree that they seem to correspond to the desired goals, they ultimately have consequences quite different from those that were desired.... People make their history, however this history might unfold; in the process, everyone pursues his or her own, consciously formulated goals. The result of these wills, acting in different directions, and of their diverse impact on the external world is history.... However ... the numerous separate wills acting in history mostly lead to results that are quite different from, and often completely opposed to, those they were intended to have...[3]

Captured exquisitely here is what Wilhelm Wundt called the law of the heterodoxy of goals.[4] This, however, is a different question, even if a related one. The goals here are definite, arising out of particular circumstances. Engels dwells on something else, on the fact that the goals are not realized, or that their realization is restricted, or that their results are the opposite of those desired. An example is provided by the crises that periodically strike capitalism. These crises are features of the economic cycle, that is, manifestations of particular laws of a social character, the "laws of motion" of capitalist society; that is, they are a category of social necessity. In relation to the individual will, however, social necessity acts here as Aristotle's "necessity" in the first sense, that is, as "that which is counter to inclination." In other words, if from the social point of view, that is, from the point of view of the movement of society, of capitalist society as a whole, we have an Aristotelian necessity of the third kind, then the same necessity applies (in relation to the individual subject, as an Aristotelian necessity of the first kind).

Anarchic, atomized commodity-capitalist society is blind, and its laws are elemental; it is not an integrated subject with a single will, not a "teleological unity." This society as a whole does not pose any goals; it is a subjectless subject, a special, historically defined type of society. Earlier types of society really did have elements, sometimes quite developed, of commodity circulation, of usurer "capital," and so forth. On the other hand, they were full of the din of class, tribal, national, and interurban struggle and warfare. In these societies the menacing anarchy was interpreted as blind fate, destiny, *moira, ananks* (for Heraclitus, *eimx smeneanage*, the preordained, ineluctable power of fate). The wonderful Greek "tragedies of fate" were an artistic-poetical reflection of this destructive social spontaneity. Dying capitalism, through its ideologues, directly presents fate as a category of "science." Spengler's *Decline of the West* set the ball rolling, and his idea of a harsh, inexorable fate has become the main principle adopted by fascist historiosophism, which combines it in paradoxical fashion with the most unrestrained voluntarism.[5]

But *revenons a nos moutons*. Engels, as is well known, described the transition to socialism as "a leap from the realm of necessity to the realm of freedom." Idle critics of Marxism have argued that this represents a transition, albeit belated, to the point of view of "free will," as idealists understand it. This, however, is an absurd objection. Engels also said that the real history of humanity would begin with socialism, and that earlier there was only prehistory. In maintaining this, he was not by any means renouncing the historical view of the society of the past, or of nature itself. The *Dialectics of Nature*, with its analysis of the "laws of nature" as historical, shows quite clearly what the real situation is here. Things are just the same with the familiar "leap." This is a leap "out of the realm of necessity into the realm of freedom" in the sense that here society and the individual are liberated from Aristotle's necessity of the first kind, that Wundt's "law of the heterodoxy of goals" is done away with. This, however, does not mean that necessity of the third kind is done away with, or that Engels performs a leap from the realm of materialism to that of idealism and pure voluntarism.

With the transition to socialism, the subjectless society becomes a subject, blind necessity ceases to be blind, the uncognized becomes cognized, the absence of a goal is transformed into its opposite, and the absurd in society is replaced by reason. This, among other things, is what lies behind Stalin's well-known formula: "The plan? We are the plan!" "We" signifies organized society, planned society, the manifestation of the collective will of society as the expression of the totality of individual wills. Here social necessity manifests itself directly in social teleology. The plan simultaneously expresses both cognized social necessity and the purpose behind the planned action, a purpose that is promptly realized. This represents a quite new relationship between necessity and the goal.

The elemental character of development, directed against individual wills, thus disappears under socialism, and in this sense a leap is made from the realm of necessity to the realm of freedom.

In the third volume of Marx's *Capital*, there is an interesting observation: that the realm of true freedom begins on the other side of material labor, in that epoch of the development of communism when the powerful forward movement of the productive forces and the immense growth of social wealth will no longer be the object of any special concern. This does not of course mean that people will attain an angelic status and cease to eat and drink. It merely signifies that the development of the productive forces will automatically, so to speak, ensure the process of public provision, and that the center of activity and of creativity will shift. What remains of the compulsory character of work will disappear completely, even if this compulsion was previously "internal" and not "external." Free creativity—invention, science, art, direct communion with nature—will sharply increase its relative weight. This represents liberation from crude concerns about people's daily bread, though again only in a certain sense of the word.

The need to eat and drink is an expression of natural necessity, revealing itself in social necessity primarily through the link of production. Social necessities are thus more complex manifestations of natural necessity; they are a new form of necessity which negates natural necessity and at the same time affirms it (this being the dialectics of the new). Under developed communism, that which was present in consciousness first and foremost as a direct social goal now becomes an automatic one. This does not mean that production has disappeared, has become unnecessary, has ceased to serve as the basis of life or to be objectively the factor defining social life. Here the dialectics of motion is such that an extremely high degree of development of production signifies a shift of goal orientations to a different area. Consequently, there is a new degree of freedom, but only in the conditional sense we were talking of. Here as well there is no "leap" into an idealist "free will," as understood by idealist philosophy. The transition to a different system of goal orientations is historically conditioned; it is an aspect of regular social development, which in turn is a feature of the historical development of nature.

It is absurd to confuse the doctrine of "unfree will" with fatalism. All fatalist doctrines proclaim that something foreordained will come to pass no matter what people do. Human creativity and human will are thus excluded from the chain of active components of the coming event that has earlier been counterposed to them. The material basis for this, distorted ideologically, has its roots in the elemental character of human prehistory. According to dialectical materialism, with its social-scientific, productive, historical essence, the will is an active factor, and through the will (in various ways, concurring with the will or not—this depends on the historical type of society) historical necessity blazes its trails.

Corresponding to this multifarious concept of freedom is a similar concept of necessity. However, we cannot touch on all these questions here. It was important for us to clarify the central problem, which is intimately related to the "necessity-teleology" controversy. *Sapienti sat.*[6]

20

The Organism

We have run ahead of ourselves somewhat, in several directions, and need to return once again to the question of living matter, the organism.

From what has gone before it is evident that the conflict between materialism and idealism, thousands of years old, is expressed not only in the counterposition of the primacy of matter to the primacy of the spirit, but also (and correspondingly) in the counterposition of the primacy of necessity to the primacy of the purpose. The latter proceeds entirely from the former. As Aristotle says in his *Physics*: "The necessary exists in matter, while the purpose is contained in the essence." (For this "essence," Aristotle also uses the word *logos*, that is, reason, the rational, spirit.) "It is clear, therefore, that matter and its motion are necessary in the objects of nature. Both must be recognized as principles, but the purpose is a principle standing on a higher level."[1]

This position stated by Aristotle is idealism. (It should be noted immediately that the works of Aristotle contain many materialist passages—he vacillates between materialism and idealism, but in the present work we are citing the passages by which modern-day idealists are guided.) In essence, Kant held to the same point of view; he explained the activity of the organism in terms of its inner conformity to purpose.

Aristotle placed great stress on the concept of the whole, asserting the primacy of the whole over the part and protesting quite correctly against regarding the whole as simply the sum of its parts. Hegel continues this Aristotelian tradition, though he takes special delight in its idealist, specific side, and especially in Aristotle's doctrine of entelechy.

"The soul is substance, like the form of the physical organic body"; it is the active principle imparting life, "entelechy."[2]

This doctrine is taken over in its entirety by Driesch, who considers causality to be a principle of natural law for the inorganic world, while for the organic world this role is played by articulation, order, and entelechy, constituting the spiritual principle, the vital force, the indispensable factor that makes the living live, and the specific feature of the organic in general. The psycho-Lamarckian Franse declares outright that "we can rightly see the cause of adaptations in the spiritual activity of plants."[3] In this, in the *vis vitalis*, in entelechy, in the "soul" of the organism, as a special integral spiritual principle, immanently directing all the development of the organism and tearing loose everything organic from the chain of natural necessity—here lies the "key" to the conception of vitalism; anything else, anything not joined with this "key" by the necessary logical bond, is completely "unspecific" from the point of view of idealism in general, and vitalism in particular.

Let us take, for example, the idea of the whole. Can it really be handed over to the monopoly ownership of idealism? Certainly not! Not in any way! Marx himself, in contrast to rationalism and mechanistic materialism, stressed the idea of totality. But unlike the modern-day worshippers of totality, who pile up all totalities in a single heap, Marx saw and understood perfectly that there are various types of totalities, and that society, for example, is not the same kind of being as an elephant (in contrast to the "organic school" then, and fascist theoreticians such as Othmar Spann and Co. now).

The idea of the whole expresses objective reality, and we have already had cause to speak of this while examining the question of reasoned thought. The whole, while not in any case the arithmetical sum of its parts, their mechanistic unification, their aggregate, nevertheless consists of parts. Each part, however, when detached from the whole, the organic whole, ceases to be part of this whole and usually dies. We say usually, since recent advances of experimental science have revealed that parts separated from an organism can be "grafted" onto another organism (the experiments on the so-called transplanting of organs have yielded truly marvelous results), sometimes not even of the same species, or else they survive for long periods in some artificial medium (the experiments of Carrel, Bryukhonenko, and others). A sexual secretion can be injected into an organism and can function as a part, an "aspect" of it. Extracted from it, and joined with a female cell, it forms a new totality. Worms can be cut into parts, and these parts carry on living! And so on. But of course, a hand when detached from a body is no longer a hand. We have no intention whatsoever, then, of surrendering to vitalism the idea of the whole, but maintain this idea in its dialectical relationship to the idea of the part.

Perhaps *Gliederung* or articulation represents an epochal discovery of vitalism? By no means. The recognition of coordination in the parts of an organism, both morphological and functional, is something age-old. If we leave out of account the "fluidities" of the ancients, in the modern era we find in Cuvier and Geoffroy Saint-Hillaire the law of correlation. Cuvier took on the task of restoring the skeleton of an exhumed body on the basis of the bones; Darwin developed this law, not to speak of what has happened since. The "service" rendered by vitalism, an extremely negative one, consists merely in the fact that it has "coordinated" this "coordination" with entelechy, as a supersensory mystical force, an immanent "goal in itself," a special-purpose vital activity outside of necessity; it has absolutely counterposed the coordination of the parts of an organism to natural necessity, viewing this coordination only from the standpoint of a teleological relationship to a "higher" principle of entelechy.

Might it be that pointing to the specific character of the organic is a service rendered by vitalism, and a particular strength of vitalism itself? Once again, the claim does not hold up. Hegel was exceedingly fond of this theme, and sought to demonstrate in all possible ways that in an organism physical and chemical processes cease to be such.

In *The Philosophy of Nature* we read:

> We can ... observe chemistry and even chemically separate out particular parts of the living whole. Nevertheless, the processes themselves *cannot be considered chemical* (author's italics), since chemical properties are inherent only in the dead; animal processes always do away with the nature of the chemical. The mediating functions that are inherent in an area of life can be investigated and uncovered at a very profound level, as in the meteorological process. Reproducing this mediation, however, is impossible.[4]

Elsewhere in the same work we find this passage:

> At this direct transition, this transformation, all chemistry and all mechanics suffer a collapse. Here they find their limits, since they perceive their object only in terms of those elements that are present and which have already possessed an identical outward form.... Neither chemistry nor mechanics, whatever contortions they might perform, can empirically follow the change that food undergoes up to the point where it enters the bloodstream.[5]

Here, however, it should be noted above all that such elementary facts as the following are reliably known to us: a plant when in the light absorbs carbon dioxide and breaks it down into carbon and oxygen, giving off oxygen, real oxygen, into the air. Whatever one might say, this is a chemical reaction in the most ordinary sense of the word. When an animal breathes, it absorbs oxygen from the air and gives off carbon dioxide—again, a chemical process of the classical type. Organic chemistry prepares organic substances by synthetic means. This is a great advance for science.

Do chemical processes occur in the same way within an organism as outside it? This is a question of fact. Probably, they all take place differently, by way of different relationships, forming correlations with specific conditions and proceeding subject to them. The organic is specific; this is why Engels wrote in *The Dialectics of Nature*: "Physiology is, of course, the physics and in particular the chemistry of the living body, but at the same time it ceases to be chemistry in particular; on the one hand, the sphere of its activity is restricted here, but on the other, it rises to a higher level." Engels also wrote: "If chemistry succeeds in preparing this protein, the chemical process will depart from its own framework," that is, a transition will have been made from chemistry to biology.[6]

But what does this show? Entelechy? Why? The fact that until now we have not constructed a living organism synthetically is easy to explain; living matter was formed over a vast time scale, and by no means under laboratory conditions. Balancing these aspects is immensely difficult. But this is not proof of entelechy either. Where is the error in the argument, put forward by dialectical materialism, that life, just like sensation, is a property of matter organized in a particular way?

Hegel answers this question—and how he answers it! Just listen! He sets out in his own words the ideas of Aristotle, and solidarizes with him (in essence, this is Hegel's own position):

> If we consider body and soul to be one, like a building consisting of many parts, or else (which, by the way, is not one and the same!—author) like things and their properties, a subject and predicate, and so forth, then this is materialism (oh, horrors! oh, gods!!—author), since both soul and body are regarded here as things (where did you get this from?!—author). Such an identity represents a superficial (of course!—author) and empty (I should think so!—author) definition, of which we do not have the right (oh, lord, what suffering!—author) to speak, since (listen, listen!—author)

form and matter do not possess identical worth in relation to being; we have to understand a truly worthy identity as being entelechy.7

Enough! "The soul is a cause, as a purpose"! A wonderful explanation! First, on the basis of a crude anthropomorphic, or more precisely, sociomorphic analogy, you have constructed an image of the universe, raised an abstraction of a goal onto a world pedestal, then you baptize everyone with its holy benison, since only this is "worthy," and it is "worthy" because on an exalted level there abides the supreme goal, the entelechy of the world. But is all this idealist hocus-pocus in the least convincing?

It is possible to turn this question around and view it, so to speak, from the opposite angle. There can be no doubt that it is an innate quality of living things to feel, and of particular living things, to think. (What kind of "lower" form of sensation exists in plants, what it consists of concretely, we do not know, but there is abundant evidence to back the hypothesis that it exists.) But be so kind as to tell us why this property of organic bodies has to be treated as a special force, and why this force has to be considered active entelechy? Why should it be supposed that this force is a *prius*, and why should it be asserted that this *prius* exists outside of natural necessity, moving in a different dimension, a dimension of goals, and that natural necessity is subordinate to this *prius*, rather than the other way round?

It is characteristic of Hegel that he revolts in every possible way against metaphysical "forces," and against tautological explanations in the category of Molière's "sleep is a soporific force." Hegel correctly objected against sound-producing and heat-producing fluids, "phlogiston" and so forth. But it is something quite different when a mystical "higher" force is introduced, a *vis vitalis*, a vital force based on nothing, supposed to explain everything, and explaining precisely nothing!

Now we shall pose the question again, in the following fashion. True, we cannot yet create organisms out of inorganic matter, although Wöhler, early in the nineteenth century, obtained urea by synthetic means. We can, however, modify organisms, breed new varieties, and in particular organisms, create new conditioned reflexes (for example, the training of animals), and so on. When we transform natural inorganic substances, we make use of natural necessity; we are guided by it, using the laws of nature, forcing nature to work upon itself. We have already analyzed this question. But tell us, if you please, does not the very same happen when we "train" a monkey or a rabbit, a dog or a pig? When we induce sea lions to play with a ball, or an ape to ride a bicycle? Does not the same happen when Michurin breeds new varieties of apples or pears? Or when Lysenko alters vegetative processes? Or when new breeds of stock are developed? In all these cases, are we not setting in motion cognized laws of nature, which "work" because they are laws of the development of organisms, laws of the interrelationships of these organisms with various factors?[8]

To this, we might immediately hear the objection: if you please, neither vitalism, nor Hegel, nor Aristotle, nor the "soul" and "entelechy," nor the "purpose" have negated or now negate external necessity in any way. They simply maintain that external necessity is a form of manifestation of inner, immanent conformity to purpose, which is the supreme principle.

You have slain me, good sirs, really slain me!

But if entelechy is fearsome, at least necessity is merciful.

Can all this argumentation really save the unfortunate vitalists? Hardly. In the examples we have cited, what has become of this notorious primacy? What is it that serves as a tool in the hands of humankind? Natural factors, laws of nature. And with their help, that is, under the impact of certain natural factors, a different direction of development ensues, a direction that was not "immanently" present in the organism. What "good" or "purpose" is there in the layers of fat that accumulate on a Yorkshire pig, and which mean that the pig is no longer able even to move? What becomes of the primacy of entelechy when it is confronted with the action of natural laws? "Entelechy" itself (in this case, the mental side of the physiological process, let us say, new conditioned reflexes) changes fundamentally. This means that the "primacy" has departed this life.

Here, however, the indefatigable critics raise a deafening howl. You have brought in a different entelechy, they cry, an entelechy of human beings, of human reason and goals. This is why you have obtained such a result! You have merely confirmed the primacy of entelechy by accepting the principle of entelechy in a higher form, the human form....

This objection too is unconvincing, since in this case there is no difference, so far as the discussion of our problem is concerned, between human and nonhuman intervention. Between "reason" and the object of the action there are natural factors. Human beings act through these, merely combining them in a particular fashion. These factors form new qualities and properties of an organism in its corporeality; therefore, they form its "entelechy" as well.

Consequently, this objection too falls away. Here as well, natural necessity scores a brilliant triumph.

The whole vitalist conception, as a conception of immanent teleology, leads ultimately to vulgar forms of teleology, which coincides with theology. This was the case with Aristotle, for whom the supreme good and supreme purpose grew over into the master of the world, that is, a god, a cosmic Alexander the Great enforcing order in the universe. Particles of this paradise, atoms and molecules of the general good, grow up as the entelechy of [each of] the organisms in hierarchical order, according to the army table of ranks (see the "forms" of St. Thomas Aquinas). Hence "every breath praises the Lord!" This is termed the "exalted," "elevated," "worthy," "beautiful," and so on, compared to which our sinful matter is a second-rank category, lowly, unworthy, ugly, dirty, and sinful. In their theological-philosophical form these ideas have at times become exceedingly widespread, and they have now been resurrected in half-witted form by the theoreticians of fascism.

The purpose—the primacy of the purpose—is pure voluntarism; the primacy of the "spiritual," and entelechy; the mystical contemplation of the world Whole; the shifting of the intellect and rational cognition to the background. *Staatsbiologie* as the main science; the mystical "voice of the blood," and the mystique of the "organic" in general. The organization of idealist order as the structural principle of the cosmos.

The special-purpose criterion of truth in the banal form of the goals of Hitler, as an organism directly in touch with cosmic entelechy (the Egyptian pharaohs had the same thing thousands of years ago!). The "spiritual possession" by the people of the means of production (material possession can stay with the capitalists—this is nothing, so long as the people have the "spiritual"!), and similar rubbish. All these are pictures of the degradation of bourgeois society. Dying in the real world, on the one hand it provokes a desperate bloodshed and places its reliance on thoroughly material means of destruction. On the other hand, it immerses itself in the mystique of the unreal, in the depths of the soul, despite the official actualism. All the while, it is fraught with the age-old words of age-old despair:

> In truth, all is vanity! For in this life everything earthly is in vain.

Or, as in Ecclesiastes:

> Vanity of vanities, all is vanity.

That is where your path leads, good sirs and mesdames.

21

Modern Science and Dialectical Materialism

On the threshold of the century there emerged a crisis of physics, and together with it, of all theoretical science. As hidden changes took place in the ideological orientations of the ruling classes, and as previous social and material relations in their turn were altered by ideological reflexes, this called forth special forms of so-called "physical idealism." This combination of words is absurd. All that is reflected in the absurdity of the phrase, however, is the "height" or "stage" of ideological distortion. Meanwhile, ideological distortion as such has been and remains a factor.

Lenin's 1908 work *Materialism and Empiriocriticism* focused on the question of the reality of the external world precisely because at that time agnosticism and idealism had received extremely wide currency, and in the depths of theoretical science, beginning with physics, theories which in essence did away with the basis of the universe, that is, matter, were wildly popular. "Matter has disappeared; equations remain." Such concepts of physics as atoms were declared to be no more than "models." These were conditional "signs," "symbols," "tools" for coordinating the elements of idealistically understood experience; nothing real corresponded to them. A sign of good form was a scornful attitude toward matter and the reality of atoms. In the theory of Vaihinger (*Die Philosophie des Als-Ob*) all the basic concepts of theoretical physics such as matter, mass, the atom, and so on were declared to be fictions, an artificial means of thought—and that was all.¹ The solipsist tendency was clearing a path for itself.

The subjective idealism of Berkeley and Hume was reborn in new forms, donning the clothes of exact science. The outstanding role in this process was played by Ernst Mach, an extremely talented and erudite physicist, historian of science, and experimenter. Here Lenin stood up "against the current" that had overwhelmed significant numbers of Marxists who were distracted by the "strictly experimental" side of the empiriocritical constructs. (We have already dealt in essence with this "doctrine of appearances" in the early parts of this work.)

It is curious now to see what the development of the natural sciences in the period since the appearance of Lenin's book has actually brought. What has the progress of theoretical physics yielded on the questions that were most contentious at the beginning of the century? In this debate, who has turned out to be objectively correct?

Whatever was said, however much idle chatter was heard, and whatever reservations were expressed, one basic fact remains: the atomic theory was brilliantly confirmed. The reality of the atom was proven. Different atoms were described; cognition penetrated into their structures. Experimental science, in the person of Rutherford, split the atom by bombarding it with streams of particles, and detected the motion of its components. The question is now arising of using the internal energy of the atom, and so forth. The atom has been experimentally substantiated. Atoms, however, exert practical influence; they bring about changes in practical-experimental fashion. Industrial technology already makes use of the achievements of microphysics, and various forms of micro-analysis serve the cause of material production on the public level.

The proof of the correctness of atomic theory, as such, has turned out to be so convincing that even Wilhelm Ostwald, the father of "energetics," has been forced to renounce all the bases of his own views, which were consistent after their fashion, and to acknowledge the correctness of the position represented by atomic physics.²

This signified a great victory for materialism, however much the idealists tried to distort the real state of affairs. The fact is that whole mountains of arguments, theories, and systems which rested on the view of the atom as a cognitive fiction crumbled into dust. The idealists were forced to retreat to other positions. They found them, and idealism now operates in forms that are even more harmful, and outright mystical. Nevertheless, in the area of theoretical science this situation, which is rooted in the social psychology of the era of profound capitalist decline, no longer rests on the same broad basis as when the question of the atom was controversial.

The development of physics and chemistry has not only provided confirmation for materialism, which for thousands of years has battled against idealism. It has also provided confirmation for dialectical materialism, for materialist dialectics.

Above all, the development of physics and chemistry has shown the qualitative nature of atoms. Quality is affirmed here as an objective property of objective things and processes. As was stated earlier on this point, we find here a fundamental difference with the ideas of mechanistic materialism and with its one-sidedness. At the same time, the dialectical law of the transition from quantity to quality is brilliantly confirmed, since depending on the quantity of electrons, the quality of the atom changes. In microphysics the categories of measure and of leaps acquire a firm basis. The proven divisibility of atoms, and the fact that atoms make up whole "systems of worlds," puts an end to the antidialectical view of the "ultimate building blocks of the universe" as a sort of absolute, where an impassable boundary will be placed, where infinity turns into finality, and where the world "in depth" proves suddenly to be boarded up. Modern physics has put an end to this view, and has again put wind in the sails of materialist dialectics, despite the physicists often not having the slightest idea of the latter.

The dialectical law of diremption, "the splitting of the whole," found expression in the interpretation of the atom as a system of positive and negative electrical charges (protons-electrons). Subsequent analysis, continually rendering the picture of atomic structure more complex and variegated, revealing more and more new features, aspects, processes, and relationships, has not done away with this polarity, in which one of the most profound and fundamental laws of dialectics is revealed. Associated with this as well is the internal motion of the atom.

The dialectical law of contradiction has manifested itself on the broadest scale in the question of interrupted (discrete) and uninterrupted character. Engels in *The Dialectics of Nature* wrote about this precisely in connection with problems of the atomic theory of that time:

> A new epoch in chemistry begins with atomic theory (therefore it is not Lavoisier but Dalton who is the father of modern chemistry). The situation in physics changed

correspondingly with the advent of molecular theory (which since the discovery of the transformation of one form of motion into another has represented a different form of this process, but in essence only another aspect of it). The new atomic theory differs from its predecessors in the respect that (if we leave asses out of account) it does not assert that matter is simply discrete, but that the discrete parts represent various stages (ether atoms, chemical atoms, masses, heavenly bodies) and different nodal points; that they condition various qualitative forms of being of matter in general, along a descending line until weight and repulsion are lost.[3]

In modern physics this unity of the intermittent and continuous, with the interpenetration of opposites, has taken the form of the unity (and of the opposition in unity) of the particle and the wave. Corpuscular theory and quanta (that is, packets of particles) on the one hand, and wave theory and waves on the other, combine in a dialectical unity in which theory (the unity of corpuscular and quantum theory) correctly reflects reality (the unity of particle and wave, their contradictory dialectical unity).

It would of course be absurd if dialectical materialism were to tie its hands by proclaiming the "picture of the world" achieved so far to be absolute truth. Cognition is going deeper and deeper all the time. What is important here, however, is the definite trend of development, which strikingly confirms the laws of dialectics. The electromagnetic theory of matter has been proven, but it is still only written in the contours of the general composition, and only partially. Nevertheless, all the new features that are revealed by the subsequent process of cognition follow the lines of objective dialectics. Protons and electrons are connected with wave motion in the ether; the discovery of uncharged particles reveals the unity and opposition of the new order where uncharged particles—neutrons—versus charged ones; positrons, that is, particles with the mass of an electron but with a positive charge, versus electrons, with their negative charge; particles with the mass of a proton, but charged negatively, versus the positively charged proton, and so forth (see the experiments of Curie, Joliot, Anderson, and others).

The development of natural science in recent times has destroyed the metaphysically one-sided concept of the permanence of chemical elements, and has provided confirmation of dialectics in a more "dialectical" form, so to speak, than existed for Hegel. Here too, Hegel sacrificed dialectics to his idealism. In protest against atomic theory, chemical elements, and so on (he himself understood "elements" in the spirit of the ancient Greeks, especially

Empedocles, that is, as earth, water, air, and fire), and from fear of materialism he overstepped the mark, bending the stick in the direction of the absolutization (that is, metaphysical restriction) of the whole, divorcing the whole from its parts.

Atomic theory, its extension into electron theory, and the powerful development of studies of the periodic system on the basis established by Dmitry Mendeleyev—the periodic table is a brilliant confirmation of the law of the transformation of quantity into quality—created a science of the transformation of elements on a quite new basis. To a significant degree, chemistry returned to alchemy, but without the philosopher's stone and without God. Atoms were drawn into this process. In this regard, the phenomena of radioactive decay provided the foundation for a whole epoch, confirming the mutability of matter (radium-helium and so forth), the historical process of the transformation of matter. (It is well known that radium has become the chronometer, so to speak, of geological history, the scale according to which the age of our venerable mother earth is determined.) The historical, that is, dialectical, view of nature has penetrated its very microstructure.

> The first breach was that achieved by Kant and Laplace (the theory of the origin of the planet from a cosmic cloud—author). The second was geology and paleontology (Lyell, slow development). The third was organic chemistry, preparing organic substances and demonstrating that chemical laws applied to living bodies. (Engels, *The Dialectics of Nature*)[4]

The "historical principle" has now penetrated even deeper and has become still more universal, creating a basis for the concept of the historical mutability of everything. This, of course, is an excellent confirmation of dialectical materialism; of materialism, since the reality of qualitative matter is evident here, and of dialectics, since the process of dialectical-historical motion, with the transition from one thing into another, is readily apparent. The materialism of Marx turns out to be more dialectical than the idealism of Hegel; the latter rejected the view that things were composed of chemical atoms, protesting against decomposition and thus fetishizing, absolutizing, the whole. Here, his dialectics passes over into metaphysics, and his philosophy into narrow-minded philistinism. All from a fear of falling into materialism! The case of Hegel proves the correctness of an assertion made by Goethe (second half of the assertion!), cited by Michelet in the appendix to his edition of Hegel's *Philosophy of Nature* (from Goethe's *Zur Morphologie*):

> A reasoning human being who notices particulars, who observes and analyzes attentively, is in a sense drawn toward everything that flows out of an idea and that returns to it. Such people feel at home in their labyrinths, and do not seek guiding threads that would lead them out more quickly. On the other hand, a person who occupies a higher vantage point is too easily filled with contempt for the particular, or individual unit, and crams into a deadening generality that which can only live in a particularized form.5

Here, Goethe was basically groping for a sort of dialectics of the opposite; the whole, being (conditionally speaking) more alive, passes over into its opposite, into a state where it is dead in relation to the living individual. A "true dialectics" has to take these aspects in their specific context, and this can only be done on a materialist basis.

The development of theoretical physics and chemistry over the past two or three decades, the creation of a new physics and microphysics, has thus confirmed the teachings of dialectical materialism. Dialectical materialism is not in the least afraid either of arguments about laws, since laws are expressions of the search for specific regularities, or of absurd idealist constructs such as the "free will" of the electron, the idealist interpretation of Heisenberg's principle, and the similar interpretation of Einstein's theory of relativity. These are ugly ideological growths on the body of science; they have to be exposed and denounced. But they no longer have long to live.

Lenin was therefore correct in his dispute with the "idealist physics," and physics itself has provided the answer to this historic question.

The situation is more complex with biology (and with physiology as a component part of it). Here, genuine mysteries are now emerging, to a significant degree connected with the fact that as we have noted, biology in the land of the swastika has been turned into *Staatsbiologie*, the basis for the state doctrine of fascism, and has therefore been hurriedly reworked both in its fundamentals and in its details. It would, however, be quite incorrect to see only this excremental aspect of modern biology.

Modern biology is characterized by the gigantic successes of experimental science, by the rise and colossal development of genetics, by the conquests of hormone theory, and indeed by astonishing experiments on the transformation of gender, on the life of organs and complexes of cells separated from the organism, and so forth. The "self-induced motion" of life and its development in the study of genes, chromosomes, and so on; the relationship—a dialectical relationship—with the external environment through the theory of mutations;

the enriched theory of Darwinism presents the process as a whole, the development of species; the studies by Pavlov present a materialist doctrine on the behavior of the individual organism in relation to its environment (that is, response to external "stimuli"). Is all this not testimony in favor of both materialism and dialectics, even though many of the workers and creative spirits in these fields have had no inkling of dialectics?

The practical application of science, and consequently the verification of its truthfulness, has occurred on an immense scale. Physics and chemistry, in their technological derivatives, have become scientific engineering. Biology has become zoo-engineering and phyto-engineering. The old maxim of Bacon, that science and human potential coincide, is being confirmed on the gigantic scale of social production and reproduction. This is demonstrating brilliantly the whole significance of the natural necessity of materialism, counterposed to idealist teleology. It is revealing the ever greater truthfulness of the tremendous power of human cognition, its ever increasing adequacy to the reality of existence.

And this power of human knowledge is being liberated by the proletariat from the bourgeois chains of metaphysical idealism and idealist metaphysics.

22

The Sociology of Thought: Labor and Thought as Social-Historical Categories

Materialist dialectics demands that thought be examined in the historical process of its rise and development, in its relation to the vital activity of social-historical humanity, that is, above all in relation to practice, to labor. Like language, thought itself—we have already addressed this question in passing, in another context—is a social product. The works of Max Müller, Laz. Geir, and Ludwig Noire contain a considerable number of arguments to show that the origin of language and thought lay in people's labor practice, and the process of formation of concepts was understood precisely in relation to this.[1]

The most recent research into the history of language and thought—in particular, the works of the late Academician N. Ya. Marr—provides an enormous amount of material to confirm these positions.[2] It is necessary to understand thoroughly, to its profoundest depths, the fundamental fact that concepts are the cells of the thought process, and that they constitute a social-historical category, the product of social history, of vast human experience. Every concept is a condenser of this experience, of the collective labor—willing or unwilling, direct or indirect, and usually proceeding in the form of struggle—of a whole series of generations, usually heaped one on the shoulders of another. When a concept is present, together with a word that has become intertwined with it, behind them stands an entire history, and from any concept and word we can wind back a whole cinema film of a complex historical process.

This was understood, for example, by Wilhelm Wundt, when he wrote in his *Questions of the Psychology of Peoples*: "... a linguist must not analyze language as a phenomenon of life isolated from human society; on the contrary, presuppositions about the development of forms of speech have to ... accord with our views about the origins and development of human beings themselves, about the origin of the forms of social life, about the rudiments of customs and of laws."[3]

Similarly Ludwig Noire wrote forthrightly in his *Ursprung der Sprache*: "Language and the life of reason flowed out of shared activity..., out of primordial labor."[4]

The given quantity that is original in historical terms, the initial relationship between humanity and the world, is in practice the labor relationship of social humanity to nature. This is shown, not by abstract considerations, but by whole mountains of factual material. Thought and language developed in the process of communication, in the generalization of experience. We have already seen how the rejection of the subjective proceeded through the comparing of individual experiences. The repeating of individual experiences and the repeating of these innumerable comparisons, the primitive "exchange of experience," led to generalizations, that is, to the shift from the "individual" to the "collective," from an individual relationship with something isolated, from a specific sensory relationship between a person and the object of labor and "the environment" in general, to the seizing upon and understanding of many "experiences" of many people. This generalization of experience was also reflected in the formation of concepts. The same with speech, which is fused indivisibly with thought. "Every word is already a generalization," notes Lenin in connection with a reference to Ludwig Feuerbach (*Philosophical Notebooks*).[5]

The practical root of the formation of concepts, as we have already seen, was located historically in the very words for "concept," since *begreifen* and *concipere* [meaning to "conceive"] both mean also "to seize"; the Russian word *ponyatie* ("concept") comes from *yati*, that is, "to take"; *videre* [Latin], *vedat'* [Russian], and *wissen* [German], coming from a common root that meant "to see" (with one's eyes), also mean "to know." And so on. We shall not multiply the examples, especially since we have already spoken of this. There is now a whole literature that elaborates on these questions, with the role of the hand

and eye in particular being explained. (Hegel also has some quite apt remarks on this subject.) Natural tools (the hand and eye; the hand as a more "practical" organ, the eye as a more "theoretical" one); artificial tools (technology); and tools of thought, or concepts (these are at the same time mental reflections of the objective world)—all operate in mutual connection.

In exactly the same way, the coordination of concepts is a social-historical process; when a certain store of concepts and words has been formed historically, a further expansion of experience will be followed by its mental reworking in terms of concepts, in their relations, in their coordination, again on the basis of a continuous relationship with the external world, primarily through the process of practical action upon it. The great error of Aleksandr Bogdanov, who developed his own doctrine of socially organized experience, consisted not in describing the generalizing of experience, but in his idealist understanding of it, that is, an understanding according to which the objective external world disappeared, while links and relations "of general significance" (for example, scientific laws) were transformed into a kind of social product to which nothing corresponded in the real world. These links and relations were themselves declared to be the objective world; the scientific picture of the world was transformed from a reflection of the world into the world itself. If for Fichte the creator of the world was "I," for Bogdanov it was "we." If for Kant the laws of the world (categories, regulating forms) were created by the transcendental subject, according to Bogdanov they were created by society. All three, however, were pure mythologizing, idealist mythologizing. Moreover, we need to note here the playing on terminology and the speculation on the triple significance of the word "objective": 1) objective as social (as opposed to the subjective-individual); 2) objective, as corresponding to reality (in contrast to any and all subjectivism, as not corresponding to reality); 3) objective, as located outside the object, and independent of the subject.[6]

Materialist dialectics holds that cognition is a social process, signifying cognition of the real world, which is located outside the subject or subjects (this does not exclude the possibility that the subject itself may also be seen as an object); that concepts, their systems, and the picture of the world, the scientific picture of the world, are products of people's social activity, but that they reflect the world, which is real and objective (in the third sense).

Cognition presupposes an object of cognition; it does not idle out of gear. The objective world is the object of mastering in its dual form, practical and theoretical. Both the process of formation of concepts and the process of their coordination include practice as their foundation. Marx in *The German Ideology* notes that consciousness cannot be other than recognized being. Consequently, theory cannot, in the final analysis, be anything other than the theory of practice.

A historical survey of this question leads one to the conclusion that theory, thought, became distinguished from practice only at a certain stage of development. Aristotle noted that theoretical reasoning appeared when elementary material needs were satisfied and time was freed up for "independent" thinking. Even earlier, thought accompanied labor (in its germinal forms), since the subject of labor is not a mechanical thing. It is true, as Hegel notes in *The Philosophy of Nature*, that "the mechanical mastering of an outside object is the beginning," but even in the process of this mastering, the subject of the mastering is a live and thinking subject (even if this "thinking" is merely embryonic).

Nevertheless, it is only the formation of a surplus product (and consequently, of "leisure") that causes intellectual functions to be singled out as a more or less independent principle. This process (a historical process) is brilliantly explained in the works of Marx and Engels, and is formulated with crystal clarity in the magnificent fragments of *The German Ideology*. The appearance of surplus labor on the basis of the growth of the productive forces; the rise of social and class differentiation on the basis of the division of labor with the isolation of mental work; the appearance of what Marx called ideological estates; the directing of thought toward particular objects under the impact of practical needs; the appearance, on this basis, of embryonic forms of science—all these processes are relatively clear, and a vast multitude of facts could be adduced to prove these propositions on the basis of the history of every science: astronomy and botany, geometry and mechanics, linguistics and theoretical physics, and so forth. This was recognized by Hegel, who by virtue of this at times came close to posing the question in a historical-materialist manner. In his *Lectures on the Philosophy of History*, he states: "Human beings with their needs relate to external nature in practical fashion," and immediately provides a definition of a tool of labor that in essence passed over into Marx's *Capital*.

Hegel regards practice as a link in the syllogism, a position which at first glance is monstrous. But Lenin notes: "This is not just a game," since here the approach to truth is by way of practice. Elsewhere, apropos the "conclusion of action," Lenin observes: "And this is true! Not, of course, in the sense that a figure of logic has human practice as its other-being (= absolute idealism), but *vice versa*, the practice of a human being, repeated billions of times, becomes fixed in human consciousness in the form of figures of logic" (*Philosophical Notebooks*).⁷

In Hegel we find extremely profound thoughts relating to the question we are discussing here. Practice has to do with the particular, with the data furnished by the senses, with the directly concrete. Theory is concerned with the general, the universal, with that which is not imparted by the senses, with the mental, the abstract. Dialectical cognition (we shall recall the doctrine of the second concrete) goes back from the abstract to the concrete, uniting analysis and synthesis, theory and practice, the unique and the general, and understanding this general in its relation to concrete definitions.

Or, as it was put exquisitely in *The Philosophy of Nature*:

> When an understanding is reached ... of the innermost essence of nature, the one-sidedness of the theoretical and practical relationship to it is removed, and at the same time the demands of both relationships are satisfied. The first relationship contains universality without definiteness, the second, individuality without universality. The cognition that occurs in concepts represents a mean.... The cognition that occurs in concepts is thus the unity of the theoretical and practical relationships to nature.⁸

It can readily be seen how correct Lenin was when, "reading Hegel," he insisted on the aspect of practice in Hegel not as something artificial and external, but as an aspect of dialectical cognition itself (the unity of theory and practice "precisely in the theory of cognition," as Ilyich stressed).

In Hegel, naturally, all this is put forward on an idealist basis. Ontologically, what Hegel is concerned with is the absolute idea. "The absolute idea is ... the identity of the theoretical and the practical ideas, each of which is in itself one-sided" (*The Science of Logic*, Ch. III).⁹

In this connection Marx answers Hegel succinctly, while dealing fully with the question ("Introduction to the Critique of Political Economy"):

> Hegel falls into the illusion that the real should be understood as the result of thought achieving an inner unity, going deeper into itself, and developing out of itself, while the method of ascent from the abstract to the concrete is simply the means by which thought masters the concrete, and reproduces it spiritually as the concrete. In no case, however, is this the process of the concrete itself coming into existence.¹⁰

The practical root of thought, its labor root, was also retained in the designations of the methods of cognition: "analysis," that is literally, "untying," a representation of the material process of the disassembling or dismemberment of an object; and "synthesis," literally "laying together," "collection of parts." In essence, all labor practice in its billion-fold repetition both in space, in many places and involving many people, and in time, is reduced to the combining of material elements of the natural world, to their dissociation into various elements, and to the composing of a whole—a physical whole, or a more complex (non-mechanical) whole of a chemical nature. This process therefore reflects and expresses both the movement of logical categories, and "figures of logic." But it is also true that such methodological concepts, and the intellectual processes such as induction and deduction which correspond to them, reflect movement from the concrete-practical to the abstractly theoretical, and from the abstractly theoretical to the concrete-practical. In precisely the same way, the cycle of Practice-Theory-Practice (P-T-P') is reflected in thought and in thinking about thought. Experience repeated billions of times; the comparing of it by many people; the direct mastering of objects of the external world by many people and the collating of these partial masterings; and the generalization of labor practice through its socialization—all this also leads to the thinking of socialized humanity, with the corresponding categories.

With the division of labor and the formation of classes, however, and with the transformation of social property into private, with the division of the integrated relation to the world into practical and theoretical relations, these disintegrated and isolated oppositions harden into oppositions between the social groups that have taken shape (in their developed form these groups are classes). In this social-class hierarchy the lower orders represent physical labor, and the upper ones mental labor. In this way the movement from practice to theory, from the concrete to the general, and from labor to thought also has a social-material correlate in terms of social-historical form, as the form of organization of divided social labor in its totality and in all its many-sided definitions (from material production to the very "highest" provinces of ideological activity).

The whole is thus divided into parallel, symmetrical oppositions:

PRACTICE—the workers who perform physical labor (the lower classes)—the concrete, the individual.

THEORY—mental labor (the upper classes, the *ideologische Stände*)—the abstract, the general.

In the isolating of theory from practice, in the forming of special class functions (the monopolization of knowledge on the basis of the monopolization of the means of production, the functions of command and the ideological role of princes, priests, and so on), in the separating out of social thought and its concentration in its "highest," differentiated forms with particular social groups, there is also the basis for the isolating of the abstract from the concrete, for the severing of the "general" from the "particular," for the hypostatizing of concepts and for their transformation into independent, self-motivating essences, that is, the basis for a fundamental ideological distortion, with the whole world beginning to dance on its head.

We now see how Hegel, though in idealist fashion putting the cart before the horse, expressed real relationships in what might seem his monstrously primitive positions on practice as part of a syllogism. This remains true even though the form of the expression was inverted and idealist. Lenin, "reading" Hegel in materialist fashion, that is, seeking out the rational kernel within Hegel's constructs, freeing it from its mystical-idealist husk and translating it into the language of materialism, immediately noted that there was profound thought within.

We thus see that the normal categories of the usual bourgeois philosophies operate in essence with phantasms, empty abstractions, explained in social-genetic terms, but empty nonetheless. The process of thought cannot be understood in isolation from objective social practice. The process of thought cannot be understood except through examining social being and social consciousness. The process of thought cannot, therefore, be understood on the basis of emaciated, one-sided abstractions of intellectual function, transformed into a supreme philosophical "I," which sometimes even imagines, like Diderot's demented piano, that all the melodies of the world are being played out within it. Robinson Crusoes, that is, isolated "I's," are no more admissible as philosophical subjects than they are as constructs in economic theory. Marxism drives them out from both areas. Consequently, the sociology of thought must act as the prolegomena for any real philosophy.

23

Sociology of Thought: Mode of Production and Mode of Presentation

Here, however, we make the shift to examining another problem, that of the well-known sociomorphism of social consciousness. In other words, we turn to addressing the question of the "mode of presentation," which according to Marx, corresponds to the "mode of production."

The dependence of thought on the social positions of the thinker, the existence of a social-historical "style of thought," "spirit of the epoch," "dominant ideas," and so on was already felt as a problem in the tropes of Pyrrho, but this was not expressed clearly. Francis Bacon, in his doctrine of the "idols of the tribe" and the "idols of the theater" posed this question in a relatively clear form as a doctrine of biased public opinion, or of the error through which every subsequent judgment passes.

In recent times, a prominent quasi-Catholic philosopher, Max Scheler, whose thought was sophisticated by Marxism, has concerned himself especially with questions of the sociology of knowledge.[1] In his fundamental work on sociologically defined forms of knowledge, he even worked out a whole table of dominant ideological orientations, specifically meant, on the one hand, for what he described as the upper class and, on the other, for the underclass.

Marx, as is well known, put forward the position that the mode of production determines the mode of presentation. By the mode of production,

Marx (*Capital*, vol. 2) understood "that particular character and method" by which the "personal and material" factors of production were united.

This mode of production "distinguishes separate economic epochs of the social structure," separate "social-economic formations." By the mode of presentation, Marx had in mind the ideological form in which cognitive material is organized.

This dependency is not sucked out of anyone's thumb, and is not the product of any a priori consideration. This dependency is a real fact, and whatever society we might care to pick, we see certain general ideas taking shape; these are the ideological reflex of a quite definite mode of production, the dominant ideas of the ruling class, the bearers of a particular mode of production, and often, the ideas of an antagonist class as well, thinking within the same general forms.

With the rise of private property, with the division of societies into class opposites and the polarization of classes, and with the division of labor into mental and physical, supervisory and subordinate, the dualism of matter and spirit became a general form of thought, a general mode of presentation, with its more concrete variants corresponding to various types of class society and to various modes of production.

A human being is divided into two essences: soul and body, spirit and flesh. "Our whole being consists of spirit and body; the spirit is like the master in us, while in the body we have, rather, a slave," we read in Sallust (*De Catilinae coniuratione*, Bk. I).[2]

The soul is an active, commanding, integral principle; the body is a passive, inert, suffering principle. In the period of the early tribal system, in the epoch of primitive animism, the soul was conceived of as a small copy of the person as a whole, present inside the person and determining his or her behavior. Later, the soul became increasingly spiritualized, and was transformed into entelechy, an invisible spiritual substance that could not be perceived with the senses and that was counterposed to the material body.

In exactly the same way, the world was divided into two principles. One of these was the world spirit, God, the creator and founder; or the "primal cause"; or providence; or an all-fulfilling, undefined, faceless spirit, a general principle of entelechy, a purpose-in-itself—at any rate, an active, determining, commanding principle. Counterposed to it was matter, which was inert, external, passive, suffering, obedient, and crude.

In essence, all thought revolved within these forms. They could be—and were—more anthropomorphic and personal, or less anthropomorphic and relatively impersonal, but they existed as a type of sociomorphism, as reflections of the basic distinguishing mark of class-divided society, all of whose real life was permeated by this profound duality. After what we have said earlier, this fact does not seem strange; if practice as a whole takes place within these forms, if they constitute the form of social life, then it follows naturally that as acknowledged being, they are also the form of social consciousness. For thought, the social structure turns out to be somewhat similar (with all the conditions that apply to the analogy!) to the structure which the sensory organs have in relation to sensation. Sensation also exists in the individual-biological, in the purely biological individual. Thought exists only in the socialized individual, in the social human being. It is abbreviated, a shortened mold, the generalization of social practice which occurs in polarities (it should be stressed that we are speaking here of class societies). Therefore, especially from the point of view of the dominant class and its *ideologische Stände*, the human being is divided, the world is divided, and even a concept, as something universal, acts as a commanding principle with relation to the individual; in this hypostatization of the general and idolization of it, we find idealism of all varieties, and in the very formation of a concept in its embryonic form, as Lenin defined it, the possibility of idealism is already present. It becomes reality because the "manufacturers of ideology" think in ways corresponding to their social position.

The great slave-owning despotisms of antiquity—Egypt, Babylon, and Assyria—were huge affairs whose internal structures were characterized by the incredibly strong, emotionally-charged distance between the ruling theocratic elite and the slaves who made up the base of the social pyramid. The main features of this social system, this order, were also reflected in the corresponding cosmogonies, which served the function of ideology. In the evolution of gods, one can even trace the evolution of the social and economic structure. Was it really not the case that Aristotle's idea of the cosmos, an idea to which we referred earlier, was cast from the mold of the state of Alexander the Great, with the appropriate "idealization" and "sublimation" of categories?

Did feudal religions, beginning with Western European feudalism and ending, for example, with the so-called "nomadic feudalism" of the Mongols, not correspond fully to the feudal social structure? One has only to take the *Summa Theologica* of St. Thomas Aquinas, with its hierarchy of "forms," to see immediately that it was cast in the mold of feudal social organization. Why, under feudalism, did God usually bear the features of a personal God? Because feudal relations were openly personal forms of dependency. Why, with the transition to capitalism, was God spiritualized? Because the impersonal power of money, the power of the market, its "elemental behavior," now appeared on the scene as a structural characteristic of society. ("Pure" social types, of course, have never existed anywhere, and therefore the modes of presentation have not been absolutely pure either.)

Why is it that at present, in the fascist countries, a shift is taking place from categorical imperatives, handed down by God as an indefinite "principle," "substance," and so on, to a hierarchically ordered cosmos with its values set out by decree and with a personal god at its head? Why is this proceeding all the way to Wotan, who is backed up by Fate, declinable in all the grammatical cases? For the reason that to the feudalization of capitalist productive relations there corresponds the feudalization of the mode of representation, on a common basis of crisis.

Why does the philosophy of the bourgeoisie, from a metaphysic of indefinite categories, make the shift to teleological mysticism? For the same reason. It is not hard to show that the elements of corporatist, hard-labor state capitalism and the monopolies that characterize fascist society have reoriented the whole ideology of the ruling class: all of science, philosophy, and religion. The central, dominant idea has become that of the hierarchical whole, with a hierarchy of values such as ranks and estates (that is, classes), and with enslavement of the lower orders as inferior. We have already seen plenty to convince us of this on the previous pages.

Why has religion died out in the USSR as a form of consciousness? Because its social base has been abolished. Why, in the USSR, is dialectical materialism becoming the world view of everyone, a universal world view? Because class society here is becoming extinct. Because theory is being united with practice. Because the abyss between mental and physical labor is being filled in. Because the thousand-year dualism of social life is being done away with. If it were not for these basic factors, no decrees would have their goals realized, no measures would suffice to destroy the accustomed mode of presentation, and religion would flourish for a long time to come.

Let us stress once again: it is not being argued that science and the world view as a whole are molded exclusively after the social life of society in the narrow sense of the word. It is not being argued that, for example, the theorems of geometry are reflections of social groups, or that botany reflects the class struggle in the study of the growing season, or that the names of medicines are the coded record of social cells. Such a view would be stupid, obtuse, and narrow-minded. Here we are talking about stylistic aspects of thought, about the forms in which thought functions on the social scale, about the mode of presentation, which does not by any means do away with the ideas themselves, just as a mode of production does not do away with the products.

As an object of cognition, the world is huge and diverse. Its reflections, the reflections of these innumerable aspects of the world in its variegated relations and mediations, are also diverse. But the effort is being made to fit all this gigantic material into a few general intellectual forms, into modes of presentation, special modes of coordination of these various aspects, while the dualist conception (in its different versions) also introduces the aspect of the ideological distortion of real things, processes, and relations.

Outside of the USSR, there is not a single known instance in which a ruling class as a whole has reasoned materialistically, that is, including atheistically. There have been periods when classes striving for power have, at particular stages, contained relatively large groupings with materialist inclinations (for example, the Encyclopedists), and this is easily explicable. There have been numerous cases of oppressed classes formulating their world view in the same way as their oppressors (see, for example, the religious gloss placed upon the peasant wars, and the corresponding ideology of all the factions of peasants, artisans, and even apprentices). One case is known in which a class striving for power has posed its ideology in forms counterposed to the ruling mode of presentation and fundamentally hostile to it; this class is the proletariat, the bearer of a new mode of production, the socialist mode of production, fundamentally hostile to the capitalism that has outlived its time.

"The opposition of the power of landed property, resting on personal relations of domination and enslavement, and the impersonal power of money is expressed perfectly in two French proverbs: *Nulle terre sans seigneur* and *L'argent n'a pas de maître*" (Marx, *Capital*, vol. 1).[3] Now, under modern capitalism, the power of capital is again personified in oligarchic families and in their political expression. Hence the change of intellectual forms and the transition from a causality which was impersonal (though with the smell of hidden anthropomorphism), and which much more faithfully reflected one of the types of real relationship in the actual world, to the open preaching of consistent teleology, which distorts this relationship of the objective world in basic, fundamental fashion. The shift to dialectical necessity as the dominant element in social thought presupposes a dialectically necessary leap into the "realm of freedom," inhabited so far only by the Soviet Union.

It is not hard to show that such ideological fetishes, popular in the capitalist market, as those of "pure" science, "pure" art, "pure" morality, and "pure" cognition are reflexes of dissociated, externally isolated functions, whose social links, as a result of the division of labor, have vanished from the field of consciousness. The corresponding types of intellectual labor are understood not as parts of the aggregate social labor, but as pure activity "in itself." Accordingly, the products of this intellectual labor also become "things-in-themselves." The longer the objective chain of separate links of labor, and the further removed a particular type of labor from direct material practice, in other words, the more abstract a given sphere of activity, the clearer the tendency to assert its "purity"; the categories of this activity are then transformed in the heads of its subjects into a substitute for the real world. Just as for Pythagoras, the symbols of mathematics became the essence of the universe, for Kantians the norms of morality are transformed into categorical imperatives, orders from the other world. Laws of nature, instead of being necessary relations between things and processes in particular combinations, become something hidden within things or standing above them and directing them, as some kind of special force. In short, the fetishization of categories is clearly evident here.

From everything that has been said earlier, it follows that in dialectical terms, that is, in rounded fashion, a concept can only be understood in relation to its material and social-material sources, that is, only from the point of view of dialectical materialism. The same must also be said of scientific or philosophical conceptions. They have to be understood in relation to the outside world: as objects of cognition both logically and socially-genetically; from the point of view of the external world; from the point of view of their truthfulness; from the point of view of their continuity and their place in the realm of ideas; from the point of view of their social-material origins; and from the point of view of their function in the life of society. Otherwise, the understanding will be dry, one-sided, and metaphysical; that is, it will be incomplete understanding, or incomprehension.

Here an insidious question arises: If in every epoch cognition, as a socially conditioned process, has its own peculiar sociomorphism, that is, a sort of social subjectivism, how is cognition of real relations possible?

After everything that has been said above, it is not hard to answer this question.

First, it should be said that the presence, figuratively speaking, of something like structural eyeglasses does not even for a minute do away with the object of cognition itself. Only an extreme degree of degeneration of a particular mode of production, with the process of cognition transformed into one of naked myth-making (this cannot, of course, exist in absolute form) will lead to the object of cognition disappearing from consciousness. Usually, an ideological distortion is present; the roots of this are located in the dual, divided social structure and in the divorce of theory from practice. Describing an enormous circle, however, real historical development is again uniting—in socialism—the functions which class society has split apart. The dialectical triad proceeds in parallel with the triad: common property—private property (of various types)—common property. This triad runs as follows: unity of theory and practice—divorce of theory and practice—unity of theory and practice. Just as in the first triad the return to the starting point is a return on a new basis, gigantically, unbelievably enriched, so with the second triad as well.

Initially, the unity of theory and practice was a wretched affair, since theory was practically nonexistent, and practice was as scanty as a beggar's purse. The unity of theory and practice in socialism, where the watershed between mental and physical work is being abolished, is arising on the basis of the gigantic wealth of the productive forces, of technology, of science, and of the personal qualifications of the workers. This is not a return to the barbarism and undifferentiated, herdlike mass of primitive communism. This is a new system of labor, rejecting the private property of the disappearing formations, but resting on all their conquests and moving labor and cognition forward at an extraordinary rate. It also follows that corresponding to this is a dialectical materialist method of cognition, the "unity of the practical and theoretical idea," to use the language of Hegel. However, this "mode of presentation" (such is its objective property) does away with the ideological distortion that has as its basis the division of labor and the disintegration of labor into mental and physical work. Together with the elimination of dualism from life, from being, dualism is also eliminated from cognition; that is, a profound and basic ideological distortion, that has existed for thousands of years, is done away with. To have wiped out religion in the consciousness of millions of people is already a gigantic step along the way to a full liberation of cognition and consciousness from its dualist fetters. In this way, and from this point of view, the position of Engels on the prehistory and history of humankind is being vindicated.

Refining and summarizing this latter question, as a question of the theory of cognition, we come up with the following dialectical movement:

PRIMITIVE COMMUNISM	CLASS SOCIETY	COMMUNISM
I. Unity of necessity and purpose	Elemental necessity as negation of the purpose (this in a commodity and commodity-capitalist economy)	Unity of necessity and purpose
II. Unity of theory and practice, with theory close to zero	Divorce of theory from practice	Unity of theory and practice on an enriched basis
III. Unity of analysis and synthesis, with their level	Divorce of analysis and synthesis	Dialectical unity of analysis and synthesis
IV. Realm of the undifferentiated concrete	Realm of the abstract	Realm of the dialectical concrete

And so forth. The new integral human beings, themselves representing the living unity of diverse functions, and the new integral society also practice a new, truly dialectical and materialist thinking. The mode of production has its own complete, historically progressive mode of presentation.

Here it is necessary to say more about an extremely important question; unless this is clarified, the whole problem of the sociomorphism of cognition cannot really be solved and may, in its incorrect interpretation, lead to curious idealistic notions such as Bogdanov's empiriomonism, that is, one of the varieties of idealism.

The question is as follows: Are the sociomorphic eyeglasses, as we described them metaphorically, no more than social-subjective forms, or is there an extra-social, objective content concealed behind them? The answer must be the latter. A natural law is something that exists objectively, and is independent of humanity. Necessity is a relationship of things and processes; it is indifferent to the presence or absence of a subject who, even if he or she exists, might discover this necessity or not discover it. If the subject discovers it, the source is the external world and its real relationships. Therefore, law and necessity, as things which objectively exist, are reflected in the social-intellectual categories of law, necessity, teleology, and so forth. But they may be reflected correctly, or in distorted fashion.

Let us examine this question here from a sociological-philosophical point of view. For this purpose, we shall take the necessity-teleology controversy. Is there something in the real world that actually exists, that is capable of directing people onto a false path? There is. In the first place, there is the practice of humanity itself. That which in its objective relationships, its extra-human relationships, represents a subjective law, in deliberate practice is transformed into a rule. Francis Bacon formulated this law as follows: That which in observation corresponds to a cause, in action corresponds to a rule. If on earth "a body expands under the influence of heat," then "to cause a body to expand, it is necessary to heat it." Secondly, it follows that the purposeful activity of a human being is a fact. Thirdly, as we have seen, in nature purposefulness exists *post factum* as adaptation or adaptability, behind the back of which lurks necessity.

Under the conditions of class-divided society, and of the sublimated ideal forms of this division, however, the sociomorphism of cognition leads to a situation in which the objective laws of nature, natural necessity, are reflected in human social consciousness as superhuman teleology. If we have, for example, the form of "animist causality," of causality as an inner, spiritual "force of things," then here there is objective causality, distorted in consciousness according to the type of human teleology; objects are divided into their "law" and "fact," with the cause interpreted as a spiritual principle relating actively to inert matter, such as ruling tribal elders issuing orders to ordinary mortals, and so forth. As a result, the very concept of "law" (natural law) has turned out to be related genetically to the concept of juridical law, and in the study of so-called natural law, one can trace the whole dialectics of development in this tangle and in distortions that have the solidity of popular prejudice.

In the philosophy of Aleksandr Bogdanov, for whom the objective world disappears, while its scientifically reworked reflection ("the scientific picture of the world," "socially organized experience") takes the place of reality existing outside ourselves, it accordingly happens that the categories of association (such as, for example, animistic causality) are not sociomorphically transformed (and in a number of cases, distorted) reflections of the objective, but merely a projection of social relations, a projection that is outside of and apart from its source in the material natural world. With Bogdanov, this (antidialectical) one-sidedness became so inflated that in this case as well it has led to the creation of real sociomorphism. Here too, only materialist dialectics can yield a correct solution to the problem.

24

On So-Called Racial Thought

From the Marxist point of view, the prolegomena of philosophy are premises of a sociological character.

From the point of view of the "theory" of modern fascism, premises of a biological, or more concretely, racial character serve as such prolegomena.

However miserable and godforsaken the ideology of the nationalist bandits of fascism, a few words must be said about it, since the logical bankruptcy and worthlessness of fascist concepts does not stop them from constituting a definite social force, the ideological force of counterrevolution.

The theoreticians of racial biology hold that the most important, decisive aspect of the type of thinking and of the type of psychological life as a whole (instinctive-unconscious, psychological-ideological, normative, and theoretical) is race, as the primary given factor determining form. Race, as "national character," *Volkstum*, determines virtues, vices, the type of thinking, and science. Einstein's theory of relativity, for example, belongs to Jewish science and is therefore subject to ostracism; fascist theoreticians speak unashamedly of Semitic and Aryan physics, mathematics, and so on. It is true that the gentleman ideologues have not managed to sort out all this rubbish with regard to basic questions; here they have sought indicators of race in external-material objects and processes (the composition of the blood, the shape of the skull, the color of hair and eyes, the length of the nose, the facial angle, the length of the trunk relative to the legs, and so forth); and there they have seized on the relationship to the land and to particular factors of geography. Or else, frightened by materialism, they have begun appealing to "inherent" properties such as "German loyalty," "honor," and other Teutonic virtues, including the virtues of the notorious "blond beast" of Nietzsche, about whom so much has been written and said in recent times. The result has been a barbaric mess. The theories concerning skulls and hair have led to unbelievable confusion, and have often had quite unexpected results. These theories have come into fundamental conflict with idealist mysticism, which requires a rejection of any materialist interpretation of biology, a rejection of the "external." Introducing greater and greater doses of inborn and unchanging mystical virtues to their warrior-gangster conception, replacing the chemical composition of the blood with the "voice of the blood," and the length of the skull with "honor" and "loyalty," the ideologues of fascism finished up in a hopeless tangle. Their theories, false through and through, quickly began turning into empty, strident verbiage.

Consequently, the "scientists" of fascism still proceed from the presence of some constant racial apperception or other—that is, of a "mode of presentation," defined not by the mode of production, but by race. What, how, and why remains obscure.

But let us cross over to analyzing the main theses of racial "theory." Here we should note the following salient points.

First, there are no pure races. Let us take, for example, the Japanese, the closest friends of German fascism, the "Prussians of the East" whom some especially zealous fascist pen-pushers have turned into Aryans. Professor Konrad (see his *Sketch of Japanese History*) reports that ethnically, the Japanese are descended from:

a) migrants from the mainland (principally via Korea), and partly from the direction of the Pacific Ocean (from the Mongolian, that is, Manchurian-Tungus world);
b) people from the Malay-Polynesian world;
c) migrants from the southern coast of China (the ancestors of the present Lolo and Myaouzy tribes); and
d) even earlier settlers on the islands: the Ebisu (Ainu) in central and northern Japan, and the Kumaso (Hayato) on Kyushu.[1]

In mythology, these processes became superimposed one upon the other as different strata of tribes: the "deities of the earth" (Tigi), the "gods of the heavens" (Tendzin), and the "descendants of heaven" (Tenseon). The center of the unifying anthropological-ethnographic process was the Tenson tribe, which along with the Idzumo tribe formed the core of the conquering Yamato tribe. It should not be thought, however, that the above-listed components were "pure." In reality, they in turn were the complex product of ethnic interbreeding. Such is the situation with the "Prussians of the East," the Japanese, who in the person of nationalist ideologues have prided themselves to an uncommon degree on their racial purity, the purity of a people chosen by God.

We shall next take the Germans, now led by the gentlemen racists. Only an absolute ignoramus could accept the thesis of the purity of the "German stock" (or of some variant such as the "Nordic race"). Germans, Celts, Slavs, Lithuanians, and Romance elements (right up to Huguenot emigrants, at one time pouring out of France) all became mixed into a single national mass (this is not to speak of Jews and other ethnic groups, such as Hungarians). Each of these constituent elements was also the product of interbreeding. It is illustrative that the parents of German racist ideology were all non-Germans by origin; Chamberlain was an Englishman, de Lagarde was French, and Eugen Dühring (earlier a fervent anti-Semite) was of Swedish descent. As for the Aryan ancestry of the Germans (the purest Aryans are usually considered to be the Persians—Iranians and Indians, although some of the "very purest" Persians, the Iranians, are close to the "purest" Semites, the Jews), recent linguistic research has shown an affinity between the Germans and the Svanetians and Etruscans, that is, people of the so-called Japhetic group, to which the late Academician N. Ya. Marr devoted a great deal of work.[2] (Compare Friedrion Braun, *Die Übervölkerung des Europas und die Herkunft der Germanen*).

We shall leave to one side the works attempting to show the Jewish origin of the Germans (Sebald Herman), mentioning this only to illustrate the hopeless confusion. Here it will suffice to point to the diffuseness of the very concept of Aryanism. What is there in the appearance of a Persian or Indian to link them to a Swede or a Prussian? What do Brahmanism and Buddhism in India have in common with the religion of Wotan and Thor as recorded in the German-Scandinavian myths? There would seem to be very little.

Any serious person, while of course recognizing the existence of historically established races and nations, would quite rightly deny their definiteness and purity. The purity of races is a myth, a made-up legend. Still more stupid is the thesis of the purity of nations. These have come together in the course of historical time, with the process also including an anthropological-ethnographic element, involving the interbreeding of diverse ethnic currents.

Secondly, the thesis that asserts the permanence of racial (or national) "spiritual properties," orientations, dominant psychological traits and ideological tendencies is quite false. Of course, there are certain relatively stable features that go to make up so-called "national character," and which are associated with peculiarities of geography and climate and with so-called "historical fate," that is, with the concrete particularities of the historical process. These features, however, are in truth a negligible quantity compared to the vast historical changes in the psychology of peoples. Germany provides the best example. At one time, during the French Revolution, the Germans were regarded as barbarians. Then they were transformed into a nation of dreamers, inhabiting a country of poets and philosophers. When railroads were first being built it was written of the Germans that they were not fit for commercial-industrial life, and that railroads would conflict with the calm patriarchal-melancholic constitution and character of the German people. The Germans, it was remarked, were not Italians, with their banks, commerce, overseas operations, industry, and so forth. Later, the German national character became that of the most industry-oriented people in Europe. Now the fascists are fostering militarism, the barracks, bloodthirsty predatory bellicosity, and so on. The country of poets and thinkers has been transformed into a country of mercenaries and praetorians. Meanwhile, what has the so-called *âme slave*, the "Slavic soul" of the Russians, been transformed into? Into its complete opposite. This is because the conditions of social existence have changed fundamentally. And what vast changes are occurring, for example, in China, which from being an inert and immobile country with immensely strong routines and an incomparable traditionalism, has been transformed into a seething cauldron of wars and revolutions, the site of an extremely tense and tragic struggle and of abrupt changes in all the country's main orientations? And so on, and so forth.

From this it is clear that to assert the permanence of dominant psychological and ideological traits which are supposedly immanent in nations (not to speak of races) is pure rubbish, with absolutely nothing to justify it. The relatively durable elements are infinitesimally small compared with the overall susceptibility to change, which is conditioned not by the stable factor of climate, but by a mutable factor, social being.

Thirdly, the arguments for anti-Semitism and the declaring of Semites to be a culture-negating quantity, an "Asiatic plague," as Dühring put it, are absolutely preposterous.

The Semites, as is well known, include:

1. the Arameans (Syrians and Chaldeans);
2. the Assyrians and Babylonians;
3. the Arabs;
4. the Phoenicians;
5. the Jews.

One would need to be a complete ignoramus not to know of the enormous cultural role played by these peoples. Chaldean astronomy is well known. So too are the great cultures of Assyria and Babylon, with their canals, wonderful roads, palaces, temples, fortresses, gigantic world cities (Babylon and Nineveh), architecture, sculpture, system of writing, literature, legislation, astronomy, medicine, mathematics, engineering, and so forth. The traditions of the Babylonian calendar, numerical system, pharmacology, and so on, not to speak of legends of Babylonian origin (by way of the Hebrew Bible), have been retained into our own times. The Arabs made remarkable discoveries in the fields of mathematics, geography, medicine, philosophy, literature, architecture, and so on. Spain under Arab rule was an extremely cultured country with famous universities. It was through the Arabs that Europe managed to obtain the works of the great thinkers of ancient Greece, including Aristotle. The Arabs during the years when they flourished in Europe were truly the flowers of culture. And what about the mysterious ancient Phoenicians? Who does not know of the Phoenician alphabet? Or the wonderful Phoenician cities and colonies? Or the daring voyages made by the Phoenicians to the Baltic Sea and Ceylon? Or great Carthage, a former Phoenician colony which was transformed into a mighty republic, fighting for dominance against Rome itself in the Punic wars, during which Hannibal Barca revealed his military genius? And did the Hebrew Bible not become the most important and familiar book of the European peoples? Was it not a semi-mythical Jewish messiah who became the God of Europe? Cromwell's Roundheads sang psalms, and the American pioneers who founded the United States went to war with these songs on their lips, not to speak of what was happening in Europe. The great mind of Spinoza, the brilliant talent of Heine, the super-genius Marx, the scientific genius Einstein—did these really bear witness to the backwardness and inferiority of Jews? Anti-Semitism is indeed the "socialism" of fools, as old August Bebel remarked.

Fourthly, history tells us of the changing historical role of various races and nations, not of a simple, straightforward process. Races and nations change places in response to very complex historical causes, and in line with this, their cultural-historical role changes as well. The black races, which in some cases possess age-old civilizations, are not an exception. The black Meros state at one time ruled all of great Egypt. China, which by the twentieth century had fallen into decay, was once the seat of a great civilization. Backward Russia became the pioneer of socialism. Races, peoples, and nations do not develop uniformly. Everything here is mobile, not shut tight by some lock consisting of a priori essences of an extrahistorical character. As for the messianic role which the fascists reserve for the "Nordic race," this ideology has been encountered in diverse historical variants and on numerous types of historical soil among a great many peoples, starting with the Jews as the "chosen people." What about the "god-bearing people" and the mission of Russia according to the Slavophiles (Khomyakov, the Kireyevs and Aksakovs, Konstantin Leontyev, and others)?[3] The messianism of the Japanese samurai and of their ideologues and practical exponents such as Araki? What about the *mania gloriosa* of Mussolini, proclaiming the world-historical role of the new Rome? It is enough to list these examples, since one could spend a great deal of time on this pursuit.

Fifthly, the concrete development of the racist position has had quite amazing results. First Alfred Rosenberg declared the entire proletarian revolution in Russia to be a revolt by Mongoloids against the Aryan elite of the German-Aryan imperial bureaucracy.[4] Then those undoubted Mongoloids, the Japanese, were transformed into Aryans to meet the demands of current fascist policy. First it was argued fiercely that John the Baptist, Jesus, and the apostle Paul were pure Aryans encircled by Jews. Then Christianity was declared a plague, and replaced by a purely Aryan-Nordic religion of the "god of the gallows," Wotan. First, from the lips of Driesmans, the creations of Dante, Michelangelo, Leonardo da Vinci, and Torquato Tasso were explained by the penetration into Italy of long-headed Germans. Then the Roman virtues of Mussolini's cohorts were lauded. First the fascists went into raptures over the achievements of German science during the war. Then the great chemist Haber, who had saved Germany with his discoveries (nitrates out of the air), was effectively driven out of the country because he was Jewish. First Luther was declared in the works of Woltmann to have been the embodiment of the victory of Germanism over the "Roman-Latin clerical principle," said to be "the bearer of

Jewish commercial and juridical morality (!)."[5] Then Luther was declared a traitor to the German people, since Christianity in general was a Jewish plague. First Goethe is declared a great example of Aryan-German genius. Then in the works of the wife of Field Marshal Ludendorff, Goethe is smeared with mud as a cosmopolitan and a Freemason, and is proclaimed the physical killer of the blond, truly German Schiller. And so forth.

The effect is even more comic when nationalists of different nations are juxtaposed. German fascists declare Bolshevism to be a Russian-Asiatic plague introduced into Europe. Meanwhile, the well-known Russian emigré philosopher Semyon Frank declares the same Bolshevism to be a Western European plague introduced into Russia.[6] All this helpless blathering, rubbish from A to Z, has nevertheless been turned into an official ideology, and is being disseminated through the use of powerful German technology.

Sixthly, the development of the world economy that has occurred under capitalism has also created a worldwide culture whose ideological elements are divided dialectically on the basis of class. There is Kantianism, Machism, pragmatism, and so forth; Shakespeare, Goethe, Heine, Tolstoy, and Dostoevsky; Darwin, Helmholtz, Haeckel, Faraday, and Maxwell; Diesel and Edison; Pavlov; Rutherford, Nils Bohr, and the Curies; Beethoven, Wagner, Debussy, Tchaikovsky, and many more. They have all entered the worldwide circulation of ideas. Marxism and Leninism, too, have become international phenomena. The explosion of rabid nationalism is not an immanent property of a race, but the ideological and political expression of imperialism in its last phase, of imperialism on the threshold of its collapse, which is linked to the dramatic sharpening of capitalist contradictions and to the general crisis of capitalism.

From this it follows that the modern fascist "mode of presentation," as the final antithesis to the socialist "mode of presentation," does not express a racial-biological antithesis, but a social-historical antithesis, a class antithesis. The ideological structures of the two camps that are fighting this last battle do not have their roots in the composition of the blood or in the color of people's hair, not in national peculiarities "in themselves," not in eternal and extrahistorical orientations of races and nations, but in socially and historically conditioned class positions. Classes that are polar opposites embody, represent, and fight for counterposed modes of production and being, for counterposed cultures and ideologies, for whole living orientations in the totality of their diverse functions.

For the solving of philosophical problems, this fascist "mode of presentation" signifies an enormous step backward, since it draws its understanding of the subject from an abstraction of a social human being (which was featured in the old bourgeois philosophy) either in the direction of a biological-racial abstraction, that is, a zoological one, or toward a medieval-teleological "mode" of hierarchically immobile thinking, of thinking in the categories of medieval scholasticism and mysticism. However much it prides itself on being anti-Christian and anti-Asian, in its anti-intellectualism it duplicates the Eastern mystics, the Church fathers, and the Christian mystics. After all, it is precisely these latter who considered thought to be a plague, an ulcer, a hell; these were the people who considered reason to be a creature of Satan, a wanton woman. In the *Upanishads* it is said that anyone who experiences the world rationally knows nothing. Lao-tze maintained that life and rational cognition were incompatible.

There is nothing that characterizes the complete rottenness of the racial-mystical orientation so thoroughly as this rejection of reason. The biological prolegomena of thought, as they are understood by the fascist philosophers, are in fact an ideological illusion. In reality, the springs of the social-historical process operate here as well. The logic of "biology" in this case reflects a concrete social and historical setting, and analysis of this logic once again confirms the fundamental truths of Marx's historical materialism. The social being of a class that is doomed and perishing, that is making desperate, brutal lunges, defines both the class itself and its social consciousness. The rejection of rational cognition and its replacement with mysticism is a testimony to intellectual poverty, which from the point of view of world history deprives this class of the right to historical existence. No one should raise petty objections to this formula; it is, of course, simply a metaphor. Nevertheless, it is an expression of reality. It signifies that tendencies of a progressive type, that is, tendencies associated with life, have become incompatible with the existence of a class which cannot go forward and which only looks backward. For precisely this reason, the class is forced to wage a struggle against reason and against reasoned cognition, whose development on a general scale poses an ever greater threat to the rotten, decadent system of the exploiters. The renewal of modern philosophical thought will not pass along these roads.

25

Social Position, Thought, and "Experience"

Racial-biological presumptions therefore have to be thrown out, or more accurately, reduced to the minimal significance that race in fact possesses. Marx's doctrine of the mode of production, which determines the mode of presentation, remains in full force. National peculiarities are merely an additional coefficient, a concrete form of manifestation of what is basic and decisive. Meanwhile, it should be noted that these peculiarities also lie in the specific features ("national" and so forth) of the material conditions of life, that is, of the mode of production itself in its particular historical concreteness. Feudalism is everywhere feudalism. Nevertheless, the so-called "nomadic feudalism" of the Mongols had its peculiar characteristics, just like Russian feudalism in comparison with that of Western Europe. American capitalism has its specific features, which can be explained by the concrete historical conditions of development of the United States (free land, relatively high wages, minimal feudal relations, the social choice of European Anglo-Saxon settlers, and so forth), just like any other capitalism. The slave-owning system of ancient Greece was not the same as the slave-owning theocracy of ancient Egypt or Babylon. The caste-based social order of India, the social system of ancient China, the Inca state, and so on—all had features in common and features that were unique. Such is the dialectics of the general and the particular. Nevertheless, within the bounds of one and the same social complex, divided into classes, professions, and so forth, different orientations inevitably arise.

The decisive role, as we have already seen, is played by class positions.

Such are the general premises of a socialist character.

In this context, we would like to pose a question which we have already analyzed to some degree in the course of this work: the question of thought, that is, of thinking in concepts, and of the so-called "experience" of the world that serves as the basis for "direct contemplation," which modern mysticism counterposes to the shortcomings of rational knowledge. We have already analyzed this question from the logical angle; here we shall pose it again from a new point of view, with the stress on the genesis and social significance of this "orientation in the world," especially as regards the fashionable enthusiasm for Indian mysticism and Eastern mysticism in general.

For Georg Simmel (see his works *Sociology*, *Philosophy of Money*, and *Social Differentiation*, as well as his work on the crisis of culture), two concepts play a major role.[1] These are the concepts of social differentiation (Simmel constantly glosses over the fundamental, decisive division into classes, a division which also expresses the dialectical bifurcation of the whole and the bipolarity of class society; he melts classes down in the concept of endless "social groups") and of position, "attitude," which determines the relations between particular individuals and the world. From this point of view the relations of a human being as subject are extremely varied. The orientations and appraisals of a human individual are diverse and changeable. He or she might relate to the world in a passive-contemplative manner; or in active, practical fashion; or aesthetically; or cognitively-critically; or naively; or in a religious way; and so on.

If we take all these definitions in their rational form, we can show 1) that social being determines social consciousness; 2) that the mode of production determines the mode of presentation; 3) that the mode of presentation has its concrete "national" peculiarities associated with the national peculiarities of the mode of production; 4) that within society each class develops its own orientations, evaluations, and so on; 5) that within classes there are varying orientations, linked to the character of various groups and the nature of the divided social labor; 6) that as social being changes, these orientations of social consciousness change as well; 7) that the range of orientations may be more or less broad within the same social group, and that this diversity may be destroyed if the social structure is such that specialization narrows life to an extreme one-sidedness.

Now that we have established these premises, we shall also find it relatively easy to analyze the question which modern-day Rousseauism of the

Indian-Chinese model takes up *con amore*. We have already spoken of this Rousseauism in Theodor Lessing's book, which the notorious Count Hermann Keyserling considers a highly authoritative source on Indian philosophy in general and Indian mysticism in particular.

At first sight it seems bizarre, paradoxical, and simply incomprehensible that Brahmanism, and later Buddhism, representing the ideology of the ruling classes, should have become established as an ascetic system, then grown into a doctrine of pure contemplation, and so on. (We are not talking here about the initial period of Buddhism, when the legendary Sakya-Muni, abandoning his palace, went among the poor and outcast, became an intercessor for the *sudra* and *brazida*, and developed his doctrine of the non-acceptance of the sensory world.)

Briefly speaking, this can be explained as follows:

In no country has there ever been as elaborate, strict, and rigid a system of caste divisions as in India, where the elite are "holy," and the pariahs are "worse than a worm in the gut of a dog." For such a social pyramid to be maintained, it was necessary to devise exceptionally effective means of acting on the masses, means that would transform the ruling theocratic oligarchy into higher beings, incommensurable with ordinary mortals. In Egypt an enthusiasm for size, embodied in the idea of rank, led to the building of colossal "eternal" pyramids and grandiose statues of pharaohs, as well as to ritual mysticism, and so forth. In India this would not be enough. Here the theocratic elite had to create things in practice that seemed like miracles to others; the elite had to show itself to be capable in fact of things of which ordinary mortals were incapable. The fact that ruling classes usually have a monopoly of knowledge had to take on an especially potent form, an unprecedented intensity that would transform the theocratic elite into beings of another order. Given the stagnant nature of economic and technical development, "progress" here could take only one direction: transforming the very physiological (and therefore psychological) nature of the rulers. The Indian theocracy achieved this in actual fact. Let us listen to our authoritative mystic:

> The Greek word *myste*, mysticism (*muo*) means "end." Here there is an end to respiration (*odem*) (Sanskrit *âtman*, Old Hebrew *ruash*):
>
> *Râya-yoga* and *tarîva* (the capacities for lucid, wakeful super-consciousness) serve to allow the sages of India to reduce inhalation and exhalation. The full suppression

and exclusion of these would mean the ending of the circulation of the blood and of the other processes of life; this coincides with the attainment of nirvana.

This origin for the concept of mysticism points the way to the ultimate profundities. Since every act (*fat*) of the spirit, such as attention, desire, self-possession, thought, and so on is characterized by self-stressing (*Sichanspannen*), which in bodily form manifests itself in an involuntary halt to respiration, all ... the secret teachings of Asia are collections of directive rules and exercises in concentration, in the mastering and suppression of the vital rhythms (*Lebens Laucher*).[2]

What follows from this?

The result of this is that the basis of the mysticism of the Indian priest-sages consists in physical training plus hypnosis, brought to a remarkable state of perfection, which mystics in Europe, where the orientation has been toward things, have not reached even approximately. The stagnation of the material culture has caused it to be replaced here by a gigantic culture of the will, aimed at surmounting the will. This is "pure contemplation," "immersion in the object," "fusion with the world," "direct experience," "mysticism," the mastering of one's body and of the realm of the passions. For centuries, from generation to generation, passing on their experience to their heirs, choosing the especially capable, cultivating *askesis*, practicing ascetic exercises, creating a whole huge culture of this training that was unknown to Europe, the Indian sages achieved such perfection that in relation to the pariahs, the *sudra* and other castes, they reached an unattainable, angel-like height. Everything else (the norms of behavior of the closed castes, with people kissing the footsteps of a Brahmin and revering his excrement, while regarding a pariah as a leper whom one cannot touch without defiling oneself; the religious doctrine of the transmigration of souls, according to which a breach of caste rules results in reincarnation as some particularly despised animal, and so forth), all mediated this social differentiation.

From this, the following characteristic features are derived: the concentration of attention on the person, on his or her desires, will, and so forth, and not on the objects of the external world; a passive relation to the external world, rather than an active position of attempting to master it; placing the will under stress in order to overcome it, that is, a culture of pure contemplation; concentration on the affective side of mental life, and not on the development of concepts; the non-logic of "spiritual experience," instead of the culture of thought as such; and so forth.

It should not, of course, be thought that all this has been "given" in its "pure" form. Only tendencies are involved. Nor should it be thought that mysticism represents the whole of Indian philosophy; the only people who tell such fables are immoderate proselytes of Indian mysticism. It would also be quite absurd to suppose that contemplation has replaced work, and that the yogi have been feeding a huge country. Such an idea of India is just as absurd as the "classical" idea of ancient Greece, according to which harmonious Greeks went about naked, carved statues, and philosophized, while their daily bread fell down ready-baked into their divine mouths. Nevertheless, since the ideas of the ruling class are normally the dominant ideas in society, it is not surprising that the contemplative position acts as a brake on an active relationship to nature and on an adequate ideological attitude, that is, on active thought in concepts. Meanwhile, the concepts which have grown up on the basis of such orientations toward life and which take shape in accordance with a mode of production whose hierarchy is disconnected and elevated to an enormous height, have become ossified in the form of universal religious-mystical systems: among the popular masses, concrete-natural-animist and fetishistic, and among the elite, more abstract. The sensory notion, the image, the fantasy, and the emotional side of life have therefore taken on a far greater specific weight than in the development of the Western European type.

For all this, it would be a grave error to lose sight of the incommensurability of different modes of production as such. It would be absurd to counterpose Indian theocracy to European capitalism. Meanwhile, precapitalist relations in Europe as well were associated with mysticism and popular romanticism, with animism and a general ascribing of animate properties to the forces of nature, with an endless variety of gods, and with shared experience of natural phenomena. Heine, in his essays on the history of religion and philosophy, provided a wonderful account of this in the case of Germany. The same, however, existed in Russia (just consider Melnikov-Pechersky),[3] in Ireland, in France, and everywhere else. To absolutize all these categories is thus quite wrong; this would be to approach these phenomena in a rationalistic, schematic, one-sided, and generally barren fashion.

The life of the senses and a sensory relationship with nature, however, do not necessarily presume mystical or mystical-religious forms. Meanwhile, the gentlemen mystics, including admirers of Indian mysticism, start out from precisely this quite incorrect premise. The religious form represents embryonic thought, and thought of a sociomorphic type; this can very easily be shown from the history of all religions without exception, beginning with the cult of ancestors, tribal elders, heroes, and so on, and finishing with kings of heaven and impersonal abstractions with their compelling force. Confucius, as we have noted, says: "In order to have a good life, it is not necessary to make a new plow, as happens in the western half of the earth, but to do some good deed for plants, animals, or people. For if we loved the sea like our own souls, we would not drown in it, and if we loved fire as we love ourselves, it would not burn us." Here we see not simply a common experience of nature, but also a rejection of concepts, goals, calculation, and account-keeping (things that Theodor Lessing finds so detestable), though all this is present in a primitive, animistic form. There is of course a difference between the life of the intellect and emotional life, between thought and feeling, between a system of concepts ("cold reason") and emotional experience ("hot blood"); or, as this dichotomy is now explained, between "spirit" and "soul," although there is no Great Wall of China separating one from the other. It is true that the specific structure of capitalism has divided city from countryside, culture from nature, theory from practice, and thought from feeling. An excellent example is provided by Kant, who never traveled beyond the outskirts of Königsberg, and who scarcely ever left his study to go out into Königsberg, except for his precisely measured daily walks. The life of capitalism, which in itself and as a whole is irrational, is rationalized down to trivial details on the individual level. The constant posing of goals and drawing up of accounts are among its characteristic properties; it turns life into a universal tactic, while emotional life is confined almost exclusively to the erotic. This impoverishment of life, and the hypertrophy of the intellectual as a result of the curtailment of the emotional (and by no means because of an "excess of mind" as such!) represents the real one-sidedness of humanity under capitalism.

Nevertheless, the question of many-sidedness and one-sidedness, of the one-sidedness or universality of vital content, is not by any means the same as the question of the type of cognition. Meanwhile, the mystics smuggle this very question in, even though in their terminology they try to muddy the waters. For them, experience (contemplation, nirvana, and so on) consists of immersion in the depths of being, in the timeless and extraspatial essence of things, in the "genuine world." If they were concerned, and only concerned, with enriching the content of human life through the shared experience of nature, with the diverse emotions linked to this experience (responses to sensory perceptions, to colors, smells, shapes, and sounds; perceptions of pleasure, joy, exaltation—everything that Avenarius termed the "positive emotional" and the "positive physio-difference"), there would be no disagreement; as we have said already, this question of the mode of living and of spiritual enrichment will be solved by socialism, which does away with the deformity represented by capitalist culture. The mystics argue, however, that rational cognition kills off the essence of the world; that it analyzes a dry mummy, transforms the world into a mathematical formula, replacing the live being with a machine, and the world with a numerical figure.

All these objections we refuted in previous discussion. What does mysticism promise us? The raptures over the Confucian formula are a mystification of Confucius, in whom everything is soberly utilitarian, though on an animist basis. If we were, however, to act according to this formula, nothing good would result. What is there that might replace intellectual cognition? Perhaps real life might, as Lessing suggests, be declared a dream, and a dream declared to be real life?

To this, Hegel in his *Phenomenology* makes a brilliant reply:

> They say that the absolute should not be understood, but felt and contemplated, and that investigation should not be directed by understanding, but by feeling and contemplation....
>
> The role of the baits that are needed to arouse the desire to bite is played by the beautiful, the holy, the eternal, by religion and love; not an idea, but ecstasy, not the coldly developing necessity of a question, but stormy inspiration ought, as they say, to serve to maintain and progressively develop the riches of substance....
>
> Surrendering to the unrestrained ferment of substance, they hope through limiting consciousness and rejecting reason to make themselves the chosen ones of substance, to whom God gives wisdom in their sleep. Nevertheless, everything that they in fact receive and engender in their sleep also belongs solely to the realm of dreams. [4]

This operation, consequently, is as old as the world, and it has not yielded anything fruitful. To put about the slogan "sleep" in the name of life is truly comic.

To urge the rejection of ideas is also to urge the rejection of words. Here the mystics quite consistently proclaim the ultimate wisdom to be ... silence. The wisest individual is the most taciturn one, who says nothing.

Such is also the achievement of Theodor Lessing:

In Sanskrit (we read in Lessing), the word for a sage is *muni*; literally, this means "dumb," no longer speaking. A particularly ancient Egyptian legend tells of the minor god Ammon, who was done reverence only in silence. All that remains to us in legend of the Greek philosopher Cratylus, a pupil of Heraclitus and teacher of Plato, is that at the height of his wisdom he sat in silence, only by turns directing the index finger of his right hand to left and right; by this, he signified the dualism of nature and the divarication of all knowledge. And truly, if I could declare myself a follower of any philosophical trend or school, I would call myself an admirer of Cratylus.[5]

As for Berkeley, so for Cratylus: the denial of the outside world for the sake of a subjective "image" and a return to the "sign language" of primitive savages. The final outcome is the rejection of thought and of human intercourse through speech. A marvelous substitute for rational cognition, and a wonderful instance of penetration into the "uttermost depths" of being! What else does mysticism have to offer? A cataleptic bliss, an indifferent ecstasy, nirvana, ataraxia? These, however, have been familiar to all peoples; even the Russian Khlysty knew them, as did the shamans of Siberia, the Iranian dervishes, and so forth. The "Dionysian" principle was at the heart of these mysteries as well. What relation, however, does this have to cognition of the real associations of the world, the real relationships? If aspects of hypnosis, of hypnotic clairvoyance, of physiological training, and of the corresponding knowledge at times enter in here, these are subject to rational explanation, and in principle there is nothing here that is either mystical or miraculous. A "miracle" is always something negative; there are no miracles, and a miracle which has really happened is not a miracle simply by virtue of the fact that it has occurred.

The mystics do battle in the name of unmediated life, rightly lamenting (and here, as we have seen, there is a real problem) the soullessness of life. But in place of the soullessness of life, they propose to render it meaningless. Pouring out a whole sea of emotions, they do their best to fetter the human intellect and hide it in a cellar. While providing a broad scope for the image of humanity, they nail shut the doors that lead into the realm of concepts. They therefore seek one-sidedness from the other direction; instead of a cultured one-sidedness of the intellect, they pursue an animal-infantile-savage one-sidedness of the emotions. For the mystics, the ideal is a vegetable-animal state as the antithesis to an artificial environment of machinism, calculation, accounting, tactics, and rational science. In other words, we are being urged here to make the transition from logical thought to the prelogical "participation" of which Levy-Bruhl speaks in his work *Les Fonctions Mentales dans les Sociétés Inférieures* (Paris, 1922).

This is not to solve the problem, but to refuse to solve it. No! Socialism will support the great Faustian tradition, the tradition of work, knowledge, struggle, intellect, and feeling, of love, nature, and art. Combining culture and nature, socialism will end the soullessness of civilization; it will create a mighty synthesis of rational cognition and rich emotional life.

26

The Object of Philosophy

Let us cross over now to attempting to provide a positive solution to the basic premises of philosophy. From everything that has been said earlier, there follows above all a historical approach to the subject. So that there should not be any subsequent misconceptions, it should immediately be noted that historically the real world itself became an object, that is, the topic of human practice and thought. The real world existed without relation to the subject, in this sense "in itself," prior to the appearance of humanity, that is, of the subject, which arose historically. The proposition "there is no object without a subject" (and vice versa) is true only when "object" and "subject" are taken in the strict sense, as correlative concepts. The object is always linked to the subject. (In parenthesis, we shall note that not so long ago in relative terms, by the "object" was understood the subject, and by the "subject," the object; the subject was the passive principle, the "object," rather than the other way round. This, however, changes nothing in essence.) From this, it does not by any means follow that the world ceases to exist when it ceases to be the object of thought and action (or has not yet become that).

In just the same way, the object of labor does not cease to be a thing when it ceases to be an object of labor, and the means of production do not cease to be means of production when they cast off the social and specifically historical form of capital. The confusing of the real world with the real world as object, that is, of the real world outside of its relationship to a subject and of the real world in relation to a subject, acts as the foundation for unrestrained quasi-philosophical speculation in which it is literally possible to suffocate.

The real world, it therefore follows, is not in any way bound to the subject by any "fundamental empiriocritical coordination." It is bound to the subject only when it figures as an object, and this position does not represent any particular philosophical wisdom, since it is nothing but a simple tautology. It is important, however, to note that the real world becomes an object historically, because its duality, the separation from it of a thinking organism, is itself a historical process, a particular stage in the development of the real world. (Here we should make the reservation that while we are concerned with the earth, this geocentrism is entirely conditional; we simply do not yet know of thinking beings on other worlds.) This means that the real world also existed without any subject; it did not in any way need a subject in order to exist, since the subject did not create it. Instead, the world and nature at a particular stage gave rise to the subject. Insofar as the latter arose and entered into active relations with the world, the world came to be transformed into an object.

The real world itself is a historically changing quantity, eternally in flux. Least of all is it an immobile and immutable absolute; it is a general process, where everything is in historical movement and undergoing change, since space and time are not subjective forms of apprehension, but objective forms of the existence of matter in motion. Nature has its history just like human society, and there is no fundamental difference here. If we take the earth and its geological history, its transition as a whole from a molten mass to its present state also includes the formation of various substances and their transformation, the formation of complex ores, the appearance of organic bodies, and the rise of thinking matter. The formation of new qualities is a vital aspect of the historical process, just like the disappearance of various others. This is the great objective dialectics of nature, presupposing "disappearing aspects" and an endless diversity of qualities, properties, forms, and relationships of the world as a whole and of its parts.

Organic nature is endowed with a series of properties that distinguish it from inorganic nature. In exactly the same way thinking matter, which has evolved into a subject, does not cease to be at the same time a part of nature with special properties. Consciousness itself, as a specific form of particular material processes, is a real fact, an objective property of matter of a certain quality. From this point of view even hallucination is fact, and it can be, and is, the object of thought. The sciences dealing with mental illnesses do not trail off into nothingness, but are involved in studying something of real substance. One could write a history of illusions and errors, since these are also facts. Hallucinations and ravings stand counterposed (or should be counterposed) to normal consciousness, since there is nothing in the outside world that corresponds to hallucination (that is, to its content). One can (and must) reject hallucination not as a fact arising from an abnormal consciousness, but from the point of view of its relationship to the external; to deny its reality as a process of consciousness would be quite absurd.

Consequently, consciousness too has a predicate of being, and at a particular stage of its development, itself becomes an object of thought; "thinking about thought" is an extremely important part of philosophy. In other words, the relationship between being and thought is a dialectical one, since these opposites interpenetrate one another, and thought exists, has a predicate of being. This being thinks, that is, has a predicate of thought; thinking matter is their real unity. But as we have seen, in this real unity of substances and in the historical *prius* there is matter, without which no spirit can exist, while without the spirit, matter can and does exist in the most diverse forms. In this regard numerous illusions arise, among other reasons because of the objectification of forms of thought. Concepts exist, as products of the mental work of humanity. Categories exist, and to some people seem to be even a priori. Religions exist, as do scientific systems, philosophies, and so forth. These are objectified forms of consciousness. They even take on material form in books and other symbols, receiving, so to speak, a tangible being. But what does all this mean? Does it mean that the spirit has the reality not of a property, but of a substance, that it becomes an independent *causa sui*, to use the old term?[1]

Of course not.

The "objectification" of intellectual forms is nothing other than an expression of their intensively socialized nature, an expression which is often (by no means always—consider the case of religious forms!) linked with the greater or lesser adequacy of their content as a reflection of reality. These forms may be accurate reflections or distorted ones. They do not exist anywhere except—to put it crudely—in the heads of socialized people. They do not fill the space between people like a sort of jelly, a special "thin" substance. Social consciousness in general is the consciousness of socialized people, not a superhuman category. To a certain degree, therefore, it is independent of each individual object of cognition. In exactly the same way, society does not cease to exist when one or another of its members dies. But if all were suddenly to die, there would be neither society nor social consciousness.

Something else needs to be said about the gigantic system of symbols. Their material being, that is, the being represented by printer's ink, for example, and by a certain spatial form, has no relation to the question of the "essence" of consciousness. The "meaning" of a book does not consist in ink and pigskin. Outside of their deciphering, that is, outside of their correlation with the subject, these are not symbols; they have no "meaning," and exist only in their crude and meaningless being, a purely external being like that of any paving stone. Only when this correlation is present is the question transferred to the plane of objectified mental forms, of which we spoke earlier. In this connection, it is curious to note that Herr Professor Werner Sombart, full of enthusiasm for the "sociology of thought" of Max Weber, without the slightest thought and as quick as a monkey, applied the corresponding categories to the external world. It emerged that the real processes of natural reality that we master are mere symbols whose meaning will never be accessible to us, while we shall never master the social processes whose meaning we do understand! According to Sombart, this devil's carousel is humanity's accursed fate.

Hence the real world, with all its properties and features, and with consciousness as a property of one of its parts, becomes an object.

The real world is historical, that is, it is situated in a process of historical change. Its properties are historical, since they are changeable. As an object, the world is historical in the sense that it becomes an object when a historical subject appears. Thinking matter, that is, this historical subject, itself becomes an object. Consciousness is a property of a particular type of matter which arose and which develops historically. Finally, an object is also historical in the sense that it 1) becomes an object historically, to the degree that the practice and theory of the subject grows, and the radius of his or her practical and theoretical orientation expands; the object is continually becoming an object, is being revealed as an object, and is not simply being dumped into this status like a cabbage into a sack; 2) the real world also in part creates itself (though not *ex nihilo*) as a subject; all of the so-called cultural landscape, the whole human-made environment, cities and villages, ditches and roads, cultivated fields, cleared forests, underground mines, and so forth—all this represents the world as transformed by humanity, the "anthropozoic period" of the planet earth, to use the language of geology. Here the historical aspect is already linked directly and immediately with human history.

The one-sidedness of almost all pre-Marxian philosophy consisted in the fact that its object was abstract, unhistorical, and at the same time an object of so-called pure consciousness. Meanwhile, we have already seen what such one-sidedness leads to, and how it is explained (both logically and socially-genetically). Consequently, at the very outset, in the interpretation of the object, a certain flaw is present. In reality, the object is an object of mastering, while the process of mastering is dual in nature; this is both practical and theoretical mastering, with practice having primacy.

As the object of practical mastering, the world is also transformed materially to one or another degree. Theoretical cognition mediates this process, expanding, enriching, and orienting it. If we take as our starting point such an interpretation of the object of philosophy, then by virtue of this all subsequent problems must inescapably be understood in a quite different light; there will be no room for the hypertrophy of the "spiritual," under the influence of which the object evaporated, as it were, being transformed (not in reality, of course, but in the heads of philosophers) into an "idea," a "concept," or some other emaciated, cachetic abstraction located on the upper contours of thought. It is true, as we know, that a series of idealist systems have interpreted the world as the object of creation; this would seem to be an active, ultra-"practical" position. However, the concepts involved here should not be confused. What these systems have been concerned with is the practice of thought, not material practice. The object in this case has not been the historically existing, material, objective world, but the product of the creative activity of the subject. Such "mastering" is illusory; it resolves itself into nothingness, into a mirage, into a mental fog.

The interpretation of an object as the object of practical and theoretical mastering is not by any means an artificial mental trick; on the contrary, it is the only correct interpretation, the only one that accords with historical and present-day reality. It does not represent one among various "points of view," depending on the "convenience of thought" or other analogous considerations. It has a firm basis in the facts of historical reality, where the object acts above all as the object of practical mastering. (Hegel's "assimilation" rests directly and immediately on this.) The object, as the object of theoretical cognition, has in general been able to manifest itself only to the degree that theoretical cognition itself has existed. (Once again we repeat and stress that prior to this the real world, let us say, the earth with all its "riches," incontestably existed, but no one had cognizance of it. Therefore, while existing as the earth, it was not yet the object of the attention of a subject; that is, it still had not become an object *stricto sensu*.)

This theoretical cognition appeared much later in historical terms, separating itself out from practice in a special and more or less autonomous process. In people's consciousness, therefore, the object became divided into two; on the one hand it became the object of practical mastering, and on the other hand, the object of theoretical mastering. "Practicians" have always more or less interpreted the world as matter, having weight, occupying space, showing resistance, requiring effort and the overcoming of resistance. "Theoreticians," to the degree that they are divorced from practice and operate in the general, that is, take as their starting point not direct contact with the real world, but reflections on a relatively exalted level, have replaced the real world with these reflections. It is amusing, for example, to see how the doctrine of the "object of cognition" took root and grew up among "pure logicians." This object consisted of "pure types" and "ideal types" (such as, for example, ideal triangles in geometry or the "ideal types" proposed by Max Weber). The trouble, however, is that these "ideal types," while abstractions, were transformed by philosophers into the "true world."

It is also hard to suppress a smile when a giant such as Hegel writes with complete seriousness, conviction, and thoughtfulness:

> The infinity of animal forms cannot ... be considered with such exactitude as if the necessity of the system were observed with absolute strictness. It is necessary, on the contrary, to elevate general definitions into a rule. If these definitions do not correspond fully to the rule, but nevertheless approximate to it ... then it is not the rule, not the characterization of the type or class and so on, that has to be changed, as if these were obliged to correspond to the given existing forms, but on the contrary, the latter must correspond to the former, since the shortcoming is in the forms. (*Philosophy of Nature.*)[2]

Logically, there is a divorce here from concrete being (since there is a divorce from material practice, from direct contact with the concrete). The "depth" here corresponds to material poverty; there is no ascent to an increasingly full-blooded second concrete, but instead, reality is systematically plucked of all its feathers. The general is torn apart from the specific, the type from the individual, the law from the fact, the abstract from the concrete, and so forth. Consequently, being is also etherealized and spiritualized. Instead of the reality of the world we have an ideal, a concept, a corporal's baton without the army, which is transformed into a shadow. In this manner, the ugly, futile vanity of the concept finds its expression.

As we have already stated, however, a concept also becomes an object of cognition at a particular stage of historical development. Concepts are not material parts of the external world, but reflections of matter organized in a particular way; if we do not accept them as processes of thought, they cannot be the direct objects of material practice. Thought occurs in people's heads, not in a milling machine and not beneath the shaft of a blooming mill. Nevertheless, since its logical make-up is a condensation of social experience, that is, of a vast historical process which also includes practice (of which we spoke earlier), thought as an object of cognition is linked to practice, and cannot be understood dialectically in isolation from this link. This is the first point; the second is that insofar as thought itself mediates the practical process, it is through the theoretical mastering of thought that the practical mastering of it occurs. Finally, the directing of thought toward particular objects is in its way a process of practical mastering of thought. Thinking about thought is also a process, in which thought itself becomes the object. Here, as we see, the aspect of practice plays a most substantial role.

The object of philosophy thus appears before us not as the object of the old philosophy, but as something diverse and materially integrated at the same time; as a fluid, historically changing quantity, as an object of theoretical and practical mastering, of mastering in its dual form.

27

The Subject of Philosophy

In parallel with its treatment of the object, pre-Marxian philosophy also saw a corresponding interpretation of the philosophical subject. As we know, this was an abstraction solely of the intellectual side of humanity's vital activity, with humanity in turn abstracted from all its social and social-historical determinants. In various philosophical schools this all-round nakedness of the subject, and its transformation into an impoverished, one-sided intellectual abstraction was formulated in various ways, but the salient features in almost all were the familiar ones of the so-called philosophical "I." In idealist systems, this was usually a "universal" "I"; among subjective idealists, an individual "I"; among agnostics and positivists, the individual taken either from a psychological or physiological angle; among mechanistic materialists, usually a physiological individual; and to Feuerbach, a physiological-biological, sensible-ancestral person, the "anthropological principle" in philosophy. The restricted nature of the old materialism, including Feuerbach's "humanism," was pitilessly exposed by Marx in his brief, sharp theses, that brilliant formulation of the fundamental principles of dialectical materialism.

If, with a certain simplification, we take the philosophizing subject, this subject represented the philosophizing side, abstracted from all social and social-historical definiteness, that is, something in essence inconceivable, since as we have already seen, thought itself presupposes a society of Aristotle's "social humanity," of Franklin's "toolmaking animal," of Marx's "socialized humanity."[1]

The sociological prolegomena to any future "philosophy" tell us that the subject of philosophy, the thinking subject, is a socialized man or woman, that is, a social-historical person in his or her many-sided vital activity. Of course, every human being is an individual member of the species. Of course, every human being is a physiological entity. Of course, every human being is therefore a biological individual. But the social-historical person is a socialized individual, possessing new qualities which are by no means dissolved in the biological and physiological. The capitalist individual, the typical bourgeois; the human individual of feudalism; socialist man and woman, and so forth—all these are categories whose specific peculiarities cannot in any way be deduced from physiology or biology. *Homo sapiens* has been transformed historically into social, tool-making man and woman. The human beings of primitive communism, with a particular type of socialization of their own personal nature, were replaced by the human beings of tribal society, of feudalism, of capitalism, and of socialism (the latter only in the USSR).

The idealist attitude toward the subject is clearly preposterous. Even the humanism of Feuerbach is quite inadequate; it is not anthropology which constitutes the prolegomena, but sociology; not biological humanity, but humanity as socialized and historically defined by specific relations of production; not one-sidedly "thinking humanity," but humanity carrying on diverse vital activities. However, it follows from the latter that for capitalist society, with its productive anarchy, atomized division of labor, broad gap between theory and practice, and so forth, it is quite impossible to understand the relations between "the person" and "the world" from the example of an individual "I." In capitalist society, to a far greater degree than in other class societies, these relations are defined only by the interconnected totality of relationships of society as a whole. If, for example, in developed socialist society every individual in his or her diverse and many-faceted activity more or less reflects the life of society as a whole, the specialized individual of capitalism embodies only one facet of social existence. Such a person is not the hub of society's relations with nature, is not their focus, since people are divided and atomized, just as capitalist society as a whole is divided and atomized.

Hypostatizing the intellectual function in its subject, idealist philosophy tears this function out of the whole context of vital activity, creating its own philosophical subject primarily as the subject of "pure reason," that is, of an isolated cognitive function taken "in itself." Meanwhile materialist theory, and Feuerbach as well, sought to find a solution by regarding humanity as a purely physiological and biological type. But by transgressing the bounds of the social-historical subject in this manner, falling into the biological or anthropological, they had inevitably to treat the subject merely as a passive product of nature, that is, to treat the subject not above all as an active principle with its own active practice, but as a passive, derivative principle, that is, not in essence as a subject in relation to a natural object, but rather, as an object on which nature acts.

Marx, as is well known, took note of this uniformity, or one-sidedness. It is connected logically with the treatment of humanity solely as an animal species, because the process of adaptation of an animal species is a process of passive adaptation, of adaptation through natural selection, while social humanity actively subdues nature, and in technology creates a specifically social mechanism for acting on nature, on matter, which in the historical process of development becomes ever more material, that is, a real object. This historical "leap" in the development of *Homo sapiens*, a leap from the animal herd to human society, from biology to sociology, from the biological individual to the socialized man or woman, from the person equipped with teeth to the person equipped with technology, took place outside of philosophy. Meanwhile, as we have seen, thought itself arises in the process of active social practice, that is, in collaboration between social individuals. Thought differentiates itself historically from this social practice, and so on.

In the philosophical doctrines of idealism, the "I" has been transformed into a deliberate spiritual-creative principle, encompassing the world and sometimes consuming it as well. In the philosophical doctrines of materialism and its variants, the "I" has been transformed into a one-sided "product," a simple point of intersection of geographical, climatic, orographic, and other influences of the so-called "natural environment." (Among French materialists of a rationalist persuasion the following, among others, are linked with this: concepts of the "natural state," the "natural order," "natural law," and also the improbable forays into the social sciences about which Marx spoke so ironically.) This is why Marx wrote that idealism developed the subjective and active side, while materialism was more passive.

Therefore, the subject is in fact the subject of mastering, just as the object is the object of mastering.

The subject of mastering is historical through and through. The subject appears as such only at a particular stage of development; consequently, it is historical from the very outset of its being. It is historical from the point of view of its growing historical might, from the point of view of its technical-practical and theoretical equipment and of the corresponding results. It is historical from the point of view of the type of social structure and of the corresponding modes of presentation.

If we look at the subject through the eyes of pre-Marxist philosophy, then what, for example, did this philosophy make of technology, whether a stone axe, a steam engine, or a diesel motor? The old philosophy regarded such prosaic objects as having nothing to do with the business at hand, as being too lowly and unworthy for philosophy even to notice. On the contrary, from the point of view of dialectical materialism, in which the subject is the subject of the mastering of the world (and of the objective transformation of the world in material practice), where practice is the process of direct intervention in the world, and where it has enormous theoretical and cognitive significance, technology is an exceedingly important aspect. Technological equipment, and the degree to which it is available, thus has a substantial significance. A savage with a stone axe and a person with socialist technology are quite different subjects, and it is simply ludicrous to speak of them as one and the same. The situation is roughly the same with the technology of experimental science. If highly sensitive modern instruments raise the sensitivity of natural organs a huge number of times; if X-ray apparatus makes the invisible visible; if instruments detect what is undetectable to our natural senses, creating, so to speak, new artificial senses (electrical instruments, for example), then in treating of the subject it is quite impermissible to leave these powerful weapons of cognition out of account.

References are made to the fact that the great minds of antiquity, for example, Aristotle, working without any technology, either productive or experimental, were able to think their way through to philosophical questions that are controversial even today, and provided some particular answers that are true even now. The fact is also cited that even atomic theory is thousands of years old. All these arguments, however, are extremely unconvincing. They are unconvincing because there is nevertheless an enormous difference here. The atoms of Democritus, Epicurus, and Lucretius were naive hypotheses, arising out of brilliant guesses. The atoms of our own time are a firm acquisition of modern science, an acquisition won experimentally and developed by theoretical scientific thought. The reasoning of Epicurus and the experiments of Rutherford, the theories of Nils Bohr, and so on, represent two different dimensions, despite everything they have in common. It is enough to read Hegel's *Philosophy of Nature* to see there a huge quantity of mystical rubbish and of rubbish pure and simple, despite the real gems shining within these heaps. Nor has it been so long since the death of this colossus.

We will be told, though, that what is involved here is science rather than philosophy. Has philosophy strayed so far from science? It has. But in the first place, one should not erect a Great Wall of China between the one and the other. Secondly, if we are to take, for example, the debate between materialism and idealism in earlier times and today, we do not see this controversy marking time, but the reproduction of the contradiction on a vastly expanded basis. Hegel is far richer than Plato; Marx is on an incomparably, immeasurably higher level than Epicurus. The fact that the question has not been resolved for everyone is rooted in the social conditioning of the world view, in the mode of presentation as a reflex of the mode of production. Therefore, the interpretation of the subject must also be historical in the sense of the historical equipping, practical and theoretical, of the subject of mastering.

Here we have once again, in a different connection, come up against the question of the mode of presentation. We have seen what an enormous role the mode of presentation plays in the world view, and have seen the law on the basis of which it arose. For us to repeat ourselves here would be out of place. We shall merely ask: if in all philosophical systems so prominent a place is assigned to the question of the physiological subjectivism (or simply subjectivism) of sensations and so forth, then where is the logical reason for going past social subjectivism, that is, the sociomorphic "mode of presentation," which can be ascertained everywhere? There are no such reasons, and there cannot be. If we had a thorough understanding of the fact that a human being is not just a biological individual, but has a social and historical being, the social and historical character of his or her consciousness also becomes quite obvious. The mode of presentation is immanent in the social and historical object. We must therefore interpret the subject of mastering, the subject of philosophy, as a historical, social subject, and interpret it from this point of view, that is, from the point of view of the mode of presentation that is peculiar to it, knowing the law of this mode of presentation, that is, its genesis, its function, its relation to the objective world, its distorting ideological role, and so forth.

But will not the subject of philosophy, when interpreted in this way, be transformed into the history of philosophy, and even into history in general? Not at all. There is no question of beginning the whole process *ab ovo*, from Adam to the present day. It would also be quite absurd to repeat the attempts to solve the problems before us from the points of view of various social-historical subjects by turns, that is, to live at the expense of the past. But it is essential to include this past, in a condensed form and in a historical-dialectical manner. This also means knowing the historical laws of correlations, being able to compare, that is, to act as a subject possessing the whole might of modern science and technology. The highest type of thought is dialectical materialist thought. The highest, historically most developed type of subject of mastering is socialist humanity, arising on a historical basis.

Hegel knew perfectly well that philosophy is an epoch captured in thought. At times he provided brilliant evidence of this understanding, when his objective idealism passed over directly into materialism. Here, for example, is how he characterized the late Roman Empire:

> ... the Roman world was a world of abstraction, in which a single cold supremacy extended over the whole educated world. The living individuality of the spirits of peoples was crushed and destroyed; the alien power bore down, like an abstract universe, on the human individual. In the midst of such a state of destruction, people felt the need to seek refuge in this abstraction ... that is, to seek refuge in this inner freedom of the subject as such. (*History of Philosophy*, II)[2]

And so forth. From this, Hegel deduced the main features of the philosophical thought of that epoch.

Hegel himself provides a telling demonstration of the social character of the subject of philosophy. Here is an example, from *The Philosophy of Nature*:

> On the whole, the new world represents an undeveloped duality: it is divided like a magnet into a northern and southern part. The old world manifests a thoroughgoing division into three parts, of which one, Africa, is a native metal, a lunar element, grown torpid from the heat, where people come to a standstill in themselves; this is a mute spirit that does not enter into consciousness. Another part, Asia, is a Bacchanalian, comet-like frenzy, arising in stormy fashion out of its surroundings, a formless product without any hope of mastering what lies about it. Finally, the third part, Europe, represents consciousness, the reasoning part of the earth, the equilibrium of rivers and valleys and mountains—and its center is Germany.[3]

This geological-poetic mysticism in the style of Jakob Böhme, in essence expressing the mode of presentation of German Christian asses, as Heine called them, cannot possibly be understood outside its historical-social context. Nor can any "pure reason" come up with such raving from within itself or from the external world alone. Hegel, however, reflecting for example on Plato, puts forward a very wise rule: "We must," he writes in *Lectures on the History of Philosophy,* "stand on a level above Plato; that is, we have to know the necessity of the thinking spirit of our time!!"4 Quite so! We need to stand higher than all, since we have to know "the necessity of the spirit of our time."

Meanwhile, "our time" is not an abstraction of time, but the flesh and blood of history, a new mode of production, a new human being and a new mode of presentation. Accordingly, the subject of our philosophy has also arisen historically; this is the historically and socially determined subject of the mastering of the world, of the mastering, simultaneously and coherently, of the practical and theoretical; the subject, diverse and multifaceted in his or her vital activity, equipped with powerful productive and experimental technology and with the modern mode of presentation, the integrated and not atomized socialist individual. To understand this means also to understand "the necessity of the thinking spirit of our time."

As we have seen, however, under socialism society itself is transformed into a deliberate subject. Society itself becomes a teleological entity, a situation that is expressed succinctly in Stalin's formula: "The plan? We are the plan!" Here we have the abolition of the primordial social spontaneity that once ruled over human beings, transforming itself into a force external in its relation to them and holding sway over them. Society as a subject masters itself, at once practically and theoretically. In socialist society the plan also expresses this mastering, which is both dual and integral. Here we find present at the same time both theoretical cognition and practical action, "cognized necessity" and teleological "freedom," mind and will, thought and practical action, scientific synthesis and purpose. Here the isolated subject simultaneously and to the greatest possible degree becomes immersed in the collective (since here we find the unity of the collectively organized will) and enriches his or her individuality to the maximum degree (since there is complete freedom of development in general, and freedom for the development of his or her special individual qualities, inclinations, bents, and talents in particular). Here, consequently, we find a dialectical interaction between the real general and the individual, the essence of the general in the individual and of the individual in the general. Such is the historically highest subject of the mastering of the world, mastering both nature and society.

28

The Interaction of Subject and Object

The process of interaction between subject and object, which overall is a process of mastering nature on the part of the subject, is itself a changing historical process. The interaction between object and subject is continually evident, but the types of this interaction are historically diverse. Just as the object and subject are historically variable, so too is the interaction between them a historically variable quantity. We have already to some degree examined this changing process in the chapters on object and subject, since it is impossible to take an object in itself (it then ceases to be an object) or to take a subject in itself (it then ceases to be a subject). As a result, the idea of correlation is already immanent in these concepts. Representing the "splitting of the whole," they act as opposites and so interpenetrate one another, just as inorganic nature in general interpenetrates organic nature, and organic nature, dying and decaying, interpenetrates the inorganic. Here, however, this "exchange of substances" between nature and society has its peculiar, specific traits. The active character of the relationship comes from the side of the subject; teleology, as we know, does not banish natural necessity, and freedom itself is "cognized necessity," according to Engels's definition.

Activity, however, represents liberation from the direct pressure of nature, from necessity in the first Aristotelian sense. If in the initial stages of human development the subject was oppressed by the "menacing" forces of nature, and was powerless and defenseless before the natural elements, now to a significant degree the subject controls them, but controls them while subject to them, since it is only possible to control the processes of nature while resting on the laws of nature. This can also be expressed in the following fashion: the subject is at one and the same time free and unfree, ruling over nature and subordinate to it. If we examine the historical process of interaction between society and nature under conditions of social growth (that is, leaving out the epochs of the social decline and fall of whole societies and "civilizations," the world-historic significance of which must never be underestimated), we will readily discover a process of liberation of humanity from oppression by the forces of nature. Technology, production, science, the economic organization of society, and so forth are taking on greater and greater significance. "Geographical factors" do not cease to operate, but they no longer determine the course of life, to a significant degree remaining constant and stable (relatively constant and relatively stable).

By contrast, the further the process of active adaptation to nature proceeds, the more rapidly society develops, alters its forms, enriches its functions, and increases its requirements; its material and spiritual culture grows more diverse. The mistake of so-called "geographical materialism," and then of its mystified and vulgarized caricature, "geopolitics," consists in the failure to understand (or in the deliberate ignoring) of the fact that in the presence of developed productive forces, "geographical factors" operate through technology and production, at the same time transforming themselves into the objects of action. Hence the subject, which has arisen in historical fashion, develops as an object; it develops historically, and insofar as the social-historical process is a process of mastering nature, this occurs with full priority given to the objective laws of nature.

As we have seen, this process as a whole can be expressed through the formula P-T-P', that is, through the formula of the cycle of theory and practice, on the constantly expanding basis of their interaction. The broadening of this basis is in turn expressed in the growth of the forces of production, including in the growth of technology, in the raising of the coefficients of technical capacities, and in the variety and speed of technological processes, including chemical reactions of all types; in the ever greater quantity and diversity of organic and inorganic substances drawn into the process of production as its raw material and material of every kind. The expansion of this basis is also expressed in the growth of science, that is, in the ever broader and more profound cognitive mastering of the world. The one here mediates the other, and their combined motion amounts to a dual process of mastering the world. The visible-sensible-material expression of this process consists of the "artificial environment" and the material changing of the face of the earth, that is, the transformation of the natural landscape into a cultured landscape, the modification of the "countryside" according to the standards of agriculture, industry, transport, tourism, cultural diversions, and so forth. Such is the culmination of the process in which the cosmos is devoured by humanity, the process of consuming the substance of the world, the process of transforming the world in line with human goals, the process of increasing the power of humanity over the substance and elements of nature.

The acceleration (or, by contrast, the slowing and stopping) of this process is linked with the conditions of functioning of the productive forces, that is, above all with the historical form of society; every historical form of society is transformed dialectically from a "form of development" into "fetters on this development" (Marx). The economy of feudalism was natural in its bases (though never completely natural!), and was limited by its slow rate of growth, stagnant technology, and in the field of thought, by its dry, rigid, and wooden theological dogmatism, which provided no opportunity for criticism or real scientific investigation. Capitalism with its principle of profit, with its competition and machines, immediately accelerated the process of mastering nature many times over, in both the material-practical and theoretical fields. This acceleration of the process of mastering the objective world proceeded both in breadth and in depth, and was truly unprecedented in human history. The creation of powerful technology, a gigantic growth of the forces of production, the formation of a world market, an unparalleled flowering of science and its transformation into world science—all these had been unknown in ancient times and to the great civilizations of antiquity. Nevertheless the interaction between nature and society, between the object and subject (in this case we are not being entirely precise, since capitalist society is not fundamentally a subject; but this is unimportant here) in the epoch of the decline of capitalism has clearly changed, both in the material sphere and in that of thought. In the latter, as we know, it is possible to observe a sharp turn from metaphysical abstractions, from spiritualistic fetishes, back to feudal theology, from "criticism" to dogmatism, from science flirting with idealism but with elements of spontaneous materialist theory, to mysticism and theology (on the extreme left flank there is an unusual interest in dialectical materialism, signifying a break with the bourgeoisie).

By contrast, the socialist form of society has dramatically accelerated the process of mastering the objective world. The assimilating of new territories; geological, botanical, zoological, and other studies of the Soviet Union; the immense growth of technology and of the forces of production, with growth rates never before witnessed anywhere in the world; the extremely rapid successes of science and its penetration into the lives of the masses through its unification with practice, and so forth—all of this is proceeding at a quite new rhythm.

Following Saint-Simon to a considerable degree, Auguste Comte, as is well known, divided the mental life of humanity (and everything else in life along with it) into three periods: "theological," "metaphysical," and "scientific." His crudest error was to take mental life as his point of departure; that is, he included in his historical construct a dose of antihistorical rationalism big enough for a horse. Of course, it was not theology that gave rise to feudalism, but feudalism that gave rise to theology. Feudalism was not the product of the theological form of thought, but the theological form of thought was the product of feudalism. The old rationalist formula of the "Enlighteners," that opinions always and everywhere govern the world, served also as the theoretical conception behind Comte's "positive science." In Comte's time, the period when science would move beyond theology and metaphysics had still on the whole to begin. It is true that Comte's teacher Saint-Simon had already written in *L'Industrie*: "Ultimately, principles are not created; they are perceived and demonstrated." Saint-Simon, however, advocated a "new Christianity" with a spiritual and secular hierarchy, while the "positivist" Comte devised a new "positivist" religion, considering himself to be its high priest. His various stages further presupposed the uninterrupted progress of society, interpreted in the manner of a living organism. And so forth. There was, however, also a rational kernel in Comte's triad, since in its basic thrust the movement from feudal theology toward the metaphysical abstractions of the epoch of capitalism, and toward the imminent period of the "irreligion of the future," when under socialism science will finally oust both theology and all types of supernatural world view, represents real progress.

The recognition of these intellectual forms as ideological distortions of reality, and the historical process of liberation from their numbing fetters, is a process of throwing off the forms of social subjectivism, of overcoming and replacing them. The logical precondition for this liberation is philosophical self-criticism, while the material-social preconditions are the class struggle of the proletariat and the transition to socialism (just as earlier, the transition from the theological world view to abstract metaphysics was an expression of the transition from the Middle Ages to the modern era, that is, from feudalism to the bourgeois world order). Ultimately, the scientific picture of the world and its philosophical generalization cease to be both anthropomorphic and sociomorphic.

Earlier, we analyzed in detail the question of the teleology of necessity. We saw that developments in human activity and victories over the natural elements do not by any means justify falling into pure voluntarism and indeterminism. Human goals are determined by necessity; in their achievements, human beings rest on the laws of nature, and any technological process, even the most complex and intricate, expresses natural necessity in all the definiteness of its concrete relationships and interpenetrations. The general conditions for human social and historical activity are also determined, however, by the phase of development of the earth; this is the framework within which human activity in general takes place. Engels, along with Fourier, considered inevitable both the decline of humanity and its extinction, together with the ending of life on the earth as a planet. In other words, human history cannot be divorced in any way from the history of the earth as the base, *locus standi* and source of nourishment of society. We are not resolved, however, to pursue our conclusions as far as this, since we do not have sufficient data either to make any assertions concerning the inevitable "aging" of the human race (this is merely a judgment by analogy), or to draw any conclusions concerning the impossibility of interplanetary communications, or to exclude the possibility of new methods being discovered for adapting to extremely slow changes in the general planetary conditions of existence. For the time being we can only say: whoever lives will see.

In the process of mastering the object from the direction of the subject, the object is increasingly revealed in its infinite diversity, qualitative and quantitative, extensive and intensive. In practice historical humanity, modern humanity, refashions huge masses of material; in cognitive terms, humanity is able to travel into infinitely vast stellar spaces and into the infinitely small (and also vast and unending) spheres of the microcosmos. For human beings, the extraordinary diversity of objective properties, qualities, relations, interdependencies, and links with humanity is continually growing, since practice and theoretical cognition are more and more revealing their inexhaustible wealth. Here we see continuing the historical transformation of the real world, independent of humanity—that is, of nature as such—into an object of mastering. We see a transition from the "indifferent" existence of the world to its collective subordination to the growing might of the subject, which coordinates, and subordinates to its purposes, great tellurian processes.

This process of mastering is an absolutely real historical fact. We refashion the substance of nature, becoming more and more cognizant of its properties; on a greater and greater scale, we are able to predict the course of objective processes. This also signifies mastering practice and theoretical cognition, in dual form. These words and concepts have no other significance, and cannot have. Idealist philosophies and agnosticism rest on the presumption that ideal essences exist, beyond the reach of practice or theory. But these "essences"—all these "ideas," "spirits," "world-souls," "monad-souls," "*logoi*," and so on—are nothing other than illusory quantities created by human beings, and located mentally in the pores of the real world or beyond its limits in the character of incognizables. Precisely because they are ideological phantasms, however, they cannot be perceived as elements of the real world. They can, on the other hand, be perceived as phantasms, as ideological distortions, and only in this way. As it happens, this is quite sufficient. To apprehend a phantasm as part of the real world is an insoluble task. Consequently, this is a false problem, about which it is not worth troubling oneself, despite the teachings of idealist philosophy. This fuss and bother is scholastic in the spirit of the well-known medieval exercises that now seem to us merely barbaric and comic. To postulate God as invisible, and then to try to see him, is a hopeless enterprise. But to see the material basis for the rise of this idea, to understand its genesis, to see something else behind the distortion, is both possible and necessary. So it is that we, in contrast to the narrowness of the rationalist metaphysicians, see in religious forms not simply naked, deliberate invention and naked deception by the priests, but a deeply rooted form of thought, in which the real laws of nature are crudely distorted in line with the mode of production, that is, sociomorphically. To understand this means to apprehend ideological phantasms in scientific fashion. In practice, doing away with their material basis means to undermine and thwart their reproduction, turning them into an element of the historical past that has neither a present nor a future.

The might of human practice and human cognition in its highest form, corresponding to the socialist subject of mastering, fills people with creative enthusiasm, and at the same time protects them from unmerited pride.

When Hegel, for example, declares that the earth is the "middle," "the best of planets," and so forth, this peculiar geocentrism is ultimately just a "province" of cognition, a God-forsaken backwater, limited and restricted. At times, beneath the cover of criticizing "evil infinity," the same Hegel betrays a yearning for calm, for the finite, for that immutably static, absolute, unitary, and constant being, "round as a sphere," of which ancient Greek thinkers spoke. Impotent, ossified, dogmatic "knowledge"—which was not knowledge, but ignorance based on "revelation"—viewed the earth as the center of the universe. By contrast, powerful practice and powerful theory demonstrate that the earth is one of an infinite number of worlds; that the situation is the same with the entire solar system; that if we proceed in the other direction, every atom consists of an infinite number of worlds; that is, that every infinite is finite, while every finite is infinite, and that everything is immersed in the infinitely-infinite universe. These expanses make some people's heads spin, and such people find they want to scratch their backs on some tiny fence. They cannot endure the world dialectics of the finite and infinite. Well, let them be! Happy scratching, gentlemen!

Meanwhile, we shall follow the path of infinite cognition, the path of endless mastering of the infinite universe, without any barriers with signs saying "Road ends here" or "Entry not permitted."

29

Society as the Object and Subject of Mastering

The question of society takes on a special significance, since here there is a very specific interrelationship. Society can be an object and a subject simultaneously. It can be an object in the fullest sense, and a subject only in part. Meanwhile, it can perform this role simultaneously in several respects with particular class-based mental orientations of an exceptionally profound and durable type, far more durable than the different variants in the field of the theoretical sciences. Society, with its whole range of social and economic formations, cannot master itself in the practical sense. This, so to speak, represents its fundamental, immanent character.

This is best demonstrated using the examples of different historical types of society, especially since we have already examined some aspects of this question in another context. Here we need to pose it, and resolve it, as a whole.

Let us take capitalist society. This is a particular type of society, which has arisen in a historical manner; a specific social and economic formation, a particular "mode of production," with its characteristic "mode of thought." Capitalism became the object of knowledge almost from the point when it first began to arise (see, for example, political economy, beginning with Petty).[1] But what kind of subject was counterposed to it? Acting as this subject were the ideologues of the ruling class. The subject here was not all of society; society was anarchic, atomized, elemental, "blind," and "irrational"; as we have already seen, it is not a goal-positing, teleological entity, since it is not organized society. There is nothing in it that corresponds to a general, overarching will, only a fictitious version of this will, created in the interests of the ruling bourgeoisie. The rational principle—the state—is a general organization of the ruling class with a restricted role; it does not define or organize the life of "civil society" in its basic economic functions, and the course of the economic process, where there is teleology in a single enterprise, that is, in a single cell within the whole, is subject to the laws of elemental chance. Society therefore cannot be the object of practical mastering. For society to become the object of successful mastering it needs to have an organized character, which makes possible a plan. This means overcoming the anarchy of capitalism, that is, of capitalism as a particular social structure. Consequently, attempts to master society as a whole require moving beyond the bounds of capitalism, and this signifies proletarian socialist revolution.

To cognize capitalist society in even minimally adequate fashion means gaining an understanding of it in its contradictions and in its dynamic, and consequently, in its shift to non-being, to a different social form—that is, historically and dialectically. But since capitalist society, by virtue of its structure, is characterized by a fundamental divergence of powerful interests, the ruling class and its ideologues are incapable of this as a matter of principle. If we are to speak of political economy, it was only in the initial period of development of this science that Adam Smith, and to an even greater degree David Ricardo, described the real relations involved, including their contradictory nature (for example, Ricardo's analysis of the relation between wages and profit). With the ending of so-called classical political economy, however, bourgeois economic thought degenerated, and was transformed into vulgar apologetics (the "historical school," the "harmonists," the "marginal utility" school, the "mathematical" school, the "social-organic" school, and the present-day organic rubbish of the fascist ideologues), and also the total decay of science, the rejection of the very possibility of theoretical cognition and its transformation into statistics through study of the specific conjuncture. We see the same process in sociology and history; Auguste Comte and Herbert Spencer were on a far higher level than the Othmar Spanns of today! The French historians of the Restoration period, and such giants as Mommsen, Niebuhr, and others, were far greater than today's puffed-up apologists for fascist nationalism, or the petty ultra-specialized scribblers who lack all horizons. The attempts at generalization and synthesis such as Spengler's *Decline of the West* come close to a skeptical rejection of science, as everyone knows who is familiar with the filigree sophistry of Spengler's constructs. Things are still worse when only capitalism is involved; it is enough to point to the evolution of Werner Sombart, who has progressed all the way from sympathy with Marxism to mystical rubbish of the lowest order.

There is no point in citing endless examples. As a subject engaging in the cognition of capitalist society, the bourgeoisie has proven powerless. Its social science has degenerated into an apology for its practice, while this practice, which expresses the anarchic functioning of capitalism, has never been able to exert control over the elemental social spontaneity of the system and overcome the irrationality of the social process that is innate to capitalism. For that matter, this practice has never even set itself such a task, and it is only now, on the basis of the decline and general crisis of capitalism, of its decay and collapse, that this practice is making desperate attempts to jump higher than its ears, and on the way down, as the productive forces decline, to solve the problem of squaring the circle; hence the utopias of a feudalized "planned capitalism," in their numerous, tedious variants. In capitalist society the social-historical process stands counterposed to its agents as an external, blind, compelling force, as "natural law," not subject to being mastered.

In socialist society, which arises historically out of capitalist society through socialist revolution and thanks to the dictatorship of the proletariat, we see something quite different. Here society is both the subject and object simultaneously. This is a teleological unity. Its necessity appears directly in its teleology, through the organized will of the masses, taking material form in the plan and being realized in the fulfilment of this plan. Here it cognizes itself. Here there is no "drift," that is, a blind and elemental principle of development. Here society takes control of itself in practical fashion, just as it takes control of itself theoretically as well. Here there is no incoherence or separate existence, in the sense of an opposition of the practical and theoretical sides of mastering. Here there is both real mastering, and the complete unity of these opposites, which exist only in sublated form.

The theory of the proletariat which has grown up within the bounds of capitalism is linked with its transforming practice, which is directed at the "whole" (the revolutionary praxis of Marx, and the "overthrowing" praxis of Engels). This theory has already proven its strength, since all its most important forecasts have already come to pass, and the practice of revolutionary transformation, that is, the practice of combative and victorious Communism, has once again proven the reality of this theory, leading to the mastering of society as a whole.

We cannot pose here a whole series of fascinating historical questions, for example, about the ancient theocracies such as Egypt; about the Inca state in Peru, which Marx (in the second volume of *Capital*) described as having an economy organized on a non-commodity basis; about the Jesuit state in Paraguay; about the problems of military-capitalist economies, and so on. All of these lead beyond the bounds of the task we have set ourselves, despite being closely related to it. Here it will be sufficient to show that in commodity society (and in its most developed form, the capitalist economy), society is not the subject, cannot be the subject, and cannot master itself either theoretically or practically. Commodity society therefore becomes a real object of cognition (where this cognition accords with reality) among its opponents, while in practice society becomes an object of mastering only in its organized form, in this case, that is, as socialist society.

The situation is thus as follows. Insofar as we are concerned with society as an object:

a) society arises on the whole before it becomes, in any form, the object of cognition and of conscious mastering in general;
b) as an object, society arises historically;
c) in the course of the historical process of development, society changes its concrete historical form, passing from one form to another and changing its modes of production;
d) each of these concrete historical societies develops the wealth of its particular, specific properties, features, qualities, and "laws of motion," which are characteristic of it alone.

Where we are concerned with the subject, we have the following:

a) the subject is historical;
b) it is historically diverse, including in the respect that in some societies it is merely partial, and the society as a whole cannot be a subject;
c) in socialist society, the whole society becomes a subject in relation to itself;
d) the capitalist subject (a bourgeois ideologue) cannot in the strict sense be the subject of mastering;
e) socialist society is a historically arising subject-object in the full sense.

Finally, insofar as we are concerned with the interrelationship between object and subject, we see that:

a) these relations are historical;
b) that in commodity-capitalist society they are extremely ill-developed, and that here in essence there is not and cannot be a process of mastering;
c) that in socialist society, where complete agreement and identity exists between the object, which is at the same time also a subject, and the subject, which is at the same time also an object, we see complete mastering. That is, we see practice which operates in accordance with goals on the social scale, and which is organized in all its aspects; we see the conscious self-motion of society, along with its self-consciousness and self-cognition, as aspects of its integrated vital activity;
d) that the birth of society as a subject is the result of the theoretically directed revolutionary practice of the proletariat, of the victory of the proletarian socialist revolution; the proletariat, as a "particular" (class), consisting of the "solitary" (individuals), masters the "universal" (society), and is transformed into the "general" (the socialist people). The concept of the subject of revolution was developed by Lenin.

From the point of view of intellectual forms, the transition to socialism signifies the abolition of fetishistic forms of social consciousness. This point needs to be examined at greater length.

Marx was the first to reveal the specific peculiarities of capitalist society, its laws of motion, the specific modes of thinking of its agents, and the social-historical specificity of its intellectual categories. We are referring here to Marx's concept of commodity fetishism.

In capitalist society every enterprise, the labor in every enterprise, and the commodity producers are formally independent of one another; they operate "freely" in the market. They are linked to one another through acts of exchange, through the metamorphoses of commodity and money, through the movement of things. Labor in this case does not represent a system of social labor, but separate complexes of it. The fact of social collaboration is concealed by the formal independence of the enterprises. Social relations between people appear to be social properties of things, of commodities. This commodity fetishism manifests itself in all the thinking of the bourgeoisie and its ideologues. In the field of political economy, where society is viewed as an object, all the categories of bourgeois science are fetishistic through and through. Capital, for example, in this case does not represent a social and historical relationship between people, a relationship that is manifested and fixed in things, but a thing in its natural form, that is, money and so forth. Hence in bourgeois political economy capital produces profit, land creates rent, and money gives birth to money; all of them possess mystical, miraculous properties. Hence the theories of the "productivity of capital," in their numerous variants. There is not even a drop here of the social or historical approach to the topic; all the real relationships are presented in a fetishized, distorted form.

The same happens in other areas as well. Because of the division of labor and the anarchy of society, the ideological spheres (for example, various fields of science and art, and also the areas of law, morals, and so on) are shrouded in exactly the same manner by a fetishistic fog.

Engels wrote to Franz Mehring (letter of July 14, 1893):

> Ideology is a process which, it is true, is carried on by the so-called thinker consciously, but with false consciousness. The real forces which set it in motion remain unknown to this thinker.... Consequently, he or she dreams up false or merely apparent motive forces. Because this is a mental process, it derives its content and form from pure thought, either the thinker's own, or that of his or her predecessors. The thinker functions exclusively with intellectual material which he or she accepts uncritically as the product of thought, without making further investigations, to the point where the process is a more remote one, independent of thought....[2]

Elsewhere, in *Ludwig Feuerbach*, Engels spoke of "work on thoughts as on independently developing essences, subject only to their own laws."

In other words, the links in the chain of divided social labor are viewed as independent. Ideas, the products of these links, are in fact connected objectively to the whole system of practice, and make up an aspect of the life of society, of its reproduction, of its life cycle. Nevertheless, ideas leap out of this association (in terms of consciousness), and turn into independent essences. Abstracted from direct contact with matter, but in one degree or another connected with material practice, they act as separate essences by virtue of the outwardly separate existence of various specialized offshoots. Just as money gives birth to money, capital gives birth to profit, and land gives rise to rent in isolation from labor (at least in the consciousness of fetishists), so pure categories, pure forms, a priori forms appear outside of practice and matter, and knowledge itself comes to represent pure knowledge, that is, knowledge in itself, and not an aspect of the mastering of the world. The rational basis of this fetishistic aberration consists in the peculiar, specifically historical structure of capitalist society. This fetishism manifests itself even more clearly in the categories of morality, where the norms of social behavior take on the character of super-sensory metaphysical categories which hang like swords of Damocles over people's heads, even though these categories are considered to be something "internal." But this theme will be dealt with in depth in another context.

Consequently, in this particular area, that is, the sphere of society, we see the necessity for a historical approach to the question of the subject and object. Neither in nature nor in society is there, or should there be, a place for empty abstractions; operating on the basis of these leads to degeneration into barren scholasticism and "drunken speculation." Only full-blooded materialist dialectics can ensure that the philosophical thought of our time functions in a genuinely fruitful manner.

30

Truth: The Concept of Truth and the Criterion of the Truthful

The question of truth is, of course, one of the central issues of philosophy. But as Pontius Pilate asked, according to gospel tradition, "What is truth?"

This question is particularly complex and many-sided, though the preceding section provided almost all the premises needed for resolving it. Here we need to concentrate first of all on eliminating at the outset the ambiguity of the term "truth," an ambiguity encountered exceedingly often, even in Marxist literature. This question needs to be addressed not from the scholastic-verbalistic-terminological angle, but in essence by proceeding from the spirit, rather than the letter, of Marx, Engels, and Lenin.

We often encounter the expression "the true world," referring to truth as objective fact, as the law, relation, quality, state, and so forth of the real world. But can any fact, if it really is a fact, be "untrue"? And how, in general, can the category of truth be applied to a fact, to the real world, taken in itself? Strictly speaking, this use of the word "truth" is absurd, since something which exists in reality exists in reality, and that is the end of the matter. That this is so appears immediately if, running ahead, we pose here the question of the criteria of truth, or, let us say, the criterion of accordance with reality. If by truth we understand reality itself, that is, the objective relations among things and processes, independent of our cognition and practical influence, then what does the question become? An obvious absurdity, since it turns out that we are asking about the relationship between reality and this particular reality; that we are speaking of one and the same thing as though it were two things! But such a situation can exist only if the external world coincides with thought, if things or "the souls of things" are concepts, that is, if we are dealing with an obvious "philosophy of identity" or variations on it—in any case, with one or another type of idealism.

This applies, for example, to Hegel, for whom, as we know, objects are real when they coincide with their idea. Analyzing the teaching of Aristotle, Hegel writes: "The speculative character of Aristotle's philosophy consists precisely in the fact that it views all things in terms of thought, and all things are turned into thoughts, with the result that, acting in the form of thoughts, they also act in their truthfulness" (*Lectures on the History of Philosophy*, vol. II).[1]

Generally speaking, it is only possible to interpret truth as a property of the real world when this world is not unique, when one presumes a duplication or multiplication of worlds, with different degrees of reality. This, of course, also pollutes the air for miles around with a mystical stench. So what is the point? The point is not hard to understand if we keep in mind that we are concerned with true, that is, accurate, cognition of the true, that is, accurate, reflection of the object in the subject. In the chapter on mediated knowledge, we discussed in detail the theory of reflection, which was developed in particular detail by Lenin in his struggle against idealist agnosticism. The reflection of the world is not the same thing as the world. Nor is it a duplicate of the world. The reflection of the world is a "picture" of it, but a picture is something quite different from what is depicted in it. A reflection may be more or less accurate, more or less full, and more or less rounded, or it may be a scandalous distortion, and so forth. But it is never the object itself, and it can never really multiply or duplicate the world. It is quite a different matter that thought can create (and does create) many reflections of varying degrees of adequacy; these can be compared on the basis of their truthfulness, that is, on the basis of the degree to which they accord with the objective world. Truthfulness is therefore nothing other than the property of a reflection in a human head such that this reflection corresponds to the real world, that is, to what is being reflected. Truth or untruth is a predicate of thought, as related to being, and not a predicate of being itself, which has absolutely no need of being approved by thought. We have already had cause to note that one must not confuse, for example, the fact of hallucination with the reality that nothing in the objective world corresponds to it. A distorting mirror distorts, but it exists, as a distorting mirror. An erroneous view reflects reality erroneously, but it exists, as an error in people's heads. The truth reflects reality accurately, but it is not this reflected reality. It is something else, a translation of reality in the heads of human beings.

What we are discussing here is reflection and correspondence. As a result, the term "coincidence" is also extremely ambiguous, since coincidence is coincidence of the identical, while there is no identity whatever between a reflection and that which is reflected. The fact that people think about the universe does not mean that the physical being of the entire cosmos, crudely speaking, is accommodated in people's heads. Nor does it mean that the universe is the same thing as the concept of it.

According to Hegel, the universe does not coincide with the representation of the universe, but with the concept of it:

> The usual definition of truth, according to which it is "the coincidence of the representation with the object," is still not contained at all within the representation. When I imagine a house, a log, and so on, I am not myself this content; I represent something quite different, and consequently, do not at all coincide with the object of my imagining. It is only in thought that a true coincidence of the objective and subjective is evident.[2]

The concepts of a house and a log, however, are neither house nor log, whatever subterfuges idealist philosophical speculation might resort to.

Now, however, the question presents itself of what the "correspondence" of the reflection to that which is reflected actually signifies. We have already seen that the most exact reflection of the world is the "scientific picture of the world," its "second concrete." (Marx in the Introduction to his *Contribution to the Critique of Political Economy*, as we recall, insisted vigorously that this "spiritual reproduction" was real, though it did not at all represent the creating of reality itself!) So what sort of correspondence is this? It is clear that what is involved is not a reflection in the sense of a mirror-calm visual image. To be blunt, it is on the whole a waste of time to try to understand this correspondence in the manner of a simple and elementary idea, such as the metaphorical mirror. The correspondence here is of a far more complex type.

Let us take our old example, the formula "bodies expand when they are heated." This formula is true; it corresponds to reality. Is it absolutely true? No! It is one-sided and incomplete. In astrophysics, in the conditions of stars, it is untrue. Even on earth there are exceptions to it (water, steel, and others). But in earthly conditions, except for a few substances, it is true; it corresponds to reality. What does it mean, to say that within these limits it "corresponds"? It means that if we see some body here on earth in relation to another factor, as a result of which the temperature of the first body rises, that is, if the energy of vibration of its molecules increases, then the volume of this body expands. Or if we say that matter has an electromagnetic nature, and if this "picture of the world" is correct, if it corresponds to reality, then this signifies as follows: whatever substance we take, and however many experiments we perform, every time we penetrate experimentally into the microstructure of a substance we will find there tiny particles with positive and negative charges. This also means that any directly practical contact with matter, aimed at altering it in accordance with the data of this theory, will confirm the theory in the concrete course of the technological process. We discussed this in detail when we were dealing with the question of the cognizability of things in themselves. A reflection is a compressed, condensed, "spiritual reproduction" of reality. An accurate, true reflection is one that precisely condenses these associations, qualities, properties, relationships, and processes, and does not create illusory ones; that is, ones which do not have a material correlate, or any real correlate existing outside of the subject. As a system of concepts, a reflection is by no means a system of arbitrarily chosen "symbols" or "signs," or of Plekhanovian "hieroglyphs." When we think about electrons, the electron is not a sign or a numerical designation of reality, but a spiritual reproduction of this reality. As we have seen, mediated significance removes subjectivity and penetrates into the objective links among things and processes. Nevertheless, we can express one and the same system of concepts in different languages, recording it in mathematical formulae, equations, letters of the alphabet, and so forth. This is now the province of symbols, of conditional designation. There is no way we can place the process of forming concepts, and of thought, on the same blackboard with the process of devising symbols and symbolic writing, and consider the two to be homogeneous.

The criterion of truth is therefore correspondence to reality. Theoretical cognition, however, is one side of the process of mastering, that is, of the theoretical mastering of the object. It follows that correspondence with reality is the criterion of the power of theoretical mastering. Truth is correspondence with reality. Truth is the power of theoretical cognition, the reality of theoretical cognition in the sense of its effectiveness.

Let us now examine the question of the effectiveness of practice. Is there some analogy here? Of course there is. Practice may be unsuccessful, feeble, mistaken. This means that in the making of cast iron, let us say, the blast furnace process does not work as anticipated. Consequently, some mistake was made here. Or, let us take another example: all the practice of the alchemists in trying to produce gold. This practice was simply in vain. Or, we might take the example of the attempts to construct a *perpetuum mobile*, a perpetual motion machine. On the other hand, productive practice is genuinely powerful in all its fields, and the increase in the power of modern-day humanity, especially socialist humanity, over nature has been immense. What is the criterion here? The objective result of the productive process, its accordance with some previously posited goal. Here we immediately find that the link between theory and practice is also revealed from the point of view of the criteria of their effectiveness, that is, the reality of their mastering of the object. The material result of the technological process is the criterion of the reality of this process, that is, of its practical might, that is, of the real objective mastering of the object. At the same time, this result also provides a test of theory, since the course of the technological process is worked out theoretically in advance. Material results disprove false theories, as for example in the case of the *perpetuum mobile*; meanwhile, theory itself confirms practice in this case, disproving the theoretical possibility of perpetual motion. A positive practical effect, that is, the practical mastering of the object, its material transformation, confirms the truthfulness of theory; practical power confirms theoretical power. But because all practice is reasoned, goal-directed activity (we are speaking here of human practice), the theoretical principle coexists within it, so to speak, whatever the system for the division of social labor might be in a given society. Precisely because practice gives rise to theory, and theory to practice, precisely because they interpenetrate one another and constitute a unity in their circulation, the practical criterion of truth coincides with the criterion of correspondence to reality. The genuine causes (indispensable links) that are revealed by theory become rules in practice; truth of cognition therefore signifies power in practice, and power in practice signifies truth of cognition, that is, its correspondence with reality. All this is correct provided we mean by practice objective changes to the world, not the illusory "practice" of mystical revelations and the soul-redeeming "benefits" of self-flagellation of various kinds, as in the *Varieties of Religious Experience* of William James. But we have already discussed this, and will not return to it again.

Let us now examine the question of the criterion of economy, set forward with such pomp by the empiriocritics ("consideration of the world from the point of view of the minimum expenditure of effort," in the works of Avenarius above all). Taken in itself, that is, without regard for the question of correspondence, this principle is at once crackpot and trivial; crackpot because it throws overboard all the increasingly diverse associations and relationships discovered in the process of cognition, and trivial because it chops away with an axe, coming at the problem in a flat, rudimentary manner. This principle can, however, be discussed—as Lenin did in *Materialism and Empiriocriticism*, devoting literally two lines to it—if we address it in accordance with the criterion of truth as the accurate reflection of reality. In this case, it acts not merely in advance, but *post factum*, not as an independent criterion, but as an expression of the productivity of mental labor, of the productivity of thought. In this case, thought which is correct, that is, which faithfully reflects reality, inevitably turns out also to be the most economical. In its production there will be nothing superfluous, that is, untrue, not corresponding to reality, confusing the question, preventing penetration into the actual relations of real processes, creating diversions onto false tracks, creating illusory links instead of forging real ones. This cannot, however, in any way mean posing in advance the demand for thinking simply and economically. Posed in so bare a form, this demand is absurd, and in cognitive terms, harmful; it leads inevitably to flat, cachectic abstractions, however these might be garnished with all manner of empiriocritical formulae about "pure description."

The question of the criteria of truth can thus be formulated as follows: the criterion of truth is correspondence with reality, which is confirmed by practice, as the correspondence of the material results of practice with its goal. The criterion of correspondence with reality coincides with the criterion of practice, just as theoretical power coincides with practical power, since these are merely two sides of the process of mastering the objective world. Correct thinking proves *post factum* to be also the most economical, that is, the most productive.

31

Truth: Absolute and Relative Truth

The universe is endless and endlessly diverse, while at the same time being a single whole. It is an immeasurable and inexhaustible sea of qualities, properties, associations, and relationships, with transitions from one to another, with uninterrupted transformations, with the demise of one entity and the rise of another, new one. The universe represents eternal coming into being and disappearance; it is an ocean of endless, mobile matter in all the magnificence of its forms. Such is the objective universe. It is quite obvious that the universe, with all its endless wealth, cannot in some final historical epoch become the object of thorough cognition and practice. The universe is revealed historically, in the thinking of the subject. Cognition is a process, and the results of this process are constantly being transformed in the historical motion of labor and thought; they are not some rigid quantity, but are constantly renewing their composition. Cognition increases both extensively, in breadth, and intensively, in depth. It assimilates ever new spheres of being, and at the same time opens up ever more general, that is, more and more profound, types of associations, relationships, and laws. The sphere of the particular, of concrete things and processes which are becoming objects of cognition, expands without interruption. At the same time cognition, growing on its practical basis, moves toward the universal, revealing more and more profound types of associations, discovering more and more general and universal laws, and proceeding from them toward the "spiritual reproduction" of a diverse intelligiblility that is now concrete. These stages of cognition correspond to the structure of being itself, to objective reality itself.

General, universal relations and an endless quantity of partial, specific ones exist objectively, quite independent of human and any other consciousness. General, universal forms of being and partial forms also exist. Necessity is a type of universal, all-natural objective bond. The laws of dialectics encompass everything: nature, society, the instant. Engels in *Anti-Dühring* described dialectics as "a law of the development of nature, history, and thought that is exceedingly general and thus exceedingly broad in its action; a law which, as we have seen, has validity in the animal and plant kingdoms, in geology, in mathematics, in history and philosophy...."[1]

As we know, there are also specific laws that are peculiar to special forms of being, for example, laws of biology that apply to the organic world and to it alone. The typology of laws thus reflects the objective types of objective relations, according to their growing or declining generality, and according to their "depth." Cognition as a process also consists in the discovery of an ever broader field of concrete things and processes and of ever more profound types of relations between them. Commenting on Hegel in his *Philosophical Notebooks*, Lenin therefore noted: "Nature is *both* concrete *and* abstract, *both* appearance *and* essence, *both* instant *and* relationship. Human concepts are subjective in their abstractness and isolation, but objective overall, in their process, sum, tendency, and source."[2]

This also makes understandable the interpretation of truth itself as a process; cognition is not able to assimilate immediately the whole endless diversity of nature and its multifarious unity, the universal relationship of the world with the infinity of its concrete mediations. Cognition, so to speak, reveals the world piece by piece, and only as a tendency comes to know the many-faceted whole, toward which it is eternally striving. In reality, there are no different universes, universes with different degrees of "truthfulness"; there is one universe with various types of association, more profound or less so. In this lies the rational core and basis for all arguments about "essence" and so forth. In particular, the universe (or more exactly, parts of it) provides a phenomenological "picture" with relation to the sensory organs of the subject, while cognition proceeds "deeper," stripping away the subjective and in terms of concepts reflecting the objective properties of the universe "in itself," "thinking away" [i.e., mentally removing] the fundamental coordination of Avenarius. This, among other things, is also expressed very clearly by Hegel in his *Science of Logic*: "What [the object] ... is like in thought, it is like only in itself and for itself; what it is like in visible form and in concept, it is like as a phenomenon."[3] In inverted form various Hegelian concepts, such as being, essence, reality, the absolute idea, and so forth, more and more reflect the profound process of cognition, of movement toward the universal, all-encompassing "absolute idea," which is absolute truth.

From the point of view of dialectical materialism, thought in this case corresponds completely to being, in the form of integral and diverse being. But cognition merely strives toward this in its historical development, constantly enriching itself, penetrating more and more deeply, and moving asymmetrically in this direction. Cognition is a reflection of human nature. It cannot reflect human nature in its entirety, but only moves toward this in the process of its historical development, proceeding out of sensible experience, stripping away its subjective side, and through human collaboration forming concepts: abstractions, laws, systems of laws, the scientific picture of the world, and so forth. This process includes the object, but conditionally, not as a whole, not fully; it grasps the universal relationship between things, but partially, incompletely, one-sidedly, and approximately. It is forever moving, however, toward a more and more complete, many-sided, profound, and universal cognition.

From the point of view of relativism, science and philosophy are able to contain only the relative. This, however, is a crude and antidialectical way of posing the question, since it absolutizes the relative itself. From the point of view of dialectical materialism, and of objective dialectics, the relative still contains the absolute, since as Lenin wrote, "... the particular does not exist except in an association that leads to the general. The universal exists only in the particular and through the particular."[4]

Here, however, it is as well to linger on an extremely important question, that is, the very concept of the relative. This concept is supremely diverse. Above all, a distinction should be drawn between what might be called the categorical relative, and the relative considered simply as incomplete. Let us take, for example, the philosophy of Kant. Its starting point is the fundamental difference between the noumenal world and the world of phenomena. Cognition proceeds, and can proceed, only within the framework of the phenomenal world. The world of "things-in-themselves," the world of noumena, is transcendental. One cannot leap across into it; it is inaccessible in principle. According to Kant it exists, but we know nothing of it, and will never know anything. In the world of noumena there are some basic causes which find expression in the diversity of the phenomenal world, but what these causes are, what their nature might be, is hidden from us as a matter of principle. Not even a single particle of the noumenal world can enter into our experience and the sphere of our cognition.

And what about practice? Kant does not resolve this question.

So here we have the relativity of our knowledge. But this is a fundamentally categorical (not in the sense of Kantian "categories") relativity, since the very category of "things-in-themselves" is inaccessible to us in principle, that is, for all time. All that is accessible to us is the world of phenomena, and here there may be a "process of knowledge," that is, a process of increasingly complete inclusion by thought, reason, and the world of "things for us." From the point of view of dialectical materialism, the relativity of truth is something quite different. Here, in complete contrast to Kant, we are concerned with cognition of the real world, which is by no means partitioned off from us by our sensory organs, but which is united with us through their agency. In the process of thought, we remove the subjective coefficient. Practically and theoretically, we take possession of the real, external, objective world, which exists independently of us. But only part of the world is the object of our mastering, and then not in the full sense. Through our production, we transform in practice no more than the infinitely small part of the cosmos that comprises our "economy," and the part that we transform, we use only partially. For example, we do not yet use the internal energy of the atom. The same is true where the theoretical side of the process of mastering is concerned. We know a great deal, but this is still an infinitely tiny amount. Both practically and theoretically, however, our strength is growing, and there are no limits to this growth. Consequently, the relativity of our cognition lies in its diminishing incompleteness and one-sidedness—something quite different from the relativism on principle of Kantian cognition, of Kant's "evil idealism," "evil subjectivism," and "evil relativism," to use Hegel's terminology.

Let us take pragmatist relativism. To pragmatism, "truth" is nothing other than "use," understood in any sense including the most subjective. If "God" consoles people, then he acts in a useful way, which means he exists, and is therefore true. Here "evil" practice and "evil" subjectivism combine in orgiastic celebrations. Here "truth" is so relative that it loses all connection with reality outside the subject. Clearly, this relativism too is something different from the relativism of incompleteness, from relativism as conceived by dialectical materialism. Different too is the relativism of the empiriocritics with their "principled coordination," from which there is no escaping, and with their phenomenology, which recognizes nothing apart from itself.

Also different is the relativism of the Sophists, for example, Gorgias. Lenin quite correctly agreed with Hegel when the latter wrote of Gorgias:

> ... Gorgias (a) polemicizes correctly against absolute realism, which when it has ideas of things, thinks it has the things themselves, when in fact it has something relative; (b) falls into the evil idealism of the new epoch: "The conceivable is always subjective; therefore, it does not exist, since through thought we transform the existing into the conceivable...."[5]

In this case, cognition has been interpreted in a purely subjective manner, and the object has evaporated. Cognition has not taken hold of it as reality, lying outside of the subject. Both for the Sophists (Protagoras and others: "man is the measure of all things"); and for Socrates (who made the addition: thinking humanity is the measure of all things) in a different fashion (since Socrates strove for the "universal"), relativism was absolutized as the subjective side of the content of the thought process. (Here, in parenthesis, it must be stressed that in expressions such as "the objective truth," and so on, the word "objective" signifies correspondence with reality, accuracy of reflection as opposed to subjective distortion, but does not at all signify objective reality itself.)

Earlier, in our discussion of the tropes of Pyrrho, we analyzed the question of the relativity of knowledge as deriving from individual, specific subjectivity, and also the question of the sociomorphism of cognition. We saw that from the point of view of dialectical materialism, all these questions are soluble. On one question, however, it is necessary to dwell once again, because of its particular significance. This is the question of the link between all the objects and processes of nature, that is, of their objective association, association outside of the subject. We also encountered this question in our critique of the Kantian "thing-in-tself." The point here is that a "thing-in-itself," that is, with no relationship either to the subject or to other things, is an empty abstraction. This needs to be specially noted and singled out, since here we are concerned not with a relativity which in some way or other is "imputed" to the subject, but with a correlation within the object itself.

However, this universal relation between things and processes, of the being of one in another and through another, is itself an object of cognition. If cognition seizes hold of this "relativity," then what is evident is not the deficient side of cognition, but on the contrary, its dialectical height. Restricted, rationalistic, metaphysical, static, wooden cognition cannot grasp this association; it isolates things and processes, turning the fluid into the frozen. Doing away with this association and this relativity would represent a retreat for cognition. Rationalist cognition expresses the scantiness and relativity that flow out of weakness. Dialectical cognition expresses the growing power of reason, resting on the might of practice.

From this it follows that the question of the objective relations between things, and of the fact that the object is always related to something else, and can only be known within this relationship, is a very special one that cannot be bracketed together with questions of the relativity of cognition as a result of one or another property of the subject. When we consider the questions that fall under this latter heading, we see that they in turn are divided into two great categories. In the first place, there are problems of relativism linked to the subjective interpretation of the cognitive process as one in which the objective world either disappears, or is declared to be inaccessible, or is condemned to eternal distortion as a result of various properties of the subject, properties which must not be left out of account and which cannot be reasoned away. Secondly, there are elements of relativism in the interpretation made by dialectical materialism; here the relativity of truth lies in its incompleteness, which diminishes as the process of cognition goes forward. This incompleteness is a deficiency which can be overcome historically, since it does not flow from the incognizability of the real world, but from its incomplete cognition. (Subjective and ideological distortions, meanwhile, can be overcome under particular cognitive conditions.)

The absolute also exists in the relative. This is best demonstrated if we take an example. It will be recalled that Aleksandr Bogdanov in his time polemicized on the basis of an absolute understanding of the absolute and relative. Among other things, he examined the proposition "Napoleon died on such-and-such a day, in such and such a year, on the island of Saint Helena," analyzing it as follows: "What is death? When does it happen? When the heart stops beating, or when all the cells die? It is well known that the hair and nails of so-called corpses keep growing. How do we measure time?" And so on. (Here we are citing the arguments from memory, and can vouch only for the faithful reproduction of the sense and spirit of the objection, not for the text.)[6]

Consequently, there is no firm, absolute, solid truth here, not to speak of the fact that we are merely concerned with a "single relationship." Still, we shall examine the question. It cannot be posed as Bogdanov does. It must be put as follows: we know that (a) if we consider death to be the ceasing of the action of the heart and similar symptoms; and (b) if time is calculated in a particular way, then Napoleon died at a particular time. This is and will be solid truth (absolute, but partial) forever. It is a different matter that we do not yet know the process of death in exact detail, and do not have mastery either theoretically or practically over life, in the sense of being able to create it, and so forth. Consequently, we do not know all the associations and relationships in this case. This is true, but it is a different question. There is an enormous amount that we do not know, but there is also a great deal that we are finding out, and coming to master. A great deal of the knowledge we have acquired will remain forever, not only "affirmations of a single relationship" such as "Napoleon is dead," and so forth. The truth is that in the future a whole series of solid conquests of science will be taken in different connections, considered from different points of view, once these points of view have been developed; it is absurd to think that in millions of years thought will be the same as it is now. But a great deal of today's science will remain alive, as solid, eternal, and absolute acquisitions.

Consequently, the counterposition of absolute and relative is itself something relative, and this opposition cannot be absolutized. It is precisely because we know a whole series of things, know them firmly, that we are really mastering the world, applying science as a lever that transforms the world of practice. Moving toward the absolute by way of the relative, in which the absolute is implicit, and conquering ever new strongpoints in the processes both of extensive and intensive cognition, we master ever greater spheres of the real world, lying outside of us, and become more and more, in actuality, lords over the forces of the earth, rulers of tellurian forces.

32

The Good

In his notes on Hegel's *History of Philosophy*, Lenin makes a comment about the Cyrenaic philosopher Hegesias. According to Lenin, Hegesias "confuses sensation as a principle of the theory of cognition and as a principle of ethics. This N.B."[1]

Such confusion is not unique to Hegesias. It was widespread in most of the philosophical schools of ancient Greece and Rome, in the East, and in Europe during the Middle Ages, as well as persisting in supposedly modern schools.

What are the roots of this confusion? They are to be found in the teleological view of the world. In fact, if at the heart of the world is purposive reason, then this reason is at the same time both truth (since this is the principle of the universe, its supreme, general entelechy), and the purpose, that is, the general good, the supreme good, to which all other "goods" must be subordinated as partial, derivative, and secondary. For pre-Socratic philosophers the Greek *nous* was the goal, "the good" in its most precise definition. For Socrates, and especially for Plato and Aristotle, this is elevated into the "general," the "type," the "Idea," and "God." Socrates, we read in Hegel, "first advanced the view that beauty, good, truth, and law are the goal and purpose of the individual person."[2]

To the Sophists, the individual was the standard against which all things were measured. Here, a clearly expressed individualism held sway. Plato and Aristotle, in stting forth their barracks-like social ideals, had to appeal to societal and state restraints, and consequently to the "universal"—that is, in the final analysis, to God—as the true good. The confusion of which Lenin spoke is an immanent law of teleological and theological idealism, reaffirmed after many centuries by Kantianism with its "postulates of practical reason," free will, immortality of the soul, God, and the categorical imperative. "God," we read in Hegel:

> is a Platonic good, in the first place a product postulated by thought. In the second instance, however, this good is to the same degree in itself and for itself. If I recognize in the capacity of the real the unchanging and eternal, something which in terms of its content is general, then this real is postulated by me, but at the same time, as something objective in itself, it is not postulated by me.[3]

Here we find "substantial rationality" counterposed to a "particular" goal. The "unchanging," the "absolute," the eternal and supreme "good," which does not need substantiation from any other, since it is itself an ultimate principle—this is how the question is posed here. The humanity of "the good," its empirical, everyday, worldly, social roots; the genesis of the social norms of behavior as something embodying the main real interests of a given historical society, its "system," "order," and "reason," to which private, secondary interests, sometimes in conflict with it, must be subordinated—deliberately or otherwise, this genesis is hidden, drowning in a sea of theological-teleological "arguments." In this respect, an argument in Hegel's *History of Philosophy*, where Hegel analyzes the doctrine of Plato, is extremely interesting. Hegel, together with Plato, objects to the discussion of all sorts of empirico-rational arguments in favor of "the good," while seeking at the same time, through the pettiness of these arguments, to compromise them completely in advance. This passage will be cited here:

> Hence, for example, they say: "Do not deceive, since you will thereby lose credit and suffer losses," or: "Be sparing in what you eat, or you will suffer a stomach upset, and will have to fast"; or in explaining a punishment, they refer to superficial reasons borrowed from the possible results of the action, and so on. By contrast, if the matter is based on firm foundations, as is the case with the Christian religion, then even if we are no longer familiar with these foundations, we nevertheless say: "Divine grace, having in view the salvation of our souls, and so forth, orders the life of humanity in this fashion." Here, the superficial reasons cited above fall away.[4]

Let no more fall away, for the sake of these wretches! This theological mysticism is wonderful after a fashion; it casts an unusually clear light on the "genesis of ideas." But enough of examples! Let us cross over to the essence of the question.

Above all, primary importance should be assigned to the question of the relationship between "truth" and "good." The illicitly cohabiting "truth-authenticity" and "truth-justice," which in Russia flourished among the late lamented "subjective sociologists," need to be divorced. As we know, truth is the accordance of the reflection with the objective world, situated outside of us. Its natural law—the most general—is necessity. The revealing of the associations and relationships, qualities and properties, and general and particular laws of the objective world is the task of theoretical cognition, as an aspect of mastering. This is on the one hand. On the other, there is in nature no "good," no general "purpose," and no "entelechy" as the supreme and universal principle, just as there is not a grain of morality, "ethics," and so on in the Pythagorean theorem, in analytical geometry, in astrophysics, or in paleontology. There is no need for us to repeat here all the arguments against both the crude "external" and the refined "innate," "immanent" teleology; we have dwelt sufficiently on this question in a special chapter of this work.

But if the teleological point of view and the teleological conception of the world cannot withstand criticism, then as a result "the good" also collapses as a principle of the universe. When we speak of truth, we speak of the correspondence of the reflection to that which is reflected, and which objectively exists. The situation with "the good" is quite different. This is something exclusively subjective and human; there is nothing that corresponds to it in the external, extrahuman world. The "universal" here has as its rational basis not the natural-universal, similar to the universal laws of nature, but a certain social and historical interest, formulated in opposition to particular interests and projected onto the cosmic screen. Human goals are merely human goals; they are embraced by people, by social-historical people. Norms of behavior, and the dominant ideas present in these norms, may in the initial stages of development be worked out unconsciously, spontaneously, and semi-instinctively, but they do not therefore cease to be human and social-historical. To seek for them an extra-human ideal sanction (such as Hegel's "divine grace") is possible only if we accept a theological-teleological conception of the world. From the opposite point of view, the human has its justification in the human, and has no need of any superhuman or supernatural sanctions.

Concepts of so general a character as that of "the good," and also the related concepts of "justice," "kindness," and "virtue," always have a specific historical content which varies depending on the economic formation, on the class, and on the particular phase of development. Outside of these concrete historical definitions, all these categories are completely formal, empty, abstract, and devoid of content. What, for example, does the ascetic "good" of Brahmanism have in common with the utilitarianism of Jeremy Bentham, that "genius of bourgeois stupidity," to use Marx's phrase? What does the virtue of the Stoics have in common with the *virtù* of Niccolo Macchiavelli, with his unrestrained perfidy for the sake of the homeland of the commercial-industrial oligarchy of Renaissance Italy? What is there in common between "the good" of early Christianity and "the good" of sensual pleasures preached by the epigones of Epicureanism? The concepts of "the good" held by Simeon Stylites or the archpriest Avvakum on the one hand, and of Heinrich Heine on the other, will scarcely recall one another in any way. And if we bring empirical historico-ethnographic material into play, ranging through different countries, peoples, and epochs, the results are truly striking; there is not even a trace of the unchanging and eternal! But using the methods of sociology, we can in each case extract, that is, explain in social-genetic fashion, this or that "good," this or that totality of coordinated moral views, arising out of the "social being," that is, from the material conditions of existence of a historically specific social formation and of its class bearer, which embodies its "system" and "order."

If we point to the historical relativity of "the good" (something that can easily be demonstrated with a thousand examples), this can, however, be parried with the following arguments. Empirically, it might be said that "the good" is revealed in the historical process, just as truth is revealed in the historical process of cognition. The fact that the concept of "the good" changes does not in the least contradict its "being in itself," does not contradict the "Absolute Good," which is cognized in the process of improving the human species; this is movement toward the universal, reposing calmly as an immutable moral law. This argument is perfectly consistent, and it would be correct but for one "minor" circumstance, that is, the incorrectness of the teleological conception of the world. When the cognition of nature takes place within sociomorphic frameworks which ideologically distort the objective content of thought, the object of cognition does not disappear, since it exists independently of cognition, and is still cognized, even though by way of distorted "reflections." But when "the good" is projected onto the world outside of humanity, there is nothing whatever that corresponds to it.

What "the good" corresponds to is not something external to human society, but something within it. This is where the roots of the "universal" are to be found; this is the general interest of a given society as such, that is, as represented by its ruling class. The changing of these classes, and the struggles among them, involve the changing of attitudes about "the good," and the struggle of these attitudes.

To this in turn, however, the following objection can be raised: Do you really think the cognition of nature is not motivated by social interests? You yourself insist that practice determines theory! Do you really not think that cognition is the mastering of the world for humanity? Is there really no interest at work here? Does not the same, in consequence, apply in this case?

No, gentlemen, you are wrong!

This question requires more sustained attention, although it is not really so difficult to resolve. In reality, interest in the case of cognition is directed toward choosing the object of cognition, just as this interest chooses the object of the physical transformation of matter. This is the teleological side of things, behind which, as we have seen, stands social necessity. Here, however, the object of cognition (the object of mastering) has been chosen, and its objective laws are revealed. In these objective laws (this is what we are really talking about!) there is "not a grain of ethics," just as there is "not a grain of ethics" in a technological process, let us say in the blast-furnace process, in the open hearth steel-making process, in the electrolytic refining of aluminum, and so forth. Orientation in the world, theoretical and practical, is society's vital function. Society is the subject of the mastering of the world; in the socialist system, it is a subject in the full sense of the world, that is, a purposeful, conscious subject. In socialist society (we shall take it here as a particularly clear example!), society as a whole, as a teleological unity, chooses the objects of mastering (theoretical and practical, in their mutual interrelation) in a planned manner. But these objects, and the processes in which they are involved, whether the technological processes of production or in the "artificial" conditions of experimental laboratories, have no "morality," "good," "interest," and so forth. Operating here are the cold and indifferent laws of physics, chemistry, and biology—and that is all. Laws of nature are used by humanity for its purposes, but this does not by any means signify that these laws embody human (or superhuman) purposes in themselves. On the whole, there is precisely nothing human in them, and these categories are completely inapplicable to them. To apply these categories here is like injecting anti-diphtheria serum into a birch log, or seeking a confirmation of Kant's categorical imperative in the production of sulphuric acid.

Everything in the world is linked to everything else by dialectical interconnections. Ultimately, therefore, it is possible to establish a connection between the most diverse things, properties, and categories. But dialectics must not be transformed into sophistry, into logical tricks, into a conceptual game.

In our example of socialist society, necessity appears directly through teleology—the need to pass over into one's own opposite. The processes of cognition and mastering are directed teleologically; objects are chosen, and the elements of nature are disposed in a particular fashion. Essential links and relations are revealed within the natural world; natural necessity acts within the technological process, where human beings themselves act as "forces of nature" (Marx), that is, as particular quantities of energy. Cognition and production, as active intellectual processes, are teleological processes, behind the back of which stands necessity. However, there is no teleology that is characteristically the object, in and of itself, of cognition and production. Teleology is not immanent to these objects, but is transcendent; it lies outside them, in the subject, not the object. Such are the real dialectical relations.

Ethical "good" arises historically on the soil of society, and affects the relationships between people. The relations between people and the objective, sensible world enter into account only to the extent that this proceeds from the relationships between the people themselves. The herd instinct and the sense of tribal solidarity in the earliest stages of human development are not yet either "ethics" or a comprehended ethical "good." The elements of ethics, the categories of "virtue," "good," "justice," and so forth, arise in historical fashion when historically formed social contradictions also emerge—contradictions between society and the group, between groups, between society and the individual, between the group and the individual, then between classes, and so on. In societies with clearly expressed personal relations, moral law is formulated directly as God-given commandments and is usually mingled with primitive law-making. Behind all this stands the sanction of the deity.

In societies with anarchic relations, that is, in commodity and commodity-capitalist society, "the good" consists of fetishized norms of behavior, expressed as metaphysical, "innately compelling" imperatives, behind which stands the sanction of an impersonal and indeterminate divine substance. These teleological concepts and the interest which is expressed in them, an interest which is prolonged and "general" (in the sense of being general for a given class society and class), represent conditions for the self-preservation of a particular social system. They constitute a principle which acts within individuals almost automatically, in near-instinctive, "innate" fashion. Suppressing the "particular" and "isolated," this principle also constitutes the "essence" of moral "good." The real source of moral "good" is hence the "general" (in the above sense) interest, behind which stands necessity as an objective category of social development, as something which determines human orientations. In most cases this earthly and social source is concealed from the consciousness of human beings, who are consumed by "duty" and with striving for "the good." The more effectively this source is hidden on earth, in society, the more zealously it is sought in heaven, in divine "good," its rays sanctifying human destinies. This is how the original *quid pro quo* came about, when the "earthly" gives birth to the "earthly," and the latter is projected onto "heaven" and from there "justifies" itself. Displays of indifference to or denial of the earthly, displays formulated as "the good," are usually a means of self-preservation for groups waiting for blows to fall on them, groups without prospects and exposed constantly to the caprices of so-called "fate," together with deliberate efforts to eradicate the outwardly-acting will from among them.

This is depicted well by the same Hegel, willingly or otherwise revealing the material underpinnings of the ethical philosophy of the Stoics, who, it need scarcely be said, in many respects also managed a real understanding of the social nature of ethical norms. To analyze these achievements, however, is not our task here.

Let us hear from the dialectical maestro:

> The principle of the Stoics is an indispensable element in the idea of absolute consciousness; at the same time (just listen!), it constitutes an essential phenomenon of their epoch. When, as occurred in the Roman world, the life of the real spirit has been lost in the abstract universal, then consciousness, the real universality of which has been destroyed, has necessarily to return to its solitude and preserve itself in thought.... Everything that is directed outward—the world, circumstances, and so on—consequently takes on a character that allows it to be done away with or ignored.[5]

In other words, the conditions of life, social collapse, life constantly beneath a sword of Damocles, without any hope of an active breakthrough, leads in intellectual terms to the "ethical" abolition of the world, to training in order to resist "fear and desire." The highest good lies in the saying "A wise man is free even in chains, since he acts from within himself, without being suborned either by fear or by desire."

However, times of social collapse have also known the philosophy of *carpe diem* (as with Horatius Flaccus); the denial of any "universal," and an absolute individualist relativism (the Sophists in Greece, Gorgias, Protagoras, and others); a decadent, intellectually barren, hedonistically distorted amoralism (the literature of the late nineteenth century), and so forth. Explaining all these particular orientations is a job for concrete analysis, a specialized task beyond the bounds of the present work.

When people realize the earthly origins of ethics and of the corresponding norms, they accept these norms consciously as standards of appropriate conduct which they themselves need. The norms are applied first and foremost to the more important and fundamental types of conduct. In the process, ethics loses its fetishistic character. For people in the new socialist epoch, this "de-deification" does not in the least diminish the strength of ethical norms. On the contrary, the struggle for real happiness on earth, for the general interests of humanity, together with victories in this struggle and a real sense of the flourishing of life, give the norms of purposive behavior a much greater force than various heavenly and metaphysical authorities gave the corresponding norms of earlier times.

From the fact that ethics expresses one or another set of interests in interpersonal relations, and that these interests are contradictory (insofar as we are concerned with fundamentally hostile classes, fundamentally contradictory), it follows that ethical norms cannot be demonstrated for everyone, since here we find a discrepancy in the very premises, in the initial positions. General formulas are empty, and tell us nothing. Barely concrete formulas are already antagonistic. For example, Lenin in his well-known speech on the education of youth defined the ethical norms of Communists as follows: everything that serves Communism is good, while everything that is harmful to it is bad.

This is the way Lenin resolved the question of "good and evil." But this solution, which is quite correct from the point of view of the proletariat, as the bearer of the new mode of production, is inevitably taken by the bourgeoisie with an opposite mathematical sign. It cannot be demonstrated to capitalists that communism is "good" or "benign," since this contradicts the fundamental interests of the capitalist class. Even consciousness of the inevitability of socialism is not an argument to sway capitalists; they would rather assume Oswald Spengler's position of so-called "courageous pessimism." Optimism is cowardice, the "valiant" philosopher of the fascist decadence proclaimed from the point of view of the decaying bourgeoisie.

For today's ultra-imperialist bourgeoisie, "the good" is concentrated in a "beautiful" predatory animal. No talk of the brotherhood of peoples, of the interests of the majority, of the masses, of humanity, and so on will move these bourgeois, since they spit on all these premises. What do such things mean to them? Their interests are directly opposite. Their "good" lies in exploitation, in brigandage, in the moaning of victims, in super-brutality, in the flourishing of an oligarchic ruling elite, in the purity of its "blood," in its bandit "exploits," and so on. If you say, "But the interests of development?" the answer will be: "Why should I be responsible for that?" If you ask, "What about the realization of equality in conditions of development for each, the flowering of life?" the reply comes back, "What use is all this equality to me? I prefer the beauty of predators, devouring their neighbors!" The antithesis of the fundamental orientations also evokes the antithesis of their sublimated forms, and in critical epochs of history, such as our own, this antagonism reaches its highest level of tension, the tension of open warfare. Here the question is not resolved by logic, but by practical force. It is in this way, and only this way, that history poses the question.

Taking particular premises as one's starting point, however, might it be possible to construct a "scientific" ethic, an ethical technology of life, so to speak? Here, of course, there cannot be any talk of science, as the totality of the formulated (reflected) laws of being, even if only of social being. All we can speak of is the systematization of norms, which would nevertheless have their foundation in necessity. Is such a "scientific" ethics possible?

We shall answer this question first with an anecdote, which is in fact quite true. Friedrich Engels once asked Georgy Plekhanov about Pyotr Lavrov: "Tell me, please! Here is your Lavrov, he seems a decent fellow, but how he loves to talk about ethics!"

In this anecdote, as in the general attitude of Marxists to questions of ethics, there is a profoundly rational kernel. The general way in which the question is posed is clear. People who in this area are afflicted with an inferiority complex, to use Freud's term, love to prattle on about this formulation. To draw up a list of virtues and deeds, a typology of cases, means to be transformed into a pedant, and to impel people into numerous errors. Compiling a catechism of behavior, a new *True Mirror of Youth*, *Domostroi*, and so forth, scarcely has any point; life nowadays is so complex that it cannot be fitted into such texts without first being anesthetized.[6] Writers solve this problem far better using lively, many-sided, concrete examples (the educational significance of literature is enormous), and it was not without cause that Stalin termed these people "engineers of human souls." Now that ethics is being defetishized, it is simultaneously being politicized; this is best seen in the political coloration of the cult of labor as "a thing of honor, a thing of glory, a thing of valor and heroism," and in the cult of Soviet heroics in general. Here there are vital forces at work, not a dry textbook, not the prescriptions of a governess, not [Samuel] Smiles or Madame Genlis in new editions.

Therefore it is more vital, more truthful, better, more successful, more purposeful!

33

Hegel's Dialectical Idealism as a System

Earlier, while discussing the question of the so-called "philosophy of identity," we touched on Hegel's system.[1] Hegel, in fact, is not absent from any page of the present work. What is essential here, however, is not to analyze the points of departure and details of Hegel's system, but to take stock of the system in its entirety.

"Just as every man is the son of his time," Hegel wrote, "so philosophy is its contemporary epoch expressed in thought."[2]

This materialist idea, in which there is even the hint of an understanding of the particular conditionality of any *type* of thought, obliges us to say a few words about the social basis of Hegel's own philosophy. Briefly speaking, this philosophy is among the great ideological reflections of the transition of society from feudalism to bourgeois rule. In it, all the preceding stages of human development are presented as stages along the way to the ultimate realm of reason, cognizant of itself and assuming fixed shape in bourgeois social institutions and the corresponding ideology. In the first place, therefore, the system is historical; secondly, it has a revolutionary sting; thirdly, it arrives finally at a peaceful conclusion; that is, it is conservative, conservative in relation to the future.

There is no need here to repeat the already hackneyed truisms about the specific historical position of Germany, about the weakness of its bourgeoisie, about the fact that unlike the situation in France, where a real conflict took place, the struggle in Germany occurred mainly in the ideological field. Countless tomes have been written on these topics. Here we would like to dwell on two facts from Hegel's own social biography.

In his youth, as is well known, Hegel welcomed the French Revolution as a sunrise and planted a "liberty tree"; his school album abounded with such inscriptions as "*In tyrannos!*" "*Vive la liberté!*" and "*Vive Jean-Jacques!*" At the height of his career, however, what he anticipated was a peaceful, "reasoned" development following the inevitable tempests of the revolution and the Napoleonic period. (He saw Napoleon as virtually the incarnation of the World Spirit, mounted on horseback.) Because of this his biographer and commentator Kuno Fischer writes:

> The July revolution and the European disturbances [of 1830], the victorious Belgian revolution, the ill-fated Polish uprising, and also disturbances of every kind in Germany, all of which followed the events in Paris, did not accord in the least with Hegel's ideas and expectations. He was certain that the era of revolutions and coups d'état had come to an end with the fall of Napoleon, and that, as he proclaimed in his introductory lectures in Heidelberg and Berlin, a time of reasoned study and progress had begun. This was to be an era of peaceful, deliberate, and considered development, an era that was also recognized in his system as the culminating act of wisdom. The new era was to see justice evolve in the world, a development which according to Kant as well constituted the task of the future. The year 1815, however, proved not to be the end of an era, but merely the end of the first act of the revolution; the fifteen-year restoration was only an interlude. Outbursts of revolution were flaring up again on the world scene, and were revealing unexpected and unpleasant [sic!—author] pictures of the future for the philosopher Hegel as for the historian Niebuhr. Revolutionary dangers even threatened the British constitution, placing reforms to the Parliament on the agenda.[3]

It is no wonder, then, that Hegel's philosophical system in its entirety is a great bourgeois theodicy, which, after an immense historical warm-up phase, with world reason passing through its various stages of development, has settled down to private property, the Prussian state, the Protestant Christian religion, and Hegel's philosophical system as the final and absolute result. This latter is the goal, attained at last through painful and contradictory historical development. All the preceding stages are way stations along this road, coexisting in "sublated" form in this ultimate historical stage; it is in this fact that the historical justification of this stage consists. Here the colossal sweep, universality of scope, and world-historical, even cosmic scale serve merely to glorify this final result. It is no accident how Hegel regards private property, outside of which he cannot conceive of true freedom, while in his view the movement of history amounts to "progress in the consciousness of freedom." In Hegel's philosophical system, we therefore have a truly classical philosophy of the bourgeoisie. The ideology of the latter had not yet degenerated into the kind of vulgar apologetics in which all, or almost all, of its scientific aspects disappear. While idealizing and distorting the picture of real development, Hegel's system nevertheless retains its valid aspects to a very large degree. This appears with particular clarity in the dialectical method and the dialectics of past development. Hegel's system, however, has now entered into conflict with this method, since for Hegel the flow of history comes to a halt in bourgeois society and its superstructures, just as Shchedrin's Ugryum-Burcheyev halts the flow of a river.[4]

Moreover, since Hegel's system views the dialectics of the past solely as a mediating feature of the rule of the bourgeoisie, and places a barricade across the road to the future, it thereby compromises the past as well. This conservative side of the system, which constitutes its essence as a system, hides everything else in its shadow.

Friedrich Engels in his time explained this brilliantly in his work *Ludwig Feuerbach*. Hegel, Engels wrote:

> was compelled to make a system and in accordance with traditional requirements, a system of philosophy must conclude with some sort of absolute truth. Therefore, however much Hegel, especially in his *Logic,* emphasized that...eternal truth is nothing but the logical, or the historical, process itself, he nevertheless finds himself compelled to supply this process with an end, just because he has to bring his system to a termination at some point or other. In his *Logic,* he can make this end a beginning again, since here the point of conclusion, the Absolute Idea—which is absolute only insofar as Hegel has absolutely nothing to say about it—"alienates itself," that is, transforms itself, into nature, and comes to itself again later in the mind, that is, in thought and in history. But at the end of the whole philosophy a similar return to the beginning is possible only in one way. Namely, by conceiving of the end of history as follows: mankind arrives at the cognition of this Absolute Idea, and declares that this cognition of the Absolute Idea is reached in Hegelian philosophy. In this way, however, the whole dogmatic content of the Hegelian system is declared to be absolute truth, in contradiction to his dialectical method, which dissolves all dogmatism. Thus the revolutionary side is smothered beneath the overgrowth of the conservative side. (*Ludwig Feuerbach und der Ausgang der klassischen deutschen Philosophie*)[5]

According to Hegel, the movement of the World Spirit, the mind of God, passes through three main stages: a) the absolute spirit in itself; b) the absolute spirit as nature, which represents an other-being of this spirit; and c) the absolute spirit, cognizant of itself. This mystical labor and creative sport of the world spirit is fanned in Hegel's account by a genuine, majestic inspiration, since beneath it, in essence, is concealed the history of the world, the history of society and of human thought, although a mighty, universal process is also played out, like a mystical masquerade. Each of the three stages is in turn divided into distinct steps; this finds its expression in the articulation of the philosophical system itself, and even in the way its exposition is divided up between Hegel's major works.

In the *Phenomenology of Spirit*, Hegel depicts the stages of the development of this spirit, beneath which is concealed the evolution of human thought from "objective consciousness" to "absolute knowledge." Here, in idealistically distorted form, a detailed view is provided of "objective consciousness," that is, the growth of the cognitive relationship between subject and object, consciousness and object, beginning with sensations ("sensory truth"); next comes the transition to perceptual consciousness (the theory of perception) and to rational definitions, with a transition from sensuous objectivity to "the peaceful realm of laws," with all the contradictions immanent in the process. Then follows a transition to self-consciousness, in which one's own consciousness becomes the object of consciousness, and where "the truth and authenticity of one's own self" is present, while the unity of self-consciousness with the self is also seen as an aspiration. Here Hegel provides an analysis, in particularly abstract form, of the historical varieties of "self-consciousness" (see, for example, the sections on master and slave, Stoicism and Skepticism, "unhappy consciousness," and so forth) and of the contradictory nature of the process. The solution lies in a shift to rational thought and rational consciousness, and also to objectified forms of consciousness (the rule of right, morality, and the state). Completing the picture are religion and absolute knowledge.

Engels, in the same work on Feuerbach, very aptly describes Hegel's phenomenology of mind as parallel to "the embryology and paleontology of the mind, a development of individual consciousness through its different stages, set in the form of an abbreviated reproduction of the stages through which human consciousness has passed in the course of history."[6] (Engels here is hinting at the well-known biogenetic law, formulated by Ernst

Haeckel, according to which the individual human embryo reproduces the evolution of the species in abbreviated form.)

The *Phenomenology* thus describes the movement toward the "rule of reason." From here, Hegel makes the shift to his *Logic*. In this work (*Die Wissenschaft der Logik*, the so-called "Great Logic," as opposed to the "Small Logic," that is, the *Encyclopedia*), the author is concerned with the movement of concepts, that is, solely with the categories of rational thought, with universal ontology and metaphysics, in which "logic" does not by any means signify only subjective logic, but also objective logic, that is, ontology. Here one should not lose sight of the philosophical conception according to which everything is spirit, that is, God. It is therefore not surprising that Hegel declares, for example: "Logic should be understood as a system of pure reason, as the realm of pure thought. This realm is truth, as it exists without any cover, in itself and for itself. It may therefore be said that this content is the depiction of God as he exists in his eternal essence, prior to the creation of nature and of his ultimate spirit" (*W. d. L.*).[7]

For Hegel, then, the subject matter consists of pure thought, outside of any sensory concreteness, that is, the highest intellectual abstractions. Nevertheless, we find a vast quantity of valuable ideas in this central part of Hegel's philosophical system, since this work is also where we find developed the dialectical logic, the "logic of contradictions," which in its "rational" form (as Marx called it), that is, when freed from its mystical cover, entered the arsenal of dialectical materialism as its most important weapon.

Here too, the "idea" undergoes development. But it develops "in the abstract element of thought." In a letter of March 29, 1866, to F.A. Lange, Engels said of Hegel's *Logic* that "his (that is, Hegel's—author) real philosophy of nature is to be found in the second part of the *Logic*—in his understanding of 'essence,' in which, properly speaking, the core of the whole doctrine is located."[8]

Here the movement of concepts proceeds from the doctrine of being to that of essence, and to the doctrine of the conception, or Notion, which culminates in the "absolute idea." The process of the emergence of ever more profound and general laws of being, which are represented in Hegel's system as relationships between abstract ideas, is depicted here in highly abstract form, with idealist distortions. Meanwhile, throughout the whole extent of the development, and at all its stages, the differentiation of the whole, the unity of opposites, and the penetration of one into another, into its opposite, appear as the motivating principles. From the initial analysis of "being" and "nothingness" and of their interrelationships there flows their unity, appearing as origin, rise, and destruction, transition into another, change, and development. This side of the *Logic* is also its revolutionary side, in which dialectics becomes the "algebra of revolution." The *Logic* concludes with the "absolute idea," which is the unity, that is, the dismembered identity, of the theoretical and practical idea. Condensed in the absolute idea are all the preceding aspects, present within it in "sublated form." The content of the absolute idea is thus the whole content of the system of Hegel's *Logic* and the essence of the dialectical method, that is, the dialectical development of concepts. Here, consequently, we find the unity of knowledge and will, of the ideas of truth and good, of the ideas of theory and practice, together with "the complete truth," in which knowledge has become its own object, and where we have "thinking about thinking" or *noesis noeseos*.[9]

Following on this is the transformation of the absolute idea into absolute spirit, by way of the intermediate stages of nature and of the so-called "ultimate spirit." For Hegel, meanwhile, the idea of good is also understood as the will to nature.

"Nature is the idea in its other-being." "The externality of space and time" is "the form of its determinateness."[10] This is how the *Logic* passes over into *The Philosophy of Nature*.

In *The Philosophy of Nature*, Hegel depicts the stages of nature, from its lowest forms to its highest. As Engels justly observes, however, nature for Hegel is not something that undergoes development, that is, development in the natural-historical sense of the word. "For him (that is, for Hegel—author), all of nature is merely a repetition of logical abstractions in sensible external form" (Marx).[11]

In a general way, Hegel expresses this as follows:

> Nature should be regarded as a system of stages, of which one proceeds necessarily out of another and constitutes the truth that is closest to the stage from which it follows. This, however, occurs within the internal idea that constitutes the ground of nature, and not in such a way that one stage gives birth naturally to another. Metamorphosis occurs only in an idea as such, since only a change in an idea is development. Intellectual investigation should reject such obscure (!!), basically sensuous ideas as, in particular, the doctrine of the so-called origin of, for example, plants and animals from water, or of more developed animal organisms from lower organisms.[12]

Meanwhile, teleological understanding is regarded as being of paramount importance. "True" teleological understanding—this conception is regarded as absolutely vital—therefore consists in viewing nature as free in its distinctive vital activity (*The Philosophy of Nature*).[13]

The entire *Philosophy of Nature*, as we have repeatedly had cause to note, is packed tightly with mystical ideas.

The three main stages of nature correspond to the movement of a concept from the general through the particular to the individual. These three stages are: general corporeality, particular corporeality, and individual corporeality. The latter, as the unity of the general and the particular, forms the living individuality, the organism. Accordingly, we are concerned with matter in general, with all its indefiniteness and formlessness, then with physical individuality, and finally, with life, that is, mechanics, physics, and organics (compare with "mechanism," "chemism," and "teleology" in the "Great Logic").

The "goal of nature," however, consists in doing away with itself, breaking through the crust of its directness and sensuousness, immolating itself like the phoenix, and then, out of this externality, having regained its youth, appearing in the form of the spirit.

Hence the transition to the philosophy of the spirit.

In *The Philosophy of the Spirit*, Hegel is concerned with an idea, but with an idea in its being for itself, that is, an idea cognizant of itself, a self-conscious idea. Hegel in this work deals with questions of psychology, and also with objectified forms of consciousness and their social-material substrate. All this is presented in the following forms:

1. The science of the subjective spirit (anthropology, the phenomenology of spirit, psychology):
2. The science of the objective spirit (law, morality).

Morality culminates in the state. The particular works that stand in the closest relationship to *The Philosophy of the Spirit* are his *Philosophy of Right* and his *Philosophy of History*.

The doctrine of absolute spirit, the final element in the philosophy of the spirit, as such, is the object of the philosophy of art (here the absolute spirit contemplates itself); of the philosophy of religion (here the absolute spirit presents itself); and of the philosophical history of philosophy (here the absolute spirit knows itself). These themes, as is well known, were the topic of Hegel's "lectures."

It is particularly interesting to note that for Hegel, the development of an idea corresponds to the development (historical development) of various philosophical systems, while these latter are for him "aspects" of his own philosophy, in which they are present in "sublated form." No philosophical system is discarded *a limine*, or is destroyed, but is instead transcended, negated in the Hegelian sense, that is, "sublated."

From this necessarily superficial review of Hegel's system one can see the grandiose and encyclopedic character of this mighty philosophical edifice, this veritable pyramid of Cheops of philosophical idealism. Hegel was a man of encyclopedic learning who had ingested the whole sum of the knowledge of his epoch, and it is not surprising that we find in his works a vast quantity of fruitful thoughts. But if we take his system as a system, it collapses and crumbles into dust.

Hegel in many ways resembled Goethe, that other giant of his age. If, as Engels remarked, *The Phenomenology of Spirit* is Hegel's embryology and paleontology, then Goethe's *Faust*, that great artistic epic, in essence has to do with the same thing. Hegel was exceedingly fond of underpinning his thoughts with ideas and artistic images from Goethe. In his own fashion, Goethe was undoubtedly a dialectician, and as we saw in the above account, Hegel took with enthusiasm to the artistic contemplation of the whole, protesting against intellectual vivisection. Goethe was impressed by the fact that Hegel stood wholeheartedly on the side of his, Goethe's, theory of color, which in its essentials was incorrect.

It should be stressed emphatically, however, that Goethe decisively objected to Hegel's idealist abstractions and theological tendencies. Eckermann reports, for example (conversation of March 23, 1827) Goethe's view of a book by Hinrichs (a Hegelian, writing on ancient tragedy):

> To tell the truth, I'm sorry that ... Hinrichs has been so spoiled by Hegelian philosophy that he has lost his capacity for unprejudiced natural contemplation and thought, the place of which has gradually been taken by an artificial and ponderous manner of thought and expression.... In his book there are quite a few places where the thought doesn't move forward, and the obscure expression revolves continually in the same circle, as with the witch's multiplication table in my *Faust*.[14]

In a letter to Müller of July 16 the same year, Goethe says: "I don't want to know anything about Hegel's philosophy, although I like Hegel himself very much."[15]

Goethe was a hylozoistic pantheist of the aesthetic type, with a marked inclination toward sensualist materialism, and to paint him with the same brush as Hegel where philosophy is concerned is quite inadmissible.

If we are to characterize Hegel's system, it is extremely important to keep in mind the system's basic aspects: 1) idealism; 2) theology; and 3) teleology.

Idealism is not a doctrine of the identity of matter and spirit, and as we spelled out in detail in the chapter on the so-called philosophy of identity, Hegel's philosophical system is not, despite common opinion, a doctrine of the identity of the corporeal and spiritual. Hegel himself understood this perfectly. In his *Logic* we find the following passage:

> Although modern philosophy is often jokingly (!) termed the philosophy of identity, in fact it is precisely this philosophy, and above all speculative logic, that has shown the worthlessness of pure rational identity, as distinct from difference. At the same time, it also demands insistently that we should not be content merely with difference, but that we should also get to know the internal unity of everything that exists.[16]

According to Hegel, this unity is such that nature is an other-being of the spirit, rather than the spirit being an other-being of nature. Matter and spirit are not modes of a single substance; nature is merely the sensual-objective expression of the universal spiritual substance, the "spirit," which is also a true *causa sui*. It is characteristic of Hegel that although his general practice is to regard the movement of philosophical thought as associated with the replacement of one system by another, with each succeeding phase "sublating" (that is, transcending, negating, but also preserving) the preceding one, he dismisses materialism in a number of places as if by way of a digression, not regarding it as a philosophy at all. "For Hegel," Marx wrote, "the process of thought, which he even transforms into an independent subject called the idea, is the demiurge of reality."[17]

The Greek *nous* and *logos* (that is, "Reason") and the Christian-Platonic "Word," as the real creative substance of the world, live on in Hegel's system. The task of philosophy is to "understand the phenomena of the spirit in their necessary sequence." From this movement of the spirit, a universal process is also constituted. Human corporeality is the embodiment of the spirit, and in the integral organism the prime place belongs to Aristotelian entelechy. History is the objectified form of movement of the same spirit. Nature is its other-being, and so forth.

Here there is no need to repeat the critique of idealism as such; this was provided earlier, from both the sociological and logical angles. For Hegel, however, objective idealism is directly expressed in theological form. In this connection it is typical of Hegel that he moves back beyond the positions occupied by Kant. As is well known, Kant in his *Critique of Pure Reason* blew to smithereens all the so-called proofs of the existence of God. It is true that in *The Critique of Practical Reason* he let God in again through the back door, but he admitted this divine being as a necessary postulate, impossible to predict by logical means. Among other "proofs" of the divine existence, Kant destroyed the so-called ontological one, which proclaims that since God is conceived of as existing in the present, and since present existence necessarily has a predicate of being, God therefore exists. Kant showed convincingly that extracting being from this idea is just as impossible as turning an imagined hundred thalers into real ones.[18]

Hegel defended the ontological proof against Kant, despite the scholastic foolishness of the argument. Here Hegel moved decisively backward, as in his philosophy of nature, where unlike Kant and in defiance of the spirit of the dialectic, he denied the historical development of nature. In Hegel's theology, anthropomorphism and sociomorphism are clearly evident. The absolute spirit "contemplates," "presents," and "cognizes" itself; that is, while constituting the universalized and hypostatized form of the human intellect, it functions as a thinking human being. The division, or differentiation, of the "idea" into the "theoretical" and "practical" idea, the "striving" of the spirit toward the world ("on the eve" of the transformation of the spirit into its other-being, nature), and so forth, all proceed along the same lines. God, the great "master" of the world, is a depiction of the creative and regulating function of humanity in extra-historical and abstract form. Hegel perpetuates Aristotle's idealist-theological doctrine of a "beatific deity," occupying himself with self-knowledge. From the modern point of view, that is, from the point of view of socialist humanity, all these fundamental aspects of the system seem childish, barbaric rubbish. To present the essence of the universe as delving into itself in solitude, and finding satisfaction in this—what naive, primitive "philosophy"! It appears strange and incomprehensible that an educated individual should be capable of such thinking. It is interesting, in this respect, to note that Hegel, while criticizing the ideology of the Enlightenment (and at times raising valid objections to aspects of rationalism), openly defends religious anthropomorphism.

In *The Phenomenology of Spirit*, for example, Hegel asserts that the anthropomorphizing of God in so-called popular religion flows from a profound and "truthful" need to have a living god, without which the immanentness of God in the world is impossible. The idea of the "supreme being" as put forward in the Enlightenment, the Robespierrean supreme *être suprême*, is flat and empty; the god here recalls the exhalation of a gas.

An antagonistic mode of production thus calls forth the corresponding mode of presentation, in which thought moves in sociomorphic categories of domination and submission. These forms prove so durable that no amount of education of the ideologues will turn the so-called higher functions (supremacy, dominion, ideological hegemony, mental labor, and so on) into the substance of the historical and cosmic process. In the history of thought there are well-known examples of even specialized branches of mental labor finding expression in the characterization of God either as master, as "initial cause" or "prime mover," as architect, as military commander, as geometrician, or as mathematician in general. To Hegel this God is above all a philosopher, since theoretical reasoning is the supreme pursuit. Divine philosophy, which is the self-consciousness and self-cognition of God, therefore views God as a theoretician....

Closely entwined with theology is teleology, in which Reason, that is, God, proposes and realizes its goals, in the process revealing the "guile of Reason" (*The Phenomenology of Spirit*):

> Reason is just as artful as it is powerful. Its guile consists in its mediating activity, which obliges objects to act on one another according to their nature and to annihilate one another in this process, while reason does not intervene, and at the same time realizes only its own purpose. In this sense it might be said that divine providence is related to the world and to its progress as an absolute guile. God obliges people to live according to their own private passions and interests, but out of this life there arises the realization of his intentions, quite different from the goals of the self-interested individuals whom he uses for this purpose.[19]

On the universal scale, what is involved is the self-cognition of the spirit in philosophy.

In nature, as we have seen, the purpose also reigns supreme.

When Hegel was traveling about the Alps, and found himself in a desolate mountain landscape, he commented:

> I doubt that the most devout theologian would venture to impute to nature here in these mountains a purpose aimed at benefiting humanity.... Amid these uninhabited wastelands, educated people would be more likely to think up quite different theories and sciences, but scarcely those elements of physico-theology that display the arrogant assumption of humanity that nature organized everything for humanity's satisfaction and delight.... This arrogance, meanwhile, is typical of our century, finding gratification in the thought that everything has been made for humanity by an outside being rather than in the consciousness that it is humanity itself that has ascribed all these purposes to nature (quotation from Kuno Fischer—author).[20]

Hegel, however, did not live "among these uninhabited wastes," and in *The Philosophy of Nature*, despite his rejection of "superficial theology," that is, of its vulgar form, he regards all of organic nature as theologically predestined for humanity. We have seen that even Hegel was not spared from this philosophy by all the jibes directed at it. Immanent theology, however, is also theology, and here too a purpose is linked with a particular subject (see the "forms" of Aristotle, entelechy, the soul, the spirit, the world spirit).

In exactly the same fashion, divine goals are discovered in history.

The entire system is therefore theological and teleological through and through. Idealism, theology, and teleology are in no way compatible with modern science, as we have shown in detail in the preceding chapters.

The historical process appears near the end of *The Phenomenology of Spirit*, in the context of the revealing of the purpose:

> The *goal*, Absolute Knowing, or Spirit that Knows itself as Spirit, has for its path the recollection of the Spirits as they are in themselves and as they accomplish the organization of their realm. Their preservation, regarded from the side of their free existence appearing in the form of contingency, is History; but regarded from the side of their philosophically comprehended organization, it is the Science of Knowing in the sphere of appearance or phenomena: the two together, comprehended History, form alike the inwardizing and the Calvary of the absolute Spirit, the actuality, truth, and certainty of his throne, without which he would be lifeless and alone. Only
>
> From the chalice of this realm of spirits
> Foams forth from Him his own infinitude.[21]

As we have seen, however, it is within Hegel's philosophical system that Absolute Spirit cognizes itself, and consequently realizes its goal of absolute truth. Here, the movement ceases. Engels, in the quotation above, reveals wonderfully this overall contradiction between a rigid system, in which development has been closed off, and the dialectical method, which constantly drives further ahead.

In the field of history, movement has become bogged down in private property, the Prussian state, and the Christian religion, and in nature things are no better. In nature there is no development whatever, merely reflection of the movement of the idea in the list of species. There is no origin of one species out of another; species are permanent. From fear of materialism, the dialectics of the continuous and discontinuous is annulled. On the one hand, atomic theory is denied while, on the other, deified light is declared to represent absolute continuity; and so forth.

Infinity is termed "evil infinity," to which is preferred a "truth" that is a closed-in infinity of circles. The fear of falling into "eternal progress" and "evil infinity" is merely the reverse side of the search for the absolute, which in essence contradicts the principle of dialectical movement.

We have already observed that as an idealist distortion of real relationships, Hegel's system depicts the historical process in a curved mirror. This depiction is distorted not just frontally, that is, not only because the relationship between thought and being, spirit and matter, is inverted. Also tied up with the idealist conception is the "subjecting to reason" of real historical progress. All of Hegel's *Phenomenology*, like his system as a whole, is constructed on a consistent succession of stages of a single whole. Meanwhile, there has never been any such integral world-historical process, just as there has never been a direct ascent from one stage to another. Such a conception of world history was characteristic of the optimistic period in the development of bourgeois ideology, and is just as false as the idea of constant degeneration, with a golden age lying in the past, or the theory of eternal circular movement. All these points of view are one-sided, and Marx was quite correct to point out that in reality, that is, in historical reality, there are movements forward, epochs of regression, periods of stagnation, movements in circles, in spirals, and so on. It is clear that the "subjecting to reason" and "logification" of the entire historical process, as of the entire world process, inevitably brings in its wake a corresponding stylization of reality, and moreover, the kind of stylization that represents a new, derivative distortion of real relationships.

Although Hegel depicts real relations, movements, and processes in cart-before-the-horse fashion, he depicts them nonetheless. "Drunken speculation" represents a break with reality, but this does not mean that Hegel came up with his philosophy "solely out of his own head." That would be quite impossible. Hegel's logical abstractions, successively linked to the whole preceding development of philosophy and resting on this development, are abstractions from reality into the sort of abstractness in which well-known defenses of reality have become "excessive" (Dietzgen), and have been transformed into parasitical categories which at the same time are as thin as Pharaoh's cows. Demonstrating theoretically the full potential of concrete abstractions, Hegel at the same time was exceedingly remote from living concreteness, despite speaking constantly of it.

In his *Notes of a Young Man*, Alexander Herzen makes the following observation:

> ...without letting ourselves be distracted by authorities, we shall have to confess that the lives of the German poets and thinkers are extraordinarily one-sided; I do not know of a single German biography that is not saturated with philistinism. For all their cosmopolitan universality, they lack a whole element of humanity, that of practical life. Although they write a great deal, especially now, about life in its concrete reality, the very fact that they write about it, and do not live it, proves their abstractness.[22]

This last aphorism is not lacking either in wit, or in the aptness of a correct characterization.

Taken as a whole, therefore, Hegel's system is:

— optimistic, since it expresses the moods of a progressive and still self-confident bourgeoisie, which sees huge prospects for development;
— idealist, since this is the ideology of the ruling class, the monopolist of mental labor, the "enlightened" class, to whose reason the inert "mass" is counterposed;
— universal in time, since the bourgeoisie feels itself to be the heir to all culture, and views its new world social order as the embodiment of reason, the final link of development, in relation to which all of world history has consisted merely of preparatory stages;
— universal in extent, since its "universality" is the reflection and expression of the world growth of capitalist productive relations, the creation of a "world market," a real forming of capitalist humanity;
— nationalist, since it is not only an expression of the creation of a world market and of the world hegemony of capitalism, but is also an aspect of

the building of the national state and of the anticipation of expansion, under the pseudonym of the special world significance of Germany;
— revolutionary in terms of method, since it embodies the struggle against feudalism and the rise of the bourgeoisie, while the entire preceding historical process is understood in its dialectical, contradictory dynamic, where old forms of being are destroyed one after another and new ones arise, in order to disappear in turn;
— conservative in its system as such, since it reflects the victory of bourgeois society, which is presented as the final stage of historical development, in which the absolute spirit comes to cognition of itself, revealing its content in Hegelian philosophy as absolute truth.

Here, therefore, we find revealed the truth of one of Hegel's remarkable aphorisms, according to which philosophy is the contemporary epoch captured in thought.

Quite naturally, however, this epoch too proved to be just as "final" as all the others. The contradictions of capitalism, the antagonism of classes and interests, were the real material spring driving the historical development of Germany, and this fact was expressed in the downfall of the Hegelian school. But since continuity in the field of ideological development is also to be observed in history, these contradictions found expression in the growing contradictions of Hegel's system itself. While the "right" Hegelians were beginning to develop the system's conservative side, and on the basis of Hegel's position on the rationality of everything that was real were creating a comprehensive apologia for historical swinishness that was totally in the spirit of the so-called "historicist school," the "left" was rising in revolt, making use of the revolutionary side of Hegelianism, and in the first instance, of the shattering, subversive power of the dialectical method. Once the stage of Feuerbachian sensualism, anthropologism, and humanism had been transcended, there arose the dialectical materialism of Marx and Engels. Meanwhile, the new ideology, expressing the strivings and hopes of an oppressed class, the proletariat, incorporated many diverse elements from preceding developments, and not only from German philosophy. Marx had an exceedingly thorough knowledge of materialist philosophy, from the Greeks (as is well known, his first work was devoted to Epicurus and Democritus), up to and including contemporary materialist doctrines. He also had an intimate knowledge of the great British materialists Bacon, Hobbes, and Locke, as well as of the French Encyclopedists and Spinoza. Here, historicism took on a completely new form, and the genius of Marx created new starting points for the development of philosophy, establishing the doctrine of social-historical humanity actively transforming the external world. The heavenly categories were brought down to earth. From standing on its head, philosophy was placed on its feet. The dams set in place by Hegel to hold back historical development were breached. Abstractions were made concrete in fact, not merely in words, and were thoroughly understood as abstractions from a reality lying outside them, as depictions of reality, and not as powerless, self-moving essences.

Marx dispersed the whole great masquerade of the most exalted figures of bourgeois ideology, forever sowing fear and agitation in all the salons of the absolute spirit, where its numerous masks dance their numbing minuets. In the subsequent epoch of degeneration of bourgeois philosophy, Marxism has continued to develop on the basis of the whole totality of modern knowledge. Engels with his *Dialectics of Nature*, and Lenin with his philosophical works, introduced a great deal that was new, continuing Marx's tradition and enriching the philosophy of Marxism, which in a particular sense is the great heir to Hegelian philosophy.

34

The Dialectics of Hegel and the Dialectics of Marx

Following a brief review of Hegel's system as a whole, it is appropriate to dwell in particular on dialectics. This is not only a method of reasoning, but above all represents the totality of the general laws of being (of nature, history, and thought). Dialectics is thus also ontology.

The specific feature of dialectics consists in the contradictory nature of movement, in the clash of opposed aspects and their unification. The splitting of the whole and the unity of opposites—*coincidentia oppositorum*—is the essence of dialectics.

Dialectics, insofar as we speak of it as a science, takes its origin from ancient Greek philosophy (especially that of Heraclitus, Aristotle, and so on); on the threshold of the modern era from Giordano Bruno; and in the modern era from Kant and Schelling. It is in Hegel, however, that dialectics is presented in its most developed form, and it is systematically expounded above all in his "Greater Logic" (*Die Wissenschaft der Logik*). The *terminology* used by Hegel, at which there is no need to be embarrassed or perplexed, is of course associated with the idealist nature of his philosophy.

The general contours of Hegel's *Logic* are as follows: a contradiction is manifested when the determinateness of an idea, which has just been affirmed, or as Hegel says, posited, is negated. The resolution of the contradiction is the unity of opposites, that is, a dual negation, which is an affirmation (thesis, antithesis, synthesis, the so-called triad).

The road to affirmation leads through two negations. The eventual result becomes the starting point for new movement. In this way, thought passes from elementary concepts to complex ones, from the immediate to the mediated, from the abstract to the concrete. This series constitutes development. The stages of concepts have the same relation to one another as the stages of consciousness in the *Phenomenology*: each contains the next in embryo. In each successive stage the preceding one is contained "in sublated form"; therefore, to use Hegel's terminology, the highest stage is the "truth" of the lowest, and constitutes the object of its urge, its striving (the mysticism of ideas!). All so-called "pure ideas" are ideas and thoughts, but they are also being; that is, logic and ontology coincide.

The changing of stages is development. All development is self-development. Hegel's *Logic* also sets out a picture of the development of the idea of development. It too is divided in a tripartite manner; it answers the questions: 1) what; 2) because of what; and 3) to what end, in the most general and abstractedly "pure" form. "What" in its most abstract form is pure being—that is, completely indeterminate being (and to this corresponds the doctrine of being); "because of what" is the ground, the substance, the essence (and to this corresponds the doctrine of essence); "to what end" is the purpose, the self-existent idea, the subject or selfhood (and to this corresponds the doctrine of the Notion).

Such are the most general contours of Hegel's dialectics, whose principal defects are readily seen even here:

1. Idealism. The basis consists of the movement of ideas. The development from the abstract to the concrete is presented, not as "the spiritual reproduction of the concrete" (Marx's *geistige Reproduktion*), but as the miraculous rise of the concrete itself.
2. Mysticism. One stage passes into another, with the lower phase having an "urge," a "desire" to transform itself into the higher. These and other analogous categories also operate in the *Logic* even when the question involved is development in general, the process of change in the world in all its forms, starting with inorganic nature.
3. Teleology. The purpose of all development, its immanent mainspring, is the idea itself, selfhood, the subject. Here both idealism and mysticism are involved simultaneously.
4. Truth is not the accuracy of the reflection of being in human consciousness, but a higher phase in relation to a lower one.

5. One-sidedness of movement, linked to idealist teleology. All that is present is progressive movement; the possibility of the process of change being regressive is excluded by the concept of divine purpose. The dialectical opposition of movement from lower forms to higher and from higher forms to lower is not grasped, and consequently, neither is their unity. Idealism in this case comes into direct conflict with dialectics.

Goethe in his time wrote: "Soon it will be twenty years that all the Germans have been subsisting on transcendental speculations. Once they realize this, they will seem to themselves to be great cranks" (Goethe, *Collected Works*, vol. 10).[1]

As we know, however, it is not at all a matter of crankery, but of powerful social determinants conditioning the relevant philosophical constructs. It needed the formation of the ideology of a new class to tear off the mask of "crankery" and extract the "rational kernel" from the "mystical shell" (Marx).

Marx did away with the above-noted flaws of Hegelian dialectics, and developed this dialectics in his own materialist fashion. From this point of view the basis of this dialectics, the splitting of the whole and the unity of opposites, is one of the most general laws of all being and thought. This is reality, the objective law of universal motion in its qualitatively different forms. Meanwhile, what is involved is not only—by no means only— mechanical movement; also involved here are counterposed mechanical forces, positive and negative electrical charges, magnetic polarity, mathematically reflected positive and negative quantities in general, the biological differentiation into the male and female sexes, the social division of society into classes, the duality of matter and spirit, and so on.

The differentiation of material reality and the motion that corresponds to it are reflected in theory. Real laws of the dialectical motion of nature, society, and thought are reflected in thought about nature, about society, and about thought itself. Dialectics is therefore cleansed of all theology, teleology, and mysticism, and of the absurd one-sidedness and one-sided adsurdities associated with this.

Hegel begins his *Logic* with an examination of being and nothingness. Being is "pure indeterminateness and emptiness." It is also nothingness. In this relationship, all subsequent categories are present in embryo. Abstract being is empty, and therefore nothingness; however, it is also distinguished from nothingness, since it indicates that thought exists, while nothingness is bare negation. Being is a thesis. Its negation is nothingness. Their unity is becoming—in which being and nothingness are found "in sublated form." The transition of nothingness into its opposite, being, is origin or emergence. The transition of being into nothingness, as its opposite, is disappearance. But origin in itself is also disappearance; the disappearance of one is the appearance of another. The result of becoming is determinate being; that is, being that is not empty and without content, but which has certain properties; this is present being, *Dasein*. (Lenin translates it as *sushchestvovanie*, "existence.") The determinateness of present being is quality.

Here the whole picture grows more complex, and the movement again shifts to a higher level. The presence of a determinateness presupposes some other, from which the given determinateness differs; in the process each is delimited from the other. Consequently, determinateness includes in itself an element of non-being, that is, the negation of this other; that is, it has two aspects, being and non-being. (*Omnis determinatio est negation*, said Spinoza.[2]) This contradictoriness is a precondition of any development. On the other hand, something and something different, something other, are interconnected. Present being presupposes its other. A thing cannot be only "in and for" itself, and the same applies to any thing. Each of them is the other of another, different from something different; each thing is delimited by another, and vice versa. To be delimited means to be finite. Hence qualitatively determinate being, present being, something, is both different from another, is related to it (being in itself, and being for another), and passes over into it. It is another, and at the same time not another. The unity of other-being and of non-distinct being—that is, unity at a higher level, when being includes determinateness and quality—is other-becoming, or change. A thing is always involved in a process of change, while it does not pass over into change.

> Something becomes different, but this different thing is itself something; consequently, it is again in its turn becoming different, and so on unto infinity.
>
> This infinity is an evil, or negative, infinity, since it is something different, the negation of the finite, which, however, thus arises again, and consequently, is by no means removed.... (*The Science of Logic*)[3]

Progressus in infinitum, endless progress, is here an unresolved contradiction. Here we find a dualism of the finite and the infinite, in which the two sides fall apart, forming irreconcilable opposites; the infinite is opposed to the finite, and in the finite has its boundary, that is, it itself becomes delimited. The truly infinite has the finite not outside of itself, but within itself. Here we have finished, complete, present being, or being for itself. The concept of the finite with no end, that is, of an irreconcilable contradiction, is illustrated by a straight line where the finite sector A to X may continue in both directions. The concept of "true infinity," meanwhile, is illustrated by the circumference of a circle, where completeness [*zavershennost*] and finishedness [*zakonchennost*] are present. True infinity is the sublation of finiteness, in the same way as true eternity is the sublation of temporality. The finite or real is sublated in infinity and is posed in ideal fashion.

> The truth of the finite is rather its idealness. This idealness of the finite is the basic proposition of philosophy, and therefore any true philosophy is idealism. The vital thing is not to accept as infinite that which in its determination immediately becomes particular and finite. Therefore, it is necessary to pay more serious attention here to this difference. The fundamental concept of philosophy, the concept of true infinity, is dependent on it.[4]

The concept of present being is thus a completed one. The other is included in it and closed off. There is no longer a transition here to the other. Change is removed. Quality is removed. Completed present being is being for itself, immutable, abiding, eternally remaining one and the same being, united and at the same time many unities. In this way, quality passes over into quantity.

Let us dwell for a time on what has been set out above.

What have we mainly been concerned with, right from the beginning? With the so-called determinants of thought, with "pure ideas." To Aristotle they were the predicates of everything thinkable. Kant considered them to be the forms of all judgments. According to Hegel, these categories act in their independent self-motion. For him, they are not the predicates of being, that is, of real and above all material being, that is, of the real world, viewed from various angles. For him, on the contrary, they act from the very beginning as independent ideas, out of which everything else develops. The most abstract concept of being is taken as the starting point. Being is taken not as the basic predicate of the world (the world exists), but on the contrary, the richness of the world, along with the whole world itself, is inferred from empty being, from nothingness. However, in being there is always *something* that *is*. Being [*bytiye*] cannot be stripped away from that which "does the being" [*bytiystvuyet*].

The "mysticism of the idea" (Lenin's phrase) leads in this case to the transformation of the predicate into the subject and to its being hypostatized.

The same must also be said of nothingness. Contrary to Hegel, however, it is never possible to obtain something out of nothing, and the old dictum that nothing arises out of nothing remains absolutely correct. From the point of view of the "mysticism of ideas," the movement of the world results from the naked negation "nothingness," and from empty being. However, this logical trick cannot be accepted as a component element of materialist dialectics.

Does this mean that in Hegel's analysis of being, the concepts *nothingness* and *becoming* are all rubbish, solely the "mysticism of ideas"? By no means. If we are to take the process of change in such a way as to regard it exclusively from the point of view of the "new," without relation to the old, then the new, as the new, has arisen for the first time. Earlier, it did not, as such, exist at all; that is, it was nothing. However, this is a completely empty abstraction, although it does illuminate one side of the matter, and that abstraction is then elevated incorrectly into a starting point. The root of the error lies in the transforming of the predicate of being into the subject, and in the distorted relationship between them. We can thus perceive the truth, if we take the problem as the abstract side of the changing of the status of the object, and not as the objectless movement of an idea. In reality, for something to arise is a change. There are not two stages here, but one and the same. They can be separated only in mental abstraction, but if the products of this artificial separation are elevated into independent essences, meanwhile being divorced from the objective world, then the "mysticism of ideas" is the inevitable result.

In dealing with the category of present being, Hegel provides a marvelous elucidation of the universal connection between things, of transitions from one into another, of the differentiation of the whole and the unity of opposites, of development and change. But the movement from present being to being for itself contains a static teleological element, concealed under the pseudonym "true infinity." The rise of things that are uniform qualitatively means that they have quantitative relationships. However, does the process of change come to a complete stop with this? Here, under the guise of a critique of "spurious infinity," a negation is put forward against the infinity of the process of change. The symbolism of the straight line and the circle is extremely unconvincing. The length of a circumference is a finite quantity. Completed infinity is a trivial, contradictory concept, while the true concept of infinity, by contrast, is also irrevocability, that is, the constant reproduction of a contradiction. What is there in this that is "spurious"?

Hegel, as he declares openly, is searching here for the absolute, for stasis, for the being of the ancient Greeks, "quiescent, round as a globe, equal to itself," that was so much to the taste of Parmenides. This in turn is linked to the idea of purpose. The "purpose" has to be attained. There needs to be an end to anxiety, in the "truly infinite" that is completion. Therefore, "true infinity" leaps out of the "spurious infinity" of change, space, and time, and is embodied in an extratemporal and extraspatial "ideal" being. Here the "idea" performs the same hocus-pocus as the absolute spirit when it cognizes itself, or as the absolute spirit performs in history, which comes to an end with the Prussian state system. This is where the narrowness of Hegel's dialectics lies, the narrowness that is closely associated with idealism and teleology. The "conclusiveness" of the struggle of the bourgeoisie against feudalism and the construction of bourgeois society as the end point of world history is reproduced in spiritual terms, as a being for itself of universal significance.

But let us continue.

Quality, as we have seen, has passed over into quantity. Quantity is the indeterminateness of magnitude, while the determinateness of quantity is magnitude. Since there is no third being between one entity and another entity, here we also find continuity, but since any magnitude can be divided, here we also find interruption, disjunction. Magnitude is thus the unity of the interrupted and the continuous, as opposing aspects; the interrupted and the continuous, consequently, are not different types of magnitude, but "aspects," coexisting in magnitude as in their unity. Continuity is not the sum of interrupted magnitudes. From a failure to understand this latter, that is, from a failure to understand the dual nature of magnitude, as the unity of opposites, there follow proofs of the impossibility of motion and so on (Zeno's aphorisms, Kant's antinomies). A determinate quantity, a magnitude, differs from other magnitudes in its boundaries, as a determinate unity of single entities, that is, as a greater or lesser quantity of units. Consequently, it has to be understandable as a number.

Increase and diminution can be continued endlessly, and here we find spurious quantitative infinity. In this connection, Hegel quotes a poem of Haller on eternity, a poem which delighted Kant, but which in Hegel aroused only "boredom":

> I heap up monstrous numbers,
> Pile mountains of millions upon millions,

> I put aeon upon aeon and huge world upon world,
> And when from that awful height
> Reeling, I look back on you,
> All the might of number multiplied a thousandfold,
> Is still not a fragment of you.
> I deduct them, and you lie whole before me.[5]

The quantitative "spurious infinity" outrages Hegel, just as the qualitative variety did, and we can endorse his sentiments. Without entering into a detailed discussion of the question, we shall merely note that in higher mathematics infinites themselves are of a diverse order, while in the modern theory of diversity, the concept of magnitude is being expanded as well. Here, consequently, a transition of quantity back into quality is being observed.

The dual transition from quality to quantity and from quantity to quality leads to the unity of these concepts. Every present being is such a unity of opposites. This unity of quantity and quality is measure. (God, however, is also measure, and assigns to all things their measure and purpose.) Measure, consequently, is qualitative quantity and quantitative quality. With quantity, quality too changes at a certain stage of development, a change of magnitude bringing altered properties. This is a transition of quantity into quality. Any present being, as the unity of quantity and quality, that is, as measure, stands in the same relation to another present being as to measure. The relationship between them is thus a relationship of measures. The transition of quantity into quality occurs in such a way that the quantitative changes are not at first accompanied by a change of quality, but at a certain point in the quantitative changes there is a break in the gradualness, a leap. The points that witness such leaps and turns, where quantity is suddenly transformed into quality, are called by Hegel "nodes."

The line that unites nodes Hegel terms the nodal line of relations of measure. Quantity, quality, and measure are essentially *states*, behind which is concealed a particular substrate:

> ... such relations are determined only as nodes of one and the same substrate. Therefore, the measures and the independent phenomena that arise with them are reduced to the level of conditions. Change is merely a variation of condition, and something which is undergoing change is considered during this to remain the same.[6]

Here, therefore, the "sublation" of all these categories is also the "sublation" of the category of being, and the transition from being to essence.

It can readily be seen that Hegel's doctrine of the transition of quantity into quality, of interruptions in gradualness, and of the uneven nature of development, along with his doctrine of measure, the nodal line of relations of measure, and so on, contains elements that have vast revolutionary significance. Confirmed by the whole development of the theory of natural science (simply consider the "critical points" in physics and chemistry, the theory of mutations, and doctrines concerning social revolution), these elements deal crushing blows to the philistine interpretation of "evolution" as it is understood by the great majority of bourgeois scientists. Despite this, interruption and continuity, gradualness and unevenness, evolution and revolution are here (that is, at the basic level of Hegel's analysis of the question) taken in their unity, as aspects (or "moments") of real movement. Of course, in this case as well it is necessary to place Hegel's dialectics "on its feet," since with Hegel the idealist point of view is adduced everywhere. This, however, is already the general, fundamental threshold, a fact which should never be forgotten.

Let us cross over now to the question of essence, which makes up the central part of Hegel's *Logic*.

"The truth of being is essence." Thought makes the transition to essence by way of mediation, or reflection:

> Striving to cognize the truth, what precisely being is in itself and for itself, knowledge does not remain within the sphere of the direct and of its definitions, but penetrates through them, presuming that behind this being there is something else, such as genuine being.... This knowledge is indirect, since it is not located directly in the sphere of essence, but begins from another being and has to traverse a preparatory pathway, a pathway of going beyond being, or rather, of entering into it.[7]

According to Hegel, the relationship between essence and being is such that the former is true, authentic being, while the latter is the untrue, inauthentic appearance. Present being is grounded in essence. Therefore, it is not simple appearance, but grounded appearance, that is, phenomenon. In their turn, phenomenon and essence are not magnitudes that have been torn apart in dualist manner, since essence expresses itself in phenomenon. Hence "essence from the beginning is located in its very self, or it is a reflection; in the second place, it exists as a phenomenon; thirdly, it reveals itself. In its movement it posits itself in the following definitions: 1) as simple essence, existing in itself in its determinants within itself; 2) as essence moving out into the sphere of present being, or in the form of existence and phenomenon; 3) as essence, united with its phenomenon, that is, as reality." (*W. d. L.*).[8]

Since in the category of essence all categories of being have been sublated, other-being has been sublated as well, and essence, as sublated other-being, is identical to itself. In this case, however, the identity is not the identity of formal logic (that is, abstract, rational identity), but concrete identity, including the aspect of difference. Formal logic puts forward the law of identity ($A=A$) and the law of contradiction (A cannot at the same time be non-A). These are empty, formal laws. However, they are nonetheless contradictory, since they embody a distinction between the subject and predicate; that is, they contain more than they wish.

Difference develops in three forms: 1) outward difference; 2) inner difference, when something differs from something else by being its other, that is, as opposition; 3) difference from itself, that is, contradiction, the essence of which consists in opposition to itself.

Contrary to formal logic, opposition contains both identity and difference. Opposites are identical, since things that are opposed can only be of similar type (positive and negative electrical charges, a distance of X miles to the west and X miles to the east, and so forth). At the same time, they are different; they are opposed (that is, they are related to one another as positive and negative). Positive and negative, however, are mutually interrelated, and presuppose one another's existence; it is possible to consider the positive to be negative, and vice versa. In this respect they are identical, but at the same time they are also different. From this it is clear that each of the two sides of the relationship we are examining is linked to the other, presupposes its being, that is, affirms it, "posits" it, and at the same time negates it, requires its non-being. Consequently, it is itself both positive and negative; it is opposite to itself, that is, contradictory. Formal logic is static logic, the logic of the immobile and isolated. Here everything has grown rigid, everything is identical with itself, and nothing contradicts itself. In dialectical logic, by contrast, everything is in motion, "all is flux," everything is contradictory, everything moves as a unity that is being revealed in opposites. "Contradiction is the moving principle."[9]

We are not concerned here with impossible contradiction (dry water, wooden iron), but with inevitable, dialectical contradiction, as the unity of being and non-being, as the principle of motion, becoming, change, rise and decline, development, and so on.

Contradiction (that is, opposition to itself) has to be resolved. Unity breaks down here into two opposing determinants, of which one posits the other (this positing element is ground); and the other is posited by the first (this is the conditioned, or the "consequent").[10] The ground and the consequent are identical (since they have one and the same content), and they are also different, developing into opposition. Hegel differentiates between 1) absolute ground (ground in general); 2) determinate ground; and 3) condition. The consequent is something grounded, not mediated. This mediated, determinate, and differentiated being is substantial determinateness, or form. "Form applies to everything that is determinate."[11] Within ground lies a substrate, essence. Essence is something indeterminate, but capable of determinateness. Form, however, is not a cap placed on matter. "Matter must ... be formed, and form must materialize itself."[12] In other words, the activity of form is at the same time the movement of matter itself. This unity of matter and form, as a unity of opposites, is content.

The unity of all conditions and of the ground, that is, the totality of all conditions, calls forth a phenomenon. This mediated, substantiated present being is existence. Present being is direct present being. Grounded present being is existence. Acting and manifesting itself in existence, that is, in a phenomenon, is that which was included in the depths of condition and ground.

We thus make the transition to phenomenon. But first of all, a few critical remarks on what has been set out above.

In the section of Hegel's *Logic* that has just been examined, the "mysticism of ideas" of course remains in full force. The formula "the truth of being is essence" thus signifies a distortion. The category of "truth" cannot pertain to objective being (being that is independent of human consciousness). As we have seen, it can express only a particular relationship between a "copy" and the "original." It is quite absurd to think that one side, part, or phase of the development and so on of objective reality is more "true" than another. On the contrary, from the point of view of the process of cognition, one can speak of the greater or lesser truthfulness of this cognition.

But since for Hegel the categories of thought take precedence, and at the same time coincide with the categories of being, they are also taken as determinants of this latter. The various "universes," the "true" and "untrue," are only different stages of cognition, corresponding to cognition of less profound and more profound associations of the one and only universe, in its various aspects and multifarious relationships (relationships between its parts, facets, and aspects, independent of the cognizing subject, and dependent on the subject, that is, in an interrelationship with it).

On the other hand, insofar as Hegel, unlike Kant, overcomes dualism, for example, to the degree that "appearance" or "phenomenon" is something grounded, in which essence manifests itself and unity is affirmed, this unity is presented here on the purely idealist basis of the spiritual world, which is also the true world, the realm of thought existing in the sensory-objective. But if we constantly keep in mind this fundamental flaw, which expresses itself in all of Hegel's terminology, a rational kernel can still be discerned: the logically reflected dialectic of real things and processes in their universal relationship and in their contradictory movement. The criticism of the rigid laws of formal logic is brilliant, and the general laws of dialectics—the unity of opposed aspects, the differentiation of the whole, and the interpenetration of opposites—are developed in exceedingly convincing and weighty form, with unusual subtlety and wit.

Let us therefore cross over now to the phenomenon, that is, to the manifestation of essence.

Existence is a thing:

> Existence is the direct unity of reflection in itself and reflection in another. Therefore, it is an undefined multitude of existences, reflected in themselves and at the same time also reflected in another, relative and constituting the world of mutual dependency and the endless association of grounds and the grounded. Grounds themselves are existences, and existences with various facets play a role as grounds, including grounds of the grounded.[13]

Outside of this association [of grounds and the grounded] the thing, that is, the "thing-in-itself," is an empty abstraction. In reality, "the thing" in general extends beyond its simple "being-in-itself," as an abstract relationship in itself, and appears in the same way, as a reflection in something else, thus acquiring properties.

As a substantial unity, a thing is a ground; as a substantial plurality and diversity, a totality of properties and changes, it is a phenomenon. A ground is a law, as something constant, and the substantial content of a phenomenon. "The realm of laws is the *stable* image of the world of Existence or Appearance."[14]

The realm of laws is a world that exists in itself and for itself, a world above the senses, in opposition to the realm of phenomena. The one, however, is the reverse side of the other; they are not divorced, as with Kant, into the world of phenomena and the world of noumena, the latter of which, moreover, is transcendental. Law is unity or identity in the diversity of phenomena; it is unity in plurality, not numerical but material. This relationship is a material one, the form taken by the unity of essence and phenomenon, a unity which is an even higher category than the preceding one, since it constitutes reality.

Material relationships appear above all in the form of a relationship between the whole and its parts, where the whole is inconceivable without the parts, and the parts unthinkable without the whole. The contradiction between the whole and the part is resolved in the conception of unity as negating the independence of the parts, "their negative unity," creating not a mechanical aggregate but an energetic unity. Hence the concept of force as a real principle, and of the exertion of force. The true relationship between these internal and external quantities is, however, one of identity. They are aspects of the same essence: "The surface appearance of an essence is the revelation of what it is in itself.... Essence is the manifestation of itself, so that this essence consists only in its revelation. In this identity of a phenomenon with its interior, or essence, the material relationship becomes actuality."[15]

We are thus given the following development of categories: being, present being (determinate being), existence (grounded present being), phenomenon (essence manifesting itself), and reality (the unity of essence and phenomenon). Reality is at the same time activity, the action of reason, the absolute. Hence, "All that is real is rational, and all that is rational is real."[16]

Reality breaks down into internal, potential reality, or possibility, and external, factual reality. Formal possibility (abstract possibility) is possibility outside of all conditions, empty potential. Differentiated from it is real possibility, with various instances. Possibility consists in the potential to be or not to be, to be thus or otherwise. When all opposing possibilities are excluded, and the totality of conditions is manifested, there appears something which, once it has happened, cannot be different. In this lies the concept of necessity, as the unity of real possibility and of something conditioned by itself; here is the character of necessity. At the same time, everything is mediated. That which is substantiated only by something else occurs by chance.

Necessary essence is absolute. "It is one and independent, and lies at the basis of all other things; it is not simply a substrate, but substance. All other things are not necessary but casual, or have the character of accidents."[17]

Substance is everything; individual things (but not their parts!) are its manifestation, and substance is power. Understood as truly unconditional, it is a primary cause, while things are no longer accidents, but actions. The relationship of causality is therefore the second substantial relationship. Insofar as the bearers of this relationship are finite substances, the chain of causes and effects, or actions and reactions, falls into a stormy eternity. The contradiction is resolved in the category of reciprocity, where cause and effect change places: "In Reciprocity ... the rectilinear movement out from causes to effects and from effects to causes is bent round and back in on itself."[18]

The cause here realizes itself; what is involved, therefore, is self-substantiation; the concept of necessity passes over into that of freedom, and the concept of substance into that of the subject (selfhood, idea). "The truth of necessity, therefore, is freedom, and the truth of substance is the Notion."[19]

By the Notion, Hegel has in mind self-consciousness, or subjectivity, bringing into being true, objective thought.

With regard to the above, apart from the general consideration of the idealism of the whole construct—and this consideration remains constantly in force—it should be noted:

First, that the interpretation of "law" and "the realm of laws" as something static is wrong. In the spirit of Parmenides, this conception presupposes an unchanging substantial world in which nothing moves, nothing changes, and everything is immobile. As we know, nothing is immobile, and law encompasses the mobile and changeable. Law, as a reflection in people's heads, is a formula of the mobile. So-called "eternal laws" are not eternal at all. The essence of the world is not a graveyard of the world. This essence is not a special world, but the very same world in its most general and profound relations and associations. These relations and associations are also mobile and relative. Searches for an absolute which is immobile in itself, and which is mobile only in appearance, represent either dualism or complete inconsistency, anti-Kantian incantations notwithstanding. In both cases idealism comes into conflict with dialectics, which is dynamic through and through.

If we take the "world in itself" (and not the Kantian "thing-in-itself"), that is, if we take the unity of things and processes not as depending on the subject, but in the associations and mediations of the objective order (of the objective in the materialist sense), this world is complex, diverse, mobile, and changeable. If, moreover, we take the most general and profound relations, for example, the laws of dialectics, these are "immobile" only in the sense that they express a universal mobility. But to draw from this any conclusions about immobility and stasis would be sophistry, not dialectics.

Second, in the doctrine of force there is a clear continuation of the tradition of ancient Greek idealism, according to which a principle that is in itself immobile sets everything in motion ("energetic unity"). This is related to the fact that in this case force itself is mystical; it is a spiritual principle, Aristotelian entelechy, the motivating energetic principle of the spiritual order.

Third, for precisely this reason, "in reality" (that is, in the Hegelian category of reality, or actuality) this principle passes over into reason, the Absolute; it is discovered and displayed here in its rational nature.

Fourth, in Hegel's analysis the transition from necessity to freedom is idealism, theology, teleology, and mysticism. All development is viewed as the realization of a purpose, as self-realization, and on the scene there appears the subject, selfhood, self-consciousness. Substance itself is transformed into a rational subject, attaining here a much higher form of its self-development. In place of universal and rounded necessity, which expresses the universal cosmic relationship of things and processes, what floats to the surface is the creative spirit, free in its goal-positing creativity. However comforting some people might find this mystical fantasizing, it too has grown obsolete in every respect, and has to be thrown out.

By the Notion, Hegel thus means subjectivity, which "sublates" necessity, revealing it, cognizing it, and by virtue of this transforming it into freedom. Therefore, the culmination of substance is no longer substance, but is the Notion, the subject. Subjectivity, however, is the basis of objectivity. Development proceeds from subjectivity to objectivity and to the unity of these opposites. This unity is the Notion (subjectivity realizing itself, selfhood, the subject-object).

The Notion, as an all-encompassing unity, is universality, the universal idea, productive and concrete (in opposition to the abstract universality of formal logic). As determinateness, it is a particular type or sort. But since the particular is in its turn the general or "universal," the rise of specific differences leads to the point where further movement is impossible. The completeness of specific differences (with relation to generic ones), or individualization, leads to the individualized idea, or the particular (*das Allgemeine, das Besondere, das Einzelne*).[20]

That which in essence was identity, difference, and ground, in the idea appears as the general, the particular, and the individual. The forms of development of the idea are judgment, passing over in its development into the syllogism. Judgment is divided into its aspects, subject and predicate; the verbal copula posits their identity. Judgment is a category, that is, a necessary form not only of thought, but also of being, and of the essence of things. When a thing reveals its properties, it manifests them as the subject of judgment, providing its predicates; in other words, a thing is revealed in the form of a judgment. Every thing is an idea, and as such, a subject developing itself. Hegel further poses the question of the degrees of judgments, and distinguishes between the judgment of existence, the judgment of reflection, the judgment of necessity, and the judgment of the Notion.

Judgment passes over into conclusion or the syllogism, which is the unity of idea and judgment. The syllogism is rational, and since everything is rational, "everything is a syllogism."[21]

Since the syllogism is mediated judgment, a distinction exists also between the syllogism of existence, the syllogism of reflection, the syllogism of necessity, and the syllogism of the Notion. (The syllogism of the Notion is already found in the most developed type of judgment, the so-called apodeictic judgment.)

Examining judgment and the syllogism, Hegel develops the dialectics of the general, the particular, and the individual, dialectics which we have encountered repeatedly in this work. Here too we find the unity of opposites, passing over from one into another, since the individual is also the general, and the general is the individual.

An internally developed, determinate, mediated idea ceases to be shut up within itself; it emerges into the outside world and becomes objective. In their generality, objects as revealed ideas are the general unity of the universe. The first form of the relationship of the totalities of things is the external relationship of the aggregate, the mechanism, and the corresponding activity, the mechanical process, or determinism. When unity ceases to be merely external, and the differences between things are really annulled and "neutralize" one another, what is evident is chemism. Universal unity cannot be either mechanical or chemical (cannot unite all objects). It is something that stands above mechanism and chemism, an all-penetrating principle, the purpose. The teleological relationship is also external, subjective, finite purposefulness from which it is essential to distinguish internal, immanent purposefulness.

The subordination of the object to a subjective purpose is judgment, and the realization of the purpose is the syllogism. The purpose here is at the same time both cause and objective, that is, an ultimate cause. Objects are the means; and the middle term serves also as the means. The relationship of the purpose to the object, as to the means, is the first premise, while the relationship of the means to the object, as to the material, is the second. The achieved purpose becomes in turn the means, and so forth; that is, we are faced here again with the "spurious infinity." This infinity is sublated by the "truly infinite" purpose, which holds the means within itself, and not externally. Subjectivity objectifies itself; the unity of subjectivity and objectivity is the Idea. In mechanism and chemism the Notion is in itself, and in the subjective purpose it is for itself; but in the Idea, the Notion is in itself and for itself simultaneously. Absolute purposes are both achieved, and demand achievement. The Idea is the absolute unity of opposites (of subjectivity and objectivity), and it is a process. In essence, unity was the stimulus for condition and for the conditioned, for cause and effect, for beginning and end, and so forth. Here the end is the beginning, the consequence is the cause, and so on. Therefore, unity in the Idea is absolute unity, extending beyond the bounds of unity. The end in itself is the soul, goal-directed entelechy; it objectifies itself in the means, which is the body. The unity of soul and body is the living individual. The objectivity of the living is the organism, which consists not of parts, but of members. "The living dies, because it includes in itself a contradiction. It is the living [which] is universal in itself, the genus, and which at the same time exists directly only as an individual." However, "the death of the individual, merely immediate life is the rise of the spirit."[22]

"The death of the individual, merely immediate life is the rise of the spirit." Subjectivity is thus spirit, reason, end-in-itself, and the idea conscious of itself. Objectivity is the world, also end-in-itself, also the ultimate goal, and also the idea. Consequently, what is involved is the subjective and objective idea. The unity of these opposites is realized in cognition, which has to do away with the one-sidedness of opposites. The one-sidedness of the subjective idea is removed through the theoretical activity of the idea, or through the idea of truth. The one-sidedness of the objective idea is removed by its entering into the world and through the realization of the rational goals of the spirit, or through practical activity (through the idea of good).

The process of ultimate cognition (the theoretical process) proceeds analytically and synthetically. Out of the process of ultimate knowledge is born the idea of necessity. "In necessity as such, ultimate knowledge itself casts off its presuppositions and starting point, the elements in its content that are given and found. Necessity in itself is the Notion relating itself to itself. In this way the subjective idea comes to itself, to determinateness in itself and for itself, to the ungiven and consequently, to the immanent in the subject, so that it crosses over into the idea of the will."[23]

Freedom appears here as an absolute goal that requires realizing in the world. The idea of good stands in opposition to "the insignificance of objectivity." The tasks of the world, however, enter into the reality of the world, and necessity into being. Therefore, contrary to Kant, the idea of good is identical to the idea of truth.

This identity of the theoretical and practical idea is also the absolute idea. Serving as the content of the absolute idea is the system of logic, the idea of development, while its form is the dialectical method, as a method of development, of contradictory tripartite development. Serving as the content is the entire system, and not "the final station." "The interest lies in the whole process of movement."[24]

The logical idea has thus culminated in the absolute idea, which subsequently, through nature as its other-being, makes its way to the absolute spirit....

After everything that has been said above, it is not hard to find "the mysticism of ideas" at every step in the part of Hegel's *Logic* dealt with here. The interpretation of real processes as judgments, syllogisms, and figures of logic clearly inverts the real relations and distorts them in idealist fashion. Lenin, however, quite rightly warned that Hegel's thoughts on these matters, thoughts which Hegel assigned such an honored place, should not be regarded as rubbish.

If we work through Hegel's thinking here at a deeper level, in all its significance, we see that it establishes an objective link between relations of reality and relations of thought, between objective laws and the laws of logic, between forms of being and forms of thought, between experience and practice on the one hand and theoretical cognition on the other. This thinking is already, in and of itself, a refutation of any and all apriorism in which the subject binds to the world of phenomena a priori forms and categories that have appeared from some unknown source. In the materialist interpretation, the real bonds between things and processes manifest themselves through the experience and practice of social humanity, and are reflected in humanity's theoretical formulas. Meanwhile, interrelationships which are confirmed by experience and practice a countless number of times, and to which there are no exceptions, are set aside in the consciousness of social humanity as axiomatic categories, which idealist philosophers later declare to be a priori.

Hegel had a good understanding of the differing worth of various types of syllogisms. In our time, for example, the classic type of syllogism, figuring in all the old and new textbooks of logic, appears in a special light. We are speaking of the syllogism: "All people are mortal. Kay is a person. Therefore, Kay is mortal." Imagine that the following new situation has arisen: Kay has managed to achieve the regeneration of cells, contrary to the ideas of Hegel on origin, life, the individual, and so forth. The first proposition, on mortality, is maintained; Kay has not yet said anything to anyone. The proposition that Kay is human still holds good. The conclusion, however, is untrue, and at the same time the first proposition also becomes untrue; it is eroded internally. An experiential origin is clearly indicated here for the word "all."

There is nothing mystical or mysterious in the fact that there are no exceptions to a whole series of relationships; these are set aside in the categories of "logical necessity." On the other hand, we have had the chance to convince ourselves that the methods of practical and experiential, or empirical, influence on nature, in accordance with its real nature, find their expression in the methods used to ascertain the character of nature (analysis, synthesis-atomization, decomposition, transformation of substance, and so on). In Hegel, of course, we nevertheless find a mystical vulgarization of these relationships (the relationship of species in *The Philosophy of Nature*, the syllogism, the solar system, and so forth) which proceeds directly from a sort of logification of the world.

This logification is clearly expressed in the relationship between subjectivity and objectivity. According to Hegel, the concept of the subject is the basis of objectivity. Here we find the priority of the spirit expressed vividly. Corresponding to this is the priority of the purpose and of freedom over necessity. In fact the idea, or subjectivity, which is the development of substance, its culmination and at the same time its basis, "sublates" necessity and turns it into creative "freedom." Subsequent movement toward objectivity and unity in the idea is nothing but subjectivity realizing itself. The idea is subject-object, but the defining principle is subjectivity; this is why this subject-object also bears the name of the idea. According to this view, the universal unity of the world has its roots not in the mechanical unity of the aggregate, not in chemical unity, and not in any material unity at all, with its necessity, but in teleological unity, the unity of the purpose, which is an all-permeating and all-encompassing principle.

The process of cognition is so decisive that it lies at the basis of the unification of the subjective and objective idea. The rational kernel of the one-sidedness of theory and practice taken "in themselves" is present here in an especially distorted form, and is deeply concealed. At times, genuinely brilliant thoughts, the germs of dialectical materialism and historical materialism, are developed here. At the same time, however, "practice" that is totally in the spirit of Kant and of the subsequent ethical babbling, and that drags behind it the ingrained traditions of Greek idealism, culminates in the idea of "the good"; this coincides in mystical fashion with the idea of truth, while practice, in the sense of the real transformation of substance, objective practice, evaporates and disappears like a mirage in the desert.

The dialectical movement of ideas that is found in Hegel, and that reflects real movement in idealist form, contains elements that are highly valuable. These are the ideas of universal relationship, of movement, of change, and the forms of this movement; here the division, or self-differentiation, of the whole, the revealing of opposites and their interpenetration, serve as the motivating principle. This is the great revolutionary side of Hegel that is restricted and smothered by the elements of idealism and by the idealist conception of the world. All form is understood here in its movement, that is, in its rise, development, downfall, and extinction, in its contradictions and the resolution of contradictions, in the rise of new forms and the revealing of new contradictions, in the peculiarities and qualities of new forms, which again and again become subject to the process of change. The great contribution made by Hegel lies in this fearlessness of thought that encompasses the objective dialectic of being, nature, and history. The basic dialectical contradiction of Hegel's own system, a contradiction noted by Engels, led to the system's collapse, and gave rise to a new historical unity, at a new stage of historical development, in the dialectical materialism of Marx.

In opposition to the materialist dialectic, modern critics of Marxism put forward a whole heap of "reasons" and "arguments," which we have touched on to some degree in other chapters of this work. The most common argument is that transferring dialectics, which Hegel developed in the logical atmosphere of idealism, into a materialist atmosphere is (as Werner Sombart puts it) an absurdity. In this connection, Troeltsch declares Marx's materialism to be non-materialist, and so on. For bourgeois critics of Marxism even to pose the question of the relationship between Hegelianism and Marxism leads to hilarious contradictions. Hence, for example, Plenge (*Marx und Hegel*) asserts that Marx and Hegel were so close that "Marx, with all of his basic theoretical positions, could have remained within the Hegelian school."[25] Meanwhile, another Herr Professor, Karl Diehl (*Über Sozialismus, Kommunismus und Anarchismus*), states that Marx retained "only a certain dialectical manner of expression."[26] Sombart (*Der Proletarische Sozialismus*) puts the view that here there are "two essentially different theoretical conceptions, which have nothing in common with one another apart from a name." Plenge contends that Marx "posed his materialism so as to include a series of earlier materialist theories." Troeltsch, by contrast, argues that Marxism is merely "extreme realism and empiricism on a dialectical basis." To Hegel's emanatist concept of natural law, Sombart counterposes the Marxist concept as causal and genetic. Troeltsch, on the other hand, counterposes Marx's dialectics, as the logic of movement, to the causal-genetic logic of positivism. Jostock (*Der Ausgang des Kapitalismus*) keeps his silence where the resolving of these contradictions is concerned; dodging the question, he cites the inadequacy of Marx's theoretical-cognitive utterances, and descends to the field of history and sociology.[27]

Meanwhile, it would seem that all these venerable gentlemen, who claim a familiarity with the topic, ought to refrain at least from a flatly antidialectical posing of the issue, as in cases where the oppositions are absolute, and do not interpenetrate one another. A genuinely dialectical understanding of the succession of ideas indicates, on the basis of a real study of the topic, that mechanistic materialism was antidialectical, that Hegelian dialectics was idealist, and that Marx's synthesis reconciled these opposites in the higher unity of dialectical materialism. This involved a critical reworking both of mechanistic materialism and of idealist dialectics; Marx thus showed himself to be the critical heir to both philosophical conceptions. To pose the question as it is posed by the contending bourgeois sides is the height of naive impotence and impotent naivety. This is an infantile way of posing the question (infantile in logical terms—its "practical" value for the bourgeoisie is another matter; but that is a question in its own right, and examining it here would be a distraction).

The argument on the basis of "atmosphere" is easily refuted both factually and logically. In reality, the center of dialectics lies in the concept of development. This is why even such commentators on Hegel as Kuno Fischer in his *History of Modern Philosophy* situate Hegel with his idea of development in the "spiritual atmosphere" of Darwin, Lyell, and the early Kant, that is, Kant in his pre-critical period with his works on natural history and above all, with his *History and Theory of the Heavens*.

And tell us, please, in these theoretical views, which constituted an entire epoch, what idealist element was there? Finally, we cannot ignore Goethe, who was undoubtedly a dialectician, and who at the same time felt a direct aversion for Hegel's theological-teleological, speculative, and abstract philosophy, about which he simply did not want to know. And what about Spencer's "status" and "contractus"? And the elements of dialectics in Saint-Simon (the "organic" and "critical" of the epoch)? That is not even to mention such things as the materialist elements in the philosophy of Aristotle, from whom Hegel scooped up wisdom in whole handfuls.

As we have already noted elsewhere, Sombart's specific argument, resting on the general concept of "atmosphere," holds that Marxists in school-pupil fashion confuse contradiction with opposition, and Hegel's emanatist logic of contradictions with Marx's empirical juxtaposition of real oppositions; the transference of one to the other, meanwhile, is absurd and stupid. For Hegel, operating on the basis of his metaphysics, dialectics is a law of thought and being, a substantial element of the world and of the historical process.... And so forth.

All that is "substantial" in this objection is its unrestrained looseness. The reality is as follows.

First: Hegel in his *Philosophy of Nature* himself decisively counterposes the emanative to the evolutionary point of view, and decisively gives his preference to the second, rejecting the first. Our not-so-venerable critic should at least have been aware of this.

Second: Sombart's counterposing of "opposition" to "contradiction" also reveals his school-pupil ignorance of the bases of Hegel's dialectical logic. As we have already seen from the account in *Die Wissenschaft der Logik,* Hegel derives contradiction itself from oppositions, interpreting contradiction as opposition to itself.

Third: The idea that for Hegel dialectics is at the same time ontology works completely against Sombart. This means that dialectics is also a law of being. But it is a law of being for Marxism as well. Materialist dialectics, however, is more consistent, since it puts an end to the limited nature of Hegel's dialectics.

Fourth: The development of the natural and social sciences shows convincingly, on the basis of concrete material, that dialectics is highly "applicable" to history and nature, including those of society. In the chapters devoted to modern physics and biology, we have seen that all the main philosophical-theoretical problems of the modern natural sciences rest on dialectics, and that Engels with his "dialectics of nature" and Lenin provided an enormous impulse to understanding the real links and relationships of nature and society. Wherever Hegel bound dialectics hand and foot with his idealism, he proved completely wrong (atomic theory; theory of light; theory of color; theory of the evolution of species; his theory of social-historical development, marked by its contentment with the bourgeois regime; and so on).

Fifth: The works of Marx, the theory of historical materialism as the application of materialist dialectics to history, and the theory of capitalism as its application to political economy, have been totally vindicated. All of *Capital* is constructed on the bases of materialist dialectics, just like Marx's brilliant historical works. In the writings of Marx, dialectical abstractions do not exist simply in words, but are genuinely concrete. This is why Marx's forecasts have been so fully borne out. History has resolved in its own fashion the controversy between Hegel's idealist dialectics and the materialist dialectics of Marx. Hegel's dialectics, with its limited idealist character, using reason and logic to try to justify everything irrational, rested content with bourgeois society and the bourgeois state. In these last of its conclusions, it was overturned by reality. Marx's dialectics, rationally cognizing the irrational anarchy of capitalist development, has been confirmed by the actual historical process. None other than Herr Werner Sombart has repeatedly been forced to admit sorrowfully that Marx's basic predictions have been fulfilled. Could one demand a greater triumph for materialist dialectics?

If an individual experiment or an individual practical act is an element in the testing of one or another proposition, then here, in the vast world-historical process, we have a great, world-historic confirmation of Marx's materialist dialectics.

In conclusion, it should be said that under developed communism, with its harmonious social structure, people's feeling of community will be a mighty force outside of any fetishistic norms. Ethics will expand to make up a sort of aesthetic, while "duty" will be transformed into a simple instinct, into a wonderful reflex of ordinary people. Everyone will save a drowning comrade, without hesitating between "self-interest" (that is, self-preservation) and "duty." No one will "make sacrifices" for the sake of their neighbor, but will simply and splendidly do what is dictated by the feeling, noble and immanent to the splendid new man and woman, of the great common character of communist people.

35

Dialectics as Science and Dialectics as Art

"A highly experienced, educated state figure ... is the one who ... has a practical mind, that is, who acts on the basis of the whole extent of the case that is before him, and not according to one of its aspects that finds expression in some maxim. On the other hand, the one who in all cases acts on the basis of a single maxim is known as a pedant, and spoils things for himself and others." This is how Hegel in *The History of Philosophy* defines "the highly experienced, educated state figure."[1]

Of course, "surrendering one's positions" is not what is involved here (although in the text as a whole Hegel also refers to the "middle"). Nor is the forgetting of the fundamental "maxim" involved. (Although Hegel does rail against basing oneself solely on a "single maxim.") The main point is that "the whole extent of the case" should be taken into account—that is, the whole concrete, multifaceted situation in which the "highly experienced and educated state figure" acts.

In this remark by Hegel it is easy to see how he poses the question of dialectics as art, practice, and action. This question has enormous importance. It is no accident that Engels says of Marxism that it is not a dogma but a guide to action. This observation by Engels should not be understood in crude fashion, that is, as though Engels were rejecting Marxism as theory. What it means is that Marxism is not a dead, abstract, scholastic, rigid system, remote from life, but a vital science, a living theory-process, developing and functioning as a weapon of struggle and practice, of that great practice that transforms the world. No one can dispute the enormous richness of Marxist theory; its content is vast. But precisely because this is a great theory, it is also capable of engendering a great practice. Here we shall pose the question of materialist dialectics both as a question of theory and a question of art.

We have already discussed dialectics in a special chapter, providing a general formulation. We shall deal with it now in a particular connection, since there is undoubtedly a certain problem here.

However often a well-known definition by Lenin has been cited, we shall adduce it here once again. The definition concerned is that of the "elements of dialectics" listed by Lenin. These are:

1. the objectivity of consideration (not examples, not digressions, but the thing itself in itself);
2. the whole totality of the diverse relations of this thing to others;
3. the development of this thing (or phenomenon), its own movement, and its own life;
4. the internally contradictory tendencies (and aspects) of this thing;
5. the thing (phenomenon, etc.) as the sum and unity of opposites;
6. the struggle and respective unfolding of these oppositions, contradictory tendencies, etc.;
7. the unification of analysis and synthesis—the sorting out of distinct parts and the totality, the sum of these parts taken together;
8. the relations of each thing (phenomenon, etc.), not only diverse and distinct, but also general and universal. Each thing (phenomenon, process, etc.) is linked to every other;
9. not only the unity of opposites, but interpenetrations of every definition, quality, feature, aspect, and property into every other (into its opposite?);
10. the endless process of the revealing of new aspects, relationships, etc.;
11. the endless process of the deepening of human cognition of things, phenomena, processes, and so on, going from appearance to essence, and from less profound essence to more profound;
12. from [mutual] existence to causality and from one form of relation and interdependency to another, more profound and more general;
13. the repetition at a higher stage of certain features, properties etc., of a lower stage;
14. [the apparent] return as though to the old (negation of the negation);
15. the struggle of content with form, and vice versa. The casting off of form, and the refashioning of content;
16. the change of quantity into quality, and vice versa.[2]

Vladimir Ilyich understood dialectics itself in dialectical terms. After he had analytically separated out the various aspects from a given whole, and conditionally dismantled this whole, taking its aspects as isolated quantities, he would then synthesize this analytical work and comprehend these definitions as a single unity: "In short, dialectics can be defined as the doctrine of the unity of opposites. This is where the core of dialectics lies...." (*Philosophical Notebooks*).[3]

Dialectical flexibility of thought, or more precisely, the flexibility of dialectical thought, makes possible an adequate reflection of objective reality. As Lenin explained brilliantly in his polemic with Struve, however, Marxist objectivism is broader and deeper than bourgeois objectivism (to the extent that the latter existed at all, it had the ephemeral existence of an ideological mayfly). Marxist objectivism is dialectical; it understands everything historical in terms of movement and becoming; it captures "fleeting moments," transitions into opposites, contradictory tendencies, and so on. Consequently, it sees not only the past, but because it reveals laws of motion, looks also into the future. To use Marx's caustic words, history shows only its *a posteriori* to the so-called "historicist school," with its apologetic for routinism, tradition, and antiquity; in contrast, Marxist objectivism grabs hold of the "sting" of movement as well, and is therefore more "real" and "objective" than the usual rational objectivism.

Dialectics is a science that objectively reflects the objective dialectics of being, ontological dialectics. Ontological dialectics encompasses everything, including the processes of thought. When we pose the question of dialectics as art, are we not posing an absurd question? Are we not charging physiology with the task of "demonstrating" how we need to digest food?

Thought can be viewed both as a process (a nervous-physiological one, and in its other-being, as thought itself, a psychological process), and from the point of view of its logical makeup—that is, of the adequacy of its concepts, as reflections, to that which they reflect, that is, to the object. The former always occurs dialectically, like any process of the universe. This does not mean, however, that the logical structure of this process captures the dialectics of reality, and accurately depicts it. If this were not so, there would be no such thing as incorrect cognition, there would not be errors or distortions, restricted forms of reasoning, or one-sided thought.

All these, however, are facts. I might engage in metaphysics with a serious belief in God and the Devil, but the flow of the corresponding associations and the correlative nervous-physiological process involved will develop in dialectical fashion. The link between the objective processes of being and their "other-being," the psychological side, is different from the link between logical concepts in their relationship with what is being reflected. Dialectics may therefore indicate how it is necessary to think (since thought in its logical makeup can also be undialectical). Physiology does not teach us that food should be digested physiologically, since the process of digestion is always physiological, and there is no problem with this. Dialectics, consequently, is both a method of thought and method of investigation. Here there is an element of a norm, and an element of art.

How, though, is the transition to practice to be carried out?

When we are concerned with technological processes, with the practice of production or of scientific experiment, everything is simplified, since the processes involved are isolated in one way or another. Theory provides objective associations. Technology transfers them from the language of necessity to the teleological language of laws and norms (the transition to action). Laws directly guide the disposition of substances and forces in accordance with a goal, coordinating everything with this goal, which is anticipated as the result of the process. If all the actions have been performed, and the result has not appeared, if the prediction has not been borne out, and the goal has not been achieved, this means that the practice was "erroneous," because the theoretical calculation was wrong; practice tested out the theory, and rejected it. If, on the other hand, the results are as predicted, "everything is in order."

In social and political practice, things are much more difficult. Here we are concerned not with an artificially isolated process (either in production or in scientific experiment), but with a diverse and extremely complex whole, with exceedingly intricate relationships that are by no means able to be expressed in mathematical-numerical fashion, since here at every step new qualities are encountered. Society is characterized by extremely complex relations between socialized individuals who themselves are very complex products of nature, and all this flows and changes with extraordinary speed. Apart from this, the subject here is a collective entity (a class) which is itself a highly complex body, and itself has a specific structure (layers within each class, parties, leaders, and so on). And all the while this subject is itself contributing to every event. Its actions are constantly objectified; thought is transformed into action, and action hardens into fact, becoming a component element in a new constellation, and immediately turning into something else. There is an endless multitude of contradictions, groups, and shadings, the realm of the concrete in its gigantic diversity and transience. Hegel at one point notes that history is so concrete that governments and peoples have never learned anything from it, since the conditions of their actions have always been unique.

Ilyich as well agreed with this remark. (His interpretation of the "subject" is the complete opposite of the phrase about the "lessons of history"; it is necessary, however, to take this position too as being relative, with a grain of salt, and not to exaggerate it!) To act correctly, that is, successfully, is possible only "in accordance with the whole extent of the case involved," that is, according to the specific, concrete conjuncture. But how is the transition to action mediated "according to the whole extent," and so forth?

Above all, it is necessary to know and understand this "whole extent." In order to do this, it is necessary to know how to think dialectically, that is, not only to understand the doctrine of dialectics but also to know how to apply it in the process of cognition. Here thought itself is viewed not only as an objective process, inevitably conditional in nature, but also as a teleological one from the point of view of its effectiveness, as the art of thinking dialectically. Theoretically understood reality can be understood correctly here only on a dialectical basis. Under the conditions of production and experiment these very conditions provide broad scope for the rational, and lend an ordinariness to thought, since in these conditions a degree of simplification is already present. In the process of theoretical cognition, however, nothing of the kind is present, and only dialectical understanding can lead to thought having a correct result. Through dialectical understanding, a correct representation of the conjuncture, "of the whole extent of the case involved," is obtained. To obtain such a representation is an achievement of the great art of dialectics, of the art of thought. The masterful, truly brilliant analyses of Lenin (including both analyses of the whole epoch, for example, in *The Development of Capitalism in Russia*, *Imperialism*, and so forth, and of distinct, often profoundly dramatic conjunctures, as for example in "The Crisis Has Matured") are masterpieces of scientific creativity, unsurpassed for their dialectical depth and acutely dynamic structure, which impels the given constellation into the future.

Here too we find the dialectical transition to practice, that is, to a system of norms in accordance with the "analysis" which is obtained, that is, ultimately, in accordance with the real conjuncture. Consequently, we find the transition to the system of actions (of diverse character, including agitational, propagandist, organizational, and directly military), and on the basis of these, and choosing the moment ("in accordance with," and so on), the transition to the actions themselves in their purposeful succession. It should not be thought, however, that everything simply follows one after the other. Action develops, but thought does not cease to function; new factors are ceaselessly coming into play, and the conjuncture is constantly changing. Complications, ruptures, unexpected elements, and so-called chance events are constantly intruding. All the actions of the revolutionary subject itself are objectivized. Even while "under way," there is an imperative need for a mental accounting, a cold analysis of new and changing objective relationships, the translation of conclusions into the language of tactics, and the transformation of all this into the impassioned activity of struggle.

Consequently, tactics and tactical action are also consonant with the whole extent of the case set out above. Here we find the art of action. (Let us recall Lenin "on insurrection as an art," where he develops Marx's brilliant conceptions on this score.)[4]

Here we have rational action, and its rationality lies in the fact that it is connected with, even fused with, the rational (that is, dialectical) understanding of the whole situation. Dialectical being, dialectical thought, and dialectical action are bound up with one another, and in this connection they represent the unity of the process of social change, that is, the sociopolitical, in this case revolutionary, transformation of society.

Here it is appropriate to dwell once again on a problem analogous to the one which we resolved while examining thought. Every historical process and goal of action is dialectical as such, as part of the being and becoming of society, in its turn making up part of nature, though also its dialectical opposite. This does not mean, however, that every action corresponds to dialectical thinking or is dialectical in its logical makeup. As we have seen, it is possible to think in a restricted, formal manner, and on the basis of these limited (that is, one-sided and hence wrong) reflections of reality, to formulate tactics and act accordingly. In these circumstances errors, political errors, will be quite inevitable; they will proceed from the mistaken positions with all the force of inevitability even in a favorable political conjuncture, and in an unfavorable one may serve to doom everything. Hence when we speak here of dialectical action, of dialectics as a practical art and as material practice, we are speaking of the kind of politics ("scientific politics") that is inseparably fused with dialectical thought.

In reality, there is no such thing as an abstraction of action; action "in itself" does not exist. There are active people, but these at the same time are thinking people; there is a certain totality here. In reality, therefore, action is inseparable from its goals; it is purposeful, rational action. The unity of this rational principle, combining all its disparate aspects, is unity of leadership, since we are concerned with the collective action of large masses. Dialectical materialism applied to society is the historical materialism of Marx. It is not a dogma, but a guide to action, since it provides a basis for the scientific politics of proletarian parties, parties of Communist revolution, Bolsheviks.

The above provides a relatively straightforward but nevertheless substantial solution to such questions as "dialectics in metallurgy," "dialectics in metal-forging," and in the sewing on of buttons. Here, adepts of dialectics have an undialectical understanding of dialectics itself. Dialectics does not do away with or cancel out so-called formal logic and rational thought. Formal logic is present "in sublated form" within dialectical logic. Higher mathematics does not by any means do away with algebra, just as algebra does not do away with arithmetic. In everyday life, formal logic has extremely wide applications. It is perfectly possible to see a knife and fork on a table as "frozen" things rather than as processes, and it is quite sufficient to perceive them in connection with your body and with food, without dragging in any "universal associations" or transitions from one to the other.

In the technological processes of production, as we noted above, a certain isolation is already present, a certain simplification of conditions, a concentration on the solitary, a tearing of one or several ultimate processes out of the whole relationship of being. It is therefore comical to strike out formal logic here, and to philosophize dialectically on a button or a steel ingot. But it is quite a different matter when we cross over to the "general," to the abstractly concrete; here, invoking dialectics is thoroughly apposite, and it is formal, rational logic which is out of place. Our judgments in such matters must themselves be dialectically concrete and must correspond to the object under scrutiny. This requires a true understanding of dialectics, not the indiscriminate "application" of it, as a "universal master key," which Engels quite rightly protested against.

It does not, of course, follow from this that we exclude production from the objects of dialectical investigation. Indeed, in all our work we are systematic in including production, technical equipment, and technological processes in the sphere of philosophy, dialectics, and the theory of cognition.

It is not hard, however, to understand the difference; when we have to sew on a button, the problem is reduced to the relationship between the jacket, the needle, and the button, and not the universal relationship of the cosmos. When the "metaphysician" in the well-known story falls into a hole, he is thrown a rope, and proceeds to reason: "Rope—a humble form of cable." He prevents his escape from the hole, since the question as he poses it has nothing to do with grabbing the rope and crawling out. But *Homo sapiens* is, to paraphrase Hegel in *The Philosophy of Nature*, "a universal, reasoning animal, that inhabits a far wider circle and reduces all objects to his own organic nature (that is, turns them into objects of practical mastery—author), and equally, into objects of his knowledge."[5]

Potentially, a person "takes in" the entire world. At a particular stage of development and in the case of certain more general or supposedly "higher" questions, this process of the broadening and deepening of practice and cognition enters into conflict with formal logic and rational thought, and here dialectics is indispensable. When we make judgments about practice and theory and their interrelationships, about practice in general, about production and the changing of its form, about the history of technology and so on, we cannot get by without dialectics. The broader and more profound the question, the more insistent is the need for it to be dealt with in dialectical fashion. The more complex the action, the more urgent the need for the art of dialectics, that is, for action directed by dialectical thought. In the field of political action, this is brilliantly confirmed by the highly fruitful theory and practice of the great founders of Communism and by those who are continuing their work. In this way, the question of theoretical dialectics and normative dialectics is resolved.

36

Science and Philosophy

The ancient thinker Aristotle said of science and philosophy: "All other sciences ... are more requisite than philosophy, but none is more excellent."[1] It is time for us now to pose the question of the relationship between science and philosophy.

As everyone knows, Marx and Engels waged a furious struggle against "drunken speculation," against the games of the self-developing Hegelian idea, against the transformation of the real world into a world of abstractions, and against the cult of thought, when this thought (within a system, naturally) devoured the world. It is also well known that Marx and Engels not only "preserved" the Hegelian dialectic, transforming it into a materialist dialectic, but also fought a bitter struggle against "vulgar empiricism" of the British type, and against the unconcern shown by the great majority of scientists for the topic of thought. Marx and Engels mocked at "creeping empiricists," "inductive asses," and so on. At the same time, they vigorously defended experimental science, showing not even a hint of the condescencion that we often find in Hegel, sometimes in very sharp form, toward "bugs, midges, and cockroaches," toward the gathering of material and its classification, and toward the broadening of even the minor sciences.

This position taken by our teachers [Marx and Engels] was thoroughly justified. The divorce from experiment and experimental data, from practice, from real contact with reality, and from all conceivable forms of historically accumulated and conserved experience—a divorce, that is, which opens the way to so-called "pure speculation," leading inevitably to idealism (according to Hegel, "substantial speculation" = "idealism" = [space left blank in manuscript], in contrast to "miserable Lockeanism")—represents the pale ideological infirmity of humanity. On the other hand, the rejection of broad and profound summarizing, of generalization, of the intellectual processing of the data of experience, of the "universal," is the narrow-mindedness of a specialized, hair-splitting scientific hack worker. Both the one and the other represent antidialectical one-sidedness, which must be overcome and which is overcome by Marx's dialectical materialism.

This approach allows us to correctly pose and resolve the question of the interrelationship of science and philosophy.

Even Hegel, for whom "nature is the idea in the form of its other-being," and for whom "nature estranged from the idea ... is merely a corpse" (*The Philosophy of Nature*), cannot deny that "we start from our sense-knowledge of nature" and gather information on the diverse forms and laws of nature (*The Philosophy of Nature*).[2]

Here, however, we also find implanted all the so-called a priori forms, categories, and other bugaboos of idealist philosophy, as has already been explained. Mediated knowledge is not the neutral gear of thought, the processing of empirical data, but a historical and social process of cognition, that is, cognition whose subjects are socialized and historically defined individuals, cognition in which both the object and the forms of the relationship with the subject are historical.

This process, as we know, is divorced from practice. In the first place, it is split up into separate sciences, and secondly, these sciences are becoming increasingly divided. Because of the social structure, different branches of the sciences are becoming specialized to the degree that all contact between them is often lost. The rational principle (as opposed to the reasoning one) is thus embodied here in the relationships themselves. Philosophy has always tried to overcome this increasing narrowness, to bring together the whole sum of knowledge, orienting itself toward the "universal." Here, however, the problem was that the thinkers themselves, as members of the ideological estates, or professions, also imagined themselves to represent an isolated branch of activity which had acquired the character of a "pure" intellectual function; therefore, the task of making such a synthesis was not for their shoulders. The Greeks, with a few exceptions, were remote from contemporary experimental science (which was weakly developed) and from the rudiments of engineering. Meanwhile, they despised the productive work of tradesmen, peasants, and slaves. Of the Greeks, the one who was best acquainted with the natural sciences, and with the sciences of his time in general, was the encyclopedic genius Aristotle; it was because of the breadth of his learning that he contributed more to philosophy than anyone else. His only equal in the modern era has been Hegel, who possessed one of the great encyclopedic minds of the nineteenth century.

In the natural sciences, however, Hegel lagged behind Kant, and was of course thousands of kilometers removed from material production and technology. Idealist philosophy, as represented by its various Kantian branches, has in recent times been oriented along the lines of high-flown ethical mumbo-jumbo, while on the other hand, philosophizing physicists have been closer to mathematics and its symbolism than to material labor with its goal of overcoming the real resistance of matter. Meanwhile, the need for synthesis has by no means disappeared, and under the planned economy of socialism, where the plan itself is the synthesis, and all of society is an organized unity, the unity of the sciences is something that flows directly from the "spirit of the times."

Let us, however, examine the problem more attentively and in a little more detail. When we are considering dialectical thought, we see how this thought moves from the first concrete through the analysis of distinct aspects and the separating-out of the general, and then rises by way of synthesis to the second concrete. In the development of human cognition, the same process occurs on a gigantic historical scale. The world, in its various disciplines and their subdivisions—large, small, and minuscule—is cognized from various angles, in its distinct and to a certain degree mutually opposing forms. These forms have their specific qualities, properties, and laws. But who or what will consider them in relation to others? Who will analyze their transitions from one into another? These "borderline" questions will knock directly on the door (physics and chemistry, chemistry and biology, physical chemistry and chemical physics, the "chemistry of the living organism," and so on). It is true that there are disciplines of a relatively general character (for example, theoretical physics in general), and scientists who work in them, but they rarely know much about biology, not to speak of social sciences such as sociology, linguistics, or history.

And yet questions of the general laws of being, of types of relationships, of the unity of the world, of transitions from one form into another, of the relations of subject and object, and so on, are now becoming especially crucial, and thrust themselves forward from every field of specialization. Scientists can now no longer maintain that all this is "metaphysics"; these matters are staring them in the face. In the past, specialists in "pure philosophy" (most of them real metaphysicians), divorced both from material labor and empirical science, would often condescend to involve themselves in science, sometimes creating monstrosities such as the "philosophy of nature." (This does not, of course, exclude the possibility of brilliant instances of guesswork, even in Schelling.) Science itself can now no longer get by without resolving a series of general questions and problems—the "higher" problems of modern physics, chemistry, biology, mathematics, and so on. How can one resolve the controversies between vitalists and Darwinists, and between mechano-Lamarckians and psycho-Lamarckians in biology? Or the problems of the laws of macro- and microstructure, of the discrete and continuous, and so forth, in physics? Or the question of history and theory, of ideography and nomography in the social sciences? Or the problem of the "physical" and "psychical" in physiology and psychology, and a whole series of other questions which are very important from the point of view of the development of science, without the resolving of broader and more general questions, that is, questions of philosophy?

It is not that another science, also taken in isolation (one that is "in itself") has to be set in place in the series of existing specialized sciences, distinguished from one another according to their object of study. To a significant degree this used to be the case with philosophy, though not in the absolute sense of the word "isolation," since the isolation of different functions was never—and could not be—absolute; here, the relative nature of the corresponding statements should not be forgotten. Now, however, when the whole historical epoch is moving toward a mighty synthesis (this is occurring through struggle, the collapse of former societies, catastrophes, and ideological crises, but it is nevertheless occurring), it is necessary to advance, with particular insistence, the idea of the synthesis of all theoretical knowledge, and of a still more mighty synthesis of theory and practice.

What does this mean for philosophy?

Hegel at one point provides a wonderful formulation: "The empirical, taken in its synthesis, is the speculative idea" (*History of Philosophy*, II).[3] We shall not forget that "speculative" in this case means "dialectical"; we shall not fear the word, knowing its meaning in this case. There you are! What we are concerned with here is that in synthesizing cognition, the empirical cognition of particular aspects and forms of being, we should synthesize them into a single harmonious whole, moving toward the general, the *Universum*, with its universal relationships and laws. This, however, also means moving toward philosophy, toward its highest and most modern form, the philosophy of dialectical materialism. This is not a separate science "in itself." It reveals and formulates the most general, universal, and profound laws and relationships, and moreover, in their relationship with the particular and isolated. It includes all sciences "in sublated form" as "aspects" of it, and is not situated above them, covering them like an external cap, an outward form.

Moreover, if the materialist dialectic becomes the method of all sciences, that is, if their methodological unity is established, then within each science, in any of its subdivisions, analogous relations appear, proceeding downwards, so to speak. Between the sciences, this philosophy establishes its links and transitions, corresponding to the links and transitions which exist in the real world. Figuratively speaking, dialectics then penetrates the whole organism of science, and this without doubt raises its vital tone sharply. The union of this philosophy with practice does away once and for all with the idealist fantasizing that grows on the soil of the divorce of intellectual functions and of their closing off "in themselves," stripping off from the process of thought its concrete, vital content.

Hegel at one point acknowledges (or lets the cat out of the bag):

> We strive to know nature that really exists, and not something nonexistent. But instead of leaving nature as it is, and taking it as it truly is, instead of perceiving it, we transform it into something quite different. Conceiving of objects, we thereby turn them into something general. Things in reality are individual, and lions in general do not exist. (*The Philosophy of Nature*, II)[4]

Bravo! The only thing is that in place of "we" throughout this passage, it is necessary to substitute "we, idealist philosophers." Materialist dialectics does not dream of replacing the king of beasts with a generic concept, an "idea," or of treating nature as a corpse and taking an "idea" as the "truth" of nature. For the materialist dialectic, therefore, such a lamentation is categorically unwarranted.

Experimenters in the natural sciences are often afraid of philosophy as something "metaphysical." In *The Dialectics of Nature*, however, Engels brilliantly formulated the observation that these brave souls are usually in thrall to the waste matter of philosophical thought, since the issues and problems that philosophy resolves cannot simply be dismissed with a wave of the hand. It is an ostrich-like, head-in-the-sand attitude to consider that these questions do not exist, a *testimonium paupertatis*, a testimony to intellectual poverty, which does no credit to those who embrace it. In particular, many natural scientists are fearful of the mysticism of Hegel, forgetting that it is not this side of his work that is important. When some materialist-minded botanist or agronomist, reading *The Philosophy of Nature*, comes upon such a piece of sententiousness as the following, his or her hair will of course stand on end: "This preserving of the seed in the earth is ... a mystical, magical action. It shows that the seed contains secret powers which are still dormant. Truly, the grain is something even higher than it appears in its immediate being...."!![5]

All this mystical rubbish, of course, has to be discarded. But in the laws of dialectics, interpreted in materialist fashion, there is not so much as an atom of this mysticism. Here, in inverted and distorted form, Hegel sets out the real content of being, its universal laws. It was no accident that Goethe wrote: "observers of nature, however different their general thinking, agree unconditionally that everything that appears to us, presenting itself to us in the form of phenomena, must display either a primary diremption or capacity for diremption, or else a primary unity that may become diremption...."[6]

This is the same unity of opposites which Lenin rightly defined as the essence of dialectics!

What is it that constitutes the proper object of dialectics? Everything, and at the same time: 1) the general laws of being; 2) the general laws of thought; and 3) the general laws of the interrelationship of subject and object. This means that dialectics, logic, and the theory of cognition coincide. We repeat, however, that the dialectic of materialism embraces everything. This is because its universal is not the universal of formal logic, not an empty abstraction, but a ball from which concrete content can be unravelled. Here, "in sublated form," are all the sciences. General laws of nature pass over into particular, specific ones, and multiply; particular laws of nature encompass the individual. Everything is connected into a single whole, but a whole that is diverse and multifaceted. At the same time, this is not a hierarchy of fixed "values," not a stairway of rigid higher and lower quantities, but the kind of diversity in which the one passes into another, eternally mobile and changing diversity, eternal transformation, disappearance and birth, the appearance of the new and the perishing of the old, a historical process. The supreme service rendered by Hegel was and remains the fact that he made a magnificent attempt to present the whole natural, historical, and spiritual world as a process. This service, of which Engels speaks with gratitude, will remain forever to the credit of the great idealist philosopher.

37

Evolution

The positive center of Hegel's whole conception is thus his interpretation of everything as a process. This view blazed trails for itself in extremely diverse fields as a tendency toward universal historicism. Historically self-developing matter was already present in Kant (*Universal Natural History and the Theory of the Heavens*); in Lamarck and Darwin in the field of biology (the term "biology" was coined almost simultaneously by Lamarck and the German Treviranius); also (before Darwin), in Goethe; in Lyell in geology; in the "historicist school" in the social sciences, and so on—all expressed the new "spirit of the times" and in logical terms were opposed to the dry rationalism of the Enlightenment. The social genesis here was relatively diverse and complex, and the very meaning of "historicization" appeared in different, often counterposed variants: from the rotten, conservative apologetics of the "historicist school" to the liberating significance of Darwinism.

Here, however, we would wish, without relating the history of how the relevant ideas developed, to dwell on a few central issues that are important for understanding Marx's historicism and the Marxist idea of "development," of "the laws of motion."

In *The Philosophy of Nature* we read:

> There are two conceptions of how certain forms are transformed into others: evolution and emanation. The evolutionary conception, according to which the initial link is imperfect and unformed, holds that at first there were moist and watery creatures, and that from the watery ones there later arose plants, polyps, molluscs, and

then fish. After this, land animals arose, and then, out of these animals, came humanity.... The idea of the emanative course of change is characteristic of Eastern viewpoints. This idea involves stages in a consistent deterioration. The initial stage is perfection, absolute wholeness, God. Then come all the less perfect creations, and finally, matter, as the "summit of evil."[1]

Hegel considers both conceptions to be one-sided, but prefers the evolutionary process of transformation of some forms into others, although he does not share this conception, since for him, species do not pass over from one into another, despite the "spirit" of dialectics.

For us, however, both of these dialectical opposites, and their unity as well, are unacceptable. They are unacceptable because their motion is played out on a distorted ideological plane, the plane of teleology. In fact, evolution is taken here as the antithesis of emanation. In emanation, God, the beneficent principle, reason, passes over dialectically into evil, sin, and matter. In evolution (as interpreted by Hegel!), by contrast, motion and the "transformation of forms" begins from a figurative end, such as the ascent from the evil, imperfect, and unformed, to the good, to the increasingly perfect, to Aristotelian "forms," to the spirit, reason, and God. Any synthesis of these (illusory, metaphysical, and false) oppositions will remain on the same plane of teleological idealism, which is a potentialized distortion, since in this case idealism is "multiplied" by teleology. Mysticism of the sort that was embraced, for example, by Paracelsus, who recognized just as many material elements as there were calculated to be principal virtues (!), appeared repeatedly, and later.[2] For example, the Swiss naturalist Charles Bonnet (1720–1793: *Traité d'Insectologie* and *Contemplation de la Nature*) worked out a whole "scale of beings," in which everything was set out in ascending order, and where human beings were followed by the ranks of angel, archangel, and God.[3] It was no accident that the caustic Voltaire, mocking this scheme and arguing that it embodied "an idea more sublime than correct," observed malevolently that it reproduced the hierarchy of the Catholic Church, that is, a feudal hierarchy (the cunning savant saw something here!).

When applied to society, evolution and emanation (here we are speaking continually of Hegel's interpretation of these concepts) corresponded to the notion of the paradisiacal state, blessed and without sin, the condition of primal man, who fell into "sin" (here we find a progression from "paradise," the "golden age," virtue, holiness, and bliss to sin, to an accursed existence, to evil and suffering, all of which corresponds to the concept of emanation). This is on the one hand; on the other is the concept of movement toward "the kingdom of god on earth," to "the city of god," to the golden age in the future. This latter idea was expressed in various eschatalogical and chiliastic conceptions, and then in the idea of "eternal improvement," rational improvement according to God's plan; this corresponded to the concept of evolution.

Of course, we have to reject *a limine* such an interpretation of "evolution," not to speak of "emanation." We have already had done both with theology and teleology, and to discuss this in detail makes absolutely no sense.

Let us now dwell on the antithesis put forward in Lenin's well-known fragment, *The Question of Dialectics*. Here Lenin speaks of two conceptions of development. The first assigns primary significance to the process of increase or decline, that is, the principle of bare quantitative change. The second gives primacy to the process of divarication of the whole. In the first case, self-motivation remains in the shade, and the whole conception is pale, dry, and lifeless. In the second, self-motivation is clearly present, and we find leaps, interruptions to gradualness, the transformation of things into their opposites, the destruction of the old and the rise of the new. Here, therefore, the question of teleology is waved aside in advance (and quite rightly), and an antithesis is put forward in which the rational-quantitative view is contrasted with the dialectical one.

The basic elements of dialectical change are to be found as far back as Aristotle; it was no accident that Engels linked dialectics to the name of this mighty Greek thinker. (The idea of transformation has played a particularly great role in the philosophy of India, but examining this would take us too far off the track; as a general thing, it should be noted that Hegel's entire interpretation of the philosophy of India, China, and so on is as far from the truth as heaven is from earth. All it embodies is arrogant, white-racist European provincialism and ignorance of the topic, which, moreover, should not surprise us.) For Aristotle, change presupposes a transition of opposites, one into the other, and their "sublation" in unity. Aristotle further posits four main categories of change: 1) from the angle of "what" (the rise and fall of a particular essence); 2) from the angle of quality (the change of properties); 3) from the angle of quantity (increase and decline); 4) from the angle of "where," that is, from the angle of place (movement in space). "Change itself is the transition from that which exists in potential to that which exists in reality" (Aristotle, *Metaphysics*), that is, in other words, becoming. Aristotle's conception is therefore much richer than the purely quantitative ones that were later destined to play so great a role in both science and philosophy: all the superiority of dialectics, even in undeveloped form, makes itself felt here.

The question of a dialectical or of a merely quantitative-rational understanding of the process of change also includes the question of the antithesis between gradualness and change by leaps, between continuity and discontinuity. This question has played and continues to play a very important role, especially in the social sciences. The usual concept of evolution excludes leaps, and the conservative enthusiasm of "the historicist school" was also expressed in a belief in gradualness as a law of nature and of the entire world (compare this with Leibniz, much earlier). It should be pointed out that the geology of Lyell also developed as the antithesis to Cuvier (the "theory of catastrophes"), and in biology, gradualism and "slow changes" formed the basis of all bases. In the social sciences, evolution was therefore interpreted as the opposite of revolution, excluding this latter or declaring it to be "unnatural." (It is precisely the category of the "unnatural" that might be of help here!) Hegel's dialectics in its rational form was able to become the algebra of revolution, however, because it demonstrated the dialectical transition of quantity into quality, of the continuous into the discontinuous, of gradual change into leaps, and gave them dialectical unity. In *The Science of Logic*, Hegel wrote:

> It is said that there are no leaps in nature ... the usual idea supposes ... that when something experiences a rise or downfall, it is sufficient to imagine this as a gradual emergence or disappearance. It has become clear, however, that in general the change of being consists not only in the transition from one magnitude into another, but also in the transition from the qualitative into the quantitative and vice versa, the rise of something other, something different; in the interruption of gradualness, in a being qualitatively different from that which has gone before.[4]

The dialectical interpretation of development thus includes both gradualness and leaps, in their transition from one into another and in their unity. The real historical process, whether in nature or in society, presupposes both gradualness and leaps, and Saint-Simon already divided epochs into "organic" and "critical." Is it really the case that the history of the earth, its geological history, has been without catastrophes, ice ages, earthquakes, "inundations," the disappearance of dry land beneath the sea, the vanishing of water, and so forth? Is it true that the universe does not know the collision of planets and stars with one another? Has human society not witnessed the downfall of whole civilizations? Has it not known wars and revolutions? Of course, we look closely at Darwin's theory of natural selection. Does it, despite the gradualness of evolution, really exclude leaps? Let us take the appearance of the adaptive feature, the concrete peculiarity, which selection "seizes upon." This peculiarity appears "by chance"; Darwin's law is a law of selection, necessity that includes fortuity. But how does it occur, the appearance of such a feature? As a mutation, that is, a leap. Furthermore, the process of selection includes struggle. When, for example, a war between ants takes place, and one ant colony destroys another, is this not a leap? And so on to infinity.

The recognition and theoretical generalization of these factors obliges us to interpret the process of change as a dialectical process, that is, as a process that unites in a higher unity the continuous and discontinuous, quantity and quality, gradualness and leaps. Development, as Marxists understand it, is not the bourgeois "pure evolution"; the Marxian concept is broader, richer, more full-blooded, and more truthful, since it better corresponds to objective reality, reflecting this reality in incomparably more truthful fashion.

As we saw much earlier, the process of evolution is not at all straightforward; it includes advances and retreats, circular and spiral movements, periods of stagnation, and destruction. The movement of the world as a whole is indifferent to "good," however lamentable this might be to idealists and to religious believers thirsting for supernatural consolation and reassurance. The unity of the world does not consist in the unity of its "purpose," nor in the single "world law" of an all-wise creator (Hegel), but in the mutual interrelatedness of all the world's aspects, in its materiality developing the endless diversity of its properties, including thought, which poses goals. Vital sensation, interest, and so forth are present in life itself and in its necessities, not beyond the bounds of nature and life. *Punctum*.

From this, there also follows the narrowness of the positivist doctrine of uninterrupted progress. When, for example, Auguste Comte in his *Sociology* goes to great lengths to show that a general progress continues without interruption throughout the whole realm of the living, starting with simple plants and the most primitive animals, and extending to humanity, whose "social evolution" in reality forms only its "concluding link," the truth is mixed with the most vulgar oversimplification. Humanity is in fact a link in the chain of natural evolution. Social development is indeed an element of development in general, just as all organic development is an aspect of the historical process of nature. The idea that progress is uninterrupted, however, is false. So too is the idea of universal progress. Comte sees neither interruptions, nor destruction, nor a descending line of development. This is a one-sided point of view. On the other hand, Marx's position that real movement includes spirals, circles, regressions, and halts should not be taken as cause for skepticism concerning the present. Here the question relates to the concretely historical conditions of social development (we are speaking in this case of society). Everything hangs on the fact that socialism is now winning its fight, and will free progress from the hobbles which decaying capitalism has placed upon it. The whole character of the situation rules out a return to the initial positions, and arguments by analogy with Rome, Greece, and so forth (see Spengler) are fruitless, superficial, primitive, and untrue. The dialectics through which immoderate worshippers of the god of progress and gloomy pessimists are transformed is itself rooted in the hopeless position not of humanity, but of capitalism. "That is the question."[5]

Hypotheses concerning a tendency toward a general world stasis (see, for example, Joseph Petzoldt: *The Picture of the World from the Point of View of Positivism*) are merely hypotheses, against which a thousand and one arguments can be marshaled; they should not in any way be taken seriously.[6] This is not a general, correct "picture of the world," since it reveals no opposing tendencies; it is one-sided, and therefore unacceptable.

The whole world is thus understood as a historical process of change, of the transformation of its diverse forms. Inorganic nature is already in itself diverse, and develops numerous qualities and properties that pass over from one into another. It "gives birth" historically to organic nature, concerning which Ernst Haeckel wrote in *Natürliche Schöpfungsgeschichte*, summarizing his basic views as follows:

> The unity of active causes in organic and inorganic nature; the ultimate basis of these causes in the chemical and physical properties of matter; the absence of a special life force or of any organic final cause (that is, entelechy—Author); the origin of all organisms in a few extremely simple initial forms or primary creatures, which arose out of inorganic substances through primary self-generation; the connected flow of the entire history of the earth, the lack of any new or forced overturnings, and in general, the impossibility of conceiving of any miracle, of any supernatural interference in the natural course of development of matter.[7]

We know how to dialectically understand "bases" and the unity of natural laws, and Haeckel in this case does not show a real fullness and precision of dialectical thought. The basis he provides, however, is correct. Let us continue: the organic world, in its "final" earthly link, is transformed into thinking humanity, a herd of which becomes society. Society is both an antagonist of nature and a part of nature, by no means torn out of its general natural relationships. Along with everything else, it is subject to a single natural necessity; like everything in the world, it develops dialectically. Within it, the laws of physics, chemistry, biology, and physiology are laws of relationship, but in a transformed, sublated manner it also has its own specific laws, which make up an "aspect" in the universal relationship of nature, and which are a specific manifestation of necessity. Such are the laws of social development. (We explored the dialectics of necessity and teleology earlier.) The whole world is changing historically, and the ancient Heraclitus was correct with his well-known saying: "Everything flows."

Finally, it is impossible not to recall once again Werner Sombart (*Proletarische Sozialismus*), who argues that the concept of dialectics in Marx's theory of development is nonsensical. Hegel, according to Sombart, is concerned with contradiction and emanation, and Marx with real opposition. Hegel is said to deal with the contradictory, and Marx with the concrete; Marxists, Sombart maintains, confuse these in "school-pupil" fashion. As we said earlier, the only thing that is correct here is the assertion that Hegel is concerned with the movement of ideas, and Marx with real movement. All the rest is indeed childish rubbish. In the first place, Hegel is opposed to the emanative interpretation; second, Hegel's works also contain contradiction and opposition; third, in Hegel's dialectics contradiction is nothing other than the opposition of an object to itself, that is, the negation of the absolute law of identity as posited by formal logic; fourth, dialectical unity is precisely the unity of opposites. And so on. This gentleman too, this weathercock, is still uttering imprecations! But such are the representatives of modern bourgeois scholarship.

38

Theory and History

Failure to understand dialectics has played, and continues to play, a major role in the theory of science where discussion of the question of theory and history is concerned. There is a doctrine which in a number of variants counterposes theory and history as absolute opposites, refusing to recognize the transition from one to the other or their dialectical unity. It is particularly interesting to pose this issue now, after we have unraveled the questions of historicism, evolution, and so forth.

The special "honor" of having erected the barricade between theory and history belongs to Heinrich Rickert.[1] Particularly in his work *Limits of the Natural-Scientific Formation of Ideas,* this author advanced roughly the following basic concepts: in the natural sciences, where everything repeats itself, what is involved is seizing upon the general, the typical, that which is characteristic of the many; here the method of science is "typifying" and "generalizing." In the "sciences of the spirit," by contrast, nothing repeats itself, and everything is individual, distinctive, and concrete; here it is only possible to speak of an individualizing method. There is a fundamental difference between the sciences of nature and the sciences of the spirit, and their structures and methods are quite heterogeneous. Or, to use the terminology of Windelband, there are sciences (of nature) that are "nomothetic" (they deduce laws), and sciences that are "ideographic," that is, descriptive (they describe the concrete course of events).

Aleksandr Chuprov the younger, in his once-celebrated *Notes on the Theory of Statistics*, delved still more deeply into this opposition, but took it not in terms of a fundamental division into sciences of "nature" and of "the spirit," but in another respect.[2] Together with a number of mathematical statisticians, including a prominent German scholar, Bortkiewicz, he put forward the argument that the "individual" is differentiated not by some special property as its necessary feature, but by its presence in a particular place and a particular time.[3] If, for example, there are before us two (imaginary) completely identical eggs, and if we consciously keep watch on them, we will always distinguish between them, that is, individualize them, since at a given time they always occupy different places, and cannot be in one and the same place at the same time. From this, the conclusion is drawn that individualization is linked with a particular time and a particular method, with position in a system of temporal and spatial coordinates. From this in turn comes the division of knowledge into two great branches: nomographic knowledge, which derives conclusions, that is, something independent of time and place ("eternal laws"); and ideographic knowledge, which is linked with time and with place simultaneously (the history of such-and-such a country in such-and-such a period, the population statistics of such-and-such a country in a particular time, and so on). Ideography is just as necessary and useful as nomography; it is merely a different form of knowledge.

Finally, it should be mentioned that in political economy the light hand of Rodbertus (by way of Tugan-Baranovsky and others) implanted a terminology that describes as "logical" categories of such an order as the means of production (capital in the "logical" sense), and as "historical" the sort of categories that are typical only of one type of economy, or at any rate, not of all types. [4]

Standing in opposition to all this is Marx's argument (in *The German Ideology*) to the effect that in essence there is only one science, that of history, which is divided into the history of nature and the history of society. Indeed, if everything is located in the historical process of change, and if general, universal movement is therefore a historical process, it is not surprising that the reflection of this movement should depict this process.

Here, undoubtedly, there is a major problem of knowledge. How is it to be resolved?

We shall begin by examining a few preliminary questions.

First, about "laws" and "facts." Are there "facts," that is, things and processes, that are outside law, that is, interconnection and relationship? No. We know very well that everything concrete is linked to the abstract, the individual with the universal, the one with another, with something different. We know that "things-in-themselves," without any relationship to anything else, are an empty abstraction, pure nothingness; that relationship and interconnection, that is, law, are immanent to things and processes. Meanwhile, do laws, interconnections, and the universal lie outside "fact," that is, outside the individual, outside things and processes? Of course not; "relationship" and "interconnection," outside of that which is related to and connected with, are also completely empty, contentless abstractions, "nothingness." Law, connection, and relationship are not something that stands alongside things and processes or hangs above them; they are not a special "force" or "factor" that directs things and processes, but a form of being of those things and processes. Connections and relationships may be more profound and broad or less so, but they never exist "in themselves"; they cannot be transformed into a sort of special reality, existing in itself and located on a higher level than things. Such an idea, which is frequently encountered, is merely a refined variant of the animist interpretation of the world.

Second, about motion and rest. The latter has to be regarded simply as a particular instance of motion, as an "aspect" of it. In fact, everything is in constant, eternal motion. From this it follows that not only society but also nature and the world as a whole are in a state of historical transformation, of historical motion. There is therefore no truth in the initial premise of Rickert's philosophy, that in nature everything repeats itself, while in society nothing does. Here there are merely different scales involved. Is it true, for example, that the earth does not have its own history? Do not its geological ages constitute distinct historical periods? Do we not find here, at every historical step, the new, the concrete, the peculiar, the specific? Of course we do. The state of the earth as a molten mass, and its present state, which has been formed historically, are not one and the same. (See Kant: *Universal History and Theory of the Heavens*.) Geology is historical through and through. And biology? What does the entire theory of biological evolution represent? Do we not see here the formation of ever new species and forms? Are we not concerned here with those "unique," "concrete," "distinctive" aspects of which Rickert talks? If it is objected that what appears here is the "particular," and not the "individual," it should be pointed out that here it is also possible to proceed to the individual, and that things are precisely the same here as in society. The "particular"—"means of production," "formations," and the "individual"—consists of even more fractional links and relations between people in the course of the historical process.

Third, both in nature and in society there exist the individual, the particular, and the universal. Both in nature and in society we find that which cannot be repeated, and that which can. If, for example, we have a historic change of periods on the earth, this is a change of epochs of which each has its own individuality. However, the process of cooling of the earth "repeats" the process of cooling of the moon; the process of cooling of Mars "repeats" the process of cooling of the earth, and so on. Here, the "universal, or general" manifests itself. The same appears in history; social structures such as feudalism or capitalism are encountered in different countries, and the "phases of development," with all their individual peculiarities, have a general essence. Individual peculiarities? Yes! But these exist in nature as well. The moon is not identical to the earth, the earth is not identical to Mars, and so on. It follows that from this point of view as well, Rickert's theory collapses. But let us continue. Rickert's conception clearly holds that "laws of nature are eternal," while history, of its own nature, is something perishable and transient. Associated with this is the idea that the sciences of nature are also the embodiment of theory, of nomographic knowledge. The eternal creative work of history is a different matter; here everything is correlated with "values" and "cultural values." In this manner, teleology creeps in.

Let us examine the question of laws from this angle as well. Law is a necessary relationship; if there are A, B, C, a, and b, then there is X (or, X is coming into existence). Here, we shall not dwell on the various types of necessity (functional dependency, causality, and so forth), since in the present case this makes no difference; what is important is the necessary relationship. If, therefore, the first half of a formula exists, the second half necessarily exists as well. This is true in every instance. Here, however, it emerges that such "eternity" applies also to any social law, for example, to the law of centralization of capital. We shall formulate this law as follows: if there is competition between capitalists, that is, aspects A, B, C, a, and b, then large capitalists will outstrip small ones, and we shall see the onset of X (the fact of centralization). Wherever and whenever the groups of conditions and causes corresponding to the first half of the formula manifest themselves, X will invariably follow. In other words, a historical, socio-historical law is in this sense "eternal," and "independent" of time and place. This, however, is an abstract way of posing the question. In reality, the conditions and causes (the first half of the formula) are associated with place and time; they are historical, even though the time scales may be vast and the historicity may escape our notice. As we have seen, the law which states that bodies expand when heated is transformed into its opposite in astrophysics, under the conditions of enormous temperatures and pressures. This means that an "eternal" law of physics is in fact historical, and is associated with place and time, since it is linked with the presence of thoroughly specific conditions. Historically speaking, the law of compression of bodies (a historical law) is replaced by the law of the expansion of bodies at increased temperatures (that is, by another historical law). But since under the conditions to which we are accustomed, that is, the usual human scale, such "history" may seem practically nonexistent (that is, does not enter into consciousness, and is not reflected, although an objective process is present), the illusion is created that laws of nature are eternal, in the sense of being ahistorical, while only the fleeting laws of history, of human history, have a historical character.

In essence, the absolute opposition of theory and history also rests on this illusion. Since we cannot yet write the history of the universe, and its historical laws appear "eternal," this is the field of theory *par excellence*. Meanwhile, from everything we have said above there also flows the relativity of this opposition. The universal dialectical process is itself universal and absolute. Hence the eternal nature of the law of motion as such, and of the general laws of this motion which are apprehended to the extent our cognition allows, such as the law of necessity and the law of dialectics. As we have seen, however, historicity is already entering into play in physics. The laws of the organic world are historical. But since the organic world exists over a prolonged period, it is possible to draw out its general laws. This is theory. This theory, however, is historical. Where do organic processes take place? On earth. When? In those epochs when life on earth has been possible. Consequently, nomography is linked here with both place and time, but with place and time on such scales that they are not felt as aspects of history, though they are accorded more recognition than the law of the expansion of bodies, since the earth is "closer" than the stars, and the history of the earth is, so to speak, more perceptible to human consciousness as presently developed.

Since biology as a whole proceeds from the general through the particular to the individual, it develops into history (let us say, the history of species). Theory, however, is historical, and history is theoretical. Theory is historical, since it embraces the historical span of being (that historical "moment" when organic life exists on earth at all); theory therefore is itself an "aspect" of a more universal history.

To take another approach, history is theoretical because it is not simply a pile, an aggregate of "facts in themselves," but includes associations, connections, and laws. As a field of knowledge, let us take political economy. Marx's *Capital* is a model of theoretical investigation; it opened up an epoch in the social sciences, and even sworn enemies do not deny, cannot deny, its theoretical power and substance. *Capital* is not the same thing as the history of capitalist relations in all its concreteness. However, it is historical to the very marrow of its bones. All its categories are historical through and through, and consciously so; such are the categories of the commodity, money, value, surplus value, capital, profit, rent, interest, and so on. Marx set out to reveal the "laws of motion" of capitalism as a particular, specifically historical phase in the development of human society. Ultimately, all the motion of categories in his works is historical, for example, the motion of the commodity, of money, of capital, and so forth. As a result, theory in this case is historical.

If, however, we apply Marx's theory to elaborating the history of capitalism in, let us say, Britain or the United States, this history will be theoretical. The laws of capitalism are linked both with place and with time (they are laws of capitalism, that is, of a temporary phenomenon). In the history of capitalism, however, both place and time are perceived in terms of different scales, in different fashion, since here there is a transition from the general via the particular to the individual, the unfolding of the whole (coherent) picture of the process of becoming in its concrete fullness, a picture which, where theory is concerned, is present only *in nuce*, in undeveloped form, *in potentia*, or in Greek, *dynamis*.

Max Weber, one of the most outstanding of the scholars whom the bourgeoisie managed to produce in—we shall not say its final period, but merely its penultimate period—attempted to create "ideal types" for the social sciences. These, however, were no more than idealistically embellished and distorted copies of Marx's "social formations." Marx came up with a brilliant solution to the problem, since he approached it dialectically, while the living spirit of dialectics has long since flown from the ideologists of the bourgeoisie.

The question of the relationship between theory and history is thus resolved.

The conception developed by Rickert, of which we spoke earlier, and which posits an absolute opposition between "the sciences of nature" and "the sciences of the spirit," sets out to prove that the laws of history are fundamentally different from those of nature. Here we find the creative activity of the unreproduced, the new, the individual, which does not exist in nature; here is the creative spirit of humanity, and therefore, what is involved is quite different. The selection of facts of which history speaks is now selection according to particular criteria; importance is assigned to that which has "cultural value," in other words, that to which value is related as a teleological aspect. In this new teleological conception (now, in fact, it is quite old—how time flies!), which has given birth to a whole mountain of arguments about the social sciences as "goal-directed sciences," we see only a variation on the same leitmotif: society is torn out of the universal relationship of nature. For all the clamor about history, society is not understood as a historical aspect of historically changing nature, but is perceived outside of this relationship. There is no mention of the dialectical relationship between society and nature. Nor is there even a hint of the dialectical relationship between necessity and teleology. There is no talk of the fact that "cultural values," as a teleological element, are themselves manifestations of social necessity, which in turn is a specifically social expression of a more general, natural necessity. Everything moves in restricted, small-scale dimensions and relationships. This narrow-mindedness and obtuseness, this one-sided reasoning, cannot act as the basis for genuine philosophical constructs. Here, the question can only be resolved by materialist dialectics, which provides an accurate reflection of the objective dialectics of historical being.

39

The Social Ideal

Marx once noted that the proletariat was incapable of realizing ideals. In observing this, he was not of course renouncing socialism or the positive assessment he made of it from all points of view, economic, cultural, "spiritual," and so on; this is shown by the whole range of his works. His formulation was intended to demarcate him in the sharpest and most decisive fashion from "moral," "ethical," and all other types of extra-historical windbaggery, which, for example, in the form of so-called "true socialism," preaching a universal sentimental love ("the socialism of old women") in a context of intensified class struggle, could lead only to the corruption, weakening, and disorganization of genuine struggles for the real cause.

Marx approaches the question objectively and historically. His method is objective not in the fashion of bourgeois objectivism, which is oblivious to trends leading to the future, but in a broader manner, that is, more objectively than commonplace objectivism. Furthermore, Marx's method is objective not in the sense that the subject slides out of view, but in the sense of revealing, including in subjective-teleological fashion, the necessary as historically formulated. This dialectics, as the highest vantage point, is beyond the comprehension both of bourgeois scholars and of the ideologues of petty-bourgeois socialism. Whole seas of ink have been expended in efforts to transform Marx either into a fatalist, or into an individual with two personas, or into a doctrinaire utopian and prophet who, in the manner of the Hebrew prophets, preaches a new "soteriology," a new doctrine of "salvation" (Sombart and company).

What is fundamental for Marx is a scientific-historical, materialist-dialectical approach to the topic. In the trends of development of capitalist society, he sees the inevitable downfall of this society, and its transition to a higher phase through the mediating process of revolution, the agency of which is the proletariat, advancing its specific interests. Such is the position of this class, and in this position there is precisely nothing of the mystical or supernatural. In the transition from feudalism to capitalism an analogous role was played by the bourgeoisie, which formulated its interests as universal through the abstractions "liberty, equality, fraternity" in the works of Montesquieu and Rousseau, of Benjamin Constant and Condorcet, and which tore down the theology of feudalism through the vanguard battles of the *Encyclopédistes*. Marx not only destroyed all illusions of an ideological type, defetishized all fetishistic categories, concepts, and systems, revealed the genuine mainsprings of development, and laid bare the material interests involved, but also destroyed for good the rationalistic, that is, narrowly rational, approach to the historical process, an approach which, while historically conditioned, was logically hostile to all historicism.

All of the rationalist "ideals" proceeded from the premise of fixed, true laws. (In theological-teleological systems this, as we have seen, coincides with the divine purpose as the highest good.) Once aware of these laws (the divine purpose, or in a quite different variant, the "natural order," corresponding to "natural law"), and once having constructed an ideal society on the basis of them, it is possible to achieve an eternal, stable "harmony," living according to "reason" or "nature."

This view distorts the very concept of law, and suffers from a complete lack of historical method, even of an inferior sort. The ideals that grow up on such a basis are rationalistically static utopias, utopias of a fixed "ideal" such as "the end of history," an absolute state, perfect and unchanging, in which the course of the historical process comes to an end, since "conformity with nature" has been discovered, and this nature is—extra-historical!

As has been explained, however, these antihistorical ideal utopias were themselves conditioned historically, and behind them were definite material conditions of existence. Living classes and living interests, unfortunately, are not always correctly understood and evaluated by historians.

The utopias of ancient times, such as Plato's *Republic*, were utopias of the slave-owning class, utopias of slave-owners. These schemes grew up on the basis of this society, which was being eaten away by the money economy, by usury, by trade, by merchant and money "capital," by an intensification of class war between commercial democrats and landowning aristocrats, by struggles between city-states, by the spread of slave revolts, and by great wars with foreign enemies. The Sophists and Socrates were already giving expression to the profound social, political, and moral crisis and disintegration of ancient Greece. Plato's utopia embodied the ideal not of the slaves (the exploited, who in his view should not be freed, but on the contrary, thrown into irons!), not of the free urban artisans, not of the commercial democrats, but of the "benevolent" aristocratic landowning slaveholders, with their patriarchal traditions and "age-old piety." Plato's criticism of private property, of money, of the family, and so on, was conducted from the angle of a criticism of commercial property, from the positions of land ownership, yearning *idealiter* for the state land ownership and state slave-holding economy of ancient Egypt. (In his philosophy as well there are Egyptian motifs, for example, the motif of the transmigration of souls in his doctrine of memory.) In Plato's writings, the foundation—the exploitation of slaves—remained completely intact. The "divine" Plato was not joking here!

We know that in Plato's time there were other "utopias," which unfortunately have not come down to us, and that thoughts were brewing about the equality of slaves; we see, for example, how Aristophanes depicts these notions in caricature form, mocking them in every conceivable fashion. We may presume that with his *Republic*, the "divine" one was also anxious to block "subjective" liberating tendencies rising up from below. It was no accident that Marx and Engels referred to Plato in quite different fashion than, for example, to Aristotle. Nor was it without cause that Lenin reproached Hegel for

> spinning out in detail Plato's "philosophy of nature," with its preposterously mystical ideas to the effect that the "essence" of sensible things consists of triangles, and other such mystical rubbish. This is totally in character! The mystic-idealist-spiritualist Hegel (like all the trite, clerical-idealist philosophy of our time) exalts and chews over the mystical idealism in the history of philosophy, while ignoring and heedlessly slighting materialism. Compare Hegel on Democritus—nothing! On Plato, a huge quantity of mystical pap.[1]

Plato's philosophy, however, is very closely linked to his political utopia, and this latter with his philosophy. To the corroding skepticism, relativism, free thought, and sometimes atheism of the Sophists, Plato in his *Republic* affixed the iron fetter of "the universal," "the idea," "God." On individualism, on disintegrating social relationships, he imposed the structures of a well-thought-out slave-owning political conception. "The main idea that lies at the basis of Plato's *Republic*," writes Hegel, "… is the idea that the moral, on the whole, has the character of substantiality, and consequently, is fixed as divine."[2] Here, individuals have to act "spontaneously out of respect and goodwill for the state institutions," that is, the state of the slaveholders.

The aims of this state are served by Plato's constitution, with its three estates, its oligarchy of rulers and warriors, its enthralment of artisans and others, its savage exploitation of slaves, its conscious perpetuation of classes (in the guise of "estates"), its collective property ownership by the slaveholders (not social property—that is something quite different!), its distribution of "virtues" among the estates (to the third estate, the toilers, there falls the virtue of … moderation, of control over desires and passions!), its raising of children within class frameworks, its suppression of any individuality or group freedom, from political freedom to freedom of copulation (in the language of Hegel, this is termed "exclusion of the principle of subjectivity"). The forces of development (and decay) of ancient society never followed these lines, and the "ideal" was never realized. Such is the irony of history, however, that Plato's criticism of private property has made his *Republic* the source of ideas, or more accurately, a source of corroboration for ideas from quite different times and of quite different historical "meanings" (for example, Thomas More's *Utopia*).

The medieval peasant utopias, the ideals of artisans and apprentices, are without philosophical significance, since for the most part they rest directly and immediately on "holy writ." Their practical and political significance, however, was enormous. They embodied the hopes and interests of huge masses, and served as the ideological banner for a vast peasant war that raged over many years in a series of countries. The various "sects" and tendencies (Taborites, Moravian Brethren, Hutterites, Bogomils, Cathari, and so on) were in essence different political factions of the toiling masses, and their leaders, such as the executed Thomas Muntzer, Jan van Leiden, and others, deserve to be recalled with gratitude by the humanity of our day as it struggles for its liberation. This is despite Lassalle's assessment of the peasant wars, an assessment that derives from the same source as Lassalle's flirtation with Bismarck.

The utopia of the great martyr Campanella bore the features of antichromatist and anticapitalist idealization of the monastery, along with features of the theocratic ideal and of exaltation of the Catholic hierarchy (although this aspect was present even in the utopia written by the author of *Gargantua*, Rabelais, whose carnal appetites are well known). But another chord was already sounding in Campanella's work. We should not forget that Campanella knew Thomas More, and that the author of *Utopia* had an extremely powerful influence on him. Nor should we forget that Campanella was an Italian of the early seventeenth century, that Italy was the first home of capitalism, and that the author of *The City of the Sun* himself directly scourges the rulers and voices indignation at the exploitation suffered by the Neapolitan workers. (The latter "exhaust themselves with backbreaking toil, while the idle die of sloth, of miserliness, of disease and dissipation," and so forth.) Here, as with More, labor is placed at the head of the table of values. At the same time, everything is directed by the "Father-Metaphysician," the incarnation of all knowledge (later, Kant would imagine himself to be just such a "Father-Metaphysician," though naturally he did not express it in this way!), with three assistants: Wisdom, Love, and Might. Meanwhile, everything such as food, clothing, love, and so on is decisively regulated: "The procreation of children is a matter for the republic," and "Love," as one of the triumvirate, "is specially concerned with everything that affects the procreation of children, that is, its purpose is that the sexual union should always yield the very best issue." Despite this, Campanella's work has many very interesting aspects (in the area of rewards for success in competition, in the field of pedagogics, and so forth). This is one of the first swallows of utopian socialism; in it, quite heterogeneous aspects are oddly intertwined.

Before Campanella, however, there lived in Italy the author of the *Discourses* and *The Prince*, Niccolo Machiavelli. He too had an ideal, but it was by no means utopian; on the contrary, here everything was constructed on the basis of a cold, sober calculation of strengths and means, on the pitiless unmasking and cynical exploitation of cynical relationships, on the complete rejection of any and all morality. We are talking about the ideal of the trading-commercial bourgeoisie of the Italian states in the sixteenth century, during the epoch of so-called "feudal reaction," when Italy was splintered into a multitude of principalities. Machiavelli sets forth a sober class analysis, understanding that people are motivated by interests (especially property, *robba*, and honor, since honors, *onori,* are linked with state power); that society is divided into classes (*dissunione*); and that within it there are "two different aspirations" (*umori diversi*), one of them popular, and the other that of the upper classes.

Machiavelli provides a quite extraordinary analysis of the uprising of the *ciompi* (the first workers' revolt) in his *History of Florence*, and a summary of norms of behavior in *The Prince* and the *Discourses*, works which are unrivalled among their kind. The moral-political side is expressed with complete frankness in the following passage from the *Discourses*: "When it is a question of saving the homeland, all considerations of what is just or unjust, merciful or cruel, praiseworthy or shameful, must be discarded. It is necessary to forget everything, and to act only in such a way that the existence of the homeland should be saved, and that its freedom should remain intact." In *The Prince*, advice is given on this score that justifies any treachery and any crime for the sake of this goal. The prince is advised to be a "fox" and a "lion" (chapter XVIII), to deceive, to lie, to dissemble, to resort to the dagger, and so forth. This "normative" section is wonderfully reminiscent of the ancient esoteric Indian collections prepared for the instruction of future rulers (compare, for example, the collection *Armachastra*). It is echoed, in more refined form, in recently published literature on reasons of state.

In Machiavelli, however, what is valuable is the analytical part, and it was no accident that Marx regarded this political thinker highly. As for the norm "the end justifies the means," it is inexpedient for broad movements and durable conquests, since those it destabilizes are first and foremost those who apply it. This is a generalization of the practice of cliques and coteries, in a musty, confined atmosphere. It is expediency for political mayflies, in conditions of political leap-frog. If Hegel in his *Philosophy of History* "approved" of *The Prince*, he spoke of the specific conditions of the age, and of the position of the forces which Machiavelli represented. Machiavelli called for reprisals against the "plebeians," that is, the common people, in the name of the interests of the so-called "people," that is, the bourgeoisie. His ideal was that of the dictatorship precisely of this class; his homeland was the homeland of the commercial-industrial bourgeoisie, uniting Italy in struggle against the feudalists, and holding the plebeians in a grip of iron.

The social ideal of the time of the French Revolution was the incarnation of the rationalist utopia: the "natural order" and "social contract" of Rousseau; "freedom, equality, and fraternity"; the thesis according to which the "free play of forces" yields the best result. If we take the words, concepts, and slogans seriously, that is, if we interpret them according to their literal meaning, then all this turned out to be an ideological myth. Behind this, however, was concealed a real, serious content: freedom for exploitation, freedom of competition, formal democratic equality before the law, freedom from all sorts of feudal encumbrances and fetters, formal independence for the commodity producer, for the new, bourgeois "economic actor," and so forth. This was the real content of the "social ideal" of the bourgeoisie, which cleaned out the Augean stables of feudalism using the hands of the petty bourgeois-plebeian Jacobin dictatorship.

The bourgeoisie conquered power, capitalism cleared paths for itself, and its own internal contradictions began to unfold. Its abysses gaped, the growth of wealth and poverty, crises, the polarization of classes. The first ideological breath of the young, still unformed proletariat was utopian socialism. Saint-Simon and Fourier, especially the latter, developed brilliant critiques of capitalism and had truly prophetic insights. Utopian socialism, however, did not see the paths of development, the real motive forces. Its constructs hung in the air; its tactics (if one can speak of them at all) were powerless, and Fourier's appeal to the strong of the world was fantastic and pitiable. Nevertheless, the services the utopian socialists performed are immortal. The members of this current voiced a criticism of capitalism, and put forward socialism, even if in immature form, as a goal.

Marx and Engels approached the question quite differently. After describing materialist dialectics and formulating the basic features of historical materialism, Marx went on in *Capital* to lay bare, with exceptional scientific scrupulousness, the characteristic "laws of motion" of spontaneously developing capitalist society. This work reaffirmed what had already been revealed in *The Communist Manifesto*, corroborating it with all the fullness of scientific argument. The historical tendencies of capitalism were explained, and its necessity was recognized; the conditions that determine the will of classes were revealed. The inevitable crash of capitalism was predicted, along with the transition through revolution to the dictatorship of the proletariat and the subsequent movement toward communism. It is a fact that some decades ago the words "capitalism" and "proletariat" were still laughed at. It is a fact that thousands and thousands of times people "disproved" the theory of the concentration and centralization of capital, the theory of crises, of the impoverishment of the masses, and of the growth in the contradictions of capitalism in general. It is a fact that people mocked the "prophecy" of the dictatorship of the proletariat, and so on. Nevertheless, all this was vindicated. Life and practice totally confirmed theory. Marx foresaw the events a hundred years in advance: just read *The Communist Manifesto* today. This was scientific clairvoyance! For Marx, the "ideal" was a conclusion derived from scientific analysis, and all of Marx's strategy, tactics, and organization of forces, like those of Lenin and Stalin in later times, always and everywhere rested, and continue to rest, on a scientific study of the epoch, the period, the moment. The approach to the "ideal" is historical, concrete, and dialectical. It is of course rubbish to argue that for Marx, socialism was a static absolute; socialism develops in the direction of communism, while communism develops, and does not stand still (we have already noted this in the analysis of the question of freedom and necessity). The movement always has a far-reaching purpose; it is profoundly principled. The concrete attributes of this goal, however, are revealed historically, and in exactly the same way, "every step of real movement" appears as a historical criterion.

All this is remote from the non-Marxist ways of posing the question. In this respect, there is a vast gulf between utopian socialism and the scientific communism of Marx. Here, for example, we find the positivist socialism of the author of "subjective sociology," Pyotr Lavrov (*From the History of Social Doctrines*).[3] Consider what scientific "laws of sociology" Lavrov advances:

1. "... A healthy society is one in which cooperation and not exploitation prevails." A thoroughly respectable truth! But is this really a law of development? Is there even a grain of science here? Even a trace of historicity? This is an empty, abstract phrase, that could simply be put as follows: exploitation is bad. Period. If there is anything else here, it is something childish, to wit: all forms of society apart from primitive communism are declared to be sick, abnormal, and unhealthy. So, was the movement out of primitive communism progressive or not? Evidently it was not. So, does that mean humanity should have remained in its savage state? And this is a "law"!
2. "At people's present-day level of development, a healthy society is one that is making progress with constructing its forms, and is not resting content with a particular set of habits." (This is Lavrov's "third real law of sociology.") Well, what are we to say about this? In the first place, what present-day "people" is Lavrov talking about? The abstraction "people" here is empty and meaningless. If we take the law as a whole, then if we think about it, it runs as follows: a healthy, that is, a good society, is one that progresses, that is, in which everything goes forward, that

is, well. A wonderfully rich law! Or, it is better to go forward than to mark time. Another "law"!

3. "Only through approximating to the methods of scientific criticism is it possible to provide real guidance for the reconstructing of social forms by way of reform or (!) revolution manifesting itself as healthy social development." (This is the "new law of socialism.") In order to act well, it is necessary to base oneself on scientific criticism. An eminently wise position. Is it perhaps necessary to base oneself on the scientific criticism that gave rise to the first two "laws"?

4. "The guiding principle for the reconstruction of social forms and for the social activity of the individual can only be the real elementary needs of the person in the harmonious development, subordination, and coordination of these needs."[4] This is the very height of wisdom! It is necessary to satisfy real needs—a truly brilliant discovery! But why only elementary needs? And what sort of person is this who serves as a scientific measuring stick? What is the "subordination" of these needs all about, if the needs are already elementary? And what sort of "law of scientific sociology" is this, when it expresses only the empty, formal, general rule that it is good to eat, sleep, and so forth, to read newspapers (or is this no longer elementary)?

Lavrov, nevertheless, is the head of a whole school, a current—he is a renowned scholar, a man of great erudition! We have dwelt on him, the more clearly to set off the whole difference between Marx's approach to the problem and that of others.

But enough of bothering with these others, especially since this is all in times past. Where the question of social ideals is concerned, the modern world provides us with a comical picture. At the dawn of capitalist development, the bourgeoisie had a social system, while the proletariat had only constructed utopias. Now, the proletariat already has a system, while the bourgeoisie, in the process of losing its decaying system, "without faith in itself," "an accursed old man," as Marx once called it, occupies itself with producing utopias of "planned capitalism." But alas, here there are no longer any leaps of the intellect, no originality, no prospects. Fascism strenuously projects its state-capitalist barracks as a "socialism" headed by capitalists, and seeks its social ideal behind and not before, in the past and not the future, as if life in the past had not already blown these "ideals" into smithereens. Organizing all the bestial ideas and forces of the past, fascism dreams of conquering the world, of releasing the energy of hundreds of millions! Such is the development of the historic epoch of the real growth of socialism, and of the downfall of doomed capitalism, as it sinks into utopia.

Socialism, however, is moving forward. Its productive forces, planned organization, and material culture are growing. The gulf between the city and the countryside is being filled in, as is another gulf, the one between mental and physical labor. Millions of people are improving their living standards at great speed, raising their level of technical culture, broadening their spiritual horizons, developing their human capacities, becoming familiar with science and art, and engaging in scientific and artistic creation. People are educating their wills, their characters, and their creative passions; they are strengthening their bodies and ridding them of disease, creating new families, working and thinking. At the same time, the organized character of the whole, that is, of socialist society, is growing, and with each day ever new conditions are established for still richer development in the future. Freedom of development—the most valuable freedom—has for the first time in history become a fact for many millions of people.

40

Lenin as a Philosopher

Lenin was a genius of the class struggle. But the class struggle, as defined by Engels, is an economic, political, and theoretical struggle. The class struggle, as revolutionary practice, as scientific revolutionary practice, also presupposes theoretical cognition. Thoroughly attuned to Marx, and uniting theory and practice, Lenin was a great master of the dialectic as science, and of the dialectic as art; his thought and action were equally consummate. Because of this, Lenin defined his epoch, just as this epoch defined him, was embodied in him, and found in him its eloquent mouthpiece.

What did Lenin bring that was new to the development of philosophical thought in general, and of Marxist philosophical thought in particular? Lenin stepped onto the philosophical field for the first time with his book *Materialism and Empiriocriticism*. The circumstances of the time are well known: the period of reaction that followed the defeat of the December uprising [of 1905]. There was a massive exodus of the intelligentsia from the revolutionary movement. It was an age of ideological confusion, "spiritual reaction," religious quests, and eroticism. Sections of the Marxists were showing enthusiasm for "modern philosophy," for positivist agnosticism and "realism"—that is, the idealism of Mach—for Avenarius, for pragmatism, and even for "god-building." In those conditions, Lenin's book was like a peal of the tocsin, gathering an army around a banner, the banner of dialectical materialism.

The logical center of the problem was the issue of the reality of the external world. What Lenin brought to this debate that was new was the fact that he solved the problem on the basis of modern natural science, principally physics, which was experiencing a crisis while at the same time being pregnant with great discoveries. After the time of Kant, who worked long and hard in the field of the natural sciences, and after the collapse of the so-called "philosophy of nature," theoretical natural science parted ways with philosophy. The empiriocritical current, however, and above all Ernst Mach, again stimulated interest in the natural sciences among philosophers. So-called "physical idealism" grew under the guise of overcoming "metaphysics," to which sphere materialism was also banished. Lenin did not attack the Kantians so much as the empiriocritics and, for the first time in Marxist literature, seriously addressed the philosophical questions of theoretical natural science; this was the first time, because there had not been any major Marxist works on these topics since *Anti-Dühring*. That marvellous work by Engels, *The Dialectics of Nature*, was not published by the philistines of German Social Democracy, and lay in the archives.[1]

The mighty materialist Plekhanov, who fought victoriously against the influence of Kant in Social Democratic circles, did not occupy himself at all with questions of natural science. Meanwhile, those who did address these questions crossed over to the positions of empiriocriticism. Lenin was thus the only Marxist to speak out against empiriocriticism (and in the process, against all forms of idealism and agnosticism) on the basis of the general conclusions of theoretical natural science. We have already seen, in a special chapter, who it was in this debate that was correct.

All the subsequent development of physics and chemistry has brilliantly vindicated Lenin, showing the correctness of dialectical materialism on the fundamental questions at issue. Experimental practice and the development of theoretical physics have proven the real existence of the atom, of electrons, and so forth. The greatest service rendered by Lenin, a genuine scientific-philosophical exploit, was the defeat he dealt to the basic positions of physical idealism, the victorious battle he waged to affirm the existence of the material world. At first distributed mainly by underground workers of the then Social Democratic movement, *Materialism and Empiriocriticism* has now, many years later, become known worldwide. Leading lights of theoretical physics, such as Max Planck, and such outstanding empirical physicists as Philippe Frank, have been obliged to define their positions in relation to Lenin; we are not speaking here of Russian physicists, who have all gone through the cleansing fire of Leninist criticism. Lenin's books have now become the center of gravity for all materialist physicists. This is a fact, and one of enormous significance. The worldwide impact of *Materialism and Empiriocriticism* is indisputable. Here Lenin appears as a thinker, turning over a new page in the history of philosophical thought, while Marxism has been enriched internally, developing its cognitive power.

Dialectical materialism appears in Lenin's book with the stress on materialism. It would, however, be wrong to suppose that the dialectical aspect is weakly represented here, although Lenin in his *Philosophical Notebooks* does not distinguish himself from those Marxists who took issue with the empiriocritics "rather in the fashion of Buchner." Is not the question of relative and absolute truth resolved in this book in brilliantly dialectical fashion? Is not the relativity of relativism itself demonstrated dialectically? Does Lenin not make a dialectical transition from one opposition to another? Cognition, as an infinite process, is superbly depicted here in its dialectical movement. In sum, within the bounds of the question of the reality of the external world and of its cognizability, Lenin in particular develops, poses, and argues the following issues:

1. The reality of the external world. What is new here is above all the link with theoretical physics, and the posing and resolving of the corresponding questions.
2. The question of matter. Matter in the philosophical and scientific senses, examined in their unity and interrelationship.
3. The theory of reflection. Here, Lenin made a huge leap forward. It could be said that, on the basis of all the conquests of science, he advanced the theory of reflection as formulated by Engels. An important point was his analysis and refutation of Plekhanov's Kantianism-embellished "theory of hieroglyphs."
4. The doctrine of truth. A brilliant analysis of the question of relative and absolute truth. A new question, and a new resolution of it: on the relation between the criteria of truth; the criterion of correspondence with reality, the criterion of the practical, and the criterion of the "economic."

This was the first time that the question of the reality of the external world, of the very existence of the objective, had been posed with such force in Marxist literature. This was understandable, since the founders of Marxism, Marx himself and Engels, were obliged to do battle with objective idealism, with the idealism of Hegel, which was an adversary even of the subjectivism of Kant ("evil idealism"), although Kant had recognized the existence of the external world as consisting of "things-in-themselves." Marx and Engels had to overthrow the "ideal" structure of objective being, translating it into the material, rather than showing the absurdity of denying existence itself. Lenin, on the other hand, was obliged to wage a victorious struggle against subjective idealism, gravitating toward solipsism. If Kantian idealism was "evil," this idealism was positively vile.

Consequently, Lenin's achievement in working through the question of the reality of the external world and the materiality of its substance, a feat achieved on the basis of and in relation to the complex problems of theoretical natural science, was a massive step forward for theoretical physics, for philosophy in general, and for the philosophy of Marxism, that is, for dialectical materialism, in particular. Lenin had to rebury all the corpses, beginning with Berkeley and Hume, and after thoroughly routing subjective idealism and solipsism, to shift practice onto the scene as a direct breakthrough into the sphere of objective being, of the objective world. There is no need to mention the convincing force of the arguments, the erudition, the revolutionary ardor, and the supreme cognitive optimism of the works of Vladimir Ilyich; in these respects *Materialism and Empiriocriticism* is an enormously gratifying "human document," an expression of the class which the late teacher led so brilliantly.

The second pole of Lenin's philosophical thought is his famous *Philosophical Notebooks*, published after his death. These notebooks are not an integral work; they consist of marginal notes, remarks, commentaries, separate fragments, and running notes of thoughts *en lisant Hegel* (as Lenin himself puts it; that is, "while reading Hegel"—and principally Hegel). Here one should not look for a connected, finished exposition, for systematized ideas. Nevertheless, this is the laboratory of Lenin's thought, its intimate side, its holy of holies, its esoteric essence, right through to self-criticism. Because of this, the notebooks are exceptionally valuable, fresh, and interesting; Lenin's "spirit" is revealed in its full force.

Above all, it should be noted that if in *Materialism and Empiriocriticism* Marxism appears as dialectical *materialism*, in the *Philosophical Notebooks* it appears as *dialectical* materialism. There, the stress is on materialism; here, on dialectics. Hence a pair of well-known aphorisms:

1. Plekhanov criticizes Kantianism (and agnosticism in general) more from the vulgar-materialist than from the dialectical materialist point of view, since he rejects Kantian reasoning only *a limine*; he does not correct this thinking (as Hegel corrected Kant),

deepening, broadening, and generalizing it, showing the connection and transitions between any and all concepts.

2. Marxists (in the early twentieth century) have criticized Kantians and Humists more in the spirit of Feuerbach (and Buchner) than in that of Hegel.[2]

Elsewhere in the *Notebooks*, Lenin reproaches Plekhanov for the fact that, while writing a great deal on philosophy, Plekhanov failed to develop the ideas of Hegel's "Great Logic" (that is, *The Science of Logic*). And so on. These cursory remarks (including the "aphorism" that no one understood *Capital* completely, since no one understood dialectics) throw light on the gigantic importance that Lenin assigned to dialectics. Marx, as is well known, intended to prepare a short summary of the rational elements of Hegelian dialectics, but did not succeed in doing this. Engels in *Anti-Dühring* affirmed dialectics in its most general features, and developed it through examples. In *The Dialectics of Nature*, we see a brilliant application of dialectics to natural science. Lenin was the first to provide a full materialist interpretation of dialectics.

As we have already indicated, Lenin understood dialectics itself in dialectical fashion, through analysis revealing its various sides and combining them synthetically into a single, diverse concept. Lenin took from Hegel everything that could and should have been taken concerning dialectics as such. It would, of course, be school-pupil pedantry to argue that the sixteen paragraphs of Lenin's definitions should be maintained in the same quantity and the same order for all time—that would be to understand neither the meaning nor the character of Lenin's notes. It cannot be denied, however, that all the important aspects, facets, and features of dialectics as a science are brilliantly captured here, captured in their interrelationships and in such a way that their cognitive significance is brought out. Also brilliantly understood and expounded are the ontological and methodological sides of dialectics. You feel directly its profoundly vital significance; that which Hegel in his idealistic interpretation formulates as an obscure game of abstract concepts, here in Lenin's work pulsates with the rhythm of diverse and contradictory reality, moving in oppositions, with all its "transitions and modulations." The corresponding universal "flexibility of concepts" acts as a natural methodological demand, without the fulfillment of which cognition is impoverished, restricted, and pale.

The theory of reflection developed by Lenin in *Materialism and Empiriocriticism* is subjected to further refinement, in particular from the point of view of dialectics. This is not the place to set out Lenin's position again; we have done that throughout the present work. It is necessary, however, to stress how Lenin interpreted mediated knowledge, appearance, as a process, as a transition to ever more profound "essences," and to more and more broad and general associations. It is also necessary to stress his treatment of the general, the individual, and the particular; to stress that for Lenin reflection is the sum total of laws, a scientific picture of the world, and not simple phenomenology in the spirit of naive realism; to stress the dialectical transition which Lenin makes from sensations to thought, and so forth. Lenin's theory of reflection is far from being elementary and naive, a simple mirror. Here, the *Philosophical Notebooks* provide enormously rich material for anyone able to read and think.

Lenin's position on the diversity of types of real relationships as aspects of the universal relationship of things and processes, rather than as mere causality, we consider exceptionally novel and important. None of the other Marxists has managed this. Lenin states this position for the first time, and its whole significance does not immediately become evident. It is fraught with extraordinary consequences; it provides a new means of overcoming the narrowness, one-sidedness, and restricted character of mechanistic materialism, with its one and only type of causative relationship, mechanistic cause and effect. Lenin does not sacrifice a single drop of monism, and does not fall into any kind of pluralism. The category of necessity, and the universality of dialectical laws, are manifestations of the unity of natural laws, and the difference between types of relationship is a manifestation of the diversity in this unity. This represents a truly dialectical understanding of the universal relationship.

In and of itself, this position of Lenin constitutes a gigantic step forward. It immediately connects dialectics with such fields as, for example, mathematics, that stumbling block for causality; it opens the way for a more subtle and correct posing of the question of the physical and the psychological (a most important question for all of philosophy!); it provides the possibility of finding rational solutions to a number of questions of modern theoretical physics, and so on. Here Lenin achieves a complete overturn and enormously enriches the philosophy of Marxism; it is necessary only to understand this Leninist position in all its depth, in all its theoretical significance. For any theoretical natural science and mathematics, this is a real contribution, and together with it, an extremely valuable contribution to the philosophy of dialectical materialism.

In the *Philosophical Notebooks*, Lenin also develops the Marxist position on the theoretical-cognitive significance of practice, technology, and so forth. This position, formulated in outline by Marx in *The German Ideology* (which Lenin could not have known, since it was published only after his death) and in the *Theses on Feuerbach*, was developed by Engels in *Anti-Dühring*. In an idealist and antidialectical manner, it was developed by Alexander Bogdanov and the supporters of pragmatism.[3] Strange as it might seem, orthodox Marxists dealt with this topic in rather superficial fashion. Lenin was the first to pose the question in both materialist and dialectical fashion simultaneously, that is, in all its philosophical depth. Technology in the theory of cognition—heavens above, what vulgarity! In Lenin's work, however, this is an eminently thought-out theoretical idea, not something casual, or a pretentious flourish. The more we follow the path of the unification of theory and practice, the more clearly the reality and efficacy of this way of posing the question will appear before us.

The connection with practice also extended throughout the whole range of Lenin's activity and thought, since for him the dialectics of thought passed over into the dialectics of action, into the practice of the revolutionary overturn and of the socialist transformation of the world. Lenin was the living embodiment of the unity of intellect and will, of theory and practice, cognition and action. In his work, the doctrine of the subject of cognition was augmented by the study of the subject of action, and no one else worked out in such remarkable, concrete fashion the theory of the proletariat as the subject of the revolutionary process. His dialectics passed over, through dialectically worked-out strategy and practice, to the dialectics of action, always intelligently conceived and successfully realized, brilliant in its scope, its principled character, its concreteness, and its complete adequacy to the given circumstances. That is, of course, a special topic, and this is not the place to elaborate on it. However, it is important to stress the unity of theory and practice, the unity in the leadership that ensured the proletariat such brilliant victories in complex and difficult circumstances.

To the lot of Lenin's genius there fell the epoch of the transition to socialism, and he embodied this turbulent epoch with its powerful dynamics. Standing in the way of the proletariat were conditions that had to be burst through, elements that had to be understood and overcome, and spontaneous forces that had to be organized. Under the leadership of Lenin, a mighty dialectical materialist and the supreme master of dialectical action, the victorious revolution of the proletariat brilliantly fulfilled its numerous and daunting tasks. Bolshevism grew into a world force, and Marxism-

Leninism into the worldwide ideology of hundreds of millions of toiling people; it became the official doctrine, the ideological side and world view of the new world, the world of socialism. Lenin did not live long enough to see the final solving of the most important question of the revolution: "Who will defeat whom?" While he was alive, socialism was only a "sector" of the economy. Elemental, anarchic forces remained strong in the economy and society. There was still a great deal that had not been subordinated to the socialist rationality of the plan.

Society had not yet been transformed into a teleological unity, in which necessity passed over directly into teleology. The preconditions for this, however, had already been established. The empty babbling about the "irrelevance" of philosophy for practice, the jabbering of the philistines and hack workers of thought and of mental vacuity, had been overcome. The genius of Lenin shone brightly. The epoch, however, creates the people it requires, and in Lenin's place, the new stage of history brought forth Stalin, at the center of whose thought and action has been the next great historical transition, when under his leadership, socialism has been victorious forever.

All of the major vital functions have been synthesized in the victorious completion of the great Stalinist five-year plans; theory has been combined with practice on an entire, gigantic social scale, and in every cell of the social organism. New questions of world significance are ripening, questions of the worldwide victory of socialism and of its youthful culture, full of the joy of life.

November 7–8, 1937, the twentieth anniversary of the great victory

Notes

INTRODUCTION: A VOICE FROM THE DEAD

1 Stephen Cohen, *Bukharin and the Bolshevik Revolution: A Political Biography* (New York: Vintage Books, 1975), p. 219.
2 Helena Sheehan, *Marxism and the Philosophy of Science: A Critical History* (New Jersey: Humanities Press, 1993), chapter 4.
3 Nikolai Bukharin, "Avtobiografiia," p. 55, cited in Cohen, *Bukharin*, p. 14.
4 Bukharin, *Historical Materialism* (Ann Arbor: University of Michigan Press, 1969).
5 Sheehan, *Marxism and the Philosophy of Science*, chapter 5.
6 Bukharin, *Science at the Crossroads* (London: Frank Cass & Co, 1971).
7 Antonio Gramsci, *Selections from the Prison Notebooks* (London: Lawrence & Wishart, 1971).
8 Bukharin, *Marxism and Modern Thought* (London: Routledge & Kegan Paul, 1935).
9 Anna Larina, *This I Cannot Forget* (London: Pandora, 1994), p. 114.
10 Ibid., p. 314.
11 Ibid.
12 Bukharin, "To a Future Generation of Party Leaders," appendix to Larina, *This I Cannot Forget*, pp. 343–55.
13 For information about these manuscripts I am indebted to the work of Stephen Cohen, primarily in the form published in his introduction to *How It All Began*. I am also grateful to him for a number of letters, telephone conversations, and a meeting in New York relating to this project.
14 Bukharin to Stalin, 1937, cited by Cohen, "Bukharin's Fate," introduction to *How It All Began* (New York: Columbia University Press, 1998), p. vii.

15 Bukharin to Larina, January 15, 1938, received in 1992, published as appendix to *How It All Began*, pp. 336–8.
16 Will Oldham, *I See a Darkness*, CD, Palace 1999.
17 Larina, *This I Cannot Forget*, p.152.
18 Cohen, "Bukharin's Fate," p. xxvii.
19 *The Case of the Anti-Soviet Block of Rights and Trotskyites* (Moscow: People's Commissariat of Justice of the USSR, 1938). It can now be found on the web at www.marxists.org/archive/bukharin/works/1938/trial/index.htm.
20 ibid.
21 ibid.
22 Larina, *This I Cannnot Forget*, p. 305.
23 I have written in much greater detail about the trajectory of Soviet intellectual life from 1917 to 1945 in chapter 4 of *Marxism and the Philosophy of Science: A Critical History*. Sections of this chapter can be found on the web indexed at www.comms.dcu.ie/sheehanh/mxphsc.htm.
24 Cohen, *Rethinking the Soviet Experience* (New York: Oxford University Press, 1985), p. 83.
25 Bertram Wolfe, *Khrushchev and Stalin's Ghost* (New York: Praeger, 1957), pp. 135, 139.
26 Cohen, "The Afterlife of Nikolai Bukharin," introduction to Larina, *This I Cannot Forget*, p. 29.
27 Bukharin to Larina, *This I Cannot Forget*.
28 This is the stance taken by Martin Amis in *Koba the Dread* (London: Jonathan Cape, 2002). Although it adds nothing to our knowledge of this period, this book has been massively reviewed and discussed as I was writing this. It seeks to drain any lingering credibility from either the old or new left as implicated in indulgent laughter at the death of twenty million. His attempt to link history to memoir is an act of smug and stunning disproportion. Most reviewers lazily acquiesced, believing that they have a right to pronounce on this period without any real study or coming to terms with it. Hitchens responded that Amis had taken a Himalayan topic and pygmified it. "Don't be silly," *Guardian*, September 4, 2002.

AUTHOR'S FOREWORD

1 Bukharin refers here to Lenin's *Philosophical Notebooks*.

AUTHOR'S INTRODUCTION

1 Bukharin quotes fragments from a range of Marx's writings, including *The Economic and Philosophical Manuscripts of 1844* (New York: International Publishers, 1964), pp. 165–166; *Capital*. Volume 1 (Harmondsworth: Penguin, 1976), p. 926; and Marx

and Engels, *The Holy Family, or Critique of Critical Criticism* (Moscow: Progress Publishers, 1975), p. 140.
2. Bukharin refers here to Denis Fonvizin's play *The Ignoramus*, first staged in 1782.
3. Francis Bacon, the English philosopher, became Lord Verulam in 1618.
4. Attempts were made to revive the ancient Germanic cult of Wotan in Nazi Germany.
5. Karl Marx and Freidrich Engels, *The Holy Family* (Moscow: Progress Publishers, 1975), p. 140.).
6. The *Domostroy* was an old Russian collection of rules for everyday life. Bukharin refers to Germany as the former land of poets and philosophers.

CHAPTER 1

1. The *solus ipse* is the isolated self posited by solipsism—the philosophical doctrine that the self alone is real and capable of being known with certainty.
2. Latin: "For the wise, that is sufficient."

CHAPTER 2

1. G. W. F. Hegel, *Phenomenology of Spirit*, tr. A. V. Miller (Oxford: Clarendon Press, 1977), p. 121.
2. G. W. F. Hegel, *Lectures on the History of Philosophy*, trans. Elizabeth S. Haldane and Frances H. Simson (Lincoln: University of Nebraska Press, 1995), vol. 2, p. 329.
3. Hegel, *Phenomenology of Spirit*, p. 125.
4. Ibid., p. 126.
5. This account of the allegory of the cave in Book VII of Plato's *Republic* is taken from Hegel, *Lectures on the History of Philosophy*, vol. 2, p. 27. Bukharin transcribes Hegel's somewhat inaccurate recollection of the allegory.
6. Karl Pearson (1857–1936), English mathematician and biologist. His book, *The Grammar of Science*, published in 1892, supported the views of Ernst Mach on epistemology.
7. The quotation from Sextus Empiricus is taken from Hegel's *Lectures on the History of Philosophy*, vol. 2, p. 348.
8. Latin, "We do not know and we shall not know."
9. Hegel, *Lectures on the History of Philosophy*, vol. 2, p. 348.
10. "Affict" is a specialized term in Kant's philosophy, describing the action of an external object on the knowing subject. The term is derived from the Latin *afficere*, "to work upon."
11. This quotation could not be located in Hegel's *Science of Logic*.
12. Cf. Hegel, *Lectures on the History of Philosophy*, vol. 2, p. 353.
13. *Caput mortuum* (Latin) is a death's head.

14 Cf. G. W. F. Hegel, *Philosophy of Nature*, trans. M. J. Petry (London: George Allen and Unwin, 1970), vol. 2, pp. 43–44.
15 Cf. Hegel, *Phenomenology of Spirit*, pp. 76–77.
16 Ibid., p. 77.

CHAPTER 4

1 Aleksandr Bogdanov was a leading Russian Marxist supporter of empiriocriticism.
2 Vladimir Aleksandrovich Bazarov (1874–1939), Russian economist and philosopher, became a Social Democrat in 1896, later turned to empiriocriticism, and was an object of Lenin's polemics in *Materialism and Empiriocriticism*.
3 Nikolai Aleksandrovich Morozov (1854–1946) was a member of the People's Will organization and took part in the attempted assassination of Tsar Alexander II. While in prison, he later turned his attention to science and education. From 1918 until the end of his life, he was director of the Lesgaft Institute of Natural Science in Moscow. It is not known whether the work Bukharin quotes was a book or an article.
4 Latin, "the part for the whole."
5 G. W. F. Hegel, *Philosophy of Nature*, trans. M. J. Petry (London: George Allen and Unwin, 1970), vol. 1, p. 223.
6 Ibid., p. 224.
7 Ibid., p. 225.
8 Bukharin probably translated the two Aristotle quotations above from G. W. F. Hegel's *Lectures on the History of Philosophy*, trans. Elizabeth S. Haldane and Frances H. Simson (Lincoln: University of Nebraska Press, 1995), vol. 2. p. 165. Cf. Aristotle, *Physics*, Book IV, section 1, in *The Complete Works of Aristotle* (revised Oxford translation), ed. Jonathan Barnes (Princeton: Princeton University Press, 1984), pp. 356–57.
9 See Hegel, *Philosophy of Nature*, vol. 1, pp. 230–231.
10 Ibid., p. 229.
11 Latin, "Nothing exists in the intellect that was not earlier present in the senses."
12 Hegel, *Philosophy of Nature*, vol. 1, pp. 197–198.
13 V. I. Lenin, "Philosophical Notebooks," in *Collected Works*, vol. 38 (Moscow: Progress Publishers, 1961), p. 209.
14 See below, Chapters 22 and 23.

CHAPTER 5

1 Sensationalism (also described as sensism or sensualism) is the doctrine that sense perceptions furnish the sole data of knowledge.

2   The quotation from Feuerbach is taken from V. I. Lenin, "Philosophical Notebooks," in *Collected Works*, vol. 38 (Moscow: Progress Publishers, 1961), p. 81.

3   Lenin, "Philosophical Notebooks," p. 71.

CHAPTER 6

1   Cf. J. W. Goethe, *The Autobiography of Johann Wolfgang von Goethe,* tr. John Oxenford (Chicago: University of Chicago Press, 1974), vol. 2, pp. 109-110.

2   G. W. F. Hegel, *Philosophy of Nature*, trans. M. J. Petry (London: George Allen and Unwin, 1970), vol. 1, p. 198.

3   Heinrich Rickert (1863-1936) was a prominent member of the Heidelberg school of neo-Kantianism.

4   Baron d'Holbach (1723-89) was a French materialist philosopher and one of the Encyclopedists.

5   Latin, "General concepts are names."

6   Latin, "General concepts are reality."

7   Cf. V. I. Lenin's "Conspectus of Aristotle's *Metaphysics*," in *Collected Works*, vol. 38, p. 372. Bukharin is mistaken in attributing this quotation to "On the Question of Dialectics," which is included in the same volume of Lenin's writings.

8   V. I. Lenin, "On the Question of Dialectics," in *Collected Works*, vol. 38, p. 361.

9   Hegel, *Philosophy of Nature*, vol. 1, p. 201.

CHAPTER 7

1   V. I. Lenin, "Philosophical Notebooks," in *Collected Works*, vol. 38 (Moscow: Progress Publishers, 1961), vol. 38, p. 233.

2   *The Complete Works of Aristotle*, ed. Jonathan Barnes (Princeton: Princeton University Press, 1995), vol. 1, p. 687. Bukharin's Russian text quotes Lenin quoting Hegel, who in turn was quoting Aristotle, *De Anima*, III, 8.

3   A paper by the German zoologist Max Standfuss on the inheritance of acquired characteristics was presented at an international congress in 1907.

4   Bukharin takes this quotation from Feuerbach from Lenin; cf. Lenin, *Collected Works*, vol. 38, p. 285.

CHAPTER 8

1   Vladimir Ivanovich Vernadsky (1836-1945), Soviet scientist who taught that the biosphere evolves to become a noosphere, or realm of reason.

2   Karl Ludwig Michelet (1801-93) was a student of Hegel and subsequently edited some of his works.
3   Cf. G. W. F. Hegel, *Philosophy of Nature*, trans. M. J. Petry (London: George Allen and Unwin, 1970), vol. 3, p. 34.
4   Here Bukharin plays on the Latin saying, *Mens sana in corpore sano* ("A healthy mind in a healthy body").

CHAPTER 9

1   Cf. G. W. F. Hegel, *Philosophy of Nature*, trans. M. J. Petry (London: George Allen and Unwin, 1970), vol. 1, pp. 201-202.
2   These lines from Part One of Goethe's *Faust* are quoted in Hegel, *Philosophy of Nature*, vol. 1, p. 202. The mixed Greek-Latin phrase used by Goethe, *encheiresis naturae*, means literally "grasping nature with one's hands."
3   Baratynsky's poem about Goethe, "On the Death of a Poet," was written in 1832.
4   Vissarion Grigoryvich Belinsky (1811-48) was an influential Russian literary critic and liberal thinker.
5   Hegel, *Philosophy of Nature*, vol. 1, p. 197.
6   Ibid., p. 200.
7   Ibid., pp. 196-197.
8   German, "mercenary soldiers."
9   Eugen Schmalenbach (1873-1955), German economist and proponent of organized capitalism.
10 Marx to P. V. Annenkov, December 28, 1846, in Karl Marx and Friedrich Engels, *Selected Works* (Moscow: Progress Publishers, 1969), vol. 1, p. 518.
11 Karl Marx, *Capital*, vol. 2 (Moscow: Progress Publishers, 1988), p. 244.
12 This quotation does not appear in the work indicated.
13 *In hoc signo vincis* (Latin, "Beneath this standard you will be victorious") was the motto of the Roman emperor Constantine, who made Christianity the official religion of the empire.

CHAPTER 10

1   G. W. F. Hegel, *Philosophy of Nature*, trans. M. J. Petry (London: George Allen and Unwin, 1970), vol. 1, p. 195-196.
2   G. W. F. Hegel, *Science of Logic*, trans. A. V. Miller (New York: Humanities Press, 1969), p. 747.
3   V. I. Lenin, "Philosophical Notebooks," in *Collected Works*, vol. 38 (Moscow: Progress Publishers, 1961), p. 219.

CHAPTER 11

1 Othmar Spann (1875–1950) was an Austrian philosopher and social theorist and an advocate of Catholic corporatism, a position close to fascism. The Nazis removed him from his university position after the Anschluss and sent him to Dachau.
2 This recommendation is not mentioned earlier in the text, as Bukharin states here.

CHAPTER 12

1 Latin, "I think, therefore I am."
2 Karl Marx and Friedrich Engels, *The Holy Family, or, Critique of Critical Criticism: Against Bruno Bauer and Company*, trans. Richard Dixon and Clemens Dutt (Moscow: Progress Publishers, 1975), pp. 225–226.
3 Quotation not found in the work cited.
4 The quotation is from Schelling, *Allgemeine Deduktion des dynamischen Prozesses* (1800), Band 1, Heft 2. No English translation available.
5 V. I. Lenin, "On the Question of Dialectics," in Lenin, *Collected Works*, vol. 38 (Moscow: Progress Publishers, 1961), p. 363. Bukharin mistakenly attributed it to the "Conspectus of Aristotle's *Metaphysics*," which starts on the next page of Lenin's *Philosophical Notebooks*. Joseph Dietzgen (1826–88) was a German Social Democrat, a shoemaker, and a philosopher.

CHAPTER 13

1 Hylozoism is the doctrine that all matter is animate and life is present in all matter. Panpsychism is the doctrine that the psyche is essential for all that exists and is present everywhere.
2 The reference is to the pre-Socratic philosophers of Ionia during the sixth and fifth centuries B.C.
3 The quotation is retranslated into English from what apparently were Bukharin's notes from a Russian edition of Jean-Baptiste Lamarck, or his own rendering into Russian from Lamarck's French text, *Philosophie zoologique* (first published in 1809). The passage is from Lamarck's chapter 6 on "degradation," in volume 1, pp. 203–204, of his *Ouvrages* (Works). Bukharin's wording differs somewhat from the version by S.V. Sapozhnikov, *Filosofia zoologii* (Moscow: Nauka, 1911), pp. 166–167.
4 Only the Russian (phonetic) spelling of the name "Franse" is given; the French spelling might be Francais, Francet, Frances, etc.
5 Cf. V. I. Lenin, "Conspectus of Hegel's *Lectures on the History of Philosophy*," in Lenin, *Collected Works*, vol. 38 (Moscow: Progress Publishers, 1961), p. 283.

6   Latin, "spontaneous generation," that is, the development of organisms without the agency of preexisting living matter.
7   The reference is to *Queen Margot* by Alexandre Dumas.
8   Ivan Afanasyevich Kuschshevsky (1847–76) was a Russian novelist. His novel *Nikolai Negorev* was reissued in Moscow in 1917.
9   Latin, "University of deeds and arts."

CHAPTER 14

1   Dmitry Ivanovich Pisarev (1840–68) was a Russian writer and revolutionary democrat. The quotation is taken from Pisarev, *Izbrannye filosofskie i obshchestvenno-politicheskie stat'i* (Selected philosophical and social-political articles), (Moscow: 1949), p. 40.
2   The Italian phrases in this sentence can be roughly translated as the "it's sweet to do nothing" attitude of the underclasses.
3   Paul Ernst (1866–1933), German essayist and novelist; Count Hermann Keyserling (1880–1946), founder of a school in Darmstadt, Germany, that promoted the wisdom of the East; Theodor Lessing (1872–1933), German philosopher, assassinated by the Nazis.

CHAPTER 15

1   This quotation could not be located in Hegel's writings.
2   The quotation has not been found in the work cited.
3   G. W. F. Hegel, *Phenomenology of Spirit*, trans. A. V. Miller (Oxford: Clarendon Press, 1977), p. 140.
4   Bukharin may have taken these lines from the young Hegel's unpublished poem from Rosenkranz's biography of Hegel. No English translation has been located.
5   The source of these quotations has not been located.
6   Hegel, *Phenomenology of Spirit*, p. 437.
7   Jacob Boehme (1575–1624), German religious mystic.
8   Hegel, *Phenomenology of Spirit*, p. 131.
9   G. W. F. Hegel, *The Logic: Being Part One of the Encyclopaedia of the Philosophical Sciences (1830)*, trans. W. Wallace (New York: Oxford University Press, 1975), p. 73.
10 G. W. F. Hegel, *Science of Logic*, trans. A. V. Miller (New York: Humanities Press, 1969), p. 70.
11 Kuno Fischer, *Geschichte der neueren Philosophie*, trans. into Russian by D. E. Zhukovsky as *Istoriia novoi filosofii*, 8 volumes (St. Petersburg, 1901–1909).

12 *Aufhebung* is often translated as sublation. It refers to a process of change in which a condition is simultaneously preserved, negated, and transcended.

CHAPTER 16

1   Plekhanov's *Beitrage zur Geschichte des Materialismus* was published in Stuttgart in 1896. It was translated into English by Ralph Fox as *Essays in the History of Materialism* (New York: H. Fertig, 1967).
2   Ludwig Büchner (1824–99) and Jacob Moleschott (1822–93) were German physiologists and extreme materialists. Buchner's *Kraft und Stoff* (Force and matter) was published in 1855.
3   In the 1860s Büchner's book *Kraft und Stoff* enjoyed great success among radical young people in Russia. Turgenev in his novel *Fathers and Sons* has the radical "nihilist" hero, Bazarov, say: "I see that [a mild, non-radical friend] is reading Pushkin for the third day.... Explain to him, please, that this won't do.... Give him something sensible to read.... I think Büchner's *Stoff und Kraft* to start off with."
4   Published in Russian in 1863.
5   Cf. V. I. Lenin, *Collected Works,* vol. 38 (Moscow: Progress Publishers, 1961), p. 179.
6   Werner Sombart (1863–1941), German economist and philosopher, became a supporter of Nazism after Hitler's rise to power.
7   Ernst Troeltsch (1865–1923), German theologian and sociologist of religion. It is not clear which work by Troeltsch was meant by Bukharin—*Historismus und Seine Probleme* (Historicism and its problems; Berlin, 1922) or *Historismus und seine Überzwindung* (Historicism and its overcoming; Berlin, 1924).

CHAPTER 17

1   V. I. Lenin, *Collected Works,* vol. 29 (Moscow: Progress Publishers, 1961), p. 162.
2   G. W. F. Hegel, *Philosophy of Nature,* trans. M. J. Petry, vol. 3 (London: George Allen and Unwin, 1970), pp. 122–123.
3   Cf. Lenin, *Collected Works,* vol. 38, p. 180.
4   First published in 1895.

CHAPTER 18

1   Aristotle, "Metaphysics," book XII, ch. 10, in *Complete Works of Aristotle,* ed. J. Barnes, vol. 2 (Princeton, N.J.: Princeton University Press, 1994), p. 1699. The passage is also quoted in wording that follows G. W. F. Hegel, *Lectures on the History of Philosophy,* trans. E. S. Haldane and F. H. Simson, vol. 2

(Lincoln: University of Nebraska Press, 1995), pp. 152–153. It is likely that Bukharin quoted and translated the passage from Hegel's German text.

2 G. W. F. Hegel, *Philosophy of Nature*, trans. M. J. Petry, vol. 1 (London: George Allen and Unwin, 1970), p. 196.

3 Bukharin is quoting Aristotle from G. W. F. Hegel, *Lectures on the History of Philosophy*, trans. Elizabeth S. Haldane and Frances H. Simson (Lincoln: University of Nebraska Press, 1995), vol. 2, p. 158.

4 *Petitio principii*, or "begging the question," is the logical fallacy of assuming a certain premise in order to prove it to be true.

5 This is Hegel's paraphrase of Aristotle, together with Aristotle's quotation of Homer, taken from Hegel, *Lectures on History of Philosophy*, vol. 2, p. 159.

6 This is a paraphrase, rather than a quotation, from Hegel, *Lectures on History of Philosophy*, vol. 2, p. 160.

7 Nikolai Yakovlevich Danilevsky (1822–55), Russian sociologist and ideologist of pan-Slavism; Hans Driesch (1867–1941), German biologist and philosopher of vitalism.

8 Latin, "I believe because it is absurd."

9 Hegel, *Philosophy of Nature*, vol. 3, p. 101.

CHAPTER 19

1 Cf. V. I. Lenin, *Collected Works*, vol. 38 (Moscow: Progress Publishers, 1961), pp. 188–189.

2 Benedictus de Spinoza, *Ethics*, trans. G. H. R. Parkinson (New York: Oxford University Press, c. 2000), p. 168.

3 Friedrich Engels, "Ludwig Feuerbach and the End of Classical German Philosophy," in *Basic Writings on Politics and Philosophy*, Karl Marx and Friedrich Engels, ed. Lewis Feuer (New York, 1959), pp. 230–231.

4 Wilhelm Wundt (1832–1920), German psychologist, linguist, and philosopher.

5 Spengler's *Decline of the West* was first published in German in 1918.

6 Latin, "For the wise, this is sufficient."

CHAPTER 20

1 Aristotle, "Physics," book II, ch. 9, in *Complete Works of Artistotle*, ed. J. Barnes, vol. 1 (Princeton, N.J.: Princeton University Press, 1994), p. 341. Bukharin's wording follows G. W. F. Hegel, *Lectures on the History of Philosophy*, trans. E. S. Haldane and F. H. Simson, vol. 2 (Lincoln: University of Nebraska Press, 1995), pp. 162–163.

2 Cf. Hegel, *Lectures on History of Philosophy*, vol. 2, p. 184, quoting Aristotle.

3   Psycho-Lamarckism (also called neovitalism) was the theory that the main source of evolution lay in conscious acts of will by organisms.
4   G. W. F. Hegel, *Philosophy of Nature*, trans. M. J. Petry, vol. 3 (London: George Allen and Unwin, 1970), p. 152.
5   Ibid., p. 156.
6   Friedrich Engels, *The Dialectics of Nature*, trans. C. Dutt (New York: International Publishers, 1940), p. 324.
7   Hegel, *Lectures on History of Philosophy*, vol. 2, pp. 182-183. The interpolated comments in parentheses are by Bukharin.
8   Ivan Vladimirovich Michurin (1855-1935) and Trofim Denisovich Lysenko (1898-1976), Soviet biologists who supported the theory of the inheritance of acquired characteristics, endorsed by Stalin and later by Khruschev.

CHAPTER 21

1   Hans Vaihinger (1852-1933), German idealist philosopher. His *Philosophie des Als-Ob* was first published in 1911 and published in English translation as *The Philosophy of "As If"* (New York: Harcourt, Brace, 1924).
2   Wilhelm Ostwald (1853-1932), German physical chemist and philosopher, awarded the Nobel Prize for chemistry in 1909.
3   Friedrich Engels, *The Dialectics of Nature*, trans. C. Dutt (New York: International Publishers, 1940), pp. 262-263.
4   Ibid., pp. 186-187.
5   Goethe, *Zur Morphologie* was first published in 1817. The quotation has not been located in any English translation of Goethe's writings.

CHAPTER 22

1   Max Muller (1823-1900) spent most of his life as a professor at Oxford University; his *Science of Language* (1861) popularized philology; he also translated major Eastern religious writings into English. Ludwig Noire (1829-89) was a German philosopher and author of a book on the origins of language. No information has been found on "Laz. Geir"; the name may have been garbled or misspelled in the process of transcription of Bukharin's manuscript.
2   Nikolai Yakovlevich Marr (1864-1934) was a Russian linguist and Orientalist.
3   The quotation was not found in the work cited.
4   Noire's work on the origin of language was first published in Mainz, Germany, in 1871.

5   V. I. Lenin, *Collected Works*, vol. 38 (Moscow: Progress Publishers, 1961), p 274.
6   Aleksandr Bogdanov (1873-1928), Russian revolutionary and philosopher and leading supporter of empiriocriticism.
7   Cf. Lenin, *Collected Works*, vol. 38, pp. 190, 217.
8   G. W. F. Hegel, *Philosophy of Nature*, trans. M. J. Petry, vol. 1 (London: George Allen and Unwin, 1970), pp. 203-204.
9   G. W. F. Hegel, *Science of Logic*, trans. A. V. Miller (New York: Humanities Press, 1969), p. 824.
10 Karl Marx, *Contribution to the Critique of Political Economy* (Chicago: Charles H. Kerr, 1904), pp. 293-294.

CHAPTER 23

1   Max Scheler (1874-1928), German philosopher, played an important role in the early development of phenomenology. The work to which Bukharin refers was published in English translation as *Problems of a Sociology of Knowledge* (Boston: Routledge & Kegan Paul, 1980).
2   Sallust's "On the Catiline Conspiracy" was written in 67 B.C.
3   "There is no land without a lord" and "Money has no master."

CHAPTER 24

1   Bukharin drew this information from N.I. Konrad, "Ocherk yaponskoy istorii s drevneiyshikh vremen do 'revolyutsii Meydzi' " (Sketch of Japanese history from ancient times to the "Meiji revolution"), in *Yaponiya* (Japan), ed. Y. Zhukov and A. Rozen (Moscow, 1934).
2   "Japhetic" is a term once used for the Indo-European language family; the term is derived from the Old Testament, which gives Japheth as the name of one of Noah's sons.
3   The Slavophiles were a group of nineteenth-century Russian writers who glorified the unique Russian and Orthodox heritage, arguing that it was superior to Western rationalism.
4   Alfred Rosenberg (1893-1946), Nazi ideologue and leading theorist of racial difference for the Nazis.
5   Ludwig Woltmann (1871-1907), German sociologist.
6   Semyon Lyudvigochich Frank (1877-1950), Russian religious thinker, exiled from the Soviet Union in 1922.

CHAPTER 25

1 Georg Simmel (1858–1918), German philosopher and sociologist.
2 Bukharin is apparently quoting here from a work by Theodor Lessing, possibly the same *Europa und Asien* that he quoted from in Chapter 14 above.
3 Pavel Ivanovich Melnikov-Perchersky (1816–83), Russian historian and ethnographer.
4 G. W. F. Hegel, *Phenomenology of Spirit*, trans. A. V. Miller (Oxford: Clarendon Press, 1977), pp. 4–6.
5 The source of this quotation has not been located.

CHAPTER 26

1 Spinoza called substance a *causa sui*—a "cause of itself."
2 G. W. F. Hegel, *Philosophy of Nature*, trans. M. J. Petry, vol. 3 (London: George Allen and Unwin, 1970), p. 180.

CHAPTER 27

1 Bukharin may be mistaken in attributing the phrase "man is a tool-making animal" to Benjamin Franklin. The phrase was used by Thomas Carlyle.
2 G. W. F. Hegel, Lectures on the History of Philosophy, trans. E. S. Haldane and F. H. Simson, vol. 2 (Lincoln: University of Nebraska Press, 1995), p. 235.
3 G. W. F. Hegel, Philosophy of Nature, trans. M. J. Petry, vol. 3 (London: George Allen and Unwin, 1970), p. 24.
4 Hegel, Lectures on History of Philosophy, vol. 2, p. 10.

CHAPTER 29

1 William Petty (1628–87), English government official, often regarded as the founder of economics in Britain.
2 Engels's letter to Mehring is in Karl Marx and Friedrich Engels, *Basic Writings on Politics and Philosophy*, ed. Lewis Feuer (New York, 1957), p. 408.

CHAPTER 30

1 G. W. F. Hegel, *Lectures on the History of Philosophy*, trans. E. S. Haldane and F. H. Simson, vol. 2 (Lincoln: University of Nebraska Press, 1995), p. 149.
2 Ibid., p. 150.

CHAPTER 31

1. Friedrich Engels, *Anti-Dühring: Herr Eugen Dühring's Revolution in Science*, trans. E. Burns (Moscow: Foreign Languages Publishing House, 1962), p. 159.
2. V. I. Lenin, *Collected Works*, vol. 38 (Moscow: Progress Publishers, 1961), p. 208.
3. This passage has not been found in the work cited.
4. Lenin, *Collected Works*, vol. 38, p. 361.
5. Ibid., p. 273.
6. This is the only instance in this book where Bukharin himself states that he is quoting from memory. There are numerous cases when his quotation does not actually match the original text or the existing Russian translation. But this instance suggests that he was generally concerned to reproduce faithfully the statements and ideas of others.

CHAPTER 32

1. V. I. Lenin, *Collected Works*, vol. 38 (Moscow: Progress Publishers, 1961), p. 279.
2. G. W. F. Hegel, *Lectures on the History of Philosophy*, trans. E. S. Haldane and F. H. Simson, vol. 1 (Lincoln: University of Nebraska Press, 1995), pp. 407, 425.
3. Hegel, *Lectures on the History of Philosophy*, vol. 1, p. 375.
4. This passage has not been found in the work cited.
5. Cf. Hegel, *Lectures on History of Philosophy*, vol. 2, p. 274.
6. *True Mirror of Youth*, a book of instructions for youth of the Russain court nobility, was first published in 1715, at the initiative of Tsar Peter the Great.

CHAPTER 33

1. See Chapter 15 above.
2. G. W. F. Hegel, *Philosophy of Right*, trans. T. M. Knox. (New York: Oxford University Press, 1967), p. 28.
3. Bukharin quotes from the Russian translation of Kuno Fischer's history of modern philosophy, *Istoriia Novoi filosofii* (St. Petersburg: 1902), vol. 8, pp. 196-197. No English translation is available.
4. Ugryum-Burcheyev was a character in Saltykov-Shchedrin's satire, "A Story of a Certain City."
5. Karl Marx and Friedrich Engels, *Basic Writings on Politics and Philosophy*, ed. Lewis Feuer (New York: Anchor Books, 1959), p. 200-201.
6. Ibid., pp. 201-202.

7   G. W. F. Hegel, *Science of Logic*, trans. A. V. Miller (New York: Humanities Press, 1969), p. 50.
8   Engels to Friedrich Albert Lange, March 29, 1865, in Marx and Engels, *Complete Works* (New York: International Publishers, 1987), vol. 42, p. 138.
9   In ancient Greek, *noein* is "to think," *noesis* is "thinking," and *nous* is "mind"—i.e., that which thinks.
10 Hegel, *Science of Logic*, p. 843.
11 The source of this quotation has not been located.
12 G. W. F. Hegel, *Philosophy of Nature*, trans. M. J. Petry, vol. 1 (London: George Allen and Unwin, 1970), p. 212.
13 Ibid., vol. 1, p. 196.
14 J. P. Eckermann, *Conversations with Goethe* (New York: E. P. Dutton, 1930), p. 141.
15 The source of this quotation has not been located.
16 G. W. F. Hegel, *The Logic: Being Part One of the Encyclopaedia of the Philosophical Sciences (1830)*, trans. W. Wallace (New York: Oxford University Press, 1975), p. 171.
17 The source of this quotation has not been located.
18 There may be an error in the Russian text in Bukharin's summary of the so-called "ontological proof of the existence of God," either in the transcription of Bukharin's handwriting or a typographical error in the printing of the Russian book. Where *sovremennoe* ("contemporary; present") appears, the word apparently should have been *sovershennoe* ("perfect"). A more correct rendering of this passage into English would then be: "...since God is thought of as perfection, and since perfection necessarily has the predicate of being, therefore, God exists."
19 This quotation is not from Hegel's *Phenomenology of Spirit*, as Bukharin believed. It is to be found in his *Encyclopaedia Logic*, pp. 272–273.
20 Bukharin quotes from the Russian translation of Fisher's work, vol. 8, p. 24. No English translation is available.
21 G. W. F. Hegel, *Phenomenology of Spirit*, trans. A. V. Miller (Oxford: Clarendon Press, 1977), p. 493.
22 No English translation is available.

CHAPTER 34

1   Bukharin quotes from volume 10 of a Russian translation of Goethe's *Works*, published in 1937. No English translation has been located.
2   Latin, "all determination is negation."

3   There is no single passage in the text cited that corresponds to Bukharin's quotation. There are similar formulations to be found in G. W. F. Hegel, *Science of Logic*, trans. A. V. Miller (New York: Humanities Press, 1969), pp. 136, 142, 149. Bukharin may have been paraphrasing these.
4   Cf. Hegel, *Science of Logic*, p. 149. Bukharin may have added his own paraphrase to the quotation.
5   Haller's poem is quoted by Hegel in *Science of Logic*, p. 230. Bukharin quotes it in the German.
6   Hegel, *Science of Logic*, p. 373.
7   Ibid., p. 389.
8   Ibid., p. 391.
9   Ibid., p. 439.
10 Ibid., p. 466.
11 Ibid., p. 448.
12 Ibid., p. 452.
13 Ibid., p. 486.
14 Ibid., p. 503.
15 Ibid., p. 528.
16 Hegel, G. W. F. Hegel, *Philosophy of Right*, trans. T. M. Knox (New York: Oxford University Press, 1967), p. 28.
17 This appears to be Bukharin's paraphrase of several formulations in Hegel, *Science of Logic*, pp. 554–557.
18 G. W. F. Hegel, *The Logic: Being Part One of the Encyclopaedia of the Philosophical Sciences (1830)*, trans. W. Wallace (New York: Oxford University Press, 1975), p. 217; cf. Hegel, *Science of Logic*, tr. Miller, p. 569.
19 Hegel, *Encyclopaedia Logic*, p. 220; cf. Hegel, *Science of Logic*, pp. 577–578.
20 These are the German terms for the general, the particular, and the individual.
21 Hegel, *Science of Logic*, p. 664.
22 Cf. Hegel, *Encyclopaedia Logic*, tr. Wallace, p. 282. Bukharin's quotation may include some paraphrase.
23 Ibid., p. 289.
24 Ibid., p. 293.
25 Johann Plenge's *Marx und Hegel* was published in Tübingen, Germany, in 1911.
26 Karl Diehl (1864–1943), German economist.
27 No information is available on the author Jostock. It is possible that this name has been mistranscribed.

CHAPTER 35

1. This quotation could not be located in the work cited.
2. V. I. Lenin, *Collected Works*, vol. 38 (Moscow: Progress Publishers, 1961), pp. 221-223.
3. Ibid.
4. Bukharin refers to Lenin's "Marxism and Insurrection: Letter to the Central Committee of the Russian Social Democratic Labor Party (Bolshevik)," September 1917.
5. The quotation could not be located in the work cited. There are similar formulations in G. W. F. Hegel, *Philosophy of Nature*, trans. M. J. Petry, vol. 1 (London: George Allen and Unwin, 1970), p. 219, and in G. W. F. Hegel, *The Logic: Being Part One of the Encyclopaedia of the Philosophical Sciences (1830)*, trans. W. Wallace (New York: Oxford University Press, 1975), p. 281.

CHAPTER 36

1. Bukharin takes this quotation from Aristotle from G. W. F. Hegel, *Lectures on the History of Philosophy*, trans. E. S. Haldane and F. H. Simson, vol. 2 (Lincoln: University of Nebraska Press, 1995), p. 136.
2. G. W. F. Hegel, *Philosophy of Nature*, trans. M. J. Petry, vol. 1 (London: George Allen and Unwin, 1970), pp. 197, 205, 207.
3. Hegel, *Lectures on the History of Philosophy*, vol. 2, p. 133.
4. Hegel, *Philosophy of Nature*, vol. 1, p. 198.
5. Ibid., vol. 3, p. 68.
6. The source of this quotation has not been located.

CHAPTER 37

1. G. W. F. Hegel, *Philosophy of Nature*, trans. M. J. Petry, vol. 1 (London: George Allen and Unwin, 1970), pp. 213-214.
2. Paracelsus (Thephrastus Bombastus von Hohenheim, 1493-1541), Swiss-German physician and natural scientist, responsible for innovations in the preparation of medicines.
3. Charles Bonnet (1720-93), Swiss naturalist and philosopher.
4. Hegel, *Philosophy of Nature*, vol. 1, p. 214.
5. The phrase from *Hamlet* is written in English in Bukharin's manuscript.
6. Joseph Petzold (1862-1929), German philosopher and supporter of empiriocriticism.
7. Ernst Haeckel (1834-1919), German biologist, philosopher, and supporter of Darwin's theory of evolution. The quotation could not be located in the work cited.

CHAPTER 38

1. Heinrich Rickert (1863–1936), German philosopher, founder of the Heidelberg school of neo-Kantianism. His book *Die Grenzen der naturwissenschaftlichen Begriffsbildung* was published in 1896–1902.
2. Aleksandr Chuprov (1874–1926), Russian statistician. The work cited by Bukharin was published in 1909.
3. Wladislaw Bortkiewicz (1868–1931), economist and statistician, professor at Berlin University, 1901–31.
4. Johann Karl Rodbertus (1805–75), German economist and historian; Mikhail Ivanovich Tugan-Baranovsky (1865–1919), Russian economist and historian, proponent of "legal Marxism" who later supported capitalism.

CHAPTER 39

1. Cf. V. I. Lenin, "Philosophical Notebooks," in *Collected Works*, vol. 38 (Moscow: Progress Publishers, 1961), pp. 281–282.
2. G. W. F. Hegel, *Lectures on the History of Philosophy*, trans. E. S. Haldane and F. H. Simson (Lincoln: University of Nebraska Press, 1995), vol. 1, p. 98.
3. Pyotr Lavrovich Lavrov (1823–1900), Russian philosopher and essayist; one of the leading ideologists of the Narodnik movement of the 1860s.
4. The quotations are from Lavrov's work *Iz istorii sotsial'nykh uchenii* (From the history of social doctrines), Moscow, 1919, pp. 57–60.

CHAPTER 40

1. Engels's *Dialectics of Nature*, edited by the Soviet Marxist scholar David Ryazanov, was first published in full, in both German and Russian, in the USSR in 1925.
2. V. I. Lenin, *Collected Works*, vol. 38 (Moscow: Progress Publishers, 1961), p. 179.
3. Aleksandr Bogdanov (1873–1928), Russian revolutionary, physician, and writer, was a leading Russian Marxist supporter of empiriocriticism.

Notes

ABC of Communism, The (Bukharin), 28
Absolute idea/spirit, 155–56, 158, 211, 280–81, 325; Hegelian dialectic and, 294–97, 298, 300, 303–4, 314
abstractions, 47, 59, 78, 128–29; concrete and, 83–91, 129, 246; dialectical, 85–86, 136; Hegelian, 305, 309, 313; things-in-themselves as, 319, 354; universality and, 88, 89, 90–91
action, dialectics of, 375. *See also* practice
aesthetics of nature, 98–103, 126–28, 129
agnosticism, 56, 57, 116, 117, 260, 270
anarchy, 190
animism, 234, 236, 237
anthropomorphism, religion and, 301–2
Anti-Dühring (Engels), 134, 174, 276, 373, 375
antinomies, 107–8. *See also* contradiction
anti-Semitism, 227–28
Arabs, 228
Aristophanes, 105, 361
Aristotle, 164, 166, 196, 210, 303; atomic theory of, 251; beatific deity of, 301; on being, 312; on change, 347–48; on the cosmos, 216; *De Anima*, 58, 93; entelechy of, 193–94, 300, 322; forms of, 346; on the good, 282; and Hegel compared, 341; Hegel on, 163, 179, 270, 329; idealism and, 193; *Metaphysics*, 177, 347; on nature, 255; on necessity, 180–81, 183, 184, 186, 187, 189–90; *Physics*, 180–81; on science and philosophy, 339; social humanity of, 248; teleology of, 177–82; on vacuum, 70
Aryan race ideology, 146, 226, 229
ataraxia, 52, 53
atomic theory, 165–66, 201–4, 251
Avenarius, 44, 59, 98, 184, 238, 274; *Critique of Pure Experience*, 140; introjection doctrine of, 79; Mach and, 74, 78, 369; on positive emotion, 238; on universality, 276

Bacon, Francis, 36, 83, 110, 164, 214, 222; *Novum Organum*, 117; on power and cognition, 150; on science, 206
Baratynsky, Yevgeny, 106, 382n3

Bazarov, Vladimir, 68, 380n2
Bebel, August, 228
being, 170-76; causality and, 170-72; Hegelian dialectics and, 309, 312, 316-17, 318, 319; monism and, 174-75; nothingness and, 310-11; phenomena and, 318, 319-20; thought and, 172-73, 243
Belinsky, Vissarion G., 106, 382n4
Bentham, Jeremy, 285
Bergson, Henri, 106
Berkeley, George, 48, 51, 159, 201, 239, 372
biological adaptation, 102, 124-25
Boehme, Jakob, 99, 159, 164, 384n7
Bogdanov, Aleksandr, 68, 209, 222-23, 375, 380n1, 394n3; on the absolute, 280-81; empiriomonism of, 78, 132, 221
Bolsheviks, 8, 30, 337
Bolshevism, 230, 376
Bonnet, Charles, 346, 393n3
Bortkiewicz, Wladislaw, 353, 394n3
bourgeois ideology, 304, 306
bourgeoisie, 36, 111, 266, 294, 314; capitalism and, 263-64, 360, 365, 367; the good and, 289-90
bourgeois philosophy, 96-97, 110, 213, 217, 328
Brezhnev, Leonid, 26
Bruno, Giordano, 308
Büchner, Ludwig, 164, 168, 171, 371, 385nn2-3
Buddhism, 50, 147, 234. *See also* Indian/Hindu mysticism
Bukharin, Nikolai Ivanovich, 8; *Marxism and Modern Thought*, 11, 12; prison writings of, 16-23, 30; rehabilitation of, 27-29; socialist humanism and, 9; trial of, 14, 23-25; *Vremena: How It All Began*, 22-23

Bukharin and the Bolshevik Revolution (Cohen), 28

Campanella, Tommaso, 363
capitalism, 21, 111, 218, 237, 262-67, 355; American, 232; bourgeoisie and, 263-64, 360, 365, 367; commodity fetishism in, 266, 267-68; crises of, 189-90, 230; laws of motion in, 357, 365; mastery of nature by, 257; socialism and, 249
capitalist class, 289. *See also* bourgeoisie
Capital (Marx), 89, 112, 184, 210, 330, 373; on dialectics, 174, 330; on freedom and necessity, 191; on laws of motion, 357, 365; on mode of production *vs.* mode of presentation, 214-15; on power of capital, 218
Cartesianism, 132-33
causality, 170-72, 194, 222, 321; Kantian view of, 57, 68-69, 119
cave allegory (Plato), 54-55, 67, 117
China, 227
Chuprov, Aleksandr, 352, 394n2
City of the Sun (Campanella), 363
class hierarchy, 212, 232-36; Indian theocracy and, 234-35, 236
class society, 19, 37, 129
class struggle, 218, 230, 231, 286, 369; socialism and, 24, 258-59, 359
cognition, 76, 78, 203, 265, 326; abstraction and, 87, 90; concept-formation and, 93, 219, 246-47; consciousness and, 64-65; dialectical materialism and, 277, 371; dialectics and, 112, 335; geocentrism and, 261; mysticism and, 231; of nature, 285-86; objective world and, 55-56, 60, 61, 246; power in, 150, 218; practice and, 209-10, 211; production and, 287;

reflection and, 77, 79; sensation and, 75, 94; socio-historical process and, 340; sociomorphism and, 219–21, 222; theoretical, 245–46; truth in, 272–73; ultimate, 324; universality and, 275–76. *See also* rational thought

Cohen, Stephen, 22, 28, 377n13

commodity society, 265, 266. *See also* capitalism

common property, 220

communism, 26, 191, 221, 264; ethics of, 289, 330; utopian socialism and, 365–66

Communist Manifesto (Marx and Engels), 365–66

Comte, Auguste, 258, 263; *Sociology*, 349–50

concepts, 207–8, 209, 236, 271–72; cognition and, 93, 219, 246–47; perception and, 97; relativity of, 62. *See also specific* concepts

Condorcet, Marquis de, 360

Confucius, 151, 237, 238

consciousness, 131–32, 173, 309; acceptance of the world, 48, 51–55, 63, 64–65; hallucination and, 242–43; objective, 63, 64–65, 244, 246; organic life and, 142–43; Plato's cave and, 54–55; self-, 64, 133, 136, 154, 295, 321, 322; social, 213, 231, 243, 325; Stoic *vs.* Skeptic, 52–54

Constant, Benjamin, 360

contemplation, 50, 108, 157; of nature, 151–52, 153. *See also* mysticism

contradiction, 202, 317, 327

corporeal being, 50–51. *See also* being

correspondence, 271–72

cosmos, 100. *See also* universality

Cratylus, 239

creative spirit, 322. *See also* Absolute idea/spirit

Crisis of Captialist Culture and Socialism, The (Bukharin), 16

Critique of Pure Experience (Avenarius), 140

Critique of Pure Reason (Kant), 55, 57, 170, 186, 301

Cuvier, Georges, 195, 348

Czechoslovakia, invasion of, 26

Danilevsky, Nikolay V., 183

Darwin, Charles, 111, 188, 195, 328, 345, 349

Darwinism, 206. *See also* evolution

De Anima (Aristotle), 58, 93

Deborin, Abram M., 11

Decline of the West (Spengler), 190, 263

Degradation of Culture and Fascism, The (Bukharin), 16

Descartes, Rene, 132–33

dialectical materialism, 38, 142, 175–76, 219, 268, 340; cognition and, 209, 221, 277; Hegelian roots of, 10, 11, 162, 296, 306–7, 327–30; human subject of, 248, 251; Lenin and, 369, 372–75; mechanistic materialism and, 98, 164, 168–69; objective world and, 80; rationalism and, 111–12; relativism and, 278, 279; science and, 174, 200–206, 343; teleology and, 176, 185; and unity of opposites, 344; will and, 192. *See also* Marx, Karl

dialectics: abstractions and, 85–86, 136; Aristotle and, 347; as art and science, 331–38; collective action and, 336–37; evolution and, 141; idealism and, 134–35, 137, 184–85, 321; interconnections of, 287; law of motion and, 356; Lenin's elements of, 332–33; of nature, 143–44, 242. *See also* Hegelian dialectics

Dialectics of Nature, The (Engels), 195, 204,

307, 370, 373; on atomic theory, 202–3; on laws of nature, 60, 190; on philosophy, 343; on universality, 89

Dichtung und Wahrheit (Goethe), 83–84

Diehl, Karl, 328

Diogenes, 55, 116

Dionysian principle, 239

diremption, 202, 344

Discourses (Macchiavelli), 364

division of labor, 19, 129, 212, 219, 267

Domostroy, 37, 290

Driesch, Hans, 183, 194

dualism, 24, 319; in social life, 214–16, 217, 220–21. *See also* dialectics

Dühring, Eugen, 226, 227

Eckermann, Johann P., 299

L'Ecole des Femmes (Molière), 136

Eddington, Arthur S., 60

Einstein's theory of relativity, 205, 224, 228

Eleusis (Schelling), 157

emotions, 237, 239

Empedocles, 180–81, 182, 204

empiricism, 43, 74, 75, 326, 342, 370, 380nn1–2. *See also* science

empiriomonism, 78, 132, 221

Encyclopedia (Hegel), 89

Engels, Friedrick, 100, 106, 259, 369, 371; *Anti-Dühring*, 134, 174, 276, 373, 375; *Communist Manifesto*, 365–66; on creeping empiricism, 43, 75; dialectics of, 304, 330, 337, 347 (*See also* dialectical materialism); *Dialectics of Nature*, 60, 89, 190, 195, 202–3, 204, 307, 343, 370, 373; essays on Feuerbach, 189, 267, 294, 295; on ethics, 290; *The German Ideology*, 113, 124, 138, 210, 353, 375; on Hegelian dialectic, 114, 339, 344; on Marxism, 123, 331–32

Enlightenment, 301–2

entelechy, 166, 178–79, 183, 185, 215; Aristotelian, 193–94, 300, 322; organism and, 193–99, 324

Epicurus, 163, 251, 252

equilibrium theory, 167

Ernst, Paul, 147, 385n3

essence, 320. *See also* being

ethics, 282, 284, 286, 287–91; of communism, 289, 330. *See also* good, the

Ethics (Spinoza), 187

Eurocommunism, 26. *See also* communism

Europa und Asien (Lessing), 148–51

evolution, 74, 111, 141, 234, 316, 345–51; Hegel on, 345–46; progress and, 349–50

experience, 45, 325. *See also* empiricism

fascism, 13, 120, 190, 290, 367; biology and, 205; class society and, 37; German, 109–10, 146, 225, 226–27, 230; militarism and, 227; mysticism and, 104, 109–11, 149, 217, 231; practice and, 121; racism and, 224–27, 229

fatalism, 190, 192

Faust (Goethe), 299

feudalism, 216–17, 232, 257, 258, 346, 360

Feuerbach, Ludwig, 76, 87, 134, 168; Engels on, 189, 267, 294, 295; humanism of, 248, 249, 306; *Lectures on the Essence of Religion*, 81–82; Lenin on, 208; on sensation, 94, 96

Fichte, Johann Gottlieb, 48, 114, 117, 159, 209; on identity, 154–55, 156

Filaret, 41

Fischer, Kuno, 293, 303; *History of Modern Philosophy*, 161, 328

five-year plan, 9, 12, 13, 120, 376
Les Fonctions Mentales dans les Sociétés (Levy-Bruhl), 240
Fonvizin, Denis, 36
Fourier, Jean Baptiste, 259, 365
Frank, Semyon, 230, 389n6
Franse, R., 140, 194.
freedom, 254, 325, 362, 365, 368; and necessity, 186–92, 255, 321
French rationalists, 167, 169
French Revolution, 293, 364–65

Geir, Laz., 207
General Deduction of the Dynamic Process (Schelling), 136–37, 156
geocentrism, 261
geopolitics, 256
German fascists, 109–10, 230; racism of, 146, 225, 226–27. *See also* fascism; Hitler, Adolf
The German Ideology (Marx and Engels), 113, 124, 138, 210, 353, 375
Germany, 20, 292; Hegel and, 305, 306
God, existence of, 301–2
Goethe, Johann Wolfgang von, 86, 113, 180, 310, 345; on cognition, 106; dialectics of, 205–6; *Dichtung und Wahrheit*, 83–84; on diremption, 344; *Faust*, 299; German fascists and, 230; Hegel and, 299–300, 329; on materialism, 87, 168; on nature, 76, 98, 99, 127; *Xenia*, 135
good, the, 128, 282–91, 297, 325, 327; bourgeoisie and, 289–90; sociohistorical process and, 284–86
Gorbachev, Mikhail, 28
Gorgias, 279
Gramsci, Antonio, 11
Greek philosophers, 105, 340–41, 361.

See also specific philosophers
Haber, Fritz, 229
Haeckel, Ernst, 66, 74, 295–96, 393n7; *Natürliche Schöpfungsgeschichte*, 350–51
Haller, Josef, 140, 314–15
Hegel, G. W. F., 127, 146, 175, 208, 252; Aristotle and, 270, 341; on atomic theory, 165–66; on being, 312; dialectics of (*See* Hegelian dialectic); on empirical cognition, 342; Feuerbach and, 81–82; geocentrism of, 261; on the good, 283; on history, 335; idealism of, 87, 114, 134, 136, 154, 162, 203, 204, 301, 309–10, 330, 371; on Kant's relativism, 278; on law of relationship, 61; Lenin on, 276, 361, 3727; on Macchiavelli, 364; materialism and, 57, 163–64; mysticism of, 135, 157–59, 251, 298, 309, 312–13, 322, 344; on nature, 84, 182; on organism, 196–97; on Plato's *Republic*, 361–62; on practice and theory, 122, 213, 220; on space and time, 70, 72–74; Stalin on, 25; on Stoicism, 288; on truth, 271; world spirit of, 133
Hegel, G. W. F., works of: *Encyclopedia*, 89; *Lectures on the History of Philosophy*, 47, 53, 67, 179, 210, 254, 270, 282–83, 331; *Phenomenology of Mind*, 64, 296, 304. *See also The Phenomenology of Spirit* (Hegel); *The Philosophy of Nature* (Hegel); *The Science of Logic* (Hegel)
Hegelian dialectics, 20, 77, 85, 160, 170, 292–330; absolute spirit and, 294–97, 298, 300, 303–4, 314; being and, 309, 312, 316–17, 318; dialectical materialism and, 10–11, 162, 169, 296, 306–7, 327–30; Marxism and, 331, 339, 351; syllogism

and, 322–23, 326
Hegesias, 282
Heine, Heinrich, 81, 127, 134, 180, 228, 285; German mysticism and, 110, 236
Henry V (Shakespeare), 112
Herzen, Alexander, 305
heterodoxy of goals, 189, 190
Hindu mysticism. *See* Indian/Hindu mysticism
Historical Materialism (Bukharin), 10, 28
historicism, 345
history, 189; race and, 227, 229; theory and, 352–58. *See also* socio-historical process
History and Theory of the Heavens (Kant), 328
History of Modern Philosophy (Fischer), 161, 328
History of Philosophy (Hegel). *See Lectures on the History of Philosophy* (Hegel)
History of the Communist Party of the Soviet Union (Bolshevik), 25
Hitler, Adolf, 37, 121, 199; mysticism and, 109–10
Hobbes, Thomas, 68, 164
Holbach, Baron d', 87, 98, 381n4
Hölderin, Friedrich, 37
The Holy Family (Marx), 37, 136, 138
Horace, 40
humanity: as abstraction, 90; as part of nature, 84, 100–102, 115, 125, 184, 237, 351; as subject of philosophy, 248–54
Hume, David, 48, 51, 159, 201, 372
hylozoism, 98; and panpsychism, 139–45
Hyperion (Hölderin), 37

idealism, 19, 36–37, 216, 260, 341; Aristotle and, 193; dialectics and, 134–35, 137, 184–85, 321; free will and, 188; Greek, 322, 327; of Hegel, 87, 114, 134, 136, 154, 162, 203, 204, 301, 309–10, 330, 371; of Kant, 62, 134, 341, 372; Lessing and, 148–49; materialism and, 57, 131–38, 164–65, 206, 250, 252; religion and, 161; subjective, 54, 78; teleology and, 176, 184–85, 346; theoretical science and, 201
"The Idealism of Plato" (Pisarev), 146–47
identity, 154–62, 300, 320; absolute spirit and, 155–56, 158; difference and, 317; Hegel's mysticism and, 157–59
ideographic knowledge, 353
imagination, 94
Indian/Hindu mysticism, 49, 50, 234–36; contemplation of nature and, 151–52, 153; and Western philosophy, 146–53. *See also* mysticism
individuality, 88, 249, 282, 352–53
L'Industrie (Saint-Simon), 258
infinite and finite, 311–14, 324
instinct, 184
intellectual labor, 219
intellectual life, 9, 12, 25
introjection, doctrine of, 79
intuition, 108, 109, 111–12
"I-spirit," 48, 51. *See also* subject

James, William, *Varieties of Religious Experience*, 120, 274
Japanese, 225–26
Jews, 226
Jostock, 328
judgment, 322–23

Kant, Immanuel, 22, 100, 182, 237, 327, 345; on being, 312; *Critique of Pure Reason*, 55, 57, 170, 186, 301; dualism of, 319; external world and, 371; on the good, 325;

History and Theory of the Heavens, 328;
idealism of, 62, 134, 341, 372; on natural
science, 134, 370; on organism, 193; on
practice, 118–20; *Prolegomena,* 119; rela-
tivism of, 277–78, 279; transcendental of,
114, 209. *See also* things-in-themselves
Keyserling, Hermann, 147, 150, 234, 384n3
Khrushchev, Nikita, 26
Kirov, Sergei M., 13
knowledge, 19, 81–82, 97, 353
Kogan, Vladimir, 20
Konrad, N. I., 225, 338n1
Korsch, Karl, 10, 11
Krylov, Ivan, 41
Kushchevsky, Ivan A., 144–45, 384n8

labor, division of, 19, 129, 212, 219, 267
Lamarck, Jean-Baptiste, 100, 139–40, 183, 342, 345
land ownership, 361
Larin, Yuri, 28
Larina, Anna, 14, 21, 24, 26, 28, 29
Lassalle, Ferdinand, 362
Lavrov, Pyotr, 290, 366–67, 394n3
law: of relationship, 59–60, 321, 326, 353–54, 355; universality and, 89. *See also* natural law
Lectures on the Essence of Religion (Feuerbach), 81–82
Lectures on the History of Philosophy (Hegel), 47, 53, 179, 210, 331, 364; on the good, 282–83; on Plato, 67, 254, 270
Leibniz, Gottfried von, 132, 133
Lenin, Vladimir Ilyich, 10, 118, 160, 171, 205, 366; agnostics and, 270; on art of insurrection, 336; Bukharin and, 20, 23; on cognition, 112; on dialectics, 174, 307, 330, 332–33, 344, 369, 372–75; on ethics, 289; on Hegel and Plato, 361; on idealism, 216; on lessons of history, 335; on living nature, 103; on materialism, 161, 164; *Materialism and Empirio-criticism,* 58, 200–201, 274; natural science and, 369–70; "On the Question of Dialectics," 87–88, 347; on percep-
tion, 93; as philosopher, 369–76; on practice and theory, 123, 213, 375; on relativism, 277, 279. *See also Philosophical Notebooks* (Lenin)
Lessing, Theodor, 147–53, 234, 237, 238–39, 384n3
Levy-Bruhl, Lucien, 240
Limits of the Natural-Scientific Formation of Ideas (Rickert), 352
logic, 156; dialectical, 337; formal vs. dialectial, 317; Hegelian: *See Science of Logic* (Hegel)
Lukacs, Georg, 10
Luther, Martin, 229–30
Lyell, Charles, 204, 345, 348
Lysenko, Trofin Denisovich, 9, 21, 198

Machiavelli, Niccolo, 285; *Discourses,* 364; *The Prince,* 363–64
Mach, Ernst, 42, 56, 201, 370; Avenarius and, 74, 78, 369
magnitude, 94, 314, 315
Marr, Nikolai Y., 207, 226, 388n2
Marx, Karl, 76, 106, 228, 266, 271, 304; on capitalist utopia, 367; *Communist Manifesto,* 365–66; dialectics of, 86, 162, 257, 351 (*See also* dialectical material-ism); on external world, 52; *The German Ideology,* 113, 124, 138, 209–10, 353, 375;

Hegelian dialectic and, 87, 169, 300, 304, 310, 327-30, 339; *The Holy Family,* 37, 136, 138; Lenin and, 369; on Machiavelli, 364; materialism of, 83, 231, 252; on mode of presentation *vs.* mode of production, 214-15, 232, 252; on mysticism, 111; objectivism of, 333; on practice, 113-14; on rational cognition, 106; on reflection of truth, 271; on representation, 78; on social ideal, 248, 250, 350, 359-60; *Theses on Feuerbach,* 117, 125, 168; on totality, 194. *See also Capital* (Marx)

Marxism, 22, 30, 135, 171, 327; Engels' view of, 331-32; Hegelian roots of, 10, 11, 81-82; intelligentsia and, 9; Lenin and, 307, 374; official history of, 25; philosophy and, 17-18, 35; unity of theory and practice in, 20, 123. *See also* communism; socialism

Marxism and Modern Thought (Bukharin, ed.), 11, 12

Marxism and the Philosophy of Science (Sheehan), 27, 28

materialism, 83, 206, 231, 256; idealism and, 57, 131-38, 164-65, 206, 250, 252; mechanistic, 98, 163-69. *See also* dialectical materialism

Materialism and Empiriocriticism (Lenin), 58, 200-201, 274, 369-72

mathematical-statistical law, 173-74

matter, concept of, 87, 90. *See also* materialism

measurement, perception and, 95-96

mechanistic materialism, 98, 163-69

Mendeleyev, Dmitry, 204

Metaphysics (Aristotle), 177, 347

Michelet, Karl Ludwig, 204, 381n2

Minkowski, Hermann, 73

mode of production, 236; Marx and, 214-15, 232, 252; and mode of presentation, 177-78, 214-15, 218, 230-33, 252, 254. *See also* productive process

Moleschott, Jacob, 164, 168, 385n2

Molière (Jean Baptiste Poquelin), 197; *L'Ecole des Femmes,* 136

monad/monism, 132, 133, 174-75. *See also* subject

Montesquieu, Baron de, 360

More, Thomas: *Utopia,* 363

Morozov, Nikolai, 69-70, 380n3

motion, 354, 356; laws of, 357, 365

Müller, Max, 207, 388n1

Mussolini, Benito, 229

mysticism, 37, 112, 135, 233-39, 283, 325; fascism and, 104, 109-11, 149, 217, 231; Hegelian, 135, 157-59, 251, 298, 309, 312-13, 322, 344; Indian/Hindu, 49, 50, 151-52, 153, 234-36; Western philosophy and, 146-53

nationalism, 230

natural law, 60, 174, 219, 222, 286, 360; diversity and, 344; necessity and, 284, 356

natural science, 12, 329, 369-70. *See also* biology; science

natural selection, 349. *See also* evolution

nature, 137, 181, 184; absolute spirit and, 155-56, 300; artistic attitude toward, 98-103, 126-28, 129; cognition of, 285-86; contemplation of, 151-52, 153; dialectics of, 143-44, 242; Hegel's concept of, 182, 300-301; human society and, 84, 100-102, 115, 184, 237, 255-57, 351, 357-58; mastery of, 260; poetry and, 101-2; scientific law and, 188;

technology and, 116–17
Natürliche Schöpfungsgeschichte (Haekel), 350–51
Nazi-Soviet pact, 16. *See also* German fascists
necessity, 176, 222, 320, 324; Aristotle on, 180–81, 183, 184, 186, 187, 189–90; freedom and, 186–92, 255, 321; law and, 284, 355, 356; purpose and, 178–79, 180, 183–84, 185; teleology and, 189, 191, 222, 255, 259, 358, 376
Newton, Isaac, 75
Nietzsche, Friederich, 37, 114, 225
Nikolai Negorev (Kushchevsky), 144–45
nirvana, 50, 52, 147, 151. *See also* Indian/Hindu mysticism
NKVD (secret police), 13, 14
Noire, Ludwig, 207, 208, 388n1
nomographic knowledge, 353
Notes of a Young Man (Herzen), 305
Notes on the Theory of Statistics (Chuprov), 352
nothingness and being, 310–11
Notion, 321–24. *See also* Absolute idea/spirit
noumena, 55, 56, 277–78. *See also* things-in-themselves

objective world, 79; cognition and, 55–56, 60, 61, 64; Marxist, 333; subject and, 255–61, 324, 326. *See also* world, acceptance of
object of philosophy, 241–47
"On the Question of Dialectics" (Lenin), 87–88, 347
organism, entelechy and, 193–99, 324; necessity and, 197, 198; vitalism and, 194, 195, 197, 199
Ostwald, Wilhelm, 201, 387n2

panpsychism, 134, 139–45
pantheism, 98
Paracelsus, 159, 346, 393n2
Parmenides, 314, 321
patriotism, 25
Pavlov, Ivan, 164, 188, 206
Pearson, Karl, 56, 117, 379n6
peasant utopias, 362
perception, sensation and, 92–97
perpetuum mobile, 273
Petzoldt, Joseph, 350
phenomena, 58, 316–17; essence and, 318, 319–20
The Phenomenology of Mind (Hegel), 64, 296, 304
The Phenomenology of Spirit (Hegel), 52–54, 63, 158, 160–61, 299; on consciousness, 295, 309; on mysticism, 238; on reason, 302
philosophical debates, 10
Philosophical Notebooks (Lenin), 11, 59, 131, 140, 208; on causality, 170; on cognition, 77; on dialectics, 333, 371, 372–75; on Hegel, 276; on human practice, 210–11; on idealism, 137; on sensation, 59, 92
philosophy: bourgeois, 96–97, 110, 213, 217, 328; dual nature of, 36; Marxism and, 17–18; object of, 241–47; religion and, 158, 160–61; science and, 339–44; subject of (*See* subject of philosophy)
The Philosophy of Nature (Hegel), 55, 210, 246, 297–98; on chemistry, 195; on dialectics, 329, 338; on evolution, 345–46; on Goethe, 99; on human place in nature, 101, 115; on laws of nature, 340; logification in, 326; mysticism in, 251, 298, 344; on organism, 100, 108–9;

on philosophical mode, 105, 343;
on relationships, 59; on space and time,
63–64, 70, 74; subjectivism in, 159;
on teleology, 179–80, 183; on theology,
303; on theory and practice, 211;
on universality, 89
The Philosophy of the Spirit (Hegel), 298–99
Philosophy of Zoology (Lamarck), 140
Phoenicians, 228
phylogenetic law, 74
physics, 71, 200, 201, 203
Physics (Aristotle), 180–81
Pisarev, Dmitry, 146–47, 164, 384n1
Plato, 79, 89, 95, 252; aesthetics and, 129;
cave allegory of, 54–55, 67, 117; on the
good, 282, 283; Hegel on, 254, 270;
idealism of, 78; *Republic*, 360–62
Plekhanov, Georgy, 41, 68–69, 117, 163, 290,
370; hieroglyphs of, 68, 272, 371; Lenin's
critique of, 372, 373; monism of, 175
Plenge, Johann, 327–28
pluralism, 174–75
positivism, 258, 328
power, 320; cognition and, 150, 218
practice, 113–23, 128, 168, 186, 264, 335;
cognition and, 209–10; Marx on, 113–14;
science and, 118; social relations and,
114–15; technology and, 116–18; time and,
119, 120. *See also* theory and practice
pragmatism, 120, 278, 369, 375
Prague spring (1968), 26
The Prince (Machiavelli), 363–64
productive process, 116, 118, 128, 287, 337.
See also mode of production; technology
progress, 349–50
Prolegomena (Kant), 119
proletariat, 264, 360, 365, 367, 375–76

property, 220, 361, 362
Proudhon, Pierre-Joseph, 111
purpose and necessity, 178–79, 180, 183–84, 185
Pyrrho, tropes of, 49, 55, 59, 214, 279;
subjectivism in, 56–57, 76
Pythagoras, 172, 219

quantity, 314; *vs.* quality, 165–66, 315
Questions on the Psychology of Peoples
(Wundt), 208

racial biology, 224–31; anti-Semitism and,
227–28; fascism and, 224–27, 229
rational thought, 104–12, 167; action and, 336;
contradiction and, 107–8; dialectical materialism and, 111–12; insufficiency of, 106–7;
intuition and, 108, 109, 111–12; mysticism
and, 148. *See also* cognition; reason
reality, 44, 79, 320; truth as reflection of,
271–72, 274. *See also* objective world
reason, 189, 302. *See also* rational thought
reciprocity, 321
reflection, 77, 79, 223; of truth, 270–71, 272
Reflexes of the Brain (Sechenov), 164
relationships, laws of, 59–66, 321, 326,
353–54, 355
relativism, 277–80, 288, 371
relativity, theory of, 205, 224, 228
religion, 217; philosophy and, 158, 160–61
religious anthropomorphism, 301–2
representation, 78, 92, 94
Republic (Plato), 54–55, 360–62
Ricardo, David, 112, 263
Rickert, Heinrich, 86, 352, 354–55, 357,
381n3, 394n1
Rodbertus, Johann Karl, 353, 394n4
Rosenberg, Alfred, 229, 389n4

Rosenkranz, Karl (Hegel's biographer), 157
Rousseau, Jean Jacques, 124, 360, 364
Rousseauism, 233-34
Russians, race and, 227, 229. *See also* Soviet Union (USSR)
Rykov, Alexei, 8, 16, 26

Saint-Hillaire, Geoffroy, 195
Saint-Simon (Claude Henri de Rouvroy), 258, 329, 348, 365
Sallust, 215
salto vitale vs. salto mortale, 41, 42, 45
Scheler, Max, 214, 388n1
Schelling, F. W. J., 108, 121, 127, 133, 342; animism of, 134; *Eleusis*, 157; *General Deduction of the Dynamic Process*, 136-37, 156; on identity, 154, 155; mysticism of, 157, 175
Schmalenbach, Eugen, 111, 382n9
Schopenhauer, Arthur, 188
science, 21, 118, 178, 316, 333; dialectical materialism and, 174, 200-206, 343; ethics and, 290; nature and, 188, 256, 258; nature *vs.* spirit in, 352, 357; philosophy and, 339-44; sensation and, 75, 76, 93-94; theory and practice in, 118, 122-23, 334. *See also* technology
Science at the Crossroads (Bukharin), 11, 12, 28
Science of Logic, The (Hegel), 58, 87, 115-16, 160-61, 300; absolute idea in, 294, 296-97; on causation, 171; on cognition, 277; Hegelian dialectics in, 308, 309-12, 316, 318, 325, 329, 348; on practice, 186, 211
Sechenov, Ivan, 164
self-consciousness, 64, 133, 136, 154, 295, 321, 322. *See also* consciousness; identity
Semites, 227-28

sensation, 57-59, 61-62, 216; Feuerbach on, 81-82; perception and, 92-97; science and, 75, 76, 93-94; solipsism and, 40, 41, 42-44, 45; things-in-themselves and, 57, 69
Sex and Character (Weininger), 49
Sextus Empiricus, 55, 56
sexual pleasure, 153
Shakespeare, William, 112
Simmel, Georg, 233, 389n1
skepticism, 52-53, 55, 60; Hegel on, 53
slavery, 361
Smith, Adam, 263
social adaptation, 125
social collaboration, 266
social consciousness, 213, 231, 243
social evolution, 349-50
social humanity, 44, 325
social ideal, 359-68; utopia, 359-65
socialism, 19-20, 249, 254, 367-68; battle of ideas and, 37; class struggle and, 258-59, 359; failure of, 29; mysticism and, 238, 240; nature and, 152-53; subject and object of, 264, 265-66; synthesis of, 341; theory and practice of, 35, 130, 220; transition to, 129-30, 190-91, 375-76; utopian, 365-66
Socialism and Its Culture (Bukharin), 16
socialist humanism, 9, 29
social necessity, 189. *See also* necessity
social position, 232-34, 235. *See also under* class
social practice, 114-15, 213. *See also* practice
social sciences, 329, 358
society: capitalism and, 262-64; mastery of, 262-68; nature and, 255-57, 358
socio-historical process, 209, 340, 350; the good and, 284-86; law and, 355

sociology: of knowledge, 19; Lavrov's laws of, 366-67; of thought, 207-13

Sociology (Comte), 349-50

sociomorphism, 214-23, 259; cognition and, 219-21, 222; dualism in society and, 214-16, 217

Socrates, 36, 279, 282, 361

solipsism, 18-19, 39-46, 159, 201, 372; acceptance of the world and, 47-49, 50, 51-52, 54; sensation and, 40, 41, 42-44, 45

Sombart, Werner, 169, 244, 264, 351, 385n6; on Hegelian dialectics, 328, 329, 330

Sophists, 279, 282, 361, 362

Soviet Union (USSR), 21, 25-28, 217, 219, 258; demise of, 29. *See also* Russia; Stalin, Joseph

space and time, 63-64, 68-80; Aristotle on, 70, 71; Hegel on, 70, 72-74; Morozov's formula and, 69-70; objective character of, 73-74; in physics, 71

Spann, Othmar, 125, 194, 263, 383n1

speculation, 339-40

Spencer, Herbert, 263, 329

Spengler, Oswald, 110, 290; *Decline of the West*, 190, 263

Spinoza, Benedictus de, 91, 133, 139, 175, 228, 311; *Ethics*, 187; *Treatise of Religions and Political Philosophy*, 111

Stalin, Joseph, 20, 23, 123, 291, 366, 376; Bukharin and, 8, 14, 24; on Hegel, 25; pact with Nazis, 16; on the plan, 191, 254; purges of, 13

Standfuss, Max, 94, 381n3

Stoicism, 52-53, 288

Struve, Otto, 333

subject of philosophy, 241-42, 248-54; identity and, 155; objective world and, 51-52, 56-63, 65, 255-61, 322, 326; sensation and, 97; sociohistorical, 244, 250-53

Summa Theologica (Aquinas), 216

syllogism, 60, 118, 210, 322-23, 326

symbols, 244, 272

Taylor, Frederick, 120

technology, 116-18, 251, 286-87; dialectics and, 334, 337; mastery of nature and, 256, 257. *See also* science

teleology, 177-85, 218, 263, 347, 358; Aristotle and, 177-82; Goethe on, 135; the good and, 284, 287; Hegel on, 163, 179-80, 183, 184, 309, 326; idealism and, 176, 184-85, 346; necessity and, 189, 191, 222, 255, 259, 358, 376; theology and, 302; universality and, 323; vitalism and, 183, 199

Tertullian, 183

theocracy, in India, 234-35, 236

theory and history, 352-58

theory and practice, 121-23, 126, 256, 261, 327, 338, 342; cycle of, 212; historical process and, 210; Lenin on, 123, 213, 375; *perpetuum mobile* and, 273; of science, 118, 122-23, 334; unity of, in Marxism, 20, 130, 220, 221

Theses on Feuerbach (Marx), 117, 125, 168, 375

things-in-themselves, 61, 78, 88, 115, 149; as abstractions, 319, 354; causality and, 57, 68-69, 119; as contradiction, 64; intellectual labor of, 219; objective world and, 56-57, 59, 60, 66, 116, 371; Plato's cave allegory and, 55, 67; relativism and, 277-78, 279, 280. *See also* noumena; subject

Thomas Aquinas, 111, 133, 179, 199; *Summa*

Theologica, 216
time, 71–72; practice and, 119, 120. *See also* space and time
Tomsky, Mikhail, 8, 15
Transformation of the World (Bukharin), 17
Treatise of Religions and Political Philosophy (Spinoza), 111
Troeltsch, Ernst, 169, 327, 328, 385n7
truth, 269–74, 309, 327, 371; absolute *vs.* relative, 275–81; and beauty, 129; cognition and, 272–73, 275–76; and the good, 284, 325; practical criterion of, 120; reality and, 271–72; reflection of, 270–71, 272; universality and, 275–76
Turgenev, Ivan, 164, 385n3

United States, capitalism in, 232
universality, 57, 70, 275–76, 305; abstraction and, 88, 89, 90–91; Hegelian dialectics and, 322, 323, 326, 342
universe, order of, 177–79
Uranovsky, Y. M., 21
Ursprung der Sprache (Noire), 208
USSR. *See* Soviet Union (USSR)
utilitarianism, 285
utopia, 359–66; Machiavelli and, 363–64; Plato's *Republic* as, 360–62; socialist, 365–66
Utopia (More), 363

Vaihinger, Hans, 200, 387n1
Varieties of Religious Experience (James), 120, 274
Vavilov, N. I., 9, 21
Vernadsky, Vladimir, 99–100, 381n1
vitalism, 141, 183, 194, 195, 197, 199
Voltaire, 346
Vremena: How It All Began (Bukharin), 22–23

Weber, Max, 244, 246, 357
Weininger, Otto, 49
will, 325; mysticism and, 235
Wöhler, 197
Wolfe, Bertram, 27
Woltman, Ludwig, 229–30, 389n5
world, acceptance of, 47–66, 116, 321; cognition and, 55–56, 60, 61, 64, 65; consciousness and, 48, 51–55, 63, 64–65; corporeal being and, 50–51; laws of relationships and, 59–63, 65, 66; solipsists and, 47–49, 50, 51–52, 54; subjectivism and, 56–57
world spirit, 133. *See also* Absolute idea/spirit
Wundt, Wilhelm, 189, 190, 208, 386n4

Xenia (Goethe), 135

Zeno, 55, 107, 116
Zinoviev, Grigori, 10, 26

www.ingramcontent.com/pod-product-compliance
Lightning Source LLC
Chambersburg PA
CBHW020239030426
42336CB00010B/541